Urgent Applications
in the Court of Protection

Urgent Applications
in the Court of Protection

Her Honour Nazreen Pearce

District Judge Sue Jackson
Nominated Judge of the Court of Protection

JORDANS

Published by
Jordan Publishing Limited
21 St Thomas Street
Bristol BS1 6JS

British Library Cataloguing-in-Publication Data

A catalogue record for this book is available from the British Library.

ISBN 978 184661 215 2

Typeset by Letterpart Ltd, Reigate, Surrey

Printed in Great Britain by CPI Antony Rowe, Chippenham, Wiltshire

FOREWORD

It is now over two years since the implementation of the Mental Capacity Act 2005. Despite some well-publicised criticisms, it has achieved the fundamental objectives of improving perceptions of incapacity and how they should be approached. It has settled the principles which underpin decision making for those who lack capacity by incorporating common law jurisprudence and best practice into statute. It has unified the previously disparate areas of finance and personal welfare (including medical treatment), and brought them under the jurisdiction of a new Court of Protection with its own specialist judges. The legislation is supported by a statutory Code of Practice, and the court procedure has a framework of rules and practice directions.

This work introduces the practitioner to the new legislation and the approach of the courts. It explores current case law. It provides a practical guide to procedure and drafting, invaluable to practitioners at any level of experience. Its emphasis on the urgent application is of particular importance. The Court of Protection has not been regarded as the first port of call for an emergency remedy. Traditionally, it provided intensive care rather than first aid. However, the new legislation has brought different challenges. Orders resolving emotionally charged disputes about health or personal welfare may need to be sought urgently. Previously, financial orders were highly restrictive and protective of the person who lacked capacity. The move towards empowerment which enables autonomy and flexibility through the use of unrestricted orders, has highlighted associated risks of misuse by the unknowing and abuse by the unscrupulous. The use of emergency powers to protect the welfare and assets of those who lack capacity is therefore of increased significance in the new arena.

This handbook provides an essential easy reference. Its success is attributable to the expertise and experience of its contributors. Nazreen Pearce is a retired circuit judge and well-known writer of legal text books. Susan Jackson is a respected nominated judge of the Court of Protection who worked with me at the Court's Central Registry in Archway for two years overseeing the implementation of the Act.

The law, so I am reliably informed, is stated as at 1 March 2010.

Denzil Lush
Senior Judge of the Court of Protection

PREFACE

Good practice is essential in all court proceedings. The Civil Procedure Rules 1998 led the way for reform of procedure and practice across all jurisdictions. The Court of Protection Rules 2007, based on the Civil Procedure Rules, provide simple clearly defined procedures from the start to the finish of the various applications which the court may be called upon to deal with. Each Part of the Rules is supplemented by a Practice Direction, which amplifies the provisions of the rules.

Although the rules are simple to follow and the Forms are prescribed for applications made in the Court of Protection, for those who are inexperienced or unfamiliar with the law which applies to this jurisdiction it can still be a maze.

The aim of this book is both to provide professionals who practice in this field and those who are called upon to advise, assist and support 'P', including family and friends, with a step-by-step guide through the law, procedure and remedies in relation to those issues that are likely to arise frequently and which may require immediate action.

We have worked together, bringing our experience from other jurisdictions alongside the publishing team at Jordans, with a view to providing a user-friendly, concise and comprehensive handbook which is accessible to all and to which they may turn to find answers. Precedents and draft orders are provided to give helpful guidance.

The authors wish to express their thanks to the nominated judges and the staff at the Court of Protection, Archway for their assistance and helpful suggestions.

We also extend our appreciation and thanks to Greg Woodgate for his efforts in paving the way for us to publish this book, to Tracy Robinson for her patience, endurance and efficiency in dealing with the amendments we made to the original draft often at short notice, and to Helen Pettet who assisted with an appropriate title for the book.

We have attempted, where possible, to illustrate the applications and orders by reference to short stories. The characters and factual circumstances relied on are purely fictional. Any apparent similarities to any real person is coincidental.

The law is stated as at 1 March 2010.

Nazreen Pearce
Sue Jackson
1 March 2010

CONTENTS

TABLE OF CASES

References are to paragraph numbers.

TABLE OF STATUTES

References are to paragraph numbers.

TABLE OF STATUTORY INSTRUMENTS

References are to paragraph numbers.

TABLE OF PRACTICE DIRECTIONS
AND CODES OF PRACTICE

References are to paragraph numbers.

LIST OF ABBREVIATIONS

ANH	Artificial Nutrition and Hydration
Code of Practice	Mental Capacity Act (2005) Code of Practice, Issued by the Lord Chancellor on 23 April 2007 in accordance with ss 42 and 43 of the 2005 Act
COP Rules	Court of Protection Rules 2007, SI 2007/1744
CPR	Cardio-pulmonary resuscitation
CPR 1998	Civil Procedure Rules 1998, SI 1998/3132
EPA	Enduring Powers of Attorney
FLA 1996	Family Law Act 1996
IMCA	Independent Mental Capacity Advocate
LPA	Lasting Power of Attorney
MCA 2005 ('the Act')	Mental Capacity Act 2005
OPG	Office of Public Guardian
PCT	Primary Care Trust
PD 7A	Practice Direction 7A – Notifying P
PD 8A	Practice Direction 8A – Permission
PD 9A	Practice Direction 9A – The Application Form
PD 9B	Practice Direction 9B – Notification of other Persons that an Application Form has been Issued
PD 9C	Practice Direction 9C – Responding to an Application
PD9E	Practice Direction 9E – Applications Relating to Serious Medical Treatment
PD 9F	Practice Direction 9F – Applications Relating to Statutory Wills, Codicils, Settlements and other Dealings with P'S Property
PD 9H	Practice Direction 9H – Applications Relating to the Registration of Enduring Powers of Attorney
PD 10A	Practice Direction 10A – Applications Within Proceedings
PD 10B	Practice Direction 10B – Urgent and Interim Applications

PD 12A	Practice Direction 12A – Court's Jurisdiction to be Exercised by Certain Judges
PD 13A	Practice Direction 13A – Hearings (Including Reporting Restrictions)
PD 14A	Practice Direction 14A – Written Evidence
PD 19B	Practice Direction 19B – Fixed Costs in the Court of Protection
PD 20A	Practice Direction 20A – Appeals
PD 21A	Practice Direction 21A – Contempt of Court
PVS	Persistent vegetative state
RCJ	Royal Court of Justice

PART I

GENERAL

CHAPTER 1

INTRODUCTION

On 1 October 2007 the Mental Capacity Act 2005 introduced a new approach to decision making for those who lack capacity. The Act not only established a new court jurisdiction supported by its own legal framework but also an entirely different way of approaching how incapacity is assessed and understood.

Historically, the High Court had exercised its *parens patriae* jurisdiction over the lives, welfare, and property and affairs of those who were deemed to be mentally incapable of making decisions for themselves. The Lunacy Act 1890 gave certain powers to the Office of the Master of Lunacy which included administrative functions in the management of the property and affairs of those who lacked capacity. In 1947 the Office of the Master in Lunacy was renamed the Court of Protection. Its role included administrative and management functions in relation to the property and affairs of those who lacked capacity. It did not include issues relating to health or personal welfare which remained within the High Court's inherent jurisdiction.

The Mental Health Act 1959 established a statutory framework which had the effect of extinguishing the High Court's jurisdiction in relation to all matters concerning an incapacitated adult with a mental disorder. They were catered for under the new legislation. The State assumed responsibility for those who lacked capacity by reason of mental disorder as defined by the Act and to manage their affairs. However, this did not include those who lacked capacity for reasons other than mental disorder, eg due to learning disabilities or dementia. This was confirmed by the House of Lords decision in *Re W*[1]. This significant group was left entirely outside statutory powers or protection.

Over the years, as the elderly population has increased, social conditions have improved and medical advances enabled those with a learning disability to survive childhood. Thus, the number of adults, who lacked capacity to make decisions concerning their personal welfare, health and property and affairs also increased. Health and Welfare services have become involved to address the resulting issues. When the Mental Health Act 1983 came into force, the Court of Protection's jurisdiction over the property and affairs of those who were incapable of managing their

---

[1]   [1971] Ch 123.

affairs was retained in Part IV of the Act but not expanded to include health and welfare issues. In 1993, following the introduction of the then government's initiative to refocus adult care under the NHS and Community Care Act 1991, there was wholesale closure of long stay hospitals (known as lunatic asylums) which had detained and treated large numbers of people who lacked capacity under an informal regime. Most were discharged to smaller residential facilities within their communities. Local authorities' social services departments became responsible for assessing and providing for the needs of those who had been discharged into the community and those who were in future to be looked after and treated in the community. The health issues of this group of individuals remained, where appropriate, with the National Health Services. The 1983 Act was sometimes deployed to achieve the detention of and provide medical treatment to those who were not mentally ill but lacked capacity. Most continued to be provided for informally, on the basis that despite incapacity they were compliant with the arrangements made for them. There were no procedures in place for the person informally detained to challenge the decision or a review procedure. There was no formal legal system or any guidelines for those who shouldered these new responsibilities which addressed the multifarious issues which were pertinent to this group, particularly in serious personal welfare and health care matters. The lacuna in the law relating to this category of individuals was filled by the Family Division of the High Court exercising its inherent jurisdiction to make declaratory orders. However, matters were in the main only referred to the High Court in the most serious or extreme cases and related to medical treatment; see *Re F (Sterilisation: Mental Patient)*;[2] *Re T (Consent to Medical Treatment)*.[3]

This jurisdiction became increasingly significant and widely used as more difficult and sensitive decisions came within the domain of health and social care providers, particularly following the decision in *Airedale NHS Trust v Bland*.[4] This jurisdiction was extended to issues concerning personal welfare and injunctive relief: see *Re S (Hospital Patient: Court's Jurisdiction)*;[5] *Re V (Declaration Against Parents)*.[6] The Court over years developed the principles, practice, procedure and guidelines which now underpin the Mental Capacity Act 2005. The overriding principles which form the foundation of the new law have their origins in decisions of the High Court.

In order to resolve the tension between domestic law and the newly adopted European Convention on Human Rights, the High Court continued to fill the gap in the law relating to deprivation of liberty of those who lacked capacity both before and after the Mental Capacity Act

---

[2]   [1989] 2 FLR 376.
[3]   [1993] 1 FLR 1.
[4]   [1993] 1 FLR 1026.
[5]   [1995] 1 FLR 1075.
[6]   [1995] 2 FLR 1003.

came into force. The new provisions of the Mental Health Act 2007 which came into force in April 2009 finally provided the necessary safeguards for the informally detained.

The Mental Capacity Act 2005 reinvented the Court of Protection. It extended its jurisdiction to enable it to deal exclusively with those who lack capacity but are not mentally ill, and with all issues relating to them. It has wide powers to deal with the personal welfare and property and affairs of those who lack capacity to make decisions for themselves. The jurisdiction is not dissimilar to the High Court's inherent jurisdiction. The Court has its own unique procedure which is governed by its own Rules, Practice Directions, Forms and Code of Practice. Initially the Court maintained its historic links with the Public Guardian (OPG), the body responsible for supervision of deputies and the registration authority for Enduring and Lasting Powers of Attorney. In April 2009 the administration of the Court was absorbed into HM Court Service and its separation from the Office of the Public Guardian was completed.

Since its inception in its current form, the Court receives on average about 1800 applications a month. It is also apparent from the recent attention that the Court has received in the media that abuse of those who lack capacity is not unusual and is an increasing problem both in relation to personal welfare and property and financial issues. Abuse concerning the property and affairs of those who lack capacity is estimated to range from between 10%–15% of all cases. Questions have been asked as to whether the OPG has sufficient teeth or resources to protect those at risk and tackle abuse effectively.

All the indications suggest that, as with the Children Act 1989 and the family justice system, the law relating to those who lack capacity will be a fast developing specialist branch of the law, with the Court of Protection taking a prominent position in the hierarchy of specialist courts. When problems or conflicts arise it will be to the lawyers that those involved will turn for advice and, where necessary, to take action. In some instances the decision will need to be made as a matter of urgency. Those who do not regularly practice in this jurisdiction and do not have an in-depth knowledge of the new law and practice and procedure may find the process unfamiliar.

This book does not seek to be an academic study of the new law. Its aim is to provide a step-by-step guide to practitioners and professionals involved with those lacking capacity, in order to deal with most issues that are likely to arise and, in particular, those which may require an urgent application. It also provides an overview of the new legislation for those who have no or little specialist knowledge.

The book is divided into six sections. The first deals with the general principles which must be considered and applied in every case by the decision maker whenever a decision has to be made, no matter how trivial or serious the issue may be. The second and third sections deal with matters relating to personal welfare and property and affairs respectively, with examples of the relief or remedy or declaration which can be applied for. The fourth section deals with mandatory and prohibitive orders which can be made by the Court and which are also likely to form part of the substantive orders applied for. The fifth section deals with the appeal process and finally all the relevant forms are included in Part IV of the book. It should also be noted that 'the person lacking capacity' is referred to as 'P' in all the statute and subsidiary legislation.

CHAPTER 2

GENERAL PRINCIPLES

LAW AND PRACTICE

2.1 INTRODUCTION

The Mental Capacity Act 2005 ('the Act') came into force in two stages on 1 April 2007 and on 1 October 2007. It provides an entirely new and comprehensive statutory framework for decision making for adults who lack capacity to make decisions for themselves, and for those who have capacity but want to make advance decisions for a time when they may lack capacity to make those decisions in the future. It covers issues and decisions relating to personal welfare, health care, property and financial affairs.

The Act builds upon best practice and guidelines laid down in case law and common law principles relating to those who lack capacity and those who have the responsibility to make decisions on their behalf.

The Act was amended by the Mental Health Act 2007 to introduce procedural safeguards where a person lacking capacity may be deprived of his/her liberty in his/her best interest and to make such actions compliant with Art 5 of the European Convention of Human Rights. These provisions came into force on 1 April 2009.

The Act, in ss 42 and 43, provides for one or more Codes of Practice to be issued by the Lord Chancellor for the guidance of those who have responsibility in relation to a person who lacks capacity and the issues identified in the section. These include:

(a) those involved in assessing capacity in relation to any matter;

(b) persons acting in connection with the care or treatment of a person lacking capacity;

(c) donees of lasting powers of attorney;

(d) deputies appointed by the Court ie the Court of Protection;

(e)   persons carrying out research in reliance on any provision made by or under the MCA 2005 concerning persons who lack capacity;

(f)   independent mental capacity advocates;

(g)   with respect to the issues relating to advance decisions and apparent advance decisions to refuse treatment;

(h)   persons involved in using deprivation of liberty procedures and those who are appointed as representatives of the person deprived of his/her liberty;

(i)   any other matter concerned with the Act as the Lord Chancellor thinks fit.

Section 42(4) of the Act imposes a legal duty on certain categories of persons to have regard to any relevant code if acting, in relation to a person who lacks capacity, in one or more of the following ways:

(a)   as the donee of a lasting power of attorney;

(b)   as a deputy appointed by the Court;

(c)   as a person carrying out research in reliance on any provision made by or under the Act;[1]

(d)   as an independent mental capacity advocate;

(e)   in exercising procedures relating to deprivation of liberty;

(f)   as a representative of a person deprived of his/her liberty;

(g)   in a professional capacity;

(h)   for remuneration.

Section 42(5) provides that a provision of a Code of Practice or a failure to comply with the code may be taken in to account by a court or tribunal conducting any criminal or civil proceedings where it is relevant to a question under consideration in the proceedings.

2.2   TO WHOM DOES THE ACT APPLY?

The Act applies to:

(a)   all adults who lack capacity; and

---

[1]   See MCA 2005, ss 30–34.

(b)   young persons, aged between 16 and 18 years, who lack capacity.

Decisions relating to persons between the ages of 16 and 18 years of age can be dealt with under the provisions of the Children Act 1989 in the county court as the definition of a 'child' in s 105 of the 1989 Act includes a child under the age of 18 years and under the High Court's inherent jurisdiction relating to children. However, the Court's jurisdiction under the Children Act 1989 in relation to children over 16 years of age is restricted by s 9(5)–(7) and more specifically in relation to specific issue and prohibited steps orders, unless it can be established that the circumstances are exceptional. When a young person lacks capacity and the issues relate to property and finance, or are of a testamentary nature which may involve the management of the person's affairs on a continuing basis into adulthood, the Court of Protection is the more appropriate venue to deal with such matters. Section 18(3) of the Act also provides that the Court of Protection may exercise jurisdiction in relation to a person's property and affairs even though that person has not reached the age of 16 years, if the Court considers it likely that the person will still lack capacity to make decisions in respect of that matter when he/she reaches adulthood. Additionally, s 21 of the Act makes provision for the transfer of proceedings relating to a person under the age of 18 years from the Court of Protection to a court having jurisdiction under the Children Act 1989 and vice versa.

2.3   KEY PRINCIPLES THAT UNDERPIN THE ACT

The Act, in s 1, sets out the fundamental principles to which regard must be had in every decision made under the Act. These are:

(1)   a person must be assumed to have capacity unless it is established that he lacks capacity;

(2)   a person is not to be treated as unable to make a decision unless all practicable steps to help him to do so have been taken without success;

(3)   a person is not to be treated as unable to make a decision merely because he makes an unwise decision;

(4)   an act done, or decision made, under this Act for or on behalf of a person who lacks capacity must be done, or made, in his best interests;

(5)   before the act is done, or the decision is made, regard must be had to whether the purpose for which it is needed can be as effectively achieved in a way that is less restrictive of the person's rights and freedom of action.

The Act thus reinforces the common law presumption that an adult person has full capacity to make decisions for himself/herself unless it is shown that he/she does not have capacity to do so. In order to assist a person in making a decision the Act provides that all practical assistance must be offered to that person. The Code of Practice[2] also draws attention to this principle by emphasising that a person should not be assumed as being unable to make a decision simply because he/she needs help or support to make and communicate the decision. Paragraphs 3.15-3.22 of the Code also alert and guide those who have to deal with a person who appears to have difficulty in making or taking a decision, to take appropriate steps to assist that person to make his/her decision. The key principle (4) reaffirms previous case law (see *Re T (An Adult) (Consent to Medical Treatment)*;[3] *Sidaway v Board of Governors of the Bethlem Royal Hospital and the Maudsley Hospital*[4]) that a person is not to be regarded as lacking capacity by reason of the fact that he/she has come to a decision which is different from that which most people would make. This is further emphasised in s 2(3) which provides that a lack of capacity cannot be established merely by reference to a person's age or appearance or a condition of his, or an aspect of his behaviour, which might lead others to make unjustified assumptions about his capacity. The Code of Practice however, draws attention to decision making which is out of character and which therefore may be evidence of P lacking capacity. Section 1(5) enshrines the common law 'best interest' practice established in *Re F (Mental Patient: Sterilisation)*.[5] Finally the principle set out in s 1(6) seeks to achieve a balance between assisting and enabling a person to make some decisions and ensuring that when the decision is taken on behalf of the person lacking capacity there are safeguards which protect that person's rights and the person from abuse.

2.4   TEST OF CAPACITY

The Act sets a definitive test for assessing whether a person has capacity to make a specific decision at the material time. It provides for a two stage process, namely the diagnostic stage which is set out in s 2(1) and the functional stage which is set out in s 3.

2.4.1   Diagnostic stage

Section 2(1) of the Act provides that:

> 'a person lacks capacity in relation to a matter if at the material time he is unable to make a decision in relation to the matter because of an impairment of, or a disturbance in, the functioning of the mind or brain.'

---

2   Mental Capacity Act (2005) Code of Practice, issued by the Lord Chancellor on 23 April 2007 in accordance with ss 42 and 43 of the 2005 Act.
3   [1992] 2 FLR 458.
4   [1985] AC 871.
5   [1990] 2 AC 1, [1989] 2 FLR 376, HL.

It thus recognises that the issue of capacity is issue specific and time specific. Before any decision is made on behalf of a person who appears to lack capacity the first question that needs to be answered is 'has the person been diagnosed as having an impairment of or disturbance in, the functioning of the mind or brain?' If they do not, they are assumed to have capacity.

The Code of Practice, para 4.12 sets out the conditions which could result in such impairment or disturbance. It includes conditions associated with some forms of mental illness, dementia, significant learning difficulties, long term effects of brain damage, physical or mental conditions which cause confusion, drowsiness or loss of consciousness, delirium, concussion following a head injury and the symptoms of alcohol and drug abuse. In order to determine this issue it may be necessary to obtain expert medical, psychiatric and/or psychological assessment of the incapacitated person (see below under **2.4.8**) unless the person is known to have been diagnosed with a well established medical condition which is not in dispute.

If the answer to the first question is in the affirmative then one needs to ask whether or not it affects the person's ability to make that particular decision at 'the material time'. It is thus acknowledged that a person's capacity may fluctuate. This is further affirmed in s 2(2), which provides that it does not matter whether the impairment or disturbance is permanent or temporary. Therefore, if the impairment is temporary and there is no urgency in making the particular decision, then applying the key principle set out in s 1(3), that all *practicable* steps to help the person must be taken and found to have failed before any decision is taken on his behalf, it may be appropriate to wait until the person is able to make a decision for himself/herself. The Code of Practice supports this interpretation as it defines 'practicable' as 'practical and appropriate' and according to 'personal circumstances', ie the kind of decision that has to be made and the time available to make that decision.

Where the circumstances require an urgent decision to be taken the Act permits the decision to be taken on behalf of the person lacking capacity but emphasises that the act done or decision made must be in his best interests.

2.4.2 The functional stage

The second stage of the test of incapacity must demonstrate that the impairment or disturbance renders the person unable to make the decision in question for himself/herself. The test is thus 'function specific' and therefore the more difficult the decision that has to be made, the higher the level of capacity which will be required to make it.

Case law[6] had established that a person may be considered as lacking capacity to make a decision when:

(a) P is unable to comprehend and retain the information which is material to the decision, especially as to the likely consequences of having or not having the treatment in question;

(b) P is unable to use the information and weigh it in the balance as part of the process of arriving at the decision.[7]

The Act, in s 3(1), confirms this test by providing that a person is unable to make a decision for himself if he is unable:

(a) to understand the information relevant to the decision;

(b) to retain that information;

(c) to use or weigh that information as part of the process of making the decision; or

(d) to communicate his decision (whether by talking, using sign language or any other means).

2.4.3   The person's ability to understand the information provided

Section 3(2) provides that a person is not be regarded as unable to understand the information relevant to a decision if he is able to understand an explanation of it given to him in a way that is appropriate to his circumstances. The information relevant to a decision includes information about reasonably foreseeable consequences of deciding one way or another or failing to make the decision.[8] In order to enable the person to understand the consequences of his decision the person must be given information about the nature of the decision to be made, the reason why the decision needs to be taken and the likely effects of making it and of refusing to make it.

2.4.4   The ability to retain information[9]

The fact that a person is able to retain the information relevant to a decision for a short period only does not prevent him/her from being regarded as able to make the decision.[10]

---

6   *Masterman-Lister v Brutton & Co* [2002] EWCA Civ 1889.
7   *Re C (Refusal of Medical Treatment* [1994] 1 FLR 31.
8   MCA 2005, s 3(4).
9   MCA 2005, s 3(1)(b).
10 MCA 2005, s 3(3).

2.4.5 The ability to use or weigh the information as a test of capacity

This has been considered in a number of decisions (for example *Re MB (Medical Treatment)*,[11] where the patient had a phobia of needles and was held to be incompetent at the point of proceeding with surgery due to the phobia, and *Bolton Hospitals NHS Trust v O*[12]).

2.4.6 The ability to communicate

If there is any indication that the person is unable to communicate this inability may be overcome with the appropriate support and assistance. In such cases, there is an obligation to provide the required support and, where appropriate, by a person who has the necessary skills. In other instances the failure to communicate may be due to a physical condition, e g unconsciousness or other such condition. The issue in such cases will be an assessment by a qualified and experienced professional on the person's condition and the likelihood of him/her regaining consciousness or the ability to communicate the information within the time limit which is relevant to the circumstances.

2.4.7 Threshold of incapacity in cases of urgency

In cases where a decision needs to be made and an act done as a matter of urgency in the best interest of a person who appears to lack capacity, but before it is possible to assess the person's capacity comprehensively, the Court is empowered, following an application, to exercise its powers on an interim basis by applying a lower threshold if the conditions set out in s 48 of the Act are met.

Section 48 provides:

> 'The court may, pending the determination of an application to it in relation to a person (P), make an order or give directions in respect of any matter if:
> (a)   there is reason to believe that P lacks capacity in relation to the matter;
> (b)   the matter is one to which its powers under this Act extend; and
> (c)   it is in P's best interest to make the order or give directions.'

Thus the Court may determine the issue without a finding of lack of capacity but it must still apply the key principles set out in s 1 of the Act when deciding what order/s to make on the issue under consideration.

The application of s 48 was considered in *Re F*[13] by HHJ Marshall a nominated circuit judge of the Court of Protection who said:

---

[11]   [1997] 2 FLR 426.
[12]   [2002] EWHC 2871, [2003] 1 FLR 824.
[13]   (Unreported) 28 May 2009.

'... it is obvious that situations can arise where the obtaining of a formal declaration or decision ... will take time, but common sense suggests that some action may be needed in the interim. Common sense also suggests that if lack of capacity in relation to any particular matter or decision is in issue (notwithstanding the presumption of capacity) then the Court should have any necessary powers to enable the proper consideration and determination of that issue, even (and in fact inevitably) if this means making orders or directions which affect the person whose capacity is in issue, before that issue has been determined.

It is the intention of s 48 to provide for those situations and to authorise the taking of urgent decisions which appear to be necessary in P's best interests "without delay" before there has been an actual determination that P does lack capacity.

The "reason to believe" test is therefore met if there is evidence to suggest that there is a real possibility that P may lack capacity ...'.

The test to be applied in such cases was considered by the judge and it was held that:

'the proper test for the engagement of Section 48 in the first instance is whether there is evidence giving good cause for concern that P may lack capacity in some relevant regard. Once that has been raised as a serious possibility the Court then moves on to the second stage to decide what action, if any, it is in P's best interest to take before a final determination of his capacity can be made.'

2.4.8   Assessment of capacity

There is no specific requirement in the Act for a professional, whether medical or otherwise, to carry out the assessment. In the majority of cases the assessment will be undertaken by the person who is responsible for providing the care or treatment and directly concerned with the person lacking capacity, and therefore has to make the decision. A Special Visitor may however, be called upon to provide an assessment. Pursuant to s 61 of the Act and for the purposes of the new jurisdiction the Lord Chancellor has appointed two panels of Court of Protection Visitors namely a panel of Special Visitors and a panel of General Visitors. A Special Visitor must be a registered medical practitioner or appear to the Lord Chancellor to have other suitable qualifications or training and to have knowledge of and experience in cases of impairment of or disturbance in the functioning of mind or brain.[14] They are usually psychiatrists who specialise in this area of work. By reason of their experience and qualification, Special Visitors are qualified to provide reports on the issue of whether or not P has capacity and to assist in ascertaining the wishes and feelings of P when there are communication difficulties.

---

[14]   MCA 2005, s 61(2).

In order to protect those who provide care and treatment and who have to make decisions on a regular basis in providing the care and treatment, s 5 provides that if a person does an act in connection with the care or treatment of another person (P) he/she will not incur any liability in relation to the act provided, before doing the act, the person takes reasonable steps to establish whether P lacks capacity in relation to the matter in question, and, when doing the act, the person reasonably believes that P lacks capacity in relation to the matter and that it will be in P's best interest for the act to be done. The nature of the care and treatment to which such acts relate are not defined in the section. The definition of 'treatment' provided in s 64(1), namely as including a 'diagnostic or other procedure' is not specific. Paragraph 6 of the Code of Practice sets out guidelines which must be followed and para 6.5 includes a list of some actions that might be covered by s 5. These involve action related to the personal care of the person concerned and health care and treatment. The latter includes:

- carrying out diagnostic examinations and tests (to identify an illness condition or other problem);

- providing professional medical, dental and similar treatment;

- giving medication;

- taking someone to hospital for assessment or treatment;

- providing nursing care (whether in hospital or in the community);

- carrying out any other necessary medical procedures (for example, taking blood sample) or therapies (for example, physiotherapy or chiropody);

- providing care in an emergency.

The protection is available only if the person providing the care and treatment reasonably believed that the patient lacked capacity to give consent and the actions taken are considered to be in the best interest of the patient after having applied the key principles (see further under the Code of Practice, paras 6.8–6.39).

The steps that are accepted as 'reasonable' will depend upon the circumstances and the urgency of the decision. Again guidance is provided in the Code of Practice (in paras 4.44–4.54) on how to assess the situation and the factors that may affect the nature of the assessment and when a professional assessment may be necessary, before any decision is made or act done.

Where the decision relates to complex and or disputed issues (see the Code of Practice, paras 3.37-4.42 and 4.53-4.54) the assessment should be undertaken by a professional who has the necessary expertise in the particular field, eg a psychiatrist, psychologist etc. In some instances an assessment by more than one expert may be needed. Where the intervention of the Court of Protection is sought, a formal assessment by an appropriately qualified professional will be required.

When assessing the person's capacity or lack of it, the person required to carry out the assessment must be given information relating to the background history and circumstances and the details of the specific decision that needs to be made by the person concerned. It is also necessary to ensure that the principles set out in the Act and the requirement of assisting the person to make the decision is considered and undertaken. The assessment should also consider how the person can be encouraged to participate, or to improve his ability to participate as fully as possible in any act done for him and any decision affecting him.[15] In deciding the issue of capacity, the factors which will need to be considered are the proposed treatment, the risk involved and the benefit to P. It will also be necessary to establish whether the condition is permanent or temporary. If temporary, the assessment should give an indication when it is likely that the person will regain capacity.

If there is any doubt about P's capacity, or lack of capacity, a declaration may be sought from the Court of Protection under s 15 of the Act which gives the Court power to make declarations as to:

(a)   whether a person has or lacks capacity to make a decision specified in the declaration;

(b)   whether a person has or lacks capacity to make decisions on such matters as are described in the declaration;

(c)   the lawfulness or otherwise of any act done, or yet to be done, in relation to that person.

The court may also be asked to make the decision(s) on P's behalf in relation to any specific matter(s), or to appoint a deputy to make the decisions on P's behalf, in relation to the specific matters under s 16(1) and (2) of the MCA 2005.

2.5   BEST INTERESTS – S 4

Where lack of capacity has been established, case law has recognised and established that any act undertaken or decision made must be in the best

---

[15]   MCA 2005, 4(4).

interests of P (see *Wyatt v Portsmouth NHS Trust;*[16] *Re Y (Mental Incapacity: Bone Marrow Transplant*[17]) and in so doing that the wishes of P, his religious beliefs and of those close to him are considered. The views of third parties, eg parents and those with responsibility for caring for P should also be taken into account, although not always followed, if it is not considered to be in the interests of P *(Re A (A Male Sterilisation):*[18] where the wish of a mother of a young man with Down's syndrome, who was on the borderline between significant and severe impairment of intelligence, was that he should be sterilised on the ground that it was in his best interest, but her application was refused on the basis that the best interests of P encompassed medical, emotional and all other welfare issues. Neither the birth of a child nor disapproval of his conduct was likely to impinge on him to a significant degree other than in exceptional circumstances).

Section 1(5) of the Act establishes that an act done or a decision made under this Act for or on behalf of a person who lacks capacity must be done or made in his best interests. Section 4 furthers this principle by setting out the best interests criteria to be applied when making any decision relating to a person who lacks capacity. The person making the determination is required to consider all the relevant circumstances (of which that person is aware and which it would be reasonable for him to regard as relevant) and in particular:

(1)   he must consider whether it is likely that the person will at some time have capacity in relation to the matter in question and if it appears likely that he will, when that is likely to be;

(2)   he must consider so far as is reasonably ascertainable:
      (a)   the person's past and present wishes and feelings (and, in particular, any written relevant statement made by him when he had capacity) (see *MM; Local Authority X v MM (By the Official Solicitor) and KM*[19]);
      (b)   the beliefs and values that would be likely to influence his decision if he had capacity, and the other factors that he would be likely to consider if he were able to do so;

(3)   he must take into account, if it is practicable and appropriate to consult them, the views of:
      (a)   anyone named by the person as someone to be consulted on the matter in question or on matters of that kind;
      (b)   anyone engaged in caring for the person or interested in his welfare;
      (c)   any donee of a lasting power of attorney granted by the person;

---

[16]   [2006] 1 FLR 554.
[17]   [1996] 2 FLR 787.
[18]   [2000] 1 FLR 549.
[19]   [2009] 1 FLR 443.

(d)   any deputy appointed for the person by the Court as to what would be in the person's best interests;

(4)   where the determination relates to life-sustaining treatment the person carrying out the assessment must not, in considering whether the treatment is in the best interests of P, be motivated by a desire to bring about his death. Life-sustaining treatment means treatment which in the view of a person providing health care for the person concerned is necessary to sustain life. Reference should be made to the Code of Practice, paras 5.29–5.36 which gives guidance on how the best interests of P should be considered.

These considerations are reinforced in the Code of Practice, para 5 and more particularly paras 5.47–5.48 in relation to the weight to be given to the interests of third parties. It also provides guidance in dealing with problematic cases. For instance, where there may be conflict of interests and concerns, where decisions are challenged. Where problems may be experienced when consulting and dealing with family members, carers and their views, guidance is provided in paras 5.62–5.69.

Section 4(4) of the Act also requires the decision-maker, so far as is reasonably practicable, to permit and encourage the person to participate, or to improve his ability to participate, as fully as possible in any act done for him and any decision affecting him.

In *Re P (Adult Patient) (Medical Treatment)*[20] the Court of Protection considered the issue of whether the best interests of P required immediate admission to a residential unit for assessment or delayed assessment at a chronic fatigue unit. P's mother's preferred option was an admission to a chronic fatigue unit. The judge approved the assessment at the chronic fatigue unit. The mother subsequently withdrew her consent. The PCT made an interim application for the immediate admission of P as an in-patient to a local unit of the PCT relying on the urgency of the need for an assessment and the risk of interference from the mother. It was considered by the experts, that overall admission to the chronic fatigue unit was the preferred option since it would involve a degree of consent rather than coercion. The court agreed that on balance it was in P's best interests to be admitted to the chronic fatigue unit, provided that the mother was willing to co-operate and would not interfere with the proposed treatment or resist any restrictions which might be imposed on her. The court also provided that, if admission to the chronic fatigue unit was unable to proceed due to the mother's lack of co-operation, P should be admitted to the local unit immediately without recourse to a further application to the Court.

---

[20]   [2009] 1 FCR 567.

2.6 INDEPENDENT MENTAL CAPACITY ADVOCATES – SS 35–39

An independent mental capacity advocate (IMCA) is the creation of the Act. The purpose of this provision is to provide an additional safeguard for P's interests in two specific situations namely:

- where serious medical treatment is proposed for P and/or

- where a change in P's residence is proposed by a NHS body or the local authority.

However, the appointment of an IMCA is only available where P has no family or friend whom it would be appropriate for the NHS body or the local authority to consult in determining what is in P's best interests (for a further discussion see **6.14.1** and **6.14.3**).

2.7 PERMISSION TO APPLY

In order to invoke the jurisdiction of the Court there is a general requirement to apply for permission as a preliminary to intervening. Section 50 of the Act sets out the categories of persons who do not require the permission of the Court before issuing an application for relief or order under the Act. They are:

(a)   a person who lacks capacity;

(b)   a person who has parental responsibility for a person who lacks capacity who is under the age of 18 years;

(c)   the donor of a lasting power of attorney to which the application relates;

(d)   a deputy appointed by the Court for a person to whom the application relates;

(e)   a person named in an existing order of the Court if the application relates to that order.

The Act, in Sch 3, para 20(1) and (2), also provides that an interested person may apply to the Court for a declaration as to whether a protective measure taken under the law of a country outside England and Wales is to be recognised in England and Wales without first seeking permission to apply.

Pursuant to s 50(2) and the COP Rules 2007, r 51, the Official Solicitor and the Public Guardian also do not require permission.

Permission is also not required:

- (subject to certain exceptions set out in r 52) where the application concerns P's property and affairs;

- for a lasting power of attorney which is, or purports to be, created under the Act;

- for an instrument which is, or purports to be, an enduring power of attorney;

- for an application made in the course of proceedings and where an acknowledgement is filed which seeks an order different from that sought in the substantive application (see Part 10 of the Rules).

All other applications require permission.[21] The Act and the Rules read together therefore require that issues relating to health and welfare will require permission even where orders relating to urgent medical treatment or withholding of such treatment are sought, unless the exemptions referred to in s 50 apply.

Where part of the application relates to a matter which requires permission and part of it does not, the applicant has a choice to either make two separate applications or one application. Provision is made for permission to be sought for that part of it which requires permission in the main application.[22] The advantage of seeking both permission and the order which does not require permission in one application is that only one fee will be payable.

2.7.1   Factors which the Court must take account of when considering an application for permission

The factors which the Court must take into consideration include:

(a)   the applicant's connection with the person to whom the application relates;

(b)   the reasons for the application;

(c)   the benefit to the person to whom the application relates of a proposed order or directions; and

(d)   whether the benefit can be achieved in any other way.

---

[21]   MCA 2005, 50(2).
[22]   COP Rules 2007, r 53(2) and PD 8A, paras 2 and 3.

These factors ensure that any application which is made is motivated by the need to promote the interest of the person who lacks capacity and to protect that person from frivolous applications. The requirement that the Court should consider whether there are other means of achieving the end result also ensures that an application is made to the Court as a last resort after all other ways of achieving the desired outcome have been tried without success.

2.7.2 Procedure for application for permission

The application must be made on Form COP2 and filed with all the supporting information and documents; ie a draft of the application in Form COP1, which the applicant seeks permission to have issued and an assessment of capacity in Form COP3, where this is required.[23] If the applicant is unable to file an assessment of capacity he must file a witness statement explaining the reasons for the absence of the assessment; the efforts that have been made to obtain an assessment and the reason why it is believed that the person lacks capacity to make a decision in relation to the subject of the proposed application. The application form must state the capacity in which the applicant is making the application if it is made in a representative capacity and state the issues which he/she requires the Court to determine and the order/s sought. It must identify the person whom lacks capacity and any person who the applicant reasonably believes may have an interest in the matter under consideration and any person who ought to be notified under r 70.

Within 14 days of the application for permission being filed the Court will consider the application and either grant the application in whole or in part, or subject to conditions without a hearing, and may also give directions in connection with the issue of the application form or refuse the application or fix a date for a hearing of the application.[24] The court may also give directions for the appointment of a Special Visitor to assess P's capacity and ascertain, in so far as it is practicable, his/her wishes and feelings. If the Court grants permission without a hearing it will give directions for the filing of all the relevant documents required under r 64 unless these have already been provided.

If the Court fixes a date for the permission hearing it will serve notice of the hearing to the applicant and any other interested party.

Any person who is notified of the application for permission and who wishes to be heard at the permission hearing must file an acknowledgement of notification within 21 days of the date on which the notification was given. The acknowledgement which must be signed by the person or his/her legal representative, must state whether the person consents to the application or opposes it, setting out the grounds for the

---

[23] COP Rules 2007, r 54 and PD 8A.
[24] COP Rules 2007, r 55.

opposition; state what if any order is considered to be more appropriate; and provide an address for service. If the person notified of the permission hearing does not file an acknowledgement he will not be able to take part in the proceedings unless the Court permits him to do so.

The order granting or refusing permission will be served by the Court on the applicant and any other person notified of the application who filed an acknowledgement of notification.[25]

Any person who is aggrieved by the decision of the Court has the right to appeal. The appeal must be dealt with in accordance with Part 20.

2.8   ALLOCATION – R 86

Before the Act came into force the jurisdiction over the affairs of a person who lacked capacity was divided between the Court of Protection and the Family Division of the High Court. The Court of Protection dealt with matters relating to the person's property and affairs. The Family Division dealt with issues relating to medical treatment and personal welfare.

The two courts approached issues in different ways. Cases heard in the Family Division involved a full hearing with oral evidence including evidence from experts taken. The person who lacked capacity was a party to the proceedings and represented by the Official Solicitor. In the old Court of Protection most cases were dealt with without an oral hearing and even when such hearings did occur they were relatively short.

Since 1 October 2007 all issues relating to an incapacitated person's property and financial affairs and personal welfare and medical treatment are now dealt with in the Court of Protection.

The Central Registry for the Court of Protection is based in Archway Towers, Archway, London, which is where all applications are processed. Regional Courts are located in Birmingham, Bristol, Cardiff, Manchester, Newcastle and Preston. In practice, regional judges will travel to courts convenient for the parties. Cases may also be heard at the RCJ. The President of the Family Division is also the President of the Court of Protection. Sir Andrew Morritt, the Chancellor of the Chancery Division has been appointed Vice-President and Denzil Lush, the former Master of the Court of Protection, is the Senior Judge. A number of High Court judges, circuit and district judges have also been nominated to hear Court of Protection cases. There is thus a three-tier judiciary who are nominated to sit in the Court of Protection. The Court of Protection's Practice Direction provide that all cases involving serious medical treatment must be heard by a nominated judge of the Family Division of the High Court. In practice, financial and management decisions are usually dealt with by

---

[25]   COP Rules 2007, r 59.

district judges with the right of appeal to a nominated circuit judge. Personal and welfare decisions are generally dealt with by the Senior Judge of the Court or a nominated circuit judge. The COP Rules apply across all tiers but the pattern followed continues to be the same as before the Act came into force. The more serious cases are assigned to the High Court as follows:

(1) An application involving the lawfulness of withholding or withdrawing artificial nutrition and hydration from a person in a permanent vegetative state, or minimally conscious state or a case involving an ethical dilemma in an untested area must be heard by the President of the Court of Protection or by a judge nominated by the President (including permission, the giving of any directions and any other hearing).[26]

(2) An application in relation to serious medical treatment or where a declaration of compatibility pursuant to s 4 of the Human Rights Act 1998 is sought (including permission, the giving of any directions, and any hearing) must be conducted by the President of the Family Division, the Chancellor or a puisne judge of the High Court.[27]

(3) A judge to whom a serious medical treatment case or a case where a declaration of incompatibility is sought under the Human Rights Act is allocated may determine that the matter is one which can be dealt with by a judge of the Court other than a designated High Court Judge.[28]

Tension may however arise where there are mixed property and finance issues and difficult welfare issues to be determined. The allocation of such cases will depend on the facts of the individual case but in most cases the Court will apply commonsense and consider issues such as proportionality; the need to avoid delay and to deal with the case expeditiously; saving the parties incurring unnecessary costs and expense; the complexity of the issues; and judicial availability and court's resources.

2.9   COSTS

The provisions relating to costs are set out in s 55 of the Act and COP Rules 2007, rr 155–168. Subject to the COP Rules, the costs of and incidental to all proceedings in the Court are in the Court's discretion. The Court has full power to determine by whom and to what extent the costs are to be paid. It may also disallow or order the legal or other

---

[26]   PD 12A, para 2.
[27]   PD 12A, para 3.
[28]   PD 12A, para 5.

representatives concerned to meet the whole of the wasted costs or such part of them as may be determined in accordance with the rules.[29]

'Wasted costs' means any costs incurred by a party:

(a)   as a result of any improper, unreasonable or negligent act or omission on the part of any legal or other representative or any employee of such a representative, or

(b)   which, in the light of any such act or omission occurring after they were occurred, the Court considers it is unreasonable to expect that party to pay.[30]

The Act, in s 56, provides for the COP Rules to make provision as to the way in fees and costs are to be paid; or charging fees and costs upon the estate of the person to whom the proceedings relate; and for the payment of fees and costs within a specified time of the death of that person to whom the proceedings relate, or the conclusion of the proceedings.

The general rule is that, where the proceedings concern the incapacitated person's property and affairs, the costs of the proceedings, or of that part of the proceedings that concerns his or her property and affairs, shall be paid by him or her or charged to his estate.[31] Where the proceedings concern the incapacitated person's personal welfare there will be no order as to costs of the proceedings or of that part of the proceedings that concern his or her personal welfare.[32] Where the proceedings concern both property and affairs and personal welfare the Court, insofar as practicable, will apportion the costs as between the respective issues.[33]

The court may however depart from this general rule if the circumstances so justify. In deciding whether to depart from the general rule the Court is will have regard to all the circumstances, including:

(a)   the conduct of the parties;

(b)   whether a party has succeeded on part of his case, even if he has not been wholly successful; and

(c)   the role of any public body involved in the proceedings.

'Conduct' of the parties includes conduct before as well as during, the proceedings and whether it was reasonable for a party to raise, pursue or contest a particular issue. It includes the manner in which a party has

---

[29]   MCA 2005, 55(1)-(4).
[30]   MCA 2005, s 55(6).
[31]   COP Rules 2007, r 156.
[32]   COP Rules 2007, r 157.
[33]   COP Rules 2007, r 158.

conducted the litigation and whether a party who has succeeded in his application or response to an application, in whole or in part, exaggerated any matter contained his application or response. Conduct therefore includes both the general conduct of the parties and conduct during litigation.[34]

COP Rules 2007, r 160 also extends Parts 44, 47 and 48 of the Civil Procedure Rules 1998 with certain modifications to proceedings in the Court of Protection, where appropriate.

If the Official Solicitor is involved in the proceedings his costs in relation to the proceedings, or in carrying out any direction given by the Court and not provided for by remuneration under r 167, must be paid by such person or out of such funds as the Court may direct.[35] Costs may also be ordered against or in favour of a third party but before doing so that person must be added as a party to the proceedings for the purposes of costs only and be given a reasonable opportunity to attend a hearing at which the Court intends to consider the matter.[36]

---

[34] COP Rules 2007, r 159.
[35] COP Rules 2007, r 163.
[36] COP Rules 2007, r 166.

PRECEDENT

PRECEDENT FOR AN ORDER MADE WITHOUT A HEARING REFUSING PERMISSION WITH REASONS FOR THE REFUSAL

IN THE COURT OF PROTECTION

IN THE MATTER OF THE MENTAL CAPACITY ACT 2005

AND IN THE MATTER OF ALFONO MARIO

BETWEEN

AB   Applicant

and

XY   Respondent

ORDER

Made by District Judge Wise

At Archway Tower, 2 Junction Road, London N19 5SZ

On ....

WHEREAS

1. Jacqueline Peacock, the 'Applicant' has sought permission to apply to the Court to be appointed joint deputy to make personal welfare decisions for Alfonso Mario.

2. The Applicant has sought to be appointed joint deputy to make property and affairs decisions for Alfonso Mario.

3. Section 5 of the Mental Capacity Act 2005 confers general authority to act without the need for any formal authorisation by the Court if a person does an act in connection with the care or treatment of a person who lacks capacity and acts in that person's best interests.

4. Section 16(4) of the Act provides that, when deciding whether it is in a person's best interests to appoint a deputy, the Court must have regard to the principles that (a) a decision of the Court is to be preferred to the appointment of a deputy and (b) the powers

conferred on a deputy should be as limited in scope and duration as is reasonably practicable in the circumstances.

5.   In the permission Form COP2, witness statement dated .... day of .... 2010 and documents filed, the Applicant has not identified with sufficient particularity the reasons why it is necessary at this stage to appoint a deputy to make personal welfare decisions and what specific personal welfare powers are sought.

IT IS ORDERED THAT

1.   The application for permission to apply to the Court to be appointed deputy to make personal welfare decisions for Alfonso Mario is refused.

2.   For the avoidance of doubt, if an issue arises upon which a personal welfare decision or direction of the Court is sought this decision does not preclude the applicant from re-applying at the material time, nor does it prejudice the applicant's application to be appointed a deputy to make decisions regarding Alfonso Mario's property and financial affairs which application is continuing.

3.   This order was made of the Court's own initiative without a hearing and without notice, pursuant to rule 89 of the Court of Protection Rules 2007. Any party or any other person affected by this order may apply to the Court for reconsideration of the order made provided any such application is made within 21 days of the order being served.

PART II

PERSONAL WELFARE AND DEPRIVATION OF LIBERTY

CHAPTER 3

WELFARE DECISIONS – RESIDENCE, CONTACT, SEXUAL RELATIONS

LAW AND PRACTICE

3.1 INTRODUCTION

The need for urgent and serious medical treatment are only two of the issues which carers of vulnerable adults encounter and on which a declaration from the Court is often sought. There are however more, general decisions, which need to be undertaken on a day-to-day basis which involve the person's personal care, such as acts involving hygiene, dressing, eating, drinking and living arrangements and social contact, on which the consent of the person concerned is essential, but that person may not have sufficient understanding of the issues or the situation to give such consent. These decisions can become urgent and, in the absence of agreement, may require recourse to the Court.

The definition of a person who lacks capacity, as set out in s 2(1) of the Act, makes it clear that capacity is issue specific and time specific and must relate to an impairment of, or disturbance in, the functioning of the mind or brain, thus involving a two stage process – the first stage is to establish that there is an impairment of, or disturbance in the functioning of the person's mind or brain and the second stage is to establish that because of the impairment or disturbance the person is unable to make the specific decision in question. Although the person may lack capacity on major issues it may nevertheless be possible to assist the person to make a decision for himself or herself in relation to everyday issues. The Act and the Code of Practice specifically provide that efforts should be made to assist the person concerned in making the decision. The Act and the Code impose a duty on those who have the care of the vulnerable person, or to make decisions on his or her behalf, to take all reasonable steps to assess the individual in order to establish whether that person lacks capacity to make a decision in relation to the specific issue in question. The Act also sets out when and by whom a formal assessment should be carried out.

Section 3(1) of the Act sets out the test that should be applied in assessing whether or not a person is able to make a decision. A person is unable to make a decision if he or she is unable:

(a)   to understand the information relevant to the decision;

(b)   to retain that information;

(c)   to use or weigh that information as part of the process of making the decision; or

(d)   to communicate his or her decision.

Those who have responsibility for the day-to-day personal care or health needs of a vulnerable person (P), whether that person is a family member or a professional carer or health care professional, will need to make decisions on behalf of the person in their care sometimes without P's consent or agreement. In respect of some of the decisions, s 5 of the Act makes provision to protect the carer if the act done is in connection with the personal care, health care or treatment of the person lacking capacity, provided the conditions in s 5 are satisfied (see Chapter 4). Other decisions will require the approval of the Court.

Before an application is made to the Court, P's needs and how it is proposed that those needs should be met or supported must be identified. Where appropriate, consultation with family members should be undertaken and the proposals shared with them and their views given due consideration, with a view to reaching agreement where possible. Where disputes remain, mediation/alternative dispute resolution process should be considered. Referral to the Court of Protection should be made as a last resort.

The Code of Practice, in Chapter 15, specifically imposes an obligation to settle disputes in a conciliatory way when there is a disagreement relating to a person's capacity, their best interests, or any decision or action taken on the person's behalf. Where the dispute arises between the professionals and family members it is good practice to set out the different options available and why the proposed option is considered to be in the person's best interests, and a case conference or meeting should be arranged where not only the options proposed but the views of the family or others who are interested in the care and welfare of the person lacking capacity are aired and discussed and given full consideration. Where appropriate, an advocate to support and represent the person who lacks capacity should be appointed so that the advocate can represent the views and interests of the person lacking capacity to the family carers or professionals and assist where mediation is considered as a way of trying to resolve the disagreement. Unless the issues require an urgent decision to be taken, time for reflection should be allowed. Mediation as a form of settling disagreements is advised (see the Code of Practice, paras 15.1–15.9).

It is obvious that this process is time consuming and therefore it is essential that consideration is given to long-term planning at an early stage. There may however, be cases where, despite attempts made to deal with the issues amicably, P's condition and needs require an immediate decision and an application to the Court as a matter of urgency, if only in the first instance to address and safeguard P's needs.

In relation to marriage issues the most likely recourse to the Courts for an emergency remedy in this context is for an order preventing an unsuitable marriage. However, if it is P who wants to marry he/she will need to be empowered to present their views. It is therefore necessary to be aware of the underlying principles associated with the celebration of a marriage by a person whose capacity is in issue.

With regard to P's social relationships, typically an application to the Court for an order urgently intervening in personal relationships, including sexual relationships, will be with the aim of preventing or restricting them. Such applications are made where there is concern for an inappropriate relationship, where P may be exploited. However, P's right to have relationships is an important concept which will be considered by the Court in exercising its discretion.

Although the Court's jurisdiction applies to adults, it is generally accepted that issues relating to those who are between the ages of 16 and 18 may be referred to the Court. In such cases the local authority, which will generally be the body that will be responsible for dealing with issues of care, residence and social and family contact, will need to consider different factors when preparing the care plans from those which apply to adults. However, whatever the issue may be on which a decision or authorisation is needed, the overriding principle set out in s 1 of the Act and the best interests of P must dictate the decision taken on P's behalf.

This chapter seeks to deal with such welfare issues relating to those who are in the 16 to 18 year bracket and those who are adults; the steps which should be taken before seeking the Court's intervention; the procedure to be followed when the decision is taken to issue proceedings; and the Court's powers in relation to both categories of incapacitated persons, particularly where interim measures are necessary whilst further investigations are undertaken.

3.2   YOUNG PERSON BETWEEN THE AGES OF 16–18 YEARS

Section 2(5) of the Act provides that no power which an individual has in relation to a person who lacks capacity, or who is reasonably believed to lack capacity, is exercisable in relation to a person aged under 16. It is therefore assumed that where a young person aged between 16 and 18 lacks capacity within the meaning of ss 2 and 3 of the Act, the provisions of the Act and the Code of Practice apply when decisions regarding the welfare needs of the young person are in issue. The Code of Practice, para 4.6 provides that the Act generally applies to individuals who are aged 16 or older. Chapter 12 of the Code of Practice also provides that most of the Act applies to young persons aged 16–17 years who lack capacity save for three exceptions, namely:

* Only people aged 18 or over can make a Lasting Power of Attorney.

* Only people aged 18 or over can make an advance decision to refuse medical treatment.

* The Court of Protection may only make a statutory will for a person aged 18 or over.

In matters relating to the admission of the young person to a psychiatric hospital the authorities should be able to rely on the provisions of ss 5 and 6 of the Act (see Chapter 4 at **4.8.2**) in conjunction and consultation with the parents of the young person or a person who has parental responsibility for him/her, to do what is in the best interests of the young person. The Code of Practice, Chapter 12 confirms this position by providing that the protection from liability provided in s 5 of the Act applies as long as the person carrying out the act has taken reasonable steps to establish that the young person lacks capacity and, when doing the act, reasonably believes that the young person lacks capacity and that the act done is in the young person's best interests and follows the general principles. In addition it requires that, when assessing the young person's best interests, the person providing care or treatment must consult those involved in the young person's care and anyone interested in his/her welfare – if it is practical and appropriate to do so. This may include the young person's parents but care should be taken not to unlawfully breach the young person's right to confidentiality. Where a young person has indicated that he/she does not want his/her parent consulted, it may not be appropriate to involve them (for example where there have been allegations of abuse).[1] In cases where the appropriate treatment proposed requires deprivation of liberty, the provisions of the Mental Health Act 1983 should be used to authorise detention.

---

[1]   Code of Practice, para 12.19.

Where the issues concern the welfare of a young person, the provisions of the Children Act 1989 should be considered alongside those of the Act in carrying out the appropriate assessments and care plans. The Code of Practice acknowledges in para 12.6 that there is an overlap with the Children Act 1989 and that where the young person lacks capacity within the meaning of the Act either MCA 2005 or the Children Act may apply, depending on the circumstances. Where neither of these Acts apply it may be necessary to look to the powers available under the Mental Health Act 1983 or the High Court's inherent jurisdiction. There are no specific rules or criteria to determine when the Act or the Children Act 1989 should apply. The Code of Practice gives some examples including that 'it may be appropriate for the Court of Protection to make a welfare decision concerning a young person who lacks capacity to decide for themselves (for example, about where the young person should live) if the Court decides that the parents are not acting in the young person's best interests. It might be appropriate to refer a case to the Court of Protection where there is disagreement between a person interested in the care and welfare of a young person and the young person's medical team about the young person's best interests or capacity. Where there is a disagreement about whether the young person lacks capacity and there is no other way of resolving the matter, a declaration or other order should be sought from the Court of Protection and if the Court considers that the issue should be dealt with in the Family Division, the Court will transfer the case to the High Court.[2]

These provisions will be of particular relevance in cases where the young person up to the age of 21 years has been the subject of a care order or is a looked after child. In such cases, conflict may arise between the young person, his/her parents and family members and the local authority and other agencies with regard to issues concerning eg accommodation, contact with, sexual relationships between the young person and a third party and what is deemed to be in the best interests of the young person and how the balance between those issues and the young person's right to autonomy and the rights of those who have parental responsibility for the child should be struck.

The Children Act 1989 imposes on the responsible local authority a statutory duty towards looked after and relevant/eligible persons between the age of 16 and 21 years. The statutory provisions which apply to persons within this category are set out in the Children Act 1989, ss 22–24D and Part II, paras 19A–19C of Sch 2 to the Act and the Children (Leaving Care) (England) Regulations 2001 and, in the case of Wales, the Children (Leaving Care) (Wales) Regulations 2001. Under these provisions the local authority has a duty to advise, assist and befriend a looked after child, and befriend him with a view to promoting his welfare when they have ceased to look after him. In relation to an eligible young person the local authority is under a duty to carry out an

---

[2]   Code of Practice, paras 12.20–12.25.

assessment of his needs with a view to determining what advice, assistance and support it would be appropriate to provide for him and to prepare a pathway plan for him.[3] Paragraph 19C imposes a duty on the local authority to arrange for such a young person to have a personal adviser.

3.2.1   The assessment

The Children (Leaving Care) Regulations 2001 provide that in carrying out an assessment and in preparing or reviewing the pathway plan the local authority must, to the extent that it is practicable, seek and have regard to the views of the young person to whom it relates and take steps to enable him to attend and participate in any meetings at which his or her case is to be considered. This includes providing the young person with copies of the results of the assessment and the pathway plan and ensuring that the contents of the documents are explained to him or her.

In carrying out the assessment the responsible local authority must take account of the following considerations:

(a)   the child's health and development;

(b)   the child's need for education, training or employment;

(c)   the support available to the child from relationships with members of his or her family and with other persons;

(d)   the child's financial needs;

(e)   the extent to which the child possesses the practical and other skills necessary for independent living; and

(f)   the child's need for care, support and accommodation.[4]

In carrying out the assessment and preparing the pathway plan the responsible local authority must, unless it is not reasonably practicable to do so, seek and take into account the views of:

(a)   the child's parents;

(b)   any person who is not a parent but has parental responsibility for the child;

(c)   any person who is caring for the child on a day-to-day basis;

(d)   any school or college attended by the child, or the local education authority for the area in which the child lives;

---

[3]   Children Act 1989, Sch 2A, Part II, paras 19A and 19B.
[4]   SI 2001/2874 and SI 2001/2189, reg 7(4).

(e)   any independent visitor appointed for the child;

(f)   the general practitioner in whose list the child is included;

(g)   the personal adviser appointed for the child; and

(h)   any other person whose views the responsible local authority or the child consider may be relevant.[5]

3.2.2   The pathway plan

Having carried out the assessment, the responsible local authority is required to prepare a pathway plan which should include the following matters:

(1)   the nature and level of personal support to be provided to the child and young person;

(2)   details of the accommodation the child or young person is to occupy;

(3)   a detailed plan for his or her education or training;

(4)   where relevant, how the responsible local authority will assist the child or young person in employment or seeking employment;

(5)   the support to be provided to enable the child or young person to develop and sustain appropriate family and social relationships;

(6)   a programme to develop the practical and other skills necessary for him or her to live independently;

(7)   the financial support to be provided to the child or young person, in particular where it is to be provided to meet his or her accommodation and maintenance needs;

(8)   contingency plans for action to be taken by the responsible local authority, should the pathway plan for any reason cease to be effective.[6]

In respect of each of the above matters the responsible local authority is required to set out the manner in which it proposes to meet the needs of the child and the date by which any action required to implement any aspect of the plan, will be carried out by the local authority.[7]

---

[5]   SI 2001/2874 and SI 2001/2189, reg 7(5).
[6]   SI 2001/2874 and SI 2001/2189, reg 8 and Schedule.
[7]   SI 2001/2874 and SI 2001/2189, reg 8(3).

3.2.3   The functions of the personal adviser

The functions of the personal adviser are set out in reg 12 and require him/her:

(a)   to provide them with advice (including practical advice and support);

(b)   to participate in their assessment and the preparation of their pathway plans;

(c)   to participate in the reviews of their pathway plans;

(d)   to liaise with the responsible local authority in the implementation of the pathway plan;

(e)   to co-ordinate the provision of services to them, and to take reasonable steps to ensure that they make use of such services;

(f)   to keep informed about their progress and wellbeing; and

(g)   to keep a written record of any of the adviser's contacts with them.

The personal adviser should not be a person who is an officer or an employee of the local authority and he/she should not be responsible for undertaking the assessment or the pathway plan.

Re (G) v Nottingham City Council and Nottingham University NHS Trust[8] and *R (J) v Caerphilly County Borough Council*,[9] although not determined by the Court of Protection, illustrate the importance of complying with the above provisions when seeking authorisation from the Court for any plan proposed for a young person, in addition to those which apply under the Act.

3.3   CAPACITY TO MARRY AND CAPACITY TO HAVE SEXUAL RELATIONS

The presumption that a person possesses capacity and the principle that the issue of capacity is subject specific and time specific is never more relevant than in cases involving the capacity to marry and to make the decision to have sexual relations with a particular person. By reason of this presumption it is not for P to establish that he/she has the capacity to marry or have sexual relations, but for those who assert the contrary to prove that P does not have capacity to marry. In such cases the Court will have to consider how far the person's capacity extends or to which specific

---

[8]   [2008] EWHC 400 (Admin).
[9]   [2005] 2 FLR 860.

areas. It does not follow that because a person is assessed as having capacity in relation to one specific area of a transaction that he/she has capacity in relation to all areas involving the same transaction. For example, a person may have capacity to make a decision in relation to a simple medical procedure but not a more complicated one. The more serious the decision, the greater the degree of capacity required.

Section 3(1) of the Act applies the same test as that which has been developed at common law in such cases as *Re C (Adult: Refusal of Treatment)*[10] and *Re MB (Medical Treatment)*.[11] This has been affirmed by Munby J (as he then was) in *MM; Local Authority X v MM (by the Official Solicitor) and KM*:[12]

> '... The section 3(1) principle therefore applies to all aspects of "personal welfare"'.

This is also confirmed in the Code of Practice, para 4.32 which includes capacity to enter into marriage:

> 'The Act's new definition of capacity is in line with the existing common law tests and the Act does not replace them. When cases come before the Court on the above issues, judges can adopt the new definition, if it thinks it is appropriate. The Act will apply to all other cases relating to financial, healthcare or welfare decisions.'

The test of a vulnerable adult's capacity to consent to marriage and sexual relations was considered in *Re E (An Alleged Patient); Sheffield City Council v E &S*[13] and *X City Council v MB, NB and MAB*.[14] It was held that a refined analysis is less important when the issue is whether someone has capacity to marry or consent to sexual relations. Any assessment of capacity to marry must take into account the question of capacity to consent to sexual relations. In assessing capacity to consent to sexual relations the threshold of understanding has been said to be low. It has been stated that it is enough that the person concerned has sufficient 'rudimentary knowledge' of what the act comprises and of its character to enable the person to decide whether to give or withhold consent. In *MM; Local Authority X v MM (by the Official Solicitor) and KM*,[15] it was held that 'capacity to consent to sexual relations is issue specific and not person or partner specific but this approach was doubted in *R v C*.[16] Although the decision in *R v C* relates to criminal proceedings and the scope of s 30(1) of Sexual Offences Act 2003 the ruling is nevertheless relevant because the Supreme Court considered the above decisions and

[10]   [1994] 1 FLR 31.
[11]   [1997] 2 FLR 426.
[12]   [2007] EWHC 2003 (Fam), [2009] 1 FLR 443.
[13]   [2004] EWHC 2808, [2005] 1 FLR 965.
[14]   [2006] EWHC 168 (Fam), [2006] 2 FLR 968.
[15]   [2007] EWHC 2003 (Fam), [2009] 1 FLR 443.
[16]   [2009] UKHL 42.

the issue of capacity and held that lack of capacity to choose can be person or situation specific and that an irrational fear that prevents the exercise of choice could amount to a lack of capacity preventing the free exercise of choice and an inability to communicate that choice (see the leading judgment of Baroness Hale of Richmond).

Consideration should also be given to Art 12 of the European Convention, which provides that men and women of marriageable age have the right to marry and found a family according to the national law governing the exercise of this right. It is recognised that the lives of those with limited or borderline capacity can still be enriched by marriage and therefore one must be careful not to set the test of capacity too high lest it operates as an unfair, unnecessary and discriminatory bar against the mentally disabled.

In *Re E (An Alleged Patient); Sheffield City Council v E & S* the local authority sought to prevent a 21-year-old woman, who was said to function at the level of a 13-year-old and for whom they had responsibility, from marrying a man who was a Schedule 1 offender. The local authority asserted that the woman lacked capacity to make decisions about where she should live, whether she should have contact with the offender or whether she should marry him. The local authority asserted that it was not in the best interests of the woman to associate with or marry the offender. A preliminary issue arose as to the appropriate questions to be put to experts in order to establish her capacity to marry. It was held that the test is whether the person has the capacity to understand the *nature* of the *contract of marriage*. The test is not the capacity to understand the *implications* of a *particular marriage*. The contract of marriage is necessarily something shared in common in all marriages. It is not something that differs as between the particular individual that P wishes to marry and is distinct from the question whether P is wise to marry the particular individual. The court does not have jurisdiction to consider whether a marriage is in an individual's best interests; whether or not that person lacks capacity, nor does it have any role to vet P's choice of suitors. It does not have the power to give consent on behalf of an adult who lacks capacity to give his or her consent. When exercising its inherent jurisdiction the Court does not give a valid consent but declares that something is lawful. The issue is simple in that an adult who lacks capacity cannot marry, so that P's 'best interests' is not relevant. It was also held that the analogy with capacity to consent to medical treatment or capacity to litigate was not appropriate because both those issues were varied, necessarily complex and involved expert advice, whereas marriage was essentially simple and the same for everyone.

Munby J (as he then was) summarised the test as follows:

(i)   The question is not whether E has capacity to marry X rather than Y. The question is not (being specific) whether E has capacity to marry S. The relevant question is whether E has the capacity to marry. If she does, it is not necessary to show that she also has capacity to take care of her own person and property.

(ii)   The question of whether E has capacity to marry is quite distinct from the question of whether E is wise to marry; either wise to marry at all, or wise to marry X rather than Y, or wise to marry S.

(iii) In relation to her marriage the only question for the Court is whether E has capacity to marry. The court has no jurisdiction to consider whether it is in E's 'best interests' to marry or to marry S. The court is concerned with E's capacity to marry. It is not concerned with the wisdom of her marriage in general or her marriage to S in particular.

(iv)   In relation to the question of whether E has capacity to marry the law remains the same today as it was set out by Singleton LJ in *The Estate of Park, deceased Park v Park*.[17]

> 'Was the deceased ... capable of understanding the nature of the contract into which he was entering, or was his mental condition such that he was incapable of understanding it? To ascertain the nature of the contract of marriage a man must be mentally capable of appreciating that it involves the responsibilities normally attaching to marriage. Without that degree of mentality it cannot be said that he understands the nature of the contract.'

(v)   More specifically, it is not enough that someone appreciates that he or she is taking part in a marriage ceremony or understands its words.

(vi)   He or she must understand the nature of the marriage contract.

(vii) This means that he or she must be mentally capable of understanding the duties and responsibilities that normally attach to marriage.

(viii) That said, the contract of marriage is in essence a simple one, which does not require a high degree of intelligence to comprehend. The contract of marriage can readily be understood by anyone of normal intelligence.

There are thus, in essence, two aspects to the inquiry whether someone has capacity to marry: (1) does he or she understand the nature of the marriage contract? (2) Does he or she understand the duties and responsibilities that normally attach to marriage?

(ix)   The duties and responsibilities that normally attach to marriage can be summarised as follows: marriage, whether civil or religious, is a

---

[17]   [1954] P 112 at 127.

contract, formally entered into. It confers on the parties the status of husband and wife. The essence of the contract being an agreement between a man and a woman to live together, and to love one another as husband and wife, to the exclusion of all others. It creates a relationship of mutual and reciprocal obligations, typically involving the sharing of a common home and a common domestic life and the right to enjoy each other's society, comfort and assistance.'

(See also the cases cited in the judgment).

In so far as P's right to have a sexual relationship is concerned the issue will relate to:

- whether P has the understanding of the nature of sexual relationship and the sexual act;

- whether P understands the risks including the risk of pregnancy and sexually transmitted diseases;

- whether P is capable of consenting to and refusing sexual intercourse, but it does not necessarily involve the capacity to understand that having a relationship with a particular individual could be harmful.

The primary objective in such cases is to make the decision which serves P's best interests. In *Re MM (An Adult)*[18] the High Court applied the test in *X City Council v MB, NB, MAB (By his Litigation Friend the Official Solicitor)*[19] to the issue of whether P had the capacity to consent to sexual relations and whether the care plans of the local authority which imposed restrictions on contact were justified. MM was a 39-year-old woman who suffered from paranoid schizophrenia. She was described has having limited insight into the nature of her illness. She also suffered from moderate learning difficulties and poor cognitive functioning, significantly impaired or non-existent verbal recall and was functionally illiterate. She had been taken into care by the local authority when she was 13. She had a male partner KM of 15 years who was diagnosed with psychopathic personality disorder and alcohol misuse. He had been violent towards MM and used her money to buy alcohol. He had also encouraged her to leave her accommodation and to follow him to various addresses and to disengage from the psychiatric services. In 2006 MM took up residence in supported accommodation at a unit. Certain restrictions were placed on her relating to her movements and inviting KM. Encouraged by KM she failed to comply with those restrictions to the detriment of her health. Ex parte orders were obtained declaring that she lacked capacity to decide where she should live and with whom she

---

[18]   [2007] EWHC 2689 (Fam), [2009] 1 FLR 487.
[19]   [2006] EWHC 168 (Fam), [2006] 2 FLR 968.

should associate and that it was not in her best interests to be removed from the unit or to have unsupervised contact with KM. This was later varied to allow her contact with KM not less than twice a week for no less than two hours. Subsequently further orders were made empowering the local authority to terminate contact at its discretion if KM was under the influence of alcohol or if he was abusive or aggressive towards MM and when she went missing ordering KM to assist the local authority to locate her. MM was found but her condition had deteriorated and her placement at the unit was at risk of breaking down. Within 3 months she had to be sectioned pursuant to s 2 of the Mental Health Act 1983. Contact was reduced to once a week for two hours and injunction orders were obtained prohibiting KM from removing her from the family placement and approaching the accommodation and from contacting her. The local authority secured a permanent placement for MM and sought a declaration that MM lacked capacity to conduct litigation and to make decisions as to where and with whom she should live, to determine with whom she could have contact or associate and to manage her financial arrangements and to enter into a contract of marriage. It was eventually conceded that she had capacity to consent to sexual relations with KM. The court however found that the local authority were seeking to control her relations with KM by imposing a care plan which prevented her from continuing her relationship with KM and hence risked her Art 8 rights. The court directed the local authority to reconsider its care plans.

3.4   RESIDENCE

Where the decision maker is a local authority, they must engage with family members in reaching a decision about where P should live. Confrontation is to be avoided and a full and comprehensive assessment carried out, not only of P and his/her capacity, but also an assessment of any person who puts himself/herself forward as a carer. In so doing, consideration must be given to all the circumstances including:

- P's vulnerability;

- the effect on P when he/she is residing with the particular carer and whether it has a damaging effect on P;

- whether if P continues to reside with the carer the support offered would be accepted;

- whether the support offered would safeguard and promote P's welfare;

- whether the staff have the skills and expertise to manage P's specific needs problems and disabilities;

- risks involved;

- P's wishes and feelings;

- the level of care available at home and during contact;

- information regarding the psychological and emotional benefit or satisfaction which the home or contact will provide;

- information relating to any physical, emotional harm which P would suffer if he/she remained with the carer;

- information on the advantages and disadvantages for P in terms of lifestyle and opportunities in the long term and medium term which would be provided;

- any other relevant factors which are specific to P;[20]

- best interests;

- striking a proper balance.

It is suggested that a proper balance sheet setting out all the advantages and disadvantages should be prepared to assist the Court. The issue of best interests must also be exercised to ensure that it is compatible with the European Convention for the Protection of Human Rights and Fundamental Freedoms with specific reference to P's Art 8 rights, which are central to the issue of protecting a person's family life but subject to Art 8(2) which provides that any restriction in accordance with the law and which is necessary in a democratic society for the protection of health or for the protection of rights and freedoms of others is permissible.

The concept of 'private life' has been described in broad terms, and is not susceptible to an exhaustive definition. It covers physical and psychological integrity of a person. It can sometimes embrace aspects of an individual's physical and social identity. 'Private life' is said to have two elements: (1) the notion of 'inner circle' in which the individual may live his own personal life as he chooses; (2) the right to establish and develop relationships with other human beings.[21]

Elements such as gender identification, sexual orientation and sexual life fall within the personal sphere protected by Art 8.[22] Article 8 also protects the right to personal development, the right to establish and develop relationships with others and generally the outside world. The right to self

---

[20] For example, see in *Re MM (An Adult)* [2007] EWHC 2689 (Fam).

[21] *Neimietz* v *Germany* (1993) 16 EHRR 97 at para 29; see also *Re S (Adult Patient) (Inherent Jurisdiction: Family Life)* [2002] EWHC 2278 (Fam), [2003] 1 FLR 292; *Re Roddy* [2004] 2 FLR 949.

[22] See *Pretty v UK* (2003) 35 EHRR 1 at para 61.

determination and the right to personal autonomy is an important principle which underlies the guarantees provided within the Article.

Any intervention must be a proportionate response to the risk presented.[23]. Applying this test to adults the assumption is that a person who lacks capacity would be better living with his/her family than in an institution and if he/she has been cared for by a family member they should continue to do so. McFarlane J in *LLBC v TG, JG and KR*[24] emphasised this presumption when he said that: 'Placement in the family should be at the top of the priority list before alternative non-family placements are considered'.

In order to over turn this presumption the local authority must establish on evidence that the care offered to the person would be better provided and be in P's best interests in accordance with the proposed care plan, and that there is a need to protect the vulnerable adult. The court will also be concerned to ensure that by removing P from one type of abuse it does not expose P to the risk of ill treatment at the hands of an institution. In order to intervene to protect a vulnerable adult from future harm there must be a real possibility of such risk, not merely a fanciful risk of such harm. It is therefore essential that the local authority should carry out a full and comprehensive assessment of family members who have cared for P, or are putting themselves forward as possible carers, and to make a genuine and reasonable attempt to carry out a full assessment of capacity of the family to meet P's needs in the community before they invoke the Court's powers to compel a family to place a relative in a residential care home: 'The court will adopt a pragmatic, common sense and robust approach to the identification, evaluation and management of perceived risk'.[25] In *LLBC v TG, JG and KR* (above) the local authority had obtained an order without notice to the family members, on the basis of inaccurate information and were criticised for failure to communicate adequately with family members, who had been confrontational and at times intractable, and without undertaking an assessment of the family members who had put themselves forward as possible carers. It also highlighted the duty of social workers to check the details of all information given to the Court particularly when draconian orders were sought on an ex parte application. Mcfarlane J endorsed Charles J's observations in *B Borough Council v S (By the Official Solicitor)*[26] that the general approach at a without notice hearing involving vulnerable adults had to be the same as that under s 44 of the Children Act 1989. The local authority's task in both cases was to evaluate, as best it could, the degree of urgency, the risk of intervening by way of making an order and the risks of not intervening at that stage.

---

[23]   See *Re L (Care: Threshold Criteria)* [2007] 1 FLR 2050.
[24]   [2009] 1 FLR 414.
[25]   See *NS v MI* [2006] EWHC 1646 (Fam), [2007] 1 FLR 444.
[26]   [2006] EWHC 2584 (Fam), [2007] 1 FLR 1600.

More recently in *Re SK*[27] the local authority had applied for a declaration as to P's capacity and injunctive relief against her family. One of the issues for consideration by the Court was the application by the elderly mother of P, who was in her 30s, for her to be returned home into her care in advance of the final hearing. The history was complicated by reason of the fact that the family were of Afghani origins and there were complex family dynamics involved. The local authority had also been involved between 1999 and 2001. The report prepared by the local authority indicated huge conflicts and conflicting and false information, which were of a recurring nature, given by the family. There were allegations that P had been imprisoned within the home, that she had been kidnapped. There was also police involvement and a place of safety order obtained.

The psychological report concluded that P 'was a vulnerable individual and could be subjected to coercion and is in danger of suffering emotional, physical, sexual and psychological harm if she marries'. The psychiatric report concluded that P was suffering from mental illness within the Mental Health Act 1983 and that she lacked capacity. The assessment of the mother highlighted several concerns. Having reviewed all the evidence, Sumner J concluded that a trial period with her mother was not in P's best interests and referred to the conflictual background, the numerous reasons given in the various professional reports, the fact that the mother had had little contact with P and her inadequate housing and inability to cope with the demands of P.

Disputes also arise between family members as to where a loved one should live. Relatives may compete to provide P with a home or disagree about a placement in residential care. The court in such cases should be asked to make orders in P's best interests settling the issue of residence.

3.5   INDEPENDENT MENTAL CAPACITY ADVOCATE – SS 38 AND 39

In any case where an NHS body or local authority proposes to make arrangements for the provision of accommodation for P in a hospital or care home (in the case of the NHS) or the provision of residential accommodation (in the case of a local authority) or a change in P's accommodation and it is satisfied that there is no family member or friend of P whom it would be appropriate for the NHS body or the local authority, as the case may be, to consult in determining what would be in P's best interests, it must instruct an IMCA to represent P. There are exceptions to this requirement. In the case of an NHS body the provision does not apply if it is satisfied that:

---

[27]   [2007] EWHC 3289 (Fam).

(a)   the accommodation is likely to be provided for a continuous period which is less than 28 days, if the accommodation is to be provided in a hospital, or 8 weeks if it is in a care home;[28] or

(b)   the arrangements need to be made as a matter of urgency.

In the case of a local authority the provision to instruct an IMCA does not apply if it is satisfied that:

(a)   the accommodation is likely to be provided for a continuous period of less than 8 weeks, or

(b)   the arrangements need to be made as a matter of urgency.

In either case, if subsequently the NHS body or the local authority (as the case may be) have reason to believe that the accommodation is likely to be provided for a continuous period which is longer than that specified above it must instruct an IMCA to represent P.[29]

In deciding what arrangements to make for P, the NHS body and the local authority (as the case may be) should take into account any information given or submission made, by the IMCA.

(For a further discussion of the role of IMCAs, see **6.14**).

3.6   CONTACT

Where there are competing interests and P lacks capacity, his/her right has to be balanced against Y's rights but P's best interests must determine the issue. The court may be asked to determine that the right should be exercised in the same way as a child's rights take priority over a parent's right.

Once again Article 8 rights have to be considered and in particular the provision that in certain circumstances the state has a duty to prevent a person interfering with another's life and that the state may intervene in order to prevent the violation of rights protected by the Convention. However such intervention must be in accordance with the law; it must be for a legitimate aim and necessary in a democratic society.

The factors which the Court took into account in restricting contact (and this will be relevant in other cases as well) in *Re MM (An Adult)*[30] included:

---

[28]   MCA 2005, s 38(3) and (9).
[29]   MCA 2005, s 38(3) and (4).
[30]   [2007] EWHC 2689 (Fam).

- P's vulnerability.

- The volatile and abusive relationship causing harm to P.

- When in the relationship P had been non-compliant with medication and support services were compromised, leading to significant harm to P.

- KM encouraged P to leave the unit and become homeless resulting in neglect to her person.

- P's partner was unable to accept responsibility for his action. He had limited insight into P's needs. He failed to co-operate and did not have the ability to prioritise her needs.

- There was a denial of violence towards P.

- P's partner disclosed P's details to her brother who had sexually abused her.

- P's partner undermined her placements.

- P's partner was hostile towards professionals and had failed to comply with the terms of contact.

- Longevity of the relationship.

- Article 8 rights.

- Whether the care plans provided and met the needs of P.

- Whether the restrictions were a proportionate interference with family life and private life.

- Whether the risk was manageable and acceptable.

In determining that the limited and restricted contact offered by the local authority was disproportionate and unjustified the Court relied on the following factors:

- Longevity of the relationship.

- Supervised contact was wholly inappropriate and disproportionate.

- The risks had to be evaluated in a pragmatic and common sense and robust way.

- Balance between the right to respect for P's physical and mental health and safety and her ongoing relationship. The court found that the risks were not such as to make it necessary for P's contact to be supervised.

- The local authority's plan did not make any provision to facilitate sexual relations between the couple.

- The court found that 'particularly serious reasons must exist particularly where the relationship has lasted a long time for denying the right to sexual relations and putting obstacles in the way'.

A Local Authority v E,[31] (a case dealt with before the Act came into force) illustrates the Court's approach to issues of residence and contact. In that case, P, who was 19 years of age, had been the subject of a care order since she was 15 years old. She had severe learning difficulties and required full time assistance in every aspect of her self care and used sign language to communicate. The local authority prepared a care plan which entailed P living in a residential unit for young adults with contact with her parents. In the absence of an agreement the local authority sought authorisation from the Court to implement the plan. Experts' evidence at the hearing recommended that P should live at the unit but have weekend staying contact with the family. Attempts made at securing an agreement failed and the parents demanded that unless P was returned into their care they would cease all contact. The court, applying the test in *Re MB (Medical Treatment)*,[32] held that the approach should be to balance all the relevant factors relating to the situation of the person who lacked capacity and to decide what solution or order would meet the best interests of P and to evaluate a welfare appraisal in accordance with the balance sheet approach suggested in *Re A (Male Sterilisation)*.[33] The court confirmed that P lacked capacity to make decisions about her future; that it was in her best interests to continue living in the residential unit and authorised that the care plan be implemented. The parents were still resisting the shared care placement which left the Court with no alternative but to authorise that the placement should be on a full-time basis until such time that the parents re-established contact.

3.7 COURT'S POWERS TO MAKE WELFARE ORDERS

Section 16 of the Act sets out the Court's powers to make decisions, in relation to a person (P), who lacks capacity on matters concerning P's welfare. These powers extend to:

- deciding where P should live;

---

[31] [2007] EWHC 2396, [2008] 1 FLR 978.
[32] [1997] 2 FLR 426.
[33] [2000] 1 FLR 549.

- deciding what contact if any, P should have with any specified person;

- making an order prohibiting a named person from having contact with P;

- giving or refusing consent to the carrying out or continuation of a treatment by a person providing health care for P;

- giving a direction that a person responsible for P's health care allow a different person to take over that responsibility.[34]

Section 16(3) makes the Court's powers subject to the general principles of s 1 and s 4 (best interests). For a discussion of how this is achieved see Chapter 2.

The court's powers to make interim orders and give directions under s 48 of the Act also applies to applications which concern the personal welfare of P. It should be noted that the threshold concerning capacity on an interim application in respect of any matter is whether:

- there is reason to believe that P lacks capacity in relation to the matter;

- the matter is one to which its powers under this Act extend; and

- it is in P's best interests to make the order, or to give directions, without delay.

Pursuant to s 49 the Court may also require reports from several sources to be prepared. It may make consequential directions for the disclosure of medical and other records and specify the scope of such reports.

Section 47 also provides that the Court has, in connection with its jurisdiction, the same powers, rights, privileges and authority as the High Court. It can thus grant injunctions, commit for contempt for non-compliance of its orders and make any other enforcement orders it considers appropriate.

3.8 WELFARE ORDERS AND DEPRIVATION OF LIBERTY

Deprivation of P's liberty by any person (D) is not permitted under the Act unless it is necessary for life-sustaining treatment and satisfies the conditions set out in s 4B of the Act or the circumstances come within the provisions of s 4A.

---

[34] MCA 2005, s 17.

Section 4B(3) provides that D may deprive P of his liberty if, by doing so, D is giving effect to a relevant decision of the Court made under s 16(2)(a) in relation to a matter concerning P's personal welfare, or if the deprivation is authorised by Sch A1 of the Act. These provisions therefore empower the Court to make a welfare order on behalf of P which includes the provision that in P's best interests P should be treated or accommodated in a way which has the effect of depriving P's liberty. The court may make such order subject to appropriate restrictions.

In *W Primary Care Trust v TB*[35] a 41-year-old woman with degenerative brain injury and delusion was considered to be in need of a complex package of intensive neuro-behavioural therapies in a residential unit and treatment was needed as a matter of urgency. She was not eligible to be detained under the Mental Health Act 1983. The woman had expressed her wish to leave the residential home where she was accommodated. There were differences of opinion on whether it was in her best interests to receive the therapy suggested and whether the residential home had the appropriate facility to provide the treatment. Interim orders had been obtained in order to secure her in the home. These included the use of reasonable restraint. Application was made on her behalf by the Official Solicitor and the Primary Care Trust that she was eligible to be detained under the provisions of s 4A. The issue the Court had to determine was whether the authorisation should be made under s 16 or Sch 1A. Roderic Wood J held that the care home was not an independent hospital nor was it part of the NHS and therefore the provisions of Sch 1A did not apply. Consequently an order could be made under the Act or the standard authorisation given pursuant to the deprivation of liberty safeguards contained in the Act (See further under Chapter 4).

3.9   PRACTICE AND PROCEDURE

Unless the provisions of s 50 of the Act apply, the applicant for any welfare order will need to apply for permission to apply in Form COP2. The substantive application in Form COP1 should be filed at the same time together with all the supporting documents required for personal welfare applications required in Form COP1B Annex B. In addition the Court will require evidence of capacity which should be in Form COP3. Where a deputy has been appointed, Form COP4 (the declaration form), and, if appropriate, a copy of any Lasting Power of Attorney should also be filed.

The Court fee of £400 will have to be paid when the application is issued.

Where permission is required the Court is required to deal with the application within 14 days. It may grant or refuse the application or list the application for a hearing and give directions including specifying who

---

[35]   [2009] EWHC 1737 (Fam).

should be given notice of the hearing (see COP Rules 2007, rr 55, 56 and 89). If a hearing is listed, a person who is notified of the hearing should file an acknowledgement of service in Form COP5.

If permission is given, the substantive application will be issued by the Court. The applicant will receive from the Court Form COP5 (the acknowledgement of service) Form COP14 (the notice of proceedings to P) with the guidance notes in Form COP14A, notice in Form COP15 and guidance notes of the issue of the application and the certificate of service Form COP20.

It is the duty of the applicant to:

• serve all the necessary documents and forms on the respondents within 21 days;

• serve P with Forms COP14 and 14A and COP5;

• notify any other relevant person of the application in Forms COP 15 and COP 5;

• file the certificate of service within 7 days of service in Form COP20.

Every respondent and any person who wishes to take part in the proceedings must file the acknowledgement of service within 21 days. The Court will then either give directions without a hearing or list the matter for a directions hearing.

If the matter is urgent the applicant must file an urgent application in Form COP9 with a draft of the orders sought and if possible a disc of the order.

In an emergency the Court may do the following:

• make an order on the papers;

• abridge time for service;

• hold a hearing without notice.

Where orders are made without notice to the respondents, the Court will list a further hearing or directions appointment and give directions for the respondent(s) to reply.

3.10 PROCEDURAL GUIDE FOR WELFARE ORDER

Permission to Apply	Required by everyone except by:	MCA 2005 s 50
	The person lacking capacity	COP Rules 2007, Part 8
	If the person lacking capacity is under 18 anyone with parental responsibility	
	Donee of a LPA to which the application relates	
	Deputy appointed by the Court	
	A person named in an existing order	
	Official Solicitor/Public Guardian	
Applicant must file	Form **COP2** if permission is required	COP Rules 2007, Part 9
	Forms **COP1** and **COP1B**	PD 9A and
	Form **COP3**	COP Rules 2007, rr 62-64
	Form **COP4** where a deputy has been assigned	
	Copy of a Lasting Power of Attorney if relevant	
Court Office	(1) Issues application and gives to the Applicant	
	• Form **COP5**	
	• Forms **COP14** and **COP14A**	
	• Forms **COP15** and **COP15A**	
	• Form **COP20**	
	(2) Judge considers the application and decides whether to give directions or list for directions/disposal hearing	COP Rules 2007, r 89
	(3) May decide to make order without a hearing in which case court will serve order on all the parties	
What the Applicant must do	(1) Serve on the respondent/s within 21 days Forms **COP1, COP1A, COP5, COP15** and **COP15A**	
	(2) Notify P on Forms **COP14, COP14A** and **COP5** of the application	COP Rules 2007, r 69

	(3) Notify any relevant party on Forms **COP15** and **COP15A**	COP Rules 2007, r 70
	(4) File certificate of service and notification in Form **COP20**	
	(5) If an urgent application is required file Form **COP9**	COP Rules 2007, Part10 PD 10A and 10B
What the Respondent must do	File an acknowledgement of service in Form **COP5**	PD 9C(3)
What the person notified must do	File an acknowledgement of notification in Form **COP5**	PD 9C(4)
Hearing	The court will consider the application	
	Give directions	COP Rules 2007, r 85
	Allocate the case	
	Set the timetable and trial window or	
	If urgent list for a disposal hearing	
	Make any other appropriate orders	
Orders that the Court may make at the interim hearing	(1) Declare whether a person lacks capacity to make a particular decision specified in the declaration	MCA 2005, s 15
And at the final hearing	(2) Declare whether the person lacks capacity on the matters set out in the declaration	
	(3) Declare the lawfulness or otherwise of any act done or yet to be done	
	(4) Authorise deprivation of liberty in certain circumstances	
	(5) Specify where P should live	
	(6) Define the extent of contact between P and others	
	(7) Grant injunctions	
	(8) Appoint a deputy where appropriate	
	(9) Make any other consequential or protective orders	

PRECEDENTS

PRECEDENT FOR A SIMPLE RESIDENCE AND CONTACT ORDER

IN THE COURT OF PROTECTION   CASE NO ....

IN THE MATTER OF THE MENTAL CAPACITY ACT 2005

AND IN THE MATTER OF JOHN SMITH

BETWEEN

HELLINIC COUNTY COUNCIL   Applicant

And

JOHN SMITH   1st Respondent

(by his litigation friend the Official Solicitor)

And

JCF   2nd Respondent

DRAFT ORDER

Made by District Judge Wise

At ....

On the day of 2010

UPON HEARING Solicitors for the Applicant and the First Respondent and the Second Respondent in person

IT IS HEREBY DECLARED AND ORDERED THAT:

1.   JS lacks capacity to make decisions on residence and contact and care provisions.

2.   It is in JS's best interests to remain living at the Paradise Residential Home and the application by JCF to remove JS to live with her at .... is dismissed.

3.   It is in JS's best interests to have contact with FCF subject to the

conditions set out in the Schedule attached to this order which may only be varied in writing by the Registered Manager of Paradise Residential Home after consultation with a representative of the Applicant's Social Services Department.

4.   JCF shall not remove JS from Paradise Residential Home.

5.   No order as to costs save that the costs of the first Respondent be subject to detailed assessment.

PRECEDENT FOR AN INTERIM ORDER REFUSING DIRECT CONTACT AND GIVING DIRECTIONS

IN THE COURT OF PROTECTION   CASE NO ....

IN THE MATTER OF THE MENTAL CAPACITY ACT 2005

AND IN THE MATTER OF MARIO SICILIANO

BETWEEN

RAYMOND SCILLIANO	Applicant
and	
GLENCARE PCT	1st Respondent
and	
NOEL FRY	2nd Respondent
and	
MARIO SCILIANO	3rd Respondent
(by his litigation friend the Official Solicitor)	

ORDER

Made by ....

At ....

On ....

UPON hearing the Applicant in person and Counsel for the Glencare PCT and the Deputy Second Respondent and solicitor instructed by the Official Solicitor

AND UPON reading the bundle prepared for this hearing, the letter from the Hellinic County Council (HCC) dated ....

IT IS DECLARED THAT:

1.   MS lacks capacity to decide whether and to what extent he should have contact with his son RS.

2.   The parties to the proceedings shall henceforth be known as 'RS' 'NF' 'MS'.

IT IS ORDERED THAT:

1.   Pursuant to ss 48,16(2)(a) and 17(1)(b) & (c) of the Mental Capacity Act 2005, there be no direct contact between MS and his son RS save as provided for in paragraph 4 of this order until further order or the determination of the Applicant's application dated the ....

2.   There be permission to the Official Solicitor to disclose to the HCC the bundle prepared for this hearing such disclosure to be made no later than 4pm on ....

3.   The Director of HCC Social Services or some other suitable person do file and serve by .... a report pursuant to s 49 of the Mental Capacity Act 2005 to address the arrangements that can be made to facilitate supervised contact between MS and his son RS outside the Paradise Nursing Home including the provision for travel arrangements and supervision.

4.   HCC do have permission if they consider it appropriate to in MS's best interests to arrange one session of supervised contact with a maximum duration of 30 minutes by the .... away from the Paradise Nursing Home and to provide a short report on such contact by ....

5.   The parties to provide updating position statements by ....

6.   The application be listed for further directions/final hearing on .... (T/E 1 Hour).

7.   The costs of the Deputy and the Official Solicitor and his solicitors shall be the subject of detailed assessment and shall be paid to the Deputy form the net proceeds of sale of 16 Great Hellinic Road and this order is to be treated as authority to the Supreme Court Costs Office to carry out a detailed assessment on the standard basis. Save as provided herein, costs be in the application.

PRECEDENT FOR A GENERAL FORM OF INTERIM ORDER ON PERSONAL WELFARE APPLICATION

IN THE COURT OF PROTECTION   CASE NO ....

IN THE MATTER OF THE MENTAL CAPACITY ACT 2005

AND IN THE MATTER OF JOHN SMITH [*insert P's forenames and surname*]

BETWEEN

HELLINIC COUNTY   Applicant
COUNCIL

And

JOHN SMITH   1st Respondent

(by his litigation friend the
Official Solicitor)

And

JCF   2nd Respondent

DRAFT ORDER

Made by ....

At ....

On ....

UPON hearing [*by telephone*] Counsel/Solicitor for the Applicant [*or the Applicant in person*] and Counsel/Solicitor for the PCT and the Deputy Second Respondent and Counsel/Solicitor instructed by the Official Solicitor

AND UPON reading the bundle prepared for this hearing, the letter from the Hellinic County Council (HCC) dated .... and considering the submissions made

AND UPON the terms of this order including the declarations having been translated for the First and Second Respondents [*or as the case may be*] and they having confirmed to the Court that they understand them

AND UPON .... [*insert name*] Second Respondent undertaking to co-operate with the Applicant moving the .... Respondent [*insert P's initials*] to the Arcacia Rehabilitation Centre [*insert name of Centre*] with all reasonable requests made by the Applicant in connection with the move, and with regard to the Applicant's assessment of the .... [*insert P's name*] which shall include the provision of information and any medical or care records within his/her possession, custody or power and with the Second Respondent further undertaking not to attempt to remove .... [*insert P's initials*] from the Arcacia Rehabilitation Centre nor to encourage .... [*insert P's initials*] to leave or to ask him/her to leave

AND UPON noting that the applicant has undertaken an assessment which concludes that JS [*insert P's initials*] is deprived of his liberty at the .... Home and this is in his best interests

AND UPON the Court indicating that all parties being present this Order shall take immediate effect for the purposes of authorising the move to Arcacia Rehabilitation Centre (such move being anticipated to take place today) notwithstanding that this Order has not been sealed

IT IS DECLARED AND ORDERED IN THE INTERIM AND FURTHER ORDER OF THE COURT THAT:

1.   JS [*insert P's initials*] lacks capacity to litigate/or on the information presently available to the Court there is reason to believe that JS [*insert P's initials*] lacks capacity to make decisions in respect of her residence care and the extent of contact with .... or

2.   By reason of his Learning Disability and Autistic spectrum disorder JS [*insert P's initials*] does not have capacity to make decisions on where he/she should reside and with whom he/she should have contact.

3.   That JS [*insert P's initials*] lacks capacity to make decisions as to his/her:

        (a)   residence;

        (b)   care; and

        (c)   contact.

Residence

4.   It is lawful and in JS's [*insert P's initials*] best interests to reside at .... [*insert name and address of Home/Rehabilitation Centre etc*] or at her current placement until further order or final determination of the application in accordance with the care plan dated .... (whether or not the same amounts to deprivation of liberty) or

5.   JS [*insert P's initials*] shall be moved immediately from .... to .... so that the Applicant may assess his/her capacity and best interests in respect of his/her residence, care and contact with ....

6.   It is in JS's [*insert P's initials*] best interests to continue to reside at accommodation at .... arranged by the .... [*name the local authority*] and to receive care arranged by the LA. In the event that the Applicant has to take steps to remove JS [*insert P's initials*] from the .... Home in order to prevent serious harm to JS [*insert P's initials*], his carers or any other person in such circumstances that it is not possible for the matter to be brought before the Court prior to his removal, then(and only then) it is lawful and in JS's [*insert P's initials*] best interests:

   (a)   for him to be removed from the .... Home [*insert the name of the Home/Centre*]; and

   (b)   thereafter pending further order of the Court, for him to reside at such other accommodation arranged by the Applicant local authority in accordance with the care plan submitted to the Court;

   (c)   the Applicant shall provide to the other parties full written details of the steps leading up to any removal in the circumstances outlined above and also shall refer the matter to the Court within 48 hours of the removal or as soon thereafter as is practicable.

7.   It is not in JS's [*insert P's initials*] best interests to reside with or be provided with care by ....

Authority to use Restraint/Deprivation of Liberty

8.   The Applicant only if necessary may use reasonable and proportionate force to effect the move. Such force may include restraining JS [*insert P's initials*] and to the extent that it deprives him/her of his/her liberty it is justified. The administration of a sedative or other medication is not authorised. Should force be used in the course of the move then the Applicant shall file and serve a report specifically addressing that within 7 days.

9.   It is lawful and in JS's [*insert P's initials*] best interests that reasonable and proportionate measures are taken to ensure that JS [*insert P's initials*] continues to reside at .... Home and in the event that he/she absents himself/herself without the approval of the manager of the Home, that reasonable and proportionate measures be taken to return him/her there [or]

10.   It is lawful and proportionate and in the best interests of JS [*insert P's initials*], for the Applicant's servants agents to separate JS [*insert P's initials*] and .... [*name person*] by the use of minimal physical contact if necessary, for example taking JS's [*insert P's*

initials] arm and leading him/her away at the end of any contact session (whether or not such measures amount to deprivation of liberty) or

11.   It is lawful being in JS's [*insert P's initials*] best interests, that whilst he/she continues to reside in accommodation arranged by the Applicant and pending future reviews, reasonable and proportionate measures (including any measures which amount to deprivation of his/her liberty) may be taken to prevent the .... Respondents [*insert name*] from removing JS [*insert P's initials*] from such accommodation) or

12.   It is lawful and in the best interests of JS [*insert P's initials*] that while he/she continues to reside at .... Hospital that reasonable and proportionate measures set out in the Applicant's Risk Assessment and Management Plan dated .... or the Risk Management Plan referred to below be taken to prevent JS [*insert P's initials*] leaving (including measures which amount to deprivation of liberty). Force in order to prevent JS [*insert P's initials*] leaving the .... Hospital shall not be used upon JS [*insert P's initials*] by any person other than officers of the Applicant and/or staff of the NHS Trust/ PCT and only such force as is absolutely necessary should be used and only by person having appropriate training in safe restraint techniques.

13.   [*where necessary*] For the purposes of its assessment at the .... Home the Applicant and those it instructs have permission to examine including physically examine him/her.

14.   It is lawful and in JS's [*insert P's initials*] interests whilst resident at the Paradise Care Home to receive health and social care in accordance with the assessment of the Applicant and those health clinicians responsible for his/her care subject to the Applicant filing and serving its proposals in respect of the future placement of JS and its care plans and restraint policy at the Paradise Care Home by .... [*insert date*].

Review of deprivation of liberty provision (where there is no authorisation in force)

15.   The Applicant/local authority shall review the deprivation of JS's [*insert P's initials*] liberty as regular intervals, the first such review shall be convened within 6 weeks of the date hereof. The Official Solicitor on behalf of JS [*insert P's initials*] shall be invited to attend all such internal reviews pending the final determination of the proceedings.

16.   Prior to each review the Applicant shall consider:

        (a)   whether JS [*insert P's initials*] has regained capacity in relation to the issue of residence care and contact and the care package that he/she should receive and what assistance, if any, could be given to assist him/her in making decisions on those issues;

(b)   whether further expert evidence, if any is required on the issue of capacity and to obtain such evidence if required;

(c)   whether the deprivation of liberty provisions remain necessary and proportionate and in JS's [*insert P's initials*] interests.

17.   in the event that the Applicant has cause to use the deprivation of liberty provisions, the applicant shall:

(a)   notify the Official Solicitor's representative as soon as reasonably practicable; and

(b)   keep proper records of the events leading up to the use of the deprivation of liberty provisions including the names of those involved, the control used to prevent JS [*insert P's initials*] leaving [*insert the reasons for using the provisions*] any injury suffered by any person involved in any such incident and the treatment, if any received.

18.   The Court shall review the deprivation of liberty provisions at a hearing on .... day of .... 2010 (T/E 1 hour). The hearing shall be by telephone unless any party indicates by midday on the .... [*insert date*] that they require the hearing to be in person. Prior to the hearing the following directions shall apply:

(a)   the HCC [*the local authority*] shall file and serve a position statement by .... ;

(b)   the Official Solicitor for JS [*insert P's initials*] shall file and serve a position statement by ....

Contact

19.   It is lawful and in JS's [*insert P's initials*] best interests for him/her to have reasonable contact with .... [*insert name*], the level and frequency of such contact to be arranged between the respective parties and the staff at the .... Home in accordance with JS's [*insert P's initials*] care plans or

20.   It is in JS's [*insert P's initials*] best interests to have contact with .... [*insert name*] in accordance with the Schedule attached to this Order.

21.   It is not in JS's [*insert P's initials*] best interests to have contact with .... [*insert name*] contrary to his expressed wishes save as provided for in the Schedule attached to this order.

22.   It is in JS's [*insert P's initials*] best interests to have only supervised contact with .... [*insert name*] in accordance with the care plan /as provided for in the Schedule attached to this order or

23.   It is in JS's [*insert P's initials*] best interests to have contact with .... [*insert name*] subject to the conditions set out in the Schedule attached to this order which may only be varied by .... after consultation with a representative of the Applicant's Social Services Department or on an application to this Court by an order of this Court.

24.   It is in JS's [*insert P's initials*] best interests to have supervised contact with .... [*insert name*] as follows:

        [*Set out the venue, frequency, duration/whether it needs to be agreed with the Official Solicitor or nor and whether the Applicant can bring contact to an end and if so in what circumstances*]

25.   There shall be a meeting attended by all parties, their legal representatives, and .... [*insert the names of the person*] at . .... [*identify the venue*] on .... [*specify the date*] for the purposes of the parties attempting to try and reach an agreement on a suitable contact schedule – such meeting is to be on a without prejudice basis save as to costs. If such contact is agreed, the parties shall inform the Court immediately. In the event that an agreement is not reached the application be listed for a final hearing before .... on .... day of .... 2010 (T/E ....). [*The court will also give directions for the filing of evidence – see below*]

Conduct of .... [*relevant persons should be named*]/*Injunctions*

26.   AB, CD .... [*name the person who are to be the subject of these orders*] shall not by themselves or by instructing encouraging or suggesting to another person.

[*See Chapter 11 Enforcement for precedents*]

Disclosure

27.   The Applicant shall disclose to the Official Solicitor's representative all social care records, assessments, care plans, reviews relating to JS [*insert P's initials*] which it has in its possession and control by the ....

28.   The Speedwell medical practice shall disclose to the Official Solicitor's representatives JS's [*insert P's initials*] medical records by the .... [*insert date*].

29.   Any third Party (including NHS Trusts, Hospitals and other bodies and GP practices) holding information relating to JS [*insert P's initials*] is herby directed to release to the Official Solicitor such information and documents (including clinical records, GP records

and social services records) as he may require on behalf of JS [*insert P's initials*] within 7 days of such request.

30.   The .... [*identify any other organization or person*] shall forthwith disclose to the Applicant copies of all records concerning JS [*insert P's initials*] from the 1 January 2000 to the date hereof and shall thereafter disclose such records to the Applicant authority on a continuing basis and the Applicant shall upon receipt of such records forthwith serve copies of those records to .... 's legal representatives.

31.   Any third party holding information relating to JS's [*insert P's initials*] finances, state benefits is directed to release to the Official Solicitor such information and documents as he may require on behalf of JS [*insert P's initials*] in the course of his investigations within 7 days of any request.

32.   The Chief Constable of Hellenic CC must within 14 days of receipt of a request from the Official Solicitor, provide full details including any printouts of the relevant incident logs in relation to all incidents involving JS [*insert P's initials*] in his possession and control subject to the following:

(a)   the Chief Constable may redact any such document to remove the sensitive details of third parties;

(b)   the Chief Constable do have permission to apply to discharge or vary this order within 7 days of receiving the order and on at least two clear days notice on the other parties;

Save that any third party may apply to the Court on 48 hours notice for further directions if they are unable to comply with this order.

33.   The Official Solicitor do provide to the legal representatives of the Second Respondent [*or as the case may be*] copies of all such disclosed documents.

34.   The Official Solicitor shall have permission to apply to the Court on notice to all the parties, for permission to redact or withhold any such document, if he considers that it would not be in the best interests of JS [*insert P's initials*] for those documents to be disclosed to the other parties.

Experts

35.   A consultant psychiatrist/psychologist agreed between the parties, shall be jointly instructed to prepare a report on JS's [*insert P's initials*] capacity (a) to litigate; (b) to make decisions about his/her residence care and contact arrangements and (d) the impact on him/her of the deprivation of liberty provisions.

36. An independent social worker agreed between the parties shall be instructed to prepare a report as to JS's [*insert P's initials*] best interests in respect of residence care and contact.

37. The Joint letter of instructions to the above experts to be drafted by the Official Solicitor/the Official Solicitor's representative shall be agreed by the parties by the .... [*insert date*].

38. All relevant documents, court papers, social services files, medical records [*set out any other records or documents*] shall be disclosed to the experts immediately.

39. There be permission to the social worker to inspect all the relevant papers filed in the proceedings and to interview JS [*insert P's initials*] for the purposes of undertaking the assessment.

40. There be permission to the psychiatrist/psychologist to inspect all the relevant papers filed in the proceedings and to interview and examine JS [*insert P's initials*] and his/her family for the purposes of providing his/her report.

41. The reasonable fees of the independent social worker and the experts shall be paid in the first instance by the Applicant [or where public funding has been granted] shall be paid by the parties in equal shares and the Court deems the costs of instructing such experts to be a reasonable and proper disbursement for the purposes of public funding certificates of the publicly funded parties.

42. The independent social worker and the experts shall file and serve and interim report by .... [*insert date*] and a final report by .... [*insert date*].

Listing

43. The matter be adjourned for further directions and consideration of whether any continuing deprivation of liberty remains justified/contact before District Judge .... sitting at .... on .... day of .... 2010 (T/E .... hour).

Directions

44. In preparation for the adjourned hearing:

    (a) the .... Respondents shall file and serve their witness statements setting out his/her/their position in respect of JS's [*insert P's initials*] removal/residence/care/contact/ assessment and in response to the Applicant's statement by 4 pm on .... [*insert date*].

(b)   the Applicant and .... shall file and serve their respective position statements and any other evidence they intend to rely on by .... [*insert date*].

45.   The final hearing be listed before a District judge/a nominated circuit judge/a judge of the Family Division of the High Court authorised to sit in the Court of Protection on a date to be fixed (T/E .... days).

46.   In preparation for the final hearing:

(a)   the applicant shall file and serve its final evidence and care plan and any supporting evidence that it intends to rely on by .... [*insert date*].

(b)   the Respondents shall file and serve their respective evidence and any supporting evidence he/she/they intend to rely on by . .... [*insert date*].

(c)   the Official Solicitor on behalf of JS [*insert P's initials*] shall file and serve a witness statement and any evidence on which he wishes to rely on by .... [*insert date*].

(d)   all parties to agree and the Applicant to file at Court not less than 4 clear working days before the hearing a paginated, indexed bundle containing a chronology, case summary, statement of issues, each party's position statement and skeleton arguments and the legal authorities relied on.

Liberty to apply

47.   If any person served with this order disagrees with any part of this order and wishes to seek to set aside or vary it, he/she/ they should make an immediate application to this court to do so and give .... [*insert time limit*] clear days notice to all other parties.

Costs

48.   No order for costs save detailed assessment of the publicly funded costs of JS [*insert P's initials*] and .... [*insert details of the parties*].

49.   Costs reserved or

50.   Cost in the application and/or

51.   The costs of the Official Solicitor and his solicitors of an incidental to these proceedings shall be paid out of JS's [*insert P's initials*] monies. All invoice ad fee notes/vouchers for disbursements on an interim basis shall be paid by JS's [*insert P's initials*] property and affairs deputy within 28 days of receipt unless prior

to such date the said Deputy applies to the Court for directions in respect of the payment of the interim invoices/fee notes/vouchers for disbursements.

PRECEDENT FOR AN ORDER APPOINTING A DEPUTY FOR PERSONAL WELFARE

IN THE COURT OF PROTECTION   CASE NO ....

IN THE MATTER OF THE MENTAL CAPACITY ACT 2005

AND IN THE MATTER OF P [*insert forename and surname*]

BETWEEN

AB	Applicant
And	
XY	Respondent

ORDER APPOINTING A DEPUTY FOR PERSONAL WELFARE

Made by ....

At Archway Tower, 2 Junction Road, London N19 5SZ

On ....

WHEREAS

(1)   An application has been made for an order under the Mental Capacity Act 2005.

(2)   The court is satisfied that P [*insert forename and surname*] is unable to make various decisions for herself in relation to a matter or matters concerning her personal welfare because of an impairment of, or a disturbance in the functioning of, her mind or brain.

(3)   The court is satisfied that the purpose for which the order is needed cannot be as effectively achieved in a way that is less restrictive of her rights and freedom of action.

IT IS ORDERED that:

(a)   Appointment of deputy

(a)   .... [*insert full name of deputy*] of [*insert full address and postcode*] is appointed as deputy ("the deputy") to make personal welfare decisions on behalf of P [*insert forename and surname*] that she is unable to make for herself subject to any conditions or restrictions set out in this order.

(b)   The appointment will last until further order.

(c)   The deputy must apply the principles set out in section 1 of the Mental Capacity Act 2005 and have regard to the guidance in the Code of Practice to the Act.

(b)   Authority of deputy

(a)   The Court authorises the deputy to make the following decisions on behalf of P [*insert forename and surname*] that she is unable to make for herself when the decision needs to be made:

    (i)   Where she should live;

    (ii)   With whom she should live;

    (iii)   Decisions on day-to-day care, including diet and dress;

    (iv)   Consenting to medical or dental examination and treatment on her behalf;

    (v)   Making arrangements for the provision of care services;

    (vi)   Whether she should take part in particular leisure or social activities;

    (vii)   Complaints about her care or treatment; [*Delete paragraph if not applicable*]

(b)   For the purpose of giving effect to any decision the deputy may execute or sign any necessary deeds or documents.

(c)   The deputy does not have authority to make a decision on behalf of P [*insert forename and surname*] in relation to a matter if the deputy knows or has reasonable grounds for believing that she had capacity in relation to the matter.

(d)   The deputy does not have the authority to make the following decisions or do the following things in relation to P [*insert forename and surname*]:

    (i)   To prohibit any person from having contact with her;

    (ii)   To direct a person responsible for her health care to allow a different person to take over that responsibility;

    (iii)   To make a decision that is inconsistent with a decision made, within the scope of his authority and in accordance with the Act, by the donee of a lasting power of attorney granted by her (or, if there is more than one donee, by any of them);

     (iv)   To consent to specific treatment if she has made a valid and applicable advance decision to refuse that specific treatment;

     (v)   To refuse consent to the carrying out or continuation of life sustaining treatment in relation to her;

     (vi)   To do an act that is intended to restrain her otherwise then in accordance with the conditions specified in the Act.

(c) Reports

(a)   The deputy is required to keep a record of any decisions made or acts done pursuant to this order and the reasons for making or doing them.

(b)   The deputy must submit an annual report to the Public Guardian.

Requested by: *[solicitors'/applicant's name]*

Your ref: «sols ref»

Our ref: NA/«COP ref no»

PRECEDENT OF ORDER APPOINTING JOINT DEPUTIES FOR PERSONAL AND WELFARE

IN THE COURT OF PROTECTION   CASE NO ....

IN THE MATTER OF THE MENTAL CAPACITY ACT 2005

AND IN THE MATTER OF P [*insert forename and surname*]

BETWEEN

	AB	Applicant
	And	
	XY	Respondent

ORDER APPOINTING JOINT DEPUTIES
FOR PERSONAL WELFARE

Made by ....

At Archway Tower, 2 Junction Road, London N19 5SZ

On .... [*insert date*]

WHEREAS

(1)   An application has been made for an order under the Mental Capacity Act 2005.

(2)   The court is satisfied that P [*insert forename and surname*] is unable to make various decisions for herself in relation to a matter or matters concerning her personal welfare because of an impairment of, or a disturbance in the functioning of, her mind or brain.

(3)   The court is satisfied that the purpose for which the order is needed cannot be as effectively achieved in a way that is less restrictive of her rights and freedom of action.

IT IS ORDERED that:

2. Appointment of deputies

(a)   .... [*insert full name of first deputy*] of .... [*insert address and postcode*] and .... [*insert full name of second deputy*] of [*insert address and postcode*] are appointed as joint deputies ("the joint deputies") to make personal welfare decisions on behalf of P [*insert forename and surname*] that she is unable to make for herself subject to any conditions or restrictions set out in this order.

(b)   The appointment will last until further order.

(c)   The joint deputies must apply the principles set out in section 1 of the Mental Capacity Act 2005 and have regard to the guidance in the Code of Practice to the Act.

3.   Authority of joint deputies

(a)   The Court authorises the joint deputies to make the following decisions on behalf of P [*insert forename and surname*] that she is unable to make for himself when the decision needs to be made:

(i)   Where she should live

(ii)   With whom she should live

(iii)   Decisions on day-to-day care, including diet and dress

(iv)   Consenting to medical or dental examination and treatment on her behalf

(v)   Making arrangements for the provision of care services

(vi)   Whether she should take part in particular leisure or social activities

(vii)   Complaints about her care or treatment

(b)   For the purpose of giving effect to any decision the joint deputies may execute or sign any necessary deeds or documents.

(c)   The joint deputies do not have authority to make a decision on behalf of P [*insert forename and surname*] in relation to a matter if the joint deputies know or have reasonable grounds for believing that she had capacity in relation to the matter.

(d)   The joint deputies do not have the authority to make the following decisions or do the following things in relation to P [*insert forename and surname*]:

(i)   To prohibit any person from having contact with her;

(ii)   To direct a person responsible for her health care to allow a different person to take over that responsibility;

(iii)   To make a decision that is inconsistent with a decision made, within the scope of her authority and in accordance with the Act, by the donee of a lasting power of attorney granted by her (or, if there is more than one donee, by any of them);

(iv)   To consent to specific treatment if she has made a valid and applicable advance decision to refuse that specific treatment;

(v)   To refuse consent to the carrying out or continuation of life sustaining treatment in relation to her;

(vi)   To do an act that is intended to restrain her otherwise then in accordance with the conditions specified in the Act.

4. Reports

(a)   The joint deputies are required to keep a record of any decisions made or acts done pursuant to this order and the reasons for making or doing them.

(b)   The joint deputies must submit an annual report to the Public Guardian.

Requested by: *[solicitors'/applicant's name]*

Your ref: «sols ref»

Our ref: NA/«COP ref no»

PRECEDENT OF ORDER APPOINTING JOINT AND SEVERAL DEPUTIES FOR PERSONAL WELFARE

IN THE COURT OF PROTECTION   CASE NO ....

IN THE MATTER OF THE MENTAL CAPACITY ACT 2005

AND IN THE MATTER OF .... [*insert forename and surname*]

BETWEEN

	AB	Applicant
	And	
	XY	Respondent

ORDER APPOINTING JOINT AND SEVERAL DEPUTIES FOR PERSONAL WELFARE

Made by ....

At Archway Tower, 2 Junction Road, London N19 5SZ

On .... [*insert date*]

WHEREAS

(1)   An application has been made for an order under the Mental Capacity Act 2005.

(2)   The court is satisfied that P [*insert forename and surname*] is unable to make various decisions for herself in relation to a matter or matters concerning her personal welfare because of an impairment of, or a disturbance in the functioning of, her mind or brain.

(3)   The court is satisfied that the purpose for which the order is needed cannot be as effectively achieved in a way that is less restrictive of her rights and freedom of action.

IT IS ORDERED that:

1.   Appointment of deputies

(a)   .... [*insert name of first deputy*] of .... [*insert full address and postcode*] and .... [*insert name of second deputy*] of .... [*insert full address and postcode*] are appointed jointly and severally as deputies to make personal welfare decisions on behalf of P (insert forename and surname) that she is unable to make for herself subject to any conditions or restrictions set out in this order.

(b)   The appointment will last until further order.

(c)   The joint deputies must apply the principles set out in section 1 of the Mental Capacity Act 2005 and have regard to the guidance in the Code of Practice to the Act.

2. Authority of joint deputies

(a) The Court authorises the deputies jointly and severally to make the following decisions on behalf of P [*insert forename and surname*] that she is unable to make for himself when the decision needs to be made:

(i)   Where she should live

(ii)   With whom she should live

(iii)   Decisions on day-to-day care, including diet and dress

(iv)   Consenting to medical or dental examination and treatment on her behalf

(v)   Making arrangements for the provision of care services

(vi)   Whether she should take part in particular leisure or social activities

(vii)   Complaints about her care or treatment [*Delete paragraph if not applicable*]

(b)   For the purpose of giving effect to any decision the joint and several deputies may execute or sign any necessary deeds or documents.

(c)   The joint and several deputies do not have authority to make a decision on behalf of P [*insert forename and surname*] in relation to a matter if the joint deputies know or have reasonable grounds for believing that she had capacity in relation to the matter.

(d)   The joint and several deputies do not have the authority to make the following decisions or do the following things in relation to P [*insert forename and surname*].

–   To prohibit any person from having contact with her

–   To direct a person responsible for her health care to allow a different person to take over that responsibility

–   To make a decision that is inconsistent with a decision made, within the scope of her authority and in accordance with the Act, by the donee of a lasting power of attorney granted by her (or, if there is more than one donee, by any of them);

– To consent to specific treatment if she has made a valid and applicable advance decision to refuse that specific treatment;

– To refuse consent to the carrying out or continuation of life sustaining treatment in relation to her

– To do an act that is intended to restrain her otherwise then in accordance with the conditions specified in the Act

3. Reports

(a) The joint and several deputies are required to keep a record of any decisions made or acts done pursuant to this order and the reasons for making or doing them.

(b) The joint and several deputies must submit an annual report to the Public Guardian.

Requested by: [*solicitors' or applicant's name*]

Your ref: «sols ref»

Our ref: NA/«COP ref no»

CHAPTER 4

DEPRIVATION OF LIBERTY

LAW AND PRACTICE

4.1 INTRODUCTION

People who lack capacity are unable to consent to their living arrangements. For those who are resident in institutional care this may mean that they are effectively deprived of their liberty. The Mental Capacity Act 2005, as amended, introduced a framework of safeguards not previously available, for those who lack capacity to agree to living arrangements which have the effect of depriving them of their liberty unlawfully.

4.2 BACKGROUND

An unlawful deprivation of a person's liberty is contrary to Art 5 of the European Convention for the Protection of Human Rights and Fundamental Freedoms. For those suffering with a mental disorder, the Mental Health Act 1983 as amended by the Mental Health Act 2007 makes provision for their hospital admission, for assessment and treatment. Section 1(2) of the Mental Health Act 1983 as amended defines 'mental disorder' as 'any disorder or disability of the mind'. The 1983 Act in its original form contained provisions which enabled the compulsory detention in hospital of persons suffering from mental disorder who were either unable or unwilling to consent to such assessment and treatment provided certain conditions set out in the Act were met.[1] The Mental Health Act 2007 extends this power to treatment within the community of patients who are discharged from hospital by introducing compulsory treatment orders. The 1983 Act as amended sets out the conditions and criteria which must be satisfied before a person can be compulsorily detained under these provisions. It also sets out a review and appeal procedure so that the patient can challenge any decision made concerning his detention against his will. These protective rights render the detention lawful. Similar protection was not available for those who lack capacity. They were subject to so-called informal admission to hospital or other institutional care by way of an administrative decision

---

[1] MHA 1983, s 2(2).

made by health or social services departments of local authorities which was not formally authorised. The nature of these placements, effectively deprived them of their liberty even if it was limited to locking of doors for safety reasons. P was in such circumstances unable to consent to the deprivation of liberty through lack of capacity and there were no safeguards in place.

This shortfall in safeguards and lack of protection of P's rights was identified by the European Court of Human Rights in *HL v UK (Bournewood)*[2] and became known as the 'Bournewood Gap'. Mr HL was an autistic man who lacked capacity. He was re-admitted to Bournewood hospital following his placement with carers in the community. He was not 'sectioned' under the Mental Health Act 1983 as he had not resisted the admission to the hospital. His carers were critical of the care and treatment he was being given by the hospital and disapproved of his continued detention. This led to an application for judicial review of the decision on the ground that HL had been unlawfully detained. The carers failed in their application. They appealed to the Court of Appeal which reversed the decision and upheld the carers' claim that he had been unlawfully detained. There was a further appeal to the House of Lords which reinstated the decision of the High Court.

The case was taken to the European Court of Human Rights. The ECtHR identified the following factual factors relating to the case which contributed to a deprivation of liberty:

(a)   the nature of the restraint which was used, including sedation, to admit Mr HL to hospital when he was resisting admission;

(b)   the staff exercised complete and effective control over his care and movement for a significant period of the day on a daily basis;

(c)   the staff exercised control over assessments, treatment, and contact with others;

(d)   a decision had been taken that he would be prevented from leaving if he attempted to do so or his carers sought to remove him;

(e)   the carers request for his discharge had been refused without any recourse for challenging that decision;

(f)   he was not able to make or maintain any outside social contacts due to the restrictions placed on his movements and access by others to him;

(g)   he was kept under constant supervision and control and hence lost autonomy.

---

[2]   (2004) 40 EHRR 761.

The Court held that Mr HL had been deprived of his liberty contrary to Art 5(1) of the Convention. His detention had been arbitrary and there was no procedure in place prescribed by law to permit such detention, nor were there any procedures available to him under which he could seek to have the decision reviewed or to challenge the merits of the decision or the conditions for his detention in breach of Art 5(4). The court referred to the safeguards which were available to a person detained under the Mental Health Act 1983 and the lack of such or any procedure for the detention of a person who did not suffer from mental disorder but lacked capacity. The court in particular highlighted the lack of any formal procedures in place: (a) on who could authorise such detention or admission; (b) for reasons to be given for such admission and whether the admission was for treatment or assessment; (c) for a continuing assessment and review; (d) for the person lacking capacity to be represented; and (e) for the person lacking disability or a representative on his behalf to seek a review of his detention or continued detention before a formal independent and appropriate tribunal.

After the decision of the European Court in *HL v UK*, (above) and implementation of the Human Rights Act 1998 the issue of deprivation of liberty took on a greater significance in the domestic courts. The domestic courts attempted to bridge the 'gap' in the cases that followed by applying the principles set out by the European Courts. Parliament also had a duty to resolve the issues raised and introduce legislation which contained the appropriate safeguards. The Mental Capacity Act 2005, s 5 addressed some of the issues raised by the Court but the decision of the ECtHR was not handed down in time for all the gaps in the legislation to be dealt with. The Mental Health Act 2007 was subsequently introduced to inter alia add new provisions to the Mental Capacity Act 2005 to fill the gaps identified by the European Court. These provisions are known as the deprivation of liberty safeguards. The Deprivation of Liberty Safeguards – Code of Practice pursuant to ss 42 and 43 of the Act has been issued to provide guidance and information for those implementing deprivation of liberty safeguards on a daily basis to ensure that by following the criteria set out, any decision taken to deprive a person, who lacks capacity, of his or her liberty can be made lawfully. The Code of Practice is intended to apply to paid staff and other professionals who have been appointed to represent the person who lacks capacity and to make decisions on that person's behalf. As with the main Code of Practice this Code has statutory force and must be followed. In addition, a number of regulations have also been issued e g the Mental Capacity (Deprivation of Liberty: Standard Authorisations, Assessments and Ordinary Residence) Regulations 2008[3] and the Mental Capacity (Deprivation of Liberty: Appointment of Relevant Person's Representative) (Amendment) Regulations 2008.[4] Guidance to and for all the relevant professionals and public bodies have also been made available by the Department of Health.

---

[3]   SI 2008/1858,
[4]   SI 2008/2368.

These can be accessed on the department's website: www.dh.gov.uk/en/
SocialCare/Deliveringadultsocialcare/MentalCapacity/
MentalCapacityActDeprivationoflibertySafeguards/index.htm.

The Court of Protection (Amendment) Rules 2009[5] and *Practice
Directions* thereunder (the Deprivation of Liberty Rules) and Forms have
also been issued to ensure that any application made to the Court is dealt
with expeditiously by a specially appointed team. The rules and Practice
Directions set out the procedure which must be followed when making an
application for a declaration for deprivation of liberty in cases of urgency.
The provisions relating to 'deprivation of liberty' (DoL) came into force
on 1 April 2009.

4.3   WHAT ARE THE ART 5 RIGHTS WHICH MUST BE RESPECTED?

The relevant provisions of Art 5 which are generally relevant to cases
involving a person lacking capacity or a vulnerable person are Art 5(1)(e),
5(4) and 5(5). Art 5(1)(e) provides that:

> 'Everyone has the right to liberty and security of person. No one shall be
> deprived of his liberty save in the following cases and in accordance with a
> procedure prescribed by law ...
> (e)   the lawful detention of persons for the prevention of the spreading of
>   infectious diseases, of persons of unsound mind, alcoholics or drug
>   addicts or vagrants.'

Article 5(4) provides that:

> 'Everyone who is deprived of his liberty by arrest or detention shall be
> entitled to take proceedings by which the lawfulness of his detention shall be
> decided speedily by a court and his release ordered if the detention is not
> lawful.'

Article 5(5) provides that:

> 'Everyone who has been the victim of arrest or detention in contravention of
> the provisions of this Article shall have an enforceable right to
> compensation.'

4.4   WHAT AMOUNTS TO A DEPRIVATION OF LIBERTY?

There is no legal definition of deprivation of liberty. For the purposes of
the Act deprivation of liberty is defined in s 6(5) as having the same
meaning as in Art 5(1) of the Human Rights Convention. Lord Hoffman

---

[5]   SI 2009/582.

in *Home Secretary v JJ*[6] said that it was not easy to discover the criterion from the majority of the decision: 'the nearest one gets is the situation that "in certain respects the treatment complained of resembles detention in an 'open prison' or committal to a disciplinary unit"', and he referred to the observations made by Judge Matcher in *Guzzardi* (see below) that deprivation of liberty was 'a concept of some complexity, having a core which cannot be the subject of argument but which is surrounded by a "grey zone" where it is extremely difficult to draw the line.'

Baroness Hale in that case said that to be deprived of liberty does not mean deprived of the freedom to live ones life as one wishes:

> 'It must mean forced or obliged to be at a particular place where one does not choose to be. But even that is not enough to amount to deprivation of liberty. There must be a greater degree of control over one's physical liberty than that.'

The European Court and the domestic courts have established certain key principles which should be applied as guidance when assessing a case. In *Guzzardi v Italy*[7] it was said:

> 'The Court recall that in proclaiming the "right to liberty" paragraph 1 of Article 5 is contemplating the physical liberty of the person; its aim is to ensure that no one should be dispossessed of this liberty in an arbitrary fashion ... the paragraph is not concerned with the mere restrictions of liberty of movement ... In order to determine whether someone has been deprived of his liberty within the meaning of Article 5, the starting point must be his concrete situation and account must be taken of a whole range of criteria such as the type, duration, effects and manner of implementation of the measure in question.'

and:

> 'The difference between deprivation of and restriction upon liberty is nonetheless merely one of degree or intensity, and not one of nature or substance.'

It is not merely one of restriction of movement.

This principle has been repeated and established in a number of decisions of the European Court. It has also been applied in cases decided by the High Court. In *JE v DE and Surrey County Council*,[8] an application was made by a wife seeking a declaration that the local authority had deprived her husband of his liberty. Her husband was 76 years of age when he was taken into care suffering from dementia after his wife had placed him in a chair on a pavement outside their home clothed only in his pyjama

---

[6] [2007] UKHL 45.
[7] (1980) 3 EHRR.
[8] [2006] EWHC 3459 (Fam).

bottoms and a shirt and slippers and refused to have him back home. Whilst in care he was repeatedly expressing a desire to go home. Whilst he was allowed contact with his wife he was restricted from leaving. It was established that he lacked capacity to decide where he should live. Munby J (as he then was) having considered the circumstances and facts in the case said at para 115 of his judgment:

> 'The crucial question in this case, as it seems to me, is not so much whether (and, if so, to what extent) DE's freedom or liberty was or is curtailed within the institutional setting. The fundamental issue in this case, in my judgment, is whether DE has been and is deprived of his liberty to leave the Y home. And when I refer to leaving the X home and the Y home, I do not mean leaving for the purpose of some trip or outing approved by SCC or by those managing the institution; I mean leaving in the sense of removing himself permanently in order to live where and with whom he chooses, specially removing himself to live at home with JE.'

In *Home Secretary v JJ*[9] the House of Lords (now known as the Supreme Court) emphasised that the borderline between restriction and deprivation remains indistinct and stated that 'it is essential not to give an over-expansive interpretation to the concept of deprivation of liberty.' The issue is therefore one of whether P was required to live in a confined area. The court held that in order to determine whether someone has been 'deprived of his liberty' within the meaning of Art 5(1):

> 'the starting point must be his concrete situation and account must be taken of the whole range of criteria such as the type, duration, effects and manner of implementation of the measure in question.'

On the facts the Court ruled that P had been deprived of his liberty. The court also added that distinction between 'restraint and deprivation of liberty was one of degree or intensity and not one of nature or substance'.

In *Ashingdane v UK*[10] the Court applied the same principle. In *Neilson v Denmark*[11] a 12 year old boy had been admitted to a psychiatric ward of a hospital for nervous disorder at the request of his mother. He remained in hospital for five and a half months. The restrictions on his movements were no different to that in any hospital. He was free to leave the ward with permission and go out accompanied by a member of the staff. The court held that his admission to hospital did not constitute deprivation of liberty and that the admission had been a responsible exercise of the mother's parental responsibility and in the best interests of the child.

In *HM v Switzerland*[12] an elderly person was placed in a nursing home to provide her with the necessary medical care and living condition. The

---

9   [2007] UKHL 45.
10   (1985) 7 EHRR 528.
11   (1988) EHRR 175.
12   (2002) 38 EHRR 314.

nursing home allowed freedom of movement and encouraged her to have social contact between others both within and outside the institution. After moving to the nursing home she had agreed to remain there. As a result of which the placement order had been lifted. In holding that she was not deprived of her liberty, the Court took into account the fact that she had been placed in the home in her own interests to provide her with medical care and living conditions which addressed her personal and welfare needs. The applicant had also been indecisive regarding whether she wanted to stay at the home or not. The court decided that the placement was a 'responsible measure taken by the competent authorities in the applicant's interests' and the situation was not of a degree or intensity to justify the conclusion that she had been deprived of her liberty.

In *HL v UK (Bournewood)*[13] the dispute was between the carers of an autistic person and the hospital and related to his care and treatment. The ECtHR followed the principles set out in *Guzzardi v Italy* and held that the patient was unlawfully deprived of his liberty as his professional carers exercised complete and effective control over his care and his movements and there was no procedure in place prescribed by law or otherwise regarding his admission, and grounds for or authorisation of his detention (see further below).

In *Storck v Germany*[14] an 18 year old was placed in a psychiatric clinic at the request of her father and cared for under constant supervision and was not permitted to leave the clinic. She had on several occasions tried to escape and was chained to a radiator to prevent her leaving. On one occasion having succeeded in escaping from the clinic she had been returned to the clinic by the police. Holding that that she had been deprived of her liberty the Court stated:

> 'the Court is unable to discern any actual basis for the assumption that the applicant – presuming that she had the capacity to consent – agreed to her continued stay in the clinic. In the alternative, assuming that the applicant was no longer capable of consenting following her treatment with strong medication, she cannot, in any event, be considered to have validly agreed to her stay in the clinic.'

Since the decision in *HL v UK* a number of cases have been decided in the domestic court in which the principles set out in the decisions of the ECtHR have been considered, applied and developed. The majority of them were decided under the High Court's inherent jurisdiction and before the amendments introduced by the Mental Health Act 2007 came into force but they are nevertheless relevant for future reference subject to any further legal developments whether statutory or in case law. In these cases, the Court has acknowledged the difficulty in assessing borderline

---

[13] (2004) 40 EHRR 761.
[14] (2005) 43 EHRR 96.

cases, suggesting that in such cases the decision was one of opinion or judgment and that there is no bright line separating the two.

Lord Bingham said that national courts must look to the jurisprudence of the Commission and the European Court in Strasbourg which the UK courts are required by s 2(1) of the Human Rights Act 1998 to take account of. But that jurisprudence must be used as laying down principles and not mandatory solutions because case law shows that the Art 5 rights have been considered in a very wide range of factual situations. Therefore, the national courts must look for guidance inter alia to the principles laid down in *Guzzardi v Italy* reiterated by the Courts on many occasions and to seek to give fair effect, on the facts of the case to those principles. Lord Bingham also warned that it was 'perilous to transpose the outcome of one case to another where the facts are different and all the relevant factors and circumstances related to that specific case must be taken into account'. The facts of the individual case must be assessed cumulatively and the question answered, whether in combination they amount to deprivation. There may be no deprivation of liberty if a single feature of an individual's situation is taken on its own, but the combination of measures considered together may have that result (see *Guzzardi v Italy*). Locked doors or institutional surroundings are not essential to the concept of deprivation of liberty. These features may be relevant in the assessment of whether a person has been deprived of his liberty.

4.4.1   Restrictions for the benefit of the person

Not all restrictions on a person's liberty will be considered as a deprivation of liberty. There needs to be an assessment of the degree or intensity of such restrictions. Restrictions designed, at least in part for the benefit of the person lacking capacity may be a relevant consideration. In *HM v Switzerland*[15] the European Court treated as relevant, restrictions which were imposed as a responsible measure in the person's best interests. In *Home Secretary v JJ*[16] (a case concerning control orders) Baroness Hale suggested that such restrictions are less likely to be considered as deprivation of liberty than are restrictions designed for the protection of society, but in *JE v DE and Surrey County Council*[17] Munby J (as he then was) observed that it was an error to confuse the question of deprivation of liberty with whether it had been justified in the interests of the person concerned. He held that the fundamental issue was whether DE was free to leave the care home permanently to live where and with whom he chose.

In *LBCC v TG, JG, and KR*[18] a 78 year old man who suffered from dementia and cognitive impairment had been resident in the L care home.

---

[15]   (2002) 38 EHRR 314.
[16]   [2007] UKHL 45.
[17]   [2006] EWHC 3459 (Fam).
[18]   [2007] EWHC 2640 (Fam).

That placement was terminated but before he could be transferred to an alternative home he was admitted to hospital with pneumonia and septicaemia. While he was in hospital one of his daughters and a granddaughter put themselves forward as possible carers for him. The local authority did not consider that he would be well placed with them as he required 24 hour care in a residential home. The local authority found him an alternative care home but before he could be placed there the hospital discharged him into the care of his daughter and granddaughter. The local authority obtained an order without notice requiring the daughter and granddaughter to deliver him to the care home. He was delivered up as ordered. At the final hearing having considered all the evidence the Court directed that he be placed with the daughter and the granddaughter. They had claimed that he had been deprived of his liberty during the period he had been placed in the care home. Their claim was rejected. While the Court accepted that it was a borderline case it found that the evidence demonstrated that the restrictions placed on the claimants' father was no different to the ones in any ordinary care home. He was able to have contact with his family and permitted to go out with them. He was compliant and had expressed that he was happy in the care home.

4.4.2 Relevance of consent

The issue of the relevance of consent will turn on the facts of the particular case. In *HM v Switzerland*[19] the fact that the person detained had not objected to her placement in the nursing home was taken into consideration when deciding the issue of degree or intensity of the restriction and reached the conclusion that in the circumstances she had not been deprived of her liberty. But in *Storck v Germany*[20] where the applicant had attempted to leave the unit on numerous occasions and was chained to a radiator to prevent her from so doing and had been returned to the home by the police when she had escaped the Court concluded that she had not consented to the placement. Similarly in *JE v DE and Surrey County Council*[21] the Court ruled that the local authority was exercising complete and effective control on the person and on every movement of his including social contact and whether he could live with his wife. Account was also taken of the numerous occasions on which he had expressed his wish to independent professionals without any prompting of his wish to live with his wife to conclude that the actions of the local authority constituted deprivation of his liberty.

In *LBCC v TG, JG, and KR*[22] the Court found that the father had spent three years in a care home. He was compliant and expressed himself as happy in the care home.

---

[19]   (2002) 38 EHRR 314.
[20]   (2005) 43 EHRR 96.
[21]   [2006] EWHC 3459 (Fam).
[22]   [2007] EWHC 2640 (Fam).

4.4.3   Relevance of the freedom to leave

Locked doors or institutional surroundings are not essential to the concept of deprivation of liberty. These features may be relevant in the assessment of whether a person has been deprived of his liberty. In *JE v DE* (above) Munby J (as he then was) considered that the question of whether the person was free to leave was a relevant factor but in *Home Secretary v JJ*[23] Baroness Hale in her judgment said that:

> 'merely being required to live at a particular address or to keep within a particular geographical area does not, without more amount to a deprivation of liberty. There must be a greater degree of control over one's physical liberty than that.'

4.5   SAFEGUARDS

The Act, as amended by the Mental Health Act 2007, now sets out the legal framework for depriving a compliant person of his liberty, previously admitted to care informally, without recourse to the Act of 1983. It puts in place safeguards to ensure that any decision, to deprive someone of his/her liberty, is made following a defined process and in consultation with the appropriate authorities. It also provides a process for an application to be made to the Court of Protection for a declaration or as a means of challenging any decision which seeks to deprive a person of his liberty.

The Deprivation of Liberty Safeguards – Code of Practice refers to the relevant cases to identify some of the factors that should in general be considered by the decision maker in considering whether an act done or proposed to be undertaken may amount to a deprivation of liberty. These are:

- All the circumstances of each and every case.

- What measures are being taken in relation to the individual? When are they required? For what period do they endure? What are the effects of any restraints or restrictions on the individual? Why are they necessary? What aim do they seek to meet?

- What are the views of the relevant person, their family or carers? Do any of them object to the measures?

- How are any restraints or restrictions implemented? Do any of the constraints on the individual's personal freedom go beyond 'restraint' or 'restriction' to the extent that they constitute a deprivation of liberty?

---

[23]   *Home Secretary v JJ* [2007] UKHL 45.

- Are there any less restrictive options for delivering care and treatment that avoid deprivation of liberty altogether?

- Does the cumulative effect of all the restrictions imposed on the person amount to a deprivation of liberty, even if individually they would not?

The Code also sets out the steps which should be taken to reduce the risk of deprivation in para 2.7.

The statutory provisions with the Code of Practice form the Deprivation of Liberty Safeguards which provide a regime for the authorities formally to authorise the deprivation of liberty and provide an appeal process to the Court of Protection in the event of challenge.

Decisions of the High Court exercising its inherent jurisdiction have set out some useful guidelines to safeguard the rights of P (see below *Sunderland v PS & Children Act 1989*[24] and *Salford County Council v GJ, MJ & BJ*[25] and under **4.5**)

The Court of Protection (Amendment) Rules 2009[26] and the Practice Directions thereunder, which came into force on 1 April 2009, set out the procedure and practice in relation to applications for deprivations of liberty and declaration in cases of urgency. The Court of Protection has a dedicated team for the speedy identification and administration of these applications.

4.6 THE COURT OF PROTECTION'S POWERS TO MAKE DECLARATION AUTHORISING DEPRIVATION OF LIBERTY

In its original form the MCA 2005 did not include a specific power to authorise an act of detention. Whether this could be implied has been considered in a number of cases. In *Re PS Incapacitated or Vulnerable Adult*[27] a case under the inherent jurisdiction of the High Court, it was held that the Court has the power to make an order authorising the minimum of force or restraint necessary for detention of an adult who lacks capacity. This issue was further advanced in *Re GJ (Incapacitated Adults)*[28] where restraint was permitted to provide medical treatment to P, but this case too was decided under the inherent jurisdiction of the High Court. The issue was further argued and considered in *Re P (Adult) Medical Treatment)*.[29] It was held that the provisions of s 15(1)(c) of the

---

[24] [2007] EWHC 623 (Fam).
[25] [2008] EWHC 1097 (Fam).
[26] SI 2009/582.
[27] [2007] 2 FLR 1083.
[28] [2008] 2 FLR 1295.
[29] [2009] 1 FCR 567.

Act which confer on the Court the general power to make declarations as to 'the lawfulness or otherwise of any act done, or yet to be done, in relation to' a person who lacks capacity to make a decision, and the provisions of s 48 (interim order and directions, see **2.4.8**) of the Act, were intended to and do empower, the Court of Protection to make orders under the Act similar to those made by the High Court under its inherent jurisdiction before the amendments to the Act by the Mental Health Act 2007 came into effect on 1 April 2009. The court therefore has power, if the circumstances and the welfare of the person concerned requires, to make a declaration under s 6(1)-(4), to render lawful an act of restraint that would otherwise amount to deprivation of liberty and to a breach under s 6(5) of the Act. The Court also relied on s 17 of the Act, which provides that, in relation to the personal welfare of P, the powers of the Court under s 16 to grant an order making a decision or decisions on behalf of P in respect of issues concerning his welfare extend to 'giving or refusing' consent to the carrying out or continuation of a treatment by a person providing health care' for P. The Code of Practice at para 6.51 also provides that:

> 'in some cases the Court of Protection might grant an order that permits the deprivation of a person's liberty, if it is satisfied that this is in the person's interests.'

> 'Thus where the facts justify, and the immediate welfare of an incapacitated adult so dictate, the Court may, by prior declaration in appropriate terms, render lawful an act of restraint under section 6(1)–(4) of the Act, which might otherwise amount to a deprivation of liberty under s 6(5), thus bridging the Bournewood Gap.' (per Sir Mark Potter P).

Since that decision, the amendments made to the Act by the Mental Health Act 2007, s 50 and Schs 7 and 8 came into force on 1 April 2009 by virtue of the Mental Health Act 2007 (Commencement No 10 and Transitional Provisions) Order 2009.[30] Section 4A now empowers the Court of Protection to make an order under the Act (as inserted by the Mental Health Act 2007). Section 4A sets out when a P may be deprived of his liberty. Section 4B of the Act also sets out the condition which must apply before a person may lawfully deprive an incapacitated person of his/her liberty while a decision is sought from the Court. These are:

(1)   there is a question about whether that person is authorised to deprive the incapacitated person of his liberty under s 4A;

(2)   the deprivation of liberty is wholly or partly for the purpose of giving life sustaining treatment or doing any act which the person doing it reasonably believes to be necessary to prevent a serious deterioration in the incapacitated person's condition; and

---

[30]   SI 2009/239.

(3)   the deprivation of liberty is necessary in order to give the life sustaining treatment or doing any act which the person undertaking it reasonably believes to be necessary to prevent a serious deterioration in the person's condition.

In any case where the person's lack of capacity is in question or the issues relate to a vulnerable person it is still possible to issue proceedings in the Court of Protection and the High Court if necessary will invoke its inherent jurisdiction to make the relevant orders as it did in cases decided before 1 April 2009. In *PS (Incapacitated or Vulnerable Adult)*[31] it was held that the Court had power to make an order authorising minimum of force or restraint necessary for detention of an adult who lacks capacity and in *Re GJ (Incapacitated Adults)*[32] the Court authorised restraint in order that medical treatment could be provided to the patient.

In *Sunderland v PS & Children Act 1989*[33] a case decided under the inherent jurisdiction of the High Court, the dispute was between the local authority and the daughter of the person concerned over the care provided for her and her wish to leave the home. The issue was whether the local authority could detain the woman and whether the Court under its inherent jurisdiction could make an order preventing the discharge of the woman from the care of the treatment unit preferred by the local authority and whether it could appoint a receiver to prevent the daughter dissipating her mother's savings and pensions in preference to the local authority applying for orders under the Mental Health Act 1983. Although not a case directly concerned with deprivation of liberty, the Court set out some guidelines which may be relevant if the High Court's powers under it inherent jurisdiction is likely to be relied on. Munby J (as he then was) set the following minimum requirements which must be satisfied:

(1)   the detention must be authorised on an application made before the detention commences;

(2)   except in an emergency, there must be evidence to establish that the person lacks capacity and that the restrictions or restraint proposed is appropriate;

(3)   any order authorising detention must contain provision for an adequate review procedure at reasonable intervals in particular to ascertain whether the lack of capacity persists or detention should continue;

---

[31]   [2007] 2 FLR 1083.
[32]   [2008] 2 FLR 1295.
[33]   [2007] EWHC 623 (Fam).

(4)   in *Salford County Council v GJ, MJ & BJ*[34] whilst accepting that safeguards would depend on the circumstances of the particular case, Munby J suggested an initial review hearing before the Court within 4 weeks of the Court order authorising deprivation of liberty or sooner if the Official Solicitor had not previously been involved in the proceedings;

(5)   regular review by the Court at or about twelve months after the hearing or sooner if so directed by the Court. The Official Solicitor should be involved at each review hearing and should be provided with up to date reports at least 4 weeks in advance of the hearing;

(6)   any party to the proceedings should be at liberty to apply for a review at any time, and where necessary at short notice;

(7)   there must be regular internal reviews as required usually every 8–10 weeks, such reviews to include the Official Solicitor.

4.7   WHAT IS MEANT BY RESTRAINT

Section 6(4) of the Act provides that a person restrains an incapacitated person if:

(a)   he uses, or threatens to use, force to secure the doing of an act which the person lacking capacity resists, or

(b)   restricts that person's liberty of movement, whether or not there is resistance.

See *Guzzardii v Italy*[35] where a suspected Mafioso had been made the subject of a compulsory residence order and taken to a small island, Asinara where he was required to live in a confined area. The court held that in order to determine whether someone has been 'deprived of his liberty' within the meaning of Art 5(1) 'the starting point must be his concrete situation and account must be taken of the whole range of criteria such as the type, duration, effects and manner of implementation of the measure in question'. On the facts, the Court ruled that he had been deprived of his liberty. The court also added that the distinction between 'restraint and deprivation of liberty was one of 'degree or intensity and not one of nature or substance'.

The Act however, permits the use of some form of restraint in limited circumstances and provided two conditions are satisfied. These are, firstly, that the person using restraint must reasonably believe that it is necessary to do the act in order to prevent harm to P and secondly, that the act done

---

[34]   [2008] EWHC 1097 (Fam).
[35]   (1980) 3 EHRR 333.

must be a proportionate response to: (a) the likelihood of P suffering harm; and (b) the seriousness of that harm.[36] The circumstances of P and the situation which necessitates the use of restraint must be assessed and if restraint is used the degree of force used must only be just enough to prevent harm to P.

The Main Code of Practice, paras 6.40–6.48 also sets out guidance about the appropriate use of restraint. The Code of Practice also makes reference to the relevant cases to assist in identifying the relevant factors that should generally be considered by the decision maker to distinguish 'restraint' from 'deprivation of liberty' (see above at **4.4**).

4.8 RESTRAINT OR DEPRIVATION OF LIBERTY IN A HOSPITAL OR CARE HOME

4.8.1 When do the deprivation of liberty safeguards apply

The position of those who lack capacity residing in institutional care by reason of administrative decision making, which effectively deprives them of their liberty, was a concern to the government following the decision of the European Court of Human Rights in *HL v UK*.[37] HL, an autistic man, lacking capacity, was readmitted to Bournewood Hospital following his placement with carers in the community. His detention was not regularised by use of the Mental Health legislation as he was compliant with the decision. It is everyday social policy for people who lack capacity and who are unable to care for themselves to be placed in care or nursing homes on the basis that they are compliant with the placement and do not resist. The route to care is by way of an administrative decision made by health or social services departments of local authorities and is not formally authorised. The nature of these placements may perforce involve a deprivation of liberty even if it is limited to the locking of doors for safety reasons (see above). The point is that P is unable to consent to the deprivation through lack of capacity. The European Court of Human Rights held that these informal arrangements contravened Art 5. The Deprivation of Liberty Safeguards provide a regime for the authorities formally to authorise the deprivation and provides an appeal process to the Court of Protection.

4.8.2 The s 5 provisions

Section 5 of the Act makes provision to allow carers and, for instance, health and social care professionals to carry out acts in connection with the care or treatment of a person lacking capacity provided before doing the act the carer takes reasonable steps to establish whether the person is lacking capacity in relation to the matter and when doing the act the carer

---

[36] MCA 2005, s 6(2) and (3).
[37] HL v UK (Bournewood) (2004) 40 EHRR 761.

reasonably believes that the person lacks capacity and that it will be in the person's best interests for the act to be done. This allows the carers to do whatever is considered necessary and in the best interests of P in order to safeguard his/her welfare and health. When carrying out such acts the carer must also apply the key principles set out in s 1 and the best interests check list set out in s 4 (see Chapter 2). Provided these conditions are met, the carer is afforded protection from liability for their actions and such acts can be carried out as if P had capacity and had given his/her consent. However, the protection from liability does not cover any act which is intended to *restrain* P.[38]

4.8.3   The Sch A1 provisions

Provision contained in Sch A1 of the Act (inserted by the Mental Health Act 2007) sets out the deprivation of liberty safeguards which came into force on 1 April 2009. A managing authority of a hospital or care home is now permitted to deprive a person lacking capacity of his/her liberty by detaining him/her provided three conditions are satisfied. These are:

(a)   the incapacitated person is detained in hospital or care home for the purpose of being given care or treatment;

(b)   that a standard or urgent authorisation is in force;

(c)   the standard or urgent authorisation relates to the incapacitated person and the hospital or care home in which that person is detained.[39]

A person who carries out any act in pursuance of such authorisation and for the purpose of giving care or treatment is excluded from liability and is placed in the same position as if the person lacking capacity had had capacity to consent in relation to the doing of the act and had consented to his/her detention.[40] However, the person is not protected from civil or criminal liability resulting from his/her negligence in doing any thing. It is also emphasised that any act done must be done for the purpose of the standard or urgent authorisation and where a standard authorisation is in force it does not authorise a person to do any act which does not comply with the conditions (if any) included in the authorisation.[41]

A standard authorisation is usually requested by the managers of the hospital or care home, where the person is or may be deprived of his/her liberty. The request is made to the supervisory authority. In order to obtain the authorisation the managing authority will have to ensure that the person in respect of whom the authorisation is sought meets the

---

[38]   MCA 2005, s 6(1).
[39]   MCA 2005, Sch A1, Part 1, paras 1 and 2.
[40]   MCA 2005, Sch A1, Part 1, para 3.
[41]   MCA 2005, Sch A1, Part 1, para 4.

qualifying requirements set out in Sch A1, Part 3, para 12 because, before the authorisation is granted, the supervisory authority will arrange for assessments to be carried out to determine whether these requirements are met in relation to the person detained (see below).

The supervisory body is in the case of a care home, the local authority where the person is ordinarily resident or where the care home is situated; or in the case of a hospital, the primary care trust in England which commissions the care, or in Wales, the National Assembly of Wales or the local health board if the care is commissioned.

4.8.4   The qualifying requirements

The following are the qualifying requirements which must be met before a standard authorisation is granted:

(a)   the age requirement;

(b)   the mental health requirement;

(c)   the mental capacity requirement;

(d)   the best interests requirement;

(c)   the eligibility requirement;

(f)   the no refusals requirement.

4.8.4.1   The age requirement

The person in respect of whom the authorisation is sought must be 18 years of age.

4.8.4.2   The mental health requirement

The person must be suffering from mental disorder within the meaning of the Mental Health Act 1983 as amended but including for these purposes a person with learning difficulties whether or not associated with abnormally aggressive behaviour or seriously irresponsible conduct.[42]

4.8.4.3   The mental capacity requirement

The person must lack capacity in relation to the question whether or not he/she should be accommodated in the relevant hospital or care home for the purpose of being given the relevant care or treatment. The key

---

[42]   MCA 2005, Sch A1, Part 3, para 14.

principles set out in s 1 of the Act and the provisions of ss 2 and 3 of the Act must be applied when assessing whether the person lacks capacity (see **2.4**).

4.8.4.3   *The best interests requirement*

Four conditions must be met to satisfy this requirement. These are:

(a)   the person is, or is to be a detained resident;

(b)   the person's detention is in his/her best interests;

(c)   the detention is necessary to prevent harm to the person; and

(d)   the detention is a proportionate response to the likelihood of the person suffering harm and the seriousness of that harm.[43]

4.8.4.4   *The eligibility requirement*

A person is ineligible if he/she is already subject to the provision of the Mental Health Act 1983 namely, he/she is detained in a hospital under the Mental Health Act 1983 or meets the criteria for detention but is objecting to being detained in the hospital or to some or all of the treatment in which case he/she should be detained under the powers contained in the 1983 Act. He would also be ineligible if on leave of absence or subject to a guardianship or a community treatment regime or conditional discharge and subject to a measure which would be inconsistent with an authorisation if granted, or if on leave of absence or subject to community treatment regime or conditional discharge and the authorisation if granted would be for deprivation of liberty in a hospital for the purpose of treatment for mental disorder.[44]

In *GJ v Foundation Trust PCT v Secretary of State for Health*[45] Charles J considered the application of the eligibility criteria in relation to a challenge by P to his detention under DoLS. Three important areas were highlighted.

Where the person detained comes within the scope of Mental Health Act 1983, this takes primacy regardless of there being alternative solutions under MCA 2005.

If detention is for the purpose of physical treatment only, then the person detained is not authorised as a mental health patient.

---

[43]   MCA 2005, Sch A1, Part 3, para 16.
[44]   MCA 2005, Sch A1, Part 3, para 17.
[45]   [2009] EWHC 2972 (Fam), [2010] Fam Law 139.

In considering eligibility/ineligibility, there must be reference to the reality of the purpose of detention and the Court must focus upon the position as it is when the case falls to be decided and not what it may have been at the time authorisation was granted.

4.8.4.5   *The no refusals requirement*

A person meets this requirement unless he/she has made an effective and valid advance decision refusing some or all of the treatment in question.

There is also a refusal if there is a valid refusal, which is within the scope of his authority, by a donee of a lasting power of attorney or deputy for the person concerned to be accommodated in the hospital or care home for the purposes of receiving some or all of the relevant care or treatment in circumstances which amount to deprivation of the person's liberty or at all.[46]

4.9   STANDARD AUTHORISATION

The managing authority must request a standard authorisation in the following cases:

(a)   if it is proposing to accommodate the person who appears to meet all the qualifying requirements, to be detained in the relevant hospital or care home, or is likely to do so within the next 28 days; or

(b)   where it appears to the managing authority that the person who is already accommodated in the relevant hospital or care home is likely at some time within the next 28 days to be a detained resident in the relevant hospital or care home or is likely at that time or at some later time within the next 28 days to meet all the qualifying requirements; or

(c)   where the person is detained resident in the relevant hospital or care home and meets all the qualifying requirements or is likely to do so at some time within the next 8 days; or

(d)   if there is or is likely to be a change in the place of detention provided that a standard authorisation has been given and remains in force.[47]

There is a change in the place of detention if the person concerned ceases to be detained in the stated hospital or care home and becomes detained

---

46   MCA 2005, Sch A1, Part 3, para 20.
47   MCA 2005, Sch 1A, Part 4, para 25.

in a different hospital or care home. In this instance the managing authority will be the managing authority of the new hospital or care home.[48]

Before a standard authorisation is given the supervisory authority must secure an assessment of all the qualifying requirements and be satisfied that these requirements are met. The Mental Capacity (Deprivation of Liberty: Standard Authorisations, Assessments and Ordinary Residence) Regulations 2008[49] provide for who should carry out the assessments, the professional skills and training which the assessors must have and the timeframe within which the assessments must be completed.

4.9.1   The best interests assessment

The assessor must decide whether a deprivation of liberty is occurring or is likely to occur. He/she must consult the managing authority of the relevant hospital or care home and have regard to the conclusions of the mental health assessor on the impact or likely impact on the person's mental health by his being detained and any relevant needs assessment and care plan. He/she must also take account of the views of any named person and anyone who has the responsibility for the care of the person or may be interested in his/her welfare and the views of any donee of a lasting power of attorney granted by the person or the Court of Protection.

The assessor must state in the assessment the name and address of every interested person consulted. If the assessor concludes that the best interests requirement is met he/she must state the maximum authorisation period not exceeding one year and may provide for different periods to apply in relation to different kinds of standard authorisations. The assessor may also include recommendations about conditions to be attached to the authorisation. If the conclusion is that the deprivation of liberty is not in the person's best interests or that there is or has been an unauthorised deprivation of liberty he must include a statement to that effect in the assessment.

4.9.2   Position where equivalent assessments have already been carried out

The supervisory body is not obliged to secure a required assessment if:

(a)   it has a written copy of an existing assessment whether or not such an assessment was carried out in connection with a request for a standard authorisation or for some other purpose, and

---

[48]   MCA 2005, Sch A1, Part 4, para 26.
[49]   SI 2008/1858.

(b)   the assessment complies with all the required requirements under Sch A1;

(c)   the existing assessments were carried out within the last 12 months; and

(d)   it is satisfied that there is no reason why the existing assessment may no longer be accurate.

If the assessment is a best interests assessment the supervisory body must take into account any information given or submissions made, by the relevant person's representative (see below), any section 39C independent mental capacity advocate (IMCA) or any section 39D IMCA.

4.9.3   Supervisory body's duty to give authorisation

*   The supervisory body must give a standard authorisation if all the assessments are positive and it has written copies of the assessments. All assessments are positive if each assessment concludes that the relevant person meets the qualifying requirements to which the assessment relates.[50]

*   The authorisation must set out the period during which the authorisation is to be in force but the period must not exceed the maximum period recommended in the best interests assessment. The commencement date of the period may be a date after the authorisation is given.

*   The authorisation may be given subject to conditions.

*   The authorisation must be in writing and must name the relevant person, the hospital or care home, the period during which the authorisation is to be in force and the purpose for which it is given, the conditions subject to which the authorisation is given and the reason why the qualifying requirement is met.

*   Appoint someone to act as the person's representative during the period of the authorisation (see below).

*   Provide a copy of the authorisation to the relevant person's representative, the managing authority; the person being deprived of his/her liberty; any IMCA and every interested person consulted by the best interests assessor.

*   Keep records.

---

[50]   MCA 2005, Sch A1, Part 4, para 50.

The supervisory body may review a standard authorisation at any time and must do so if requested by the person detained under its provision, his/her representative or the managing authority. If a request is made, the supervisory body must decide whether any of the qualifying requirements appear to need a review and if so commission review assessments.

4.9.4   Duty of the managing authority

It must comply with any conditions attached to the authorisation. In the event of any material change in the detained person's circumstances it must request a review. If the conditions on which the authorisation was requested persist when the authorisation expires it may apply for a further authorisation to begin on the date when the original authorisation expires. In this event the full assessment process must be repeated.

4.9.5   Rights of third party to require consideration of unauthorised detention by the supervisory body

An eligible third party may request the supervisory body to decide whether or not there is an unauthorised deprivation of liberty, provided the following conditions are met:

(a)   the eligible person must have notified the managing authority that it appears that there is an unauthorised deprivation of liberty;

(b)   the eligible person must have asked the managing authority to request a standard authorisation;

(c)   the managing authority has failed to make a request for standard authorisation within a reasonable period of the request having been made.

Where a request is made by an eligible third party the supervisory body must select and appoint a person to carry out an assessment of whether or not the person to whom the request relates is a detained resident unless it appears to the supervisory body that the request is frivolous or vexatious, or where the issue has already been decided and since that decision there has been no change of circumstances which would merit the question being decided again. The supervisory body's decision must be notified to the eligible person, the person to whom the request relates, the managing authority and any IMCA.[51]

---

[51]   MCA 2005, Sch A1, Part 4, paras 67–69.

4.10   URGENT APPLICATIONS

The managing authority of the relevant hospital or care home may give an urgent authorisation to provide a lawful basis for deprivation of liberty before a request for a standard authorisation is made, if it is required to make a request for a standard authorisation and they believe that the need for the relevant person to be a detained resident is so urgent that it is appropriate for the detention to begin before they make the request, or where they have made the request for a standard authorisation and they believe that the need for the relevant person to be a detained resident is so urgent that it is appropriate for the detention to begin before the request is disposed of. If the managing authority decide to give an urgent authorisation they must:

- Specify the period during which the authorisation is to be in force not exceeding 7 days.

- Give the urgent authorisation in writing.

- State the name of the relevant person, the name of the relevant hospital or care home, the period of authorisation and the purpose for which the authorisation is given.

- Keep a written record of why they have given the urgent authorisation.

- As soon as practicable after giving the authorisation, give a copy of the authorisation to the relevant person and any section 39A IMCA.

- Take such steps as are practicable to ensure that the relevant person understands the effect of the authorisation and the right to make an application to the Court to exercise its jurisdiction under s 21A and give the appropriate information both orally and in writing.[52]

The managing authority may seek an extension of the duration of the urgent authorisation. They must keep a written record of the reasons for the request and give the relevant person notice of the request for an extension. The supervisory body may on request grant an extension of the period of urgent authorisation only if they are satisfied that a request for a standard authorisation has been made; that there are exceptional reasons why it has not yet been possible for the request to be disposed of, and that it is essential for the existing detention to continue until the request is disposed. The extension must not exceed 7 days. If an extension is granted the supervisory body must notify the managing authority stating the period of the extension keep a written record of the outcome of the request and the period of the extension.

---

[52]   MCA 2005, Sch A1, Part 5, paras 77–83.

4.11   APPOINTMENT OF RELEVANT PERSON'S REPRESENTATIVE

The provision for the appointment of a representative to a person in respect of whom a standard authorisation has been issued are set out in the Act at Sch A1, paras 139–140. It provides that the supervisory body must appoint a person to be the relevant person's representative and that person must if appointed maintain, represent and support the relevant person in matters relating to or connected with his/her deprivation of liberty. The functions of a representative are in addition to and do not affect the authority of any donee, the powers of a deputy or any powers of the Court.[53] The Mental Capacity (Deprivation of Liberty: Appointment of Relevant Person's Representative) Regulations 2008, as amended by SI 2008/2368, provide for the selection and termination of appointment of a representative, and the formalities of the appointment and termination of a representative's appointment.

4.12   THE COURT'S POWERS IN RELATION TO STANDARD AND URGENT AUTHORISATION UNDER SCH A1

The Court of Protection has jurisdiction to ensure that Art 5(4) of the European Convention is complied with by reviewing the lawfulness of the detention of anyone for whom authorisation has been granted to provide care or treatment. The application for a review may be made by the person who has been deprived of his/her liberty or a representative for that person.

Section 21A of the Act provides that where a standard authorisation has been given the Court may determine any questions relating to:

(a)   whether the relevant person meets one or more of the qualifying requirements;

(b)   the period during which the standard authorisation is to be in force;

(c)   the purpose for which the standard authorisation is given;

(d)   the conditions subject to which the standard authorisation is given,

and may make an order varying or terminating the standard authorisation or directing the supervisory body to vary or terminate the standard authorisation.[54]

---

[53]   MCA 2005, Sch A1, Part 10, para 141(1) and (2).
[54]   MCA 2005, s 21A(2) and (3).

Where an urgent authorisation has been given, the Court may determine any question relating to:

(a) whether the urgent authorisation should have been given;

(b) the period during which the urgent authorisation is to be in force;

(c) the purpose for which the urgent authorisation is given;

and may make an order varying or terminating the urgent authorisation or directing the managing authority of the relevant hospital or care home to vary or terminate the urgent authorisation.[55]

A court may, in relation to either of the above applications, consider a person's liability for any act done in connection with the standard or urgent authorisation before its variation or termination, and make an order excluding a person from liability.[56]

4.13 PROCEDURE

The procedure and practice in relation to deprivation of liberty applications are set out in Part 10A of the Court of Protection Rules 2007 and the Practice Directions relating to such applications. Deprivation of Liberty (DoL) application means applications for orders under s 21A of the Act relating to standard or urgent authorisation under Sch A1 of the Act. It is acknowledged that by their nature such applications are of special urgency. The procedure set out hereunder relates to only such applications. They do not apply to applications concerning other matters, which may also raise issues relating to deprivation of liberty and require urgent attention. This should be explained to the DoL team at the Court so that the applications are handled appropriately.

The Practice Direction relating to applications for a deprivation of liberty identifies the key features of the special DoL procedure as follows:

(a) special DoL forms ensure that DoL court papers stand out as such and receive special handling by the Court office;

(b) the application is placed before a judge as soon as possible – if necessary before the application is issued – for directions to be given as to the steps to be taken in the application and who is to take each step and by when;

(c) the usual COP Rules will apply only so far as consistent with the judicial directions given for the particular case;

---

[55] MCA 2005, s 21A(4) and (5).
[56] MCA 2005, s 21A(6) and (7).

(d)   a dedicated team in the Court office ('the DoL team') will deal with such application at all stages including liaison with would be applicants/other parties;

(e)   the progress of each DoL case will be monitored by a judge assigned to that case, assisted by the DoL team.

4.13.1   When can an application be made to the Court of Protection

In order to comply with the provisions of Art 5(4) of the European Convention an application made by the person who is deprived of his liberty or on his behalf must be dealt with expeditiously. However, whenever there are concerns about a person being deprived of his liberty, in the first instance attempts must be made to resolve the issue through a conciliatory process than through litigation. The main Code of Practice sets out, in Chapter 15, the best ways to settle disagreements and disputes. Where possible these guidelines should be followed. The complaint procedure of the managing authority and the supervisory body should also be used where appropriate and where there is sufficient time to do so. However, since the issue of someone being deprived of his/her liberty relates to a breach of a person's human rights under the European Convention it is important that the vulnerable person or those who are acting on his behalf or concerned about his welfare should not be discouraged from applying to the Court for a declaration and appreciate that an application can be made at any stage of the safeguarding process set out in the Act. The Act, in s 21A, sets out the circumstances in which an application may be made to the Court. In summary the application can be made:

•   before standard authorisation is given;

•   after a standard authorisation is given;

•   where an urgent authorisation is given;

•   where an extension of the authorisation is sought.

Where the application is considered before the standard authorisation is given the Court may be asked to declare whether the relevant person has capacity and whether the act done or proposed to be done is lawful and in the best interests of the incapacitated person.

Where an application is made after the supervisory body has given authorisation the relevant person or his/her representative deputy or donee may apply to the Court to determine:

- whether the relevant person meets one or more of the qualifying requirements for deprivation of liberty;

- the period for which the standard authorisation is to remain in force;

- the purposes for which the standard authorisation has been given;

- the conditions attached to the standard authorisation.

Where an urgent authorisation has been given an application to the Court may be made to determine any question relating to:

- whether the authorisation should have been given;

- the period during which the authorisation is to remain in force;

- the purpose for which the urgent authorisation has been given.

4.13.2 Who can apply without permission

The following person can apply without permission:

- The person who lacks or may lack capacity.

- A donor of a Lasting Power of Attorney to whom an application relates or their donee.

- A deputy who has been appointed by the Court to act for the person concerned.

- A person named in an existing order.

- A person appointed by the supervisory body as the relevant person's representative.

- The Official Solicitor in certain circumstances.

- A Public Guardian.

Permission to apply for the substantive application will need to be applied for by any other person.

4.14   HOW TO APPLY

4.14.1   Steps to be taken before issuing an application

The applicant must contact the Deprivation of Liberty Team (DoL) at the earliest opportunity before making the application to inform the team that the application is to be made and how quickly the Court's decision is required on the merits of the application and when the application is likely to be lodged. Where this is not possible, the applicant should liaise with the DoL team either by telephone or fax at the time when the application is lodged. The information that the DoL team will need in advance is:

(1)   that the DoL application is to be made;

(2)   how urgent the application is (by when should the Court's decision, or interim decision on the merits be given); and

(3)   when the Court will receive the application papers.

In very urgent cases arrangements can be made by the team for directions to be given or an interim order to be obtained by telephone conference before the application is issued. In such cases the Court will require brief details including the following:

(a)   the parties' details and where they live;

(b)   the issue to be decided;

(c)   the date of the urgent or standard authorisation;

(d)   the date of effective detention;

(e)   the parties' legal representatives;

(f)   details of any interested parties, such as a relative; and

(d)   whether there have been any previous proceedings relating to the parties and, if so, details of the same.

In cases of emergency, where it is necessary to make an application out of office hours, the security office at the RCJ should be contacted on 020 7947 6000. The security officer should be informed of the nature of the case. In the Family Division the procedure involves the judge being contacted through the Family Division duty Officer, and the RCJ security officer will need to contact the duty officer and not the judge's clerk. In all other cases the DoL team should be contacted at:

The Court of Protection
DoLs Application Branch
Archway Towers
2 Junction Road
London N19 5FZ
DX 141150 Archway 2
Telephone 0845 330 2900
Fax: 020 7664 7712

In all cases relating to an application for deprivation of liberty, the prescribed forms for such applications must be used. If in such a case it is anticipated that other issues may arise, the DoL forms should identify and describe briefly those issues and any relief which may be sought in respect of them should be set out in the sections 3.5 and 5 of the DLA Form under the heading 'other issues'. This will enable the Court to deal with them immediately or by giving directions for how they should be dealt with. Therefore, unless the Court expressly directs, applicants should not issue a second and separate application (using the standard court forms) relating to any 'other issues'.

Where the application seeks relief concerning a deprivation of liberty other than under s 21A in respect of standard or urgent authorisation eg under s 16(2)(a) the standard court forms and not the DoL forms should be used but it should be made clear on the standard form that relief relating to deprivation of liberty is also being sought and the proposed applicant should contact the DoL team to discuss the handling of the application before the application is issued

4.14.2 Issuing an application

To make an application where permission to make the DoL application is required:

(1) the applicant is required to file the following forms:
    (a) Form DLC where the applicant needs permission to make a DoL.
    (b) A draft form DLA.
    (c) Form DLB (if the application is urgent) in which the reasons for the application and the urgency must be set out. If the applicant considers that the application needs to be dealt with within a shorter time scale this should be indicated on the form and a proposed timetable should be set out. The directions and order sought must be identified with a draft of the order attached. The DLB should always be placed at the top of the papers and (where this is appropriate) mention that the permission is required and that a completed DLC form is attached.

Only P and his appointed representative, attorney or deputy have the right to make an application without leave. All other persons including family members are required to seek permission to apply;

(2)   pay the court fee of £400;

(3)   if possible an electronic version of the draft order on disc should be lodged;

(4)   where an application is made out of hours before the application is lodged, an undertaking will be required that the appropriate forms will be lodged and the court fee paid unless an exemption applies.

4.14.3   The Court Office

As soon as the DoL team is notified of the application the team will ensure that the application is placed before a nominated judge. During office hours the application will be placed before a judge at Archway Towers. During out of office hours the application will be placed before the judge who is most immediately available. Initially, the application will be dealt with by the judge and any orders made without attendance of the applicant or his representatives. Possible directions which the Court may need to give include:

(a)   upon whom and by when and how service of the application should be effected;

(b)   dispensing with acknowledgement of service of the application or allowing a short period of time for so doing, which in some cases may amount to a few hours only;

(c)   whether further lay or expert evidence should be obtained;

(d)   whether the detained person should be a party and represented by the Official Solicitor and whether any other person should be a party;

(e)   whether any family members should be formally notified of the application and of any hearing and joined as parties;

(f)   fixing a date for the first hearing and giving the time estimate;

(g)   allocation of the case to the level of judge appropriate to hear the case;

(h)   whether the case is such that should be immediately transferred to the High Court for directions;

(i)   directions relating to the preparation of a bundle for the judge

As soon as the order is made the DoL team will notify the applicant of the order and carry out any other directions given by the judge and make arrangements for any transfer of the case to another court and for a first hearing

4.14.4   After issue/directions given

After issue and any directions given, the applicant or his legal representatives must:

(1)   ensure that any directions given by the judge are complied with;

(2)   ensure that the application, any orders made and the acknowledgement of service in Form DLE are served on the respondents to the application;

(4)   prepare an indexed and paginated bundle of documents which should include a case summary, skeleton arguments and draft order for the hearing on notice; and

(5)   serve an index of the bundle on all parties to the application and, where a party appears in person, serve a copy of the bundle on that person.

4.14.5   The first hearing

The first hearing will be listed for the Court to fix a date and or give directions, make an interim order or final order if appropriate or make such other orders as the appropriate in the case. The hearing is as a general rule held in private.[57] The court may direct that the hearing takes place in public if the criteria in r 93 apply.

4.14.6   Orders the Court can make

The court may make any appropriate orders, grant an injunction and given directions. These will include:

(a)   a declaration whether or not the person who is the subject of the proceedings lacks capacity;

(b)   a declaration whether the act done or proposed to be done is lawful or in the best interests of the person who lacks capacity;

(c)   authorising acts which deprive a person of his liberty;

---

[57]   COP Rules 2007, r 90 and PD 13A.

(d)   authorising appropriate restraint to be used;

(e)   orders varying or terminating the standard or urgent authorisation and;

(f)   orders directing the managing authority or supervisory body to comply with any directions the Court gives;

(g)   prohibiting a person from doing certain acts.

The general rule in all cases concerning health and welfare is that there will be no order as to costs of the proceedings.[58] This also applies to DoL applications.

4.15   APPEALS

Part 20 of the COP Rules applies to appeals from the Court's decision. Permission to appeal will be required.[59] Permission will only be granted if the Court considers that the appeal would have a real prospect of success or there is some other compelling reason why the appeal should be heard.[60]

4.15.1   Practice in relation to without notice applications

Concerns have been expressed by the Court that practitioners too regularly do not follow the guidance on the information to be provided and the procedure to be followed in seeking without notice relief and that such failure shows an insufficient appreciation of the exceptional nature of without notice relief and the impact it has or could have on the rights, life and emotions of the person concerned in relation to whom and others against whom the order is made. It is only in exceptional circumstances and in accordance with the guidance set out in the relevant case law and practice guidance should without notice applications be made.[61] It is therefore important to ensure that the evidence in support of an application for deprivation of liberty gives a balanced, fair and particularised account of the events leading up to the application and the facts upon which it is based. Where possible it should include what the applicant thinks the respondent's case is or is likely to be. It should also include an account of the steps the applicant proposes concerning services, the giving of explanation of the order and the implementation of the order. This is of particular importance where emotional issues are involved and family members of a person who lacks capacity are the

---

[58]   COP Rules 2007, r 157.
[59]   COP Rules 2007, r 172.
[60]   COP Rules 2007, r 173.
[61]   *B Borough Council v S (By the Official Solicitor)* [2006] EWHC 2584 (Fam), [2007] 1 FLR 1600.

subject of injunctions and orders. In such cases information of the applicant's intentions is likely to inform issues as to the need, form and the proportionality of the relief sought and granted.[62] Where an order is obtained on a without notice application the term 'liberty to apply' should be replaced with the terms:

> 'If any person served with this order disagrees with any part of this order and wishes to seek to set aside or vary it, they should make an immediate application to this court to do so.'

This suggestion endorses the observation made in *B Borough Council v S (By the Official Solicitor)*[63] by Charles J in relation to without notice applications:

> 'There is a natural temptation for applicants to seek, and the Court to grant, relief to protect vulnerable person whether they are children or vulnerable adults. In my view this can lead (and experience as the applications judge confirms that it does lead) to practitioners making without notice applications which are not necessary or appropriate, or which are not properly supported by appropriate evidence. Also there is in my view a general practice of asking the Court to grant without notice orders over fairly extended period with expression permission to apply to vary or discharge on an inappropriately long period of notice (often 48 hours). It seems to me that on occasions this practice pays insufficient regard to the interests of both the person in respect of whom and against whom the orders are made, and that therefore on every occasion without notice relief is sought and granted the choice of the return date and the provisions as to permission to apply should be addressed with care by both applicants and the Court. Factors in that consideration will be an estimation of the effect on the person against whom the order is made of service of the order and how that is to be carried out.'

4.16 EXAMPLE OF ORDERS

(1)   The first Respondent ... is eligible to be deprived of his/her liberty at V pursuant to an authority under section 4A of the Mental Capacity Act 2005.

(2)   Notwithstanding ... P's inability to consent, it shall be lawful and in his/her best interests for his/her clinicians and care workers including the Applicant's and the ... Respondents employees servants or agents to:

(a)   admit the first Respondent ... to units provided by ... At either the A care home or the B Care home for the purpose of caring for his/her welfare and providing him/her with psychological, behavioural and psychiatric treatment.

---

[62]   *LLBC v TG, JG and KR* [2007] EWHC 2640 (Fam) (para 38 of the judgment).
[63]   [2006] EWHC 2584 (Fam), [2007] 1 FLR 1600.

(b)   Provide him/her with psychological, behavioural and psychiatric treatment in accordance with the care plans provided by …

(c)   Use such reasonable restraint as may be necessary in conveying the First Respondent … to and preventing him/her from leaving the unit, including measures that may amount to the deprivation of liberty for the purpose of caring for his/her welfare and providing him/her with psychological, behavioural and psychiatric treatment.

4.17 PROCEDURAL GUIDE FOR DEPRIVATION OF LIBERTY ORDER

When can an application be made	Before standard authorisation is given	
	After standard authorisation is given	
	After urgent authorisation is given	
Steps to be taken		
Before the application is issued	The applicant must contact the DoL team or at the same time as lodging the application and give the team the following information:	
	(1) that an application is to be made	
	(2) how urgent it is	
	(3) by when the decision should be given	
If an urgent application is to be made	(4) details of the parties and their addresses	
	(5) issue to be decided	
	(6) date of standard/urgent authorisation	
	(7) details of parties' legal representatives	
	(8) details of family members	
	(9) details of previous court proceedings	
Is permission needed	Only the patient and his appointed representative, attorney or deputy have the right to make an application without leave. All other persons including family members must seek permission	MCA 2005, s 50 COP Rules 2007, Parts 8 and 10A
In an emergency	Application can be made out of hours by calling security officer at the RCJ on 020 7947 6000	PD 10A, para 2.5
	In the Family Division judge can be contacted through the FD duty officer. The security officer will contact the duty officer	
How to apply		
The applicant must file	Form DLA Form DLB (plus draft) Form DLC (if permission required) If possible an electronic version of order sought on disc	PD 10A, para 4.1

	In an emergency an undertaking will be required that Forms will be filed and fee paid	
Court Fee	£400	PD 10A, para 4.1
Possible directions which may be sought on issue	(1) Upon whom, by whom and how service should be effected	PD 10A, para 5.1
	(2) Dispensing with acknowledgement of service or seeking abridgement of time	
	(3) Whether lay or expert evidence required whether P or OS or other persons should be made parties	
	(4) Whether family member should be notified and joined as a party	
	(5) Fixing trial window or date for hearing allocation	
	(6) Whether it is appropriate to transfer to the High Court	
	(7) Directions for the preparation of bundles	
Court Office	Take steps to place application before a Nominated judge to hear DoL cases will notify the judge to put him/her on stand by and the judge will consider the application and give directions if appropriate	PD 10A, paras 6.1 and 6.2
Steps after judge's order	DoL team will notify parties of order Action every point on judge's note Refer queries to the judge Make arrangements for transfer	
Steps to be taken by applicant	Comply with the order made File DLD if appropriate Serve Form DLE with other documents Prepare indexed and paginated Court bundle to include skeleton arguments and draft order Provide a copy of index to all parties and a copy of bundle to unrepresented party	PD 10A, paras 7.2 and 8.4
First Hearing	Court will attempt to hear case within 5 days. The hearing will be in private unless r 93 applies and court so directs	PD 10A, para 8.2 COP Rules, r 90
Orders that may be made	See **4.11**, **4.13.6**, **4.15** above and s 21A of MCA 2005	
Costs	No order	COP Rules 2007, r 157 PD 10A, para 10.1

Appeal	Permission to appeal required	PD 10A, para 11.1 COP Rules 2007, r 172
	Permission will only be granted if court considers it has a real prospect of success or there are some other compelling reasons	COP Rules 2007, r 173 PD 10A, para 11.1

CHAPTER 5

URGENT MEDICAL TREATMENT

LAW AND PRACTICE

5.1 INTRODUCTION

At common law any intrusive medical treatment constitutes an unlawful act unless authorised by statute such as the Mental Health Act 1983 or it is done with the person's consent or as a matter of necessity. In the case of a competent adult his/her consent must be respected no matter how unwise or absurd the decision may appear to others. Common law did not give any other person the right or the power to make decisions for or on behalf of a person who lacked capacity.

The Mental Health Acts make provision for the assessment and treatment of those persons with a mental illness or disorder. The treatment provided must, however, be related to the mental disorder which the person is or believed to be suffering from. These provisions include compulsory powers, provided the strict criteria set out in the Mental Health Act 1983 are met. Generally these powers are exercised irrespective of whether or not the person has capacity to consent to the treatment. The powers do not authorise intrusive treatment generally.

The High Court however, under its inherent jurisdiction as parens patriae exercised its declaratory jurisdiction to declare whether an adult person lacks capacity to consent to treatment and whether a particular treatment or withholding of treatment is lawful as being in the person's best interests. Since the House of Lords decision in *Re F (Mental Patient)*[1] the High Court under its inherent jurisdiction has dealt with many cases in which the common law has been developed and which eventually formed the basis of the statutory provisions contained in the Mental Capacity Act 2005. These decisions developed the concept of respecting a competent person's autonomy to make decisions, the test of capacity and the fact that it is issue specific, and the best interests principle not only in relation to medical treatment but other welfare issues.

---

[1]   [1990] 2 AC 1.

In addition, the coming into force of the Human Rights Act 1998 made it necessary for appropriate provisions to be made to ensure that a person's rights under the European Convention were respected and protected.

The Mental Capacity Act 2005 as amended seeks to provide a comprehensive legal framework which covers all matters relating to an adult person (P) who lacks capacity.

The Act seeks to provide a clear and consistent legal basis and authority for decisions which need to be taken on behalf of and acts to be done to, a person who lacks capacity. It reinforces the common law principle that the autonomy of a person who has capacity to make decisions must be respected. It ensures that proper assessments are made to test whether a person lacks capacity to make the specific decision in question and that appropriate steps are taken to enable the person to make a decision for himself/herself and that the person's wishes and feelings are taken into account. The Act and the Code of Practice ensures that a uniform best practice is followed and it provides for a careful planning process to enable advance decisions to be made and for members of the person's family to be consulted.

The key principles set out in s 1 of the Act which underpin the entire statutory provision and the Code of Practice under s 42 must be considered in all applications relating to medical care and treatment as they apply to all other matters. The provisions set out in s 2 which relate to issue of capacity and the best interests test as provided in s 3 must also be applied both before any application to the Court is made for a declaration and by the Court when determining any issue which relates to providing medical treatment. Since these sections reinforce the principles developed under common law in decisions of the High Court those decisions will remain relevant but subject to the specific provisions of the Act.

5.2   PERSONS WHO LACK CAPACITY – S 2

For the purposes of the Act a person lacks capacity in relation to a matter if at the material time he is unable to make a decision himself in relation to the matter *because of an impairment of, or disturbance in the functioning of, the mind or brain*. Although there is no legal requirement under the Act that lack of capacity has to be established by medical evidence it is submitted that in relation to issues relating to medical treatment the question of whether a person has the capacity to make the decision in question should be provided by expert evidence which may include evidence from a psychiatrist and or a psychologist. It is possible that a person who is suffering from a mental disorder within the Mental Health Act 1983 is nonetheless able to make the specific decision in relation to medical treatment which is not related to his mental illness (see *Re C (Adult: Refusal of Treatment)*[2] and cases referred to below).

The standard of proof required is the civil standard ie on the balance of probabilities. The Act specifically provides that lack of capacity cannot be decided simply by reference to a person's age or appearance or an aspect of behaviour which might lead others to make unjustified assumptions about his capacity.

5.3 INABILITY TO MAKE DECISION – S 3

The criteria to be applied remains similar to that which was applied under common law and set out in the decision in *Re C (Refusal of Medical Treatment)*[3] (see further in Chapter 2).

5.4 BEST INTERESTS – S 4

The position under the Act is not dissimilar to that under common law. The test remains an objective one in that the emphasis is on what is in the best interests of the person concerned and not what the person would have decided to do had he had capacity. In deciding this issue the Act requires the decision maker to have regard to the person's wishes and feeling, his beliefs and values and those of others. Existing case law will be relevant in determining this issue when there is a difference between the best interests assessment and the expressed wishes of the incapacitated person.

The Act sets out a new statutory framework and it may therefore be argued that in determining issues that arise under it the Court should approach such cases uninfluenced by previous decisions made under the High Court's inherent jurisdiction. However, since the statutory framework is based on and in some respects replicates case law it is inevitable that some reliance will be placed on such cases if for no other reason than as a guide and tool to interpret the statutory provision and develop this area of the law. An example of a case where existing law has been relied on in this way is the observations of McFarlane J in *LLBC v TG, JG and KR*.[4] Additionally, there are bound to be cases which are border line or involve a number of issues and it is determined that the person has capacity to make decisions in relation to some matters but not others. In such cases the High Court will need to consider the issues under its dual jurisdiction ie under the Act and its inherent jurisdiction and thus there is likely to be an overlap.[5] The following paragraphs therefore set out

---

[2]   [1994] 1 WLR 290.
[3]   [1994] 1 FLR 31.
[4]   [2007] EWHC 2640 (Fam).
[5]   See *Re MM (An Adult)* [2007] EWHC 2689 (Fam).

how various difficult issues have been dealt with by the High Court under its inherent jurisdiction both to assist decision makers and advisers should the matter be litigated.

5.5   REFUSAL OF ASSESSMENT/TREATMENT

If the person has capacity but refuses to consent he/she cannot be forced to do so. The position is the same in the case of a person who is incapable and resists intervention.[6] In the past the Mental Health Act 1983 provisions have been resorted to in order to forcibly treat a patient. However, in this event, it would have to be established that the criteria under the relevant provision of that Act are met.

The general principle is that the consent of a mentally competent adult must be obtained before medical or surgical treatment is administered to him.[7] 'Prima facie every adult has the right and capacity to decide whether or not he will accept medical treatment, even if a refusal may risk permanent injury to his health or even lead to premature death' per Lord Donaldson MR in *Re T (An Adult) (Consent to Medical Treatment)*.[8]

Thus, an adult has the right to choose whether he will consent to treatment, refuse it or choose one form of treatment rather than another. This right exists notwithstanding that the reason for making the choice may be rational, irrational, unknown or even non-existent.[9] This principle has been recognised in the MCA 2005 which in s 1(4) provides that a person is not to be treated as unable to make a decision merely because he makes an unwise decision. This widely drawn principle is, however, subject to exceptions and the presumption of the 'capacity to decide' is rebuttable.

In *Re B (Consent to Treatment: Capacity)*[10] the President of the Family Division set out the following guidelines:

(a)   There is a presumption that a patient has the mental capacity to make decisions whether to consent to or refuse medical or surgical treatment offered to him or her.

(b)   If mental capacity is not in issue and the patient, having been given the relevant information and offered the available options, chooses to refuse the treatment that decision has to be respected by the

---

6   Code of Practice, para 4.59.
7   *Re F (Sterilisation: Mental Patient)* [1989] 2 FLR 376.
8   [1992] 2 FLR 458, at 473.
9   *Re T (An Adult) (Consent to Medical Treatment)* above and see also *Sidaway v Board of Governors of Bethlem Royal Hospital and the Maudsley Hospital* [1985] AC 871.
10   [2002] EWHC 429, [2002] 1 FLR 1090.

doctors. Considerations, that the best interest of the patient would indicate that the decision should be to consent to treatment, were irrelevant.

(c)   If there is concern or doubt about the mental capacity of the patient, that doubt should be resolved as soon as possible, by the doctors within the hospital or NHS Trust or by other normal medical procedures.

(d)   Meanwhile, while the question of capacity is being resolved, the patient, of course, has to be cared for in accordance with the judgment of the doctors as to the patient's best interests.

(e)   If there are difficulties in deciding whether the patient has sufficient mental capacity, particularly if the refusal might have grave consequences for the patient, it is important that those considering the issue should not confuse the question of mental capacity with the nature of the decision made by the patient, however grave the consequences. The view of the patient might reflect a difference in values rather than an absence of competence and the assessment of capacity should be approached with that firmly in mind. The doctors could not allow their emotional reaction to, or strong disagreement with, the decision of the patient to cloud their judgment in answering the primary question whether the patient had the mental capacity to make the decision.

(f)   In the rare case where disagreement still exists about competence, it is of the utmost importance that the patient is fully informed of the steps being taken and made a part of the process. If the option of enlisting independent outside expertise is being considered, the doctor should discuss that with the patient so that any referral to a doctor outside the hospital would be, if possible, on a joint basis with the aim of helping both sides to resolve the disagreement. It might be crucial to the prospects of a good outcome that the patient is involved before the referral is made and feels equally engaged in the process.

(g)   If the hospital is faced with a dilemma which the doctors do not know how to resolve, it has to be recognised and further steps taken as a matter of priority. Those in charge cannot allow a situation of deadlock or drift to occur.

(h)   If there is no disagreement about competence but the doctors are for any reason unable to carry out the wishes of the patient, their duty is to find other doctors who would do so.

(i)   If all appropriate steps, to seek independent assistance from medical experts outside the hospital fail, the NHS Trust should not hesitate to make an application to the High Court (the Court of Protection) or seek the advice of the Official Solicitor.

(j)   The treating clinicians and the hospital should always have in mind that a seriously physically disabled patient who is mentally competent has the same right to personal autonomy and to make decisions as any other person with mental capacity.

In *Re JT (Adult: Refusal of Medial Treatment)*[11] the patient was suffering from mental disability involving learning difficulties and extremely disturbed behaviour. There was, however, clear evidence that she understood the information given to her regarding the treatment, its nature, and that she realised the consequences of refusal to continue the treatment in accordance with the three-stage test laid down in *Re C* (see above). It was held that she had capacity to refuse treatment and her condition did not justify bringing the case within s 63 of the Mental Health Act 1983; it would be a criminal and tortious act to perform physically invasive treatment without her consent.

In *Re SA (Vulnerable Adult with Capacity: Marriage)*[12] Munby J (as he then was) referred to a number of circumstances where intervention by the Court in relation to a vulnerable adult is exercisable:

> '... even if not incapacitated by mental disorder or mental illness (but who) is, or is reasonably believed to be either (i) under constraint or (ii) subject to coercion or undue influence or (iii) for some other reason deprived of the capacity to make the relevant decision, or disabled from making a free choice, or incapacitated or disabled from giving or expressing a real and genuine consent.'

Issues will arise whether a person who is under some disability, for example due to alcohol or drug abuse, should be regarded as having an impairment or disturbance in the functioning of mind or brain. Case law as demonstrated below would suggest that they are likely to be regarded as temporarily incapacitated. Whether such cases will in future be covered under the provisions of MCA 2005 will depend on whether the requirement 'because of impairment or disturbance in the functioning of mind and brain' is construed widely or restrictively. In a number of cases decided under the inherent jurisdiction, the Court has been satisfied that the competent person was unable to make the relevant decision due to factors which destroyed or disabled the person's will and capacity. It is submitted that it is arguable that such cases would come within the definition of 'impairment or disturbance in the functioning of mind and brain'.

---

[11]   [1998] 1 FLR 48.
[12]   [2005] EWHC 2942 (Fam).

Where a person is deprived of capacity or has it reduced by reason of temporary factors such as unconsciousness, confusion, shock, severe fatigue, the effects of drugs, or by panic induced by psychological fear and anxiety, it will be necessary to scrutinise the evidence very carefully because fear may be a rational reason for refusing to undergo an operation. On the other hand it may also have the effect of paralysing the will to the point at which refusal and irrationality tips the usually competent person over into a situation where the capacity to make a decision is destroyed.[13] Sometimes it may be difficult to ascertain whether a person has, in fact, exercised a right to decide and, if so, what that decision was. This is particularly the case in emergency situations. In such cases, although the next of kin have no right to consent or refuse consent on another person's behalf, contact with them may reveal what the patient's anticipated decision would be. If this is clearly established, it would be legally binding on the doctor.

In every case, the doctor must give careful and detailed consideration of the patient's capacity to decide at the time the decision was made. The fact that a person is suffering from mental illness does not preclude him from giving a valid consent. The question is whether the patient is capable of understanding and understands what he is deciding; the more serious the decision, the greater the capacity required. The level of the person's ability to decide will inevitably depend on the nature of treatment to be administered, and the information he is given about the proposed treatment. There is a duty on the doctors to give the patient full information as to the nature of the treatment proposed and the likely risks (including any special risks attaching to the treatment). Having given the information, the doctor faced with a refusal of consent must give careful consideration to the patient's capacity to make the decision, the true scope and basis of the decision and whether the decision has been or could have been vitiated as a result of the undue influence of others. (For the test of competency see Chapter 2).

5.6 UNDUE INFLUENCE IN DECISION MAKING

A decision made by an otherwise competent person could have been vitiated as a result of the undue influence of others and cause the person to lack capacity temporarily as occurred in *Re T (An Adult) (Consent to Treatment)*[14] where a woman, who was in the late stages of her pregnancy, was involved in a road traffic accident. Her refusal to undergo a Caesarean operation was overruled because it was found on the facts that the decision had been made under the influence of her mother who was a Jehovah's Witness. Lord Donaldson MR, at 474 said:

---

[13] *Bolton Hospital NHS Trust v O* [2002] EWHC 2871 (Fam), [2003] 1 FLR 824; *Re MB (Medical Treatment)* [1997] 2 FLR 426.

[14] [1992] 2 FLR 458.

'In cases of doubt as to the effect of a purported refusal of treatment, where failure to treat threatens the patient's life or threatens irreparable damage to his health, doctors and health authorities should not hesitate to apply to the Courts for assistance.'

For the test of capacity see s 2 of the Act and **2.4**. Practitioners' attention is also drawn to the Code of Practice, para 4.12. In cases where the issue may be very borderline the application should be issued in the Court of Protection with an application for the case to be allocated to the High Court and immediately transferred up.

5.7   PHOBIA

In *Re L (Patient: Non-Consensual Treatment)*[15] a declaration was sought that a patient in labour could be anaesthetised by means of an injection before her child was delivered by emergency operation. The patient had refused to give her consent because she had an extreme phobia against needles. The evidence was that in the absence of intervention the foetus was at risk, deterioration was inevitable and that death would follow. It was held that the patient's fear put her life and that of her unborn child at risk and that her phobia was such, as to deprive her of the mental competence to make a decision. The treatment proposed to be administered was in the best interests of the patient as it was necessary in order to save the patient's life and that of her child. It should be noted that the decision turned on whether the patient had 'mental competence' whereas the issue under the Act is one of 'capacity' and the person's lack of capacity to make a decision has to be due to an 'impairment of, or disturbance in the functioning of, the mind or brain'. It is submitted that since the provisions in ss 1–3, which deal with the issue of capacity and how lack of capacity is to be determined, are not dissimilar to the principles developed in case law upon which the decision in *Re L* was made, it is arguable, subject to psychiatric and or psychological evidence in support, that in similar circumstances, the decision on an application under the Act would be the same.

In *Re MB (Medical Treatment)*[16] the patient was a young woman who was pregnant. She had a phobia of needle pricks. This was known to the doctors and those who attended upon her from the 33rd week of the pregnancy because she had refused to allow blood samples to be taken by reason of the phobia. Subsequently, obstetric complications with potential serious consequences for the unborn child developed. The risk to the unborn child was assessed at 50% but there was little physical risk to the mother. A Caesarean section was recommended. The mother consented to the operation but she refused to provide blood samples and refused to allow the anaesthetist to insert the veneflon or allow anaesthesia by way of injection or by mask and eventually withdrew her

---

[15]   [1997] 2 FLR 837.
[16]   [1997] 2 FLR 426.

consent to the operation. The doctor's view was that the patient clearly understood the reasons for the operation and accepted them without reservation. He did not, however, think that the full implications of not being able to accept the advice of the impact of her refusal on her and her baby was as clear to her as he would have wished and his impression was that she lacked the capacity to see very far beyond the immediate situation. She was a naive frightened young woman but was not exhibiting any psychiatric disorder. It was the phobia of needles and the irrational fear of needles that got in the way. By reason of this the doctor confirmed that she was suffering from the abnormal mental condition of needle phobia and that at the moment of panic, her fear dominated all; that at the actual point of and for a period of time after the panic, she was not capable of making a decision at all, ie she was not able to hold the information in the balance and make a choice. The Court of Appeal confirmed the decision at first instance that she was temporarily incompetent and incapable of making a decision. The court held that in an emergency the doctors would be free to administer the anaesthetic if that was in her best interests. In considering the scope of best interests, the patient has to be treated on similar principles to the welfare of a child since the Court and the doctors are concerned with a person unable to make the necessary decision for himself. In coming to such a decision, relevant information about the patient's circumstances and background should be made available to the Court.

A similar dilemma as under *Re L* (above) arises both in relation to the test of capacity and best interests. However, it is clear that in assessing her capacity the four criteria set out in s 3 was applied in the case. Since it was accepted that her incapacity was a temporary one the question arises whether if a similar situation were to arise in an application under the Act it would be appropriate to wait until the patient was in a better frame of mind and/or whether it is essential in the circumstances to take further steps to help the patient to make a decision. On the particular facts of the case an assessment of the need for urgency for a decision and the impact on both the patient and the unborn child of any delay would be relevant particularly in assessing the best interests principle. Additionally, there was evidence of other events during her pregnancy to suggest that even if the case had been delayed the situation would not have altered.

5.8 FEAR, PANIC AND ANXIETY

In *Bolton Hospitals NHS v O*[17] the patient who was 39 weeks pregnant had given birth four times, each time by Caesarean section. She required a Caesarean section to deliver the child she was carrying and, if she did not, there was a greater than 95% chance that she and her baby would die. The patient wished to have the operation but on four occasions, having given her consent, when she had gone down to the theatre to have the operation

---

[17]   [2002] EWHC 2871 (Fam), [2003] 1 FLR 824.

she experienced panic and withdrew her consent. She was diagnosed as suffering from post-traumatic stress disorder with symptoms of flashbacks, anxiety, and fear arising from previous Caesarean sections. When granting the declaration sought that the patient temporarily did not have capacity to consent to the treatment due to psychological fear and anxiety, the Court held that whilst the patient was entitled to refuse consent without giving any good reason for so doing, there was a point at which refusal and irrationality tipped the usually competent person over into a situation where the capacity to see through the consequences was inhibited by the panic situation in which the patient found him or herself. However panic, indecisiveness and irrationality in itself does not as such amount to incompetence, but they may be symptoms or evidence of incompetence.

5.9   PAIN

In *Rochdale Healthcare (NHS) Trust v C*[18] the patient was admitted to hospital for the birth of her child. The consultant obstetrician was of the view that a Caesarean section was necessary but the patient would not agree to the operation being carried out as she had previously had a section and had suffered backache and pain around the resulting scar. The consultant obstetrician was also of the opinion that the mental capacity of the patient was not in question and that she seemed to be fully competent. She was able to comprehend and retain information and to believe the information she was given. Although there was no psychiatric evidence available, the Court, however, concluded that she was not capable of weighing-up the information she was given because she was in the throes of labour and that:

> '... a patient who could, in those circumstances, speak in terms which seemed to accept the inevitability of her own death, was not a patient who was able properly to weigh up the considerations that arose so as to make any valid decision, about anything of even the most trivial kind, surely still less one which involved her life.' (Per Johnson J)

The operation in this case was in fact carried out with the patient's consent before the Court had made the decision.

5.10   ABUSE OF DRUGS

In *A Metropolitan Borough Council v DB*[19] the Court found that a 17-year-old crack-cocaine addict, who had refused ante-natal treatment care until shortly before the birth of her child, was not competent to give her consent to medical treatment. The court permitted reasonable force to be used for the purpose of imposing intrusive medical treatment on her as

---

[18]   [1997] 1 FCR 274.
[19]   [1997] 1 FLR 767.

a life-threatening situation had arisen or a serious deterioration to her health might occur if appropriate treatment was not administered.

5.11   RELIGIOUS BELIEFS

In *Re S (Adult: Surgical Treatment)*[20] the High Court, exercising its inherent jurisdiction, granted a declaration that an emergency Caesarean section, despite the mother's refusal on religious grounds, was lawful where it was necessary in order to protect the patient and her unborn child. The mother in that case had been in labour for 2 days. Her situation and that of her unborn child was described as desperately serious. There was the gravest risk of a rupture of the uterus if the section was not carried out. It was described as a life and death situation. The doctors had done their utmost to persuade the mother that the only means of saving her life and that of the unborn child was to allow the operation to be carried out. Although there was no other English authority directly on the point the Court granted the declaration. The reported judgment is short and does not set out any principles upon which the consent of the mother who was of sound mind was overruled. It is thus contrary to the general principle that treatment cannot be imposed upon a competent person because it is believed to be in the patient's interests. It is unlikely that, in an application brought under the Act, the Court would interfere with a person's right to autonomy and right to self determination, in the absence of any evidence to suggest that the person was under pressure or undue influence of another, or other factors which establishes that the person's will was destroyed, even when his/her life depended on receiving treatment and even though the decision appears to be morally repugnant. In any case where there is doubt regarding a person's capacity and the decision relates to surgical intervention or invasive treatment, application should be made to the Court for a declaration as to capacity and for authorisation. See further under Chapter 6 and *Re T (An Adult) (Consent to Medical Treatment)*.[21]

5.12   THE UNBORN CHILD

At common law an unborn child has no legal status or rights and the unborn child has not been treated as a person. Any rights accorded to the foetus have been held to be contingent upon its subsequent live birth. In *Re MB (Medical Treatment)*,[22] however, although the Court was asked to consider the interests of the unborn child and balance them against the mother's interests, the Court's decision was made on the finding that the mother was not competent. The court gave consideration to the written submissions made and concluded that, on the present state of English law, the Court did not have the jurisdiction to take the interests of the foetus

---

[20]   [1993] 1 FLR 26.
[21]   [1992] 2 FLR 458.
[22]   [1997] 2 FLR 426.

into account and the judicial exercise of balancing those interests did not arise in such cases. The Court of Appeal outlined the statutory provisions which protected the rights of the unborn child but nevertheless held that:

> '... on the present state of law, it is clear that a competent woman who has the capacity to decide may, for religious reasons, other reasons, or for no reasons at all, choose not to have medical intervention, even though the consequences may be the death or serious handicap of the child she bears or her own death. She may refuse to consent to the anaesthesia injection in the full knowledge that her decision may significantly reduce the chance of the unborn child being born alive. The foetus up to the moment of birth does not have any separate interests capable of being taken into account when a court has to consider an application for a declaration in respect of a Caesarian section operation. The court does not have the jurisdiction to declare that such medical intervention is lawful to protect the interests of the unborn child even at the point of death.'

The observation made by Butler-Sloss LJ was obiter but in *St George's Healthcare NHS Trust v S; R v Collins and others, ex parte S*,[23] the Court of Appeal reviewed the cases on the status of the foetus and confirmed the decision of the Supreme Court in Canada in *Winnipeg Child and Family Services (Northwest Area) v G*,[24] and the observation made in *Re MB* (above) and in *A-G's Reference (No 3 of 1994)*[25] Judge LJ said:

> 'Although human, and protected by the law in a number of different ways set out in the judgment in Re MB, an unborn child is not a separate person from its mother. Its need for medical assistance does not prevail over her rights. She is entitled not to be forced to submit to an invasion of her body against her will, whether her own life or that of her unborn child depends on it. Her right is not reduced or diminished merely because her decision to exercise it may appear morally repugnant. The declaration in this case involved the removal of the baby from within the body of her mother under physical compulsion. Unless lawfully justified, this constituted an infringement of the mother's autonomy. Of themselves, the perceived needs of the foetus did not provide the necessary justification.'

The basis of this decision reflects the principles which are now set out in ss 1–3 of the Act.

In *St George's Healthcare NHS Trust v S; R v Collins and Others, ex parte S*[26] a declaration had been obtained without notice to the mother dispensing with her consent to medical treatment. The mother was detained under the Mental Health Act 1983 and delivered of her child by Caesarean section, although she had, with full knowledge and understanding of the risk to her and the baby, and after having taken legal advice, clearly indicated that she wanted her baby to be delivered

---

[23]   [1998] 2 FLR 728, [1998] 3 All ER 673.
[24]   [1997] 3 BHRC 611.
[25]   [1998] AC 245, [1997] 3 All ER 936.
[26]   [1998] 2 FLR 728, [1998] 3 All ER 673.

naturally. The application was nevertheless made without notice to the mother and without her knowledge. No attempt had been made to inform her or her solicitors of the application. No evidence was submitted to the Court and the order did not contain any provision that the mother could apply to vary or discharge the order. The Court of Appeal held that having regard to the right of an individual to autonomy and the right of self-determination, an adult of sound mind was entitled to refuse medical treatment even when his or her own life depended on receiving such treatment (at p 685E). In the case of a pregnant woman, whilst the pregnancy increased her personal responsibilities, it did not diminish her entitlement to decide whether or not to undergo medical treatment, even though her decision to exercise it might appear morally repugnant (at p 692). To avoid any recurrence of the unsatisfactory procedure that was followed, the Court of Appeal repeated and expanded the guidelines set out in *Re MB*. The Court of Appeal also emphasised that the guidelines applied not only to Caesarean section cases, but also to any case involving capacity when surgical or invasive treatment may be needed by a patient, whether female or male. It also extended to medical practitioners and health professionals generally as well as to hospital authorities. However, those who represent the mother/patient in such cases should ensure that the hearing takes place on proper notice; that the fullest information as possible on the mother/patient is given by the applicants; that all the medical documents on the mother/patient are disclosed; that information is received on the practice of the profession and, in particular, on the hospital and medical team concerned, and that the opportunity is made available for a second opinion to be obtained on behalf of the mother.

It is appropriate to point out that at the time when these decisions were made, concerns and misgivings were expressed by some in the medical profession regarding the recent cases. Practitioners' attention is drawn to the commentaries which have appeared in the BMJ No 7088 [1997] 19 April pp 1143 and 1183–1187. As to the failure to provide in an order that the respondent in whose absence the order was made has the right to apply for a variation or discharge of the order, see *LLBC v TG, JG, and KR*[27] and *B Borough Council v S (By the Official Solicitor)*.[28]

5.13 THE COMMON LAW DOCTRINE OF 'NECESSITY' AND THE POSITION UNDER THE MENTAL CAPACITY ACT 2005

The general rule has been that it is unlawful to carry out any invasive medical treatment on a person without his/her consent unless it is an act specifically authorised by statute law or under the doctrine of necessity.

---

[27] [2007] EWHC 2640 (Fam).
[28] [2006] EWHC 2584 (Fam), [2007] 1 FLR 1600.

The common law doctrine of necessity has in the past been relied on to render lawful any treatment carried out by a medical professional, if it could be shown that the treatment was necessary as a matter of urgency and that the act was done in the best interests of the patient notwithstanding the absence of consent. The Act, in ss 5 and 6, confirms that position but the provisions appear to be slightly wider. It remains to be seen how the provisions are interpreted if challenged.

Section 5 of the Act provides that if a person does an act in connection with the care or treatment of another person he will be placed in the same position as if he had done the act on the person who had capacity to consent in relation to the matter and had consented to the particular act or treatment, provided that before doing the act he had taken reasonable steps to establish whether the person lacked consent in relation to the matter and that it was in the person's best interests for the act to be done. In future, (save for cases which come within the category of serious medical treatment) where a decision has to be taken which relates to the care and medical treatment of an incapacitated person the decision can be made and the act done without seeking prior authorisation from the Court. Section 6 of the Act however, excludes the use of restraint unless it is necessary to prevent harm to the patient and the act is a proportionate response to the likelihood of the patient suffering harm and the seriousness of that harm (see further under **3.6** and **4.6**). Whatever the circumstances the restraint which amounts to deprivation of liberty within the meaning of Art 5(1) is prohibited unless it is used to provide life-sustaining treatment or the act is done to prevent a serious deterioration in the patient's condition while a decision is sought from the Court. Where such a situation is anticipated an application should be made to the Court of Protection as a matter of urgency for authorization or declaration. In all other cases, if there is any doubt in relation to the capacity of the patient or the nature of the care or treatment to be provided or whether the treatment proposed (eg where there is a difference of opinion) is in the best interests of the patient, it is desirable to seek the prior approval of the Court. In *D v NHS Trust (Medical Treatment: Consent)*.[29] Coleridge J approved this as an appropriate course to take when he said:

> 'In cases of controversy and cases involving momentous and irrevocable decisions, the courts have treated as justiciable any genuine question as to what the best interests of a patient require or justify.'

5.14   PRACTICE AND PROCEDURE

Applications to the Court must follow the procedure set out in COP Rules, Parts 8–10 and the relevant practice directions. The appropriate COP Forms must be used with such variations as the case requires. All

---

[29]   [2004] 1 FLR 1110.

information required in the forms must be provided. Every application must be made in Form COP1 and must be filed with Form COP1B. If the applicant is applying in a representative capacity, he/she must state what that capacity is. The application form must identify the issue/s which the applicant wishes the Court to determine and set out the order/s sought. The parties to the application must be identified. The name of the person in respect of whom the application is made (P) must also be identified. The applicant must also file all the supporting documents required under COP Rules, r 64.

5.14.1   Is permission required – s 50 and Part 8

No permission is required if an application is made by:

(a)   a person who lacks or is alleged to lack capacity;

(b)   anyone with parental responsibility for a person who lacks capacity and is under 18 years of age;

(c)   the donor or donee of a lasting power of attorney to which the application relates;

(d)   a deputy appointed by the Court for a person to whom the application relates; or by a person named in an existing order of the Court;

(e)   where the application is made by the Official Solicitor or the Public Guardian.

Permission is required for any other applicant.

5.14.2   How to apply – Parts 8–10 of the COP Rules and PD 9C and 10A

If permission to apply is required the applicant should file Form COP2 together with the substantive application in Form COP1. The applicant must also file an assessment of capacity in Form COP3. Where a deputy has been appointed the deputy's declaration in Form COP4 should also be filed.

The applicant should indicate on the application form that the application:

•   is urgent;

•   or should be dealt with by a particular judge or level of judge within the Court;

- requires a hearing; or

- any combination of the above.[30]

5.14.3   What will the Court do if permission is granted to make the application

If permission is granted the Court will issue the application and give the applicant the following Forms:

- the acknowledgment of service Form COP5;

- notice of proceedings to P Form COP14 and the guidance notes COP Form 14A;

- notice that the application has been issued in Form COP15 and the guidance notes COP15A; and

- certificate of service and notification Form COP20.[31]

The court must also consider the application as soon as practicable after issue to identify whether there are important and or urgent issues which need to be considered immediately. The Court may deal with the application or part of it with or without a hearing. In considering whether to hold a hearing the Court is required to have regard to the following:

(a)   the nature of the proceedings and the orders sought;

(b)   whether the application is opposed by a person who appears to the Court to have an interest in matters relating to P's best interest;

(c)   whether the application involves a substantial issue of facts;

(d)   the complexity of the facts and the law;

(e)   any wider public interest in the proceedings;

(f)   the circumstances of P and any party, particularly as to whether their rights would be adequately protected if a hearing were not held;

(g)   whether the parties agree that the Court should dispose of the application without a hearing;

(h)   any other matter specified in PD 10A.

---

[30]   PD 10A, para 17.
[31]   COP Rules 2007, r 65.

If the Court considers that a hearing is necessary it will give notice of the hearing date to the parties and to any other relevant person and state on the notice whether the hearing is to dispose of the matter or for directions. Where the Court decides that the matter can be dealt with without a hearing it will make such orders as it thinks fit and serve a copy of the order on all the parties and any relevant person. If the Court makes an order without a hearing the order must contain a provision that the order was made in the absence of the parties and that any party may apply within 21 days of the order being served (or such other period as the Court may direct) for the Court to reconsider the order.[32]

Any party to the proceedings who wishes the Court to reconsider the order made without a hearing must make an application to the Court to do so as required by COP Rules, r 89(3).

The court may also direct that an application or any part of it will be dealt with by a telephone conference. Where video conferencing is required the person requesting it must apply to the Court for such a direction (see Part 14 of PD 14A).

P will be joined as a party to the proceedings and representation ordered usually by the Official Solicitor as litigation friend.

5.14.4   What the applicant must do if the application is granted

The applicant must:

(1)   Serve on the respondent/s the following documents within 21 days:
   (a)   the application Form COP1 and COP1A
   (b)   the accompanying documents Form COP5 and COP15 and COP15A.[33]

(2)   Notify the following persons that an application has been issued:
   (a)   P if he is not a party to the proceedings. P must be served with Forms COP 14, 14A and COP5.[34]
   (b)   Any other relevant person who may have an interest in the proceedings of the application. Any other person must be served with Forms COP15 and 15A and Form COP5.[35]

(3)   Within 7 days of service and notification file at court the certificate of service and notification in Form COP20.[36]

---

[32]   COP Rules 2007, r 89(9).
[33]   COP Rules 2007, r 66.
[34]   COP Rules 2007, r 69.
[35]   COP Rules 2007, r 70.
[36]   COP Rules 2007, r 70(3).

(4)   If an urgent application is required the applicant must make an application for an urgent hearing in Form COP9.[37]

Any person who is served or notified of the application and who wishes to be heard must file an acknowledgement of service within 21 days of service in Form COP5.[38]

5.14.5   What the person served with or notified of the application should do

Where the person is served with the application form he must if he wishes to be a party to the proceedings file an acknowledgement of service, using Form COP5.[39] Where a person is notified of the application he must if he wishes to apply to the Court to be joined as a party file an acknowledgement of notification using Form COP5.[40]

Where a person is neither served nor notified of the application, he must, if he wishes to be a party to the proceedings, apply to the Court to be joined by filing an application in Form COP10.[41]

In the event of an emergency the Court is empowered to make orders:

- on the papers without a hearing;

- at a without notice hearing;

- abridging time.

Where orders are made without notice to respondents a further hearing will be fixed and directions given for the respondents to file a response.

5.14.6   Hearing

The court will list a hearing to consider the application and give directions and make an interim or final order. At a directions hearing the Court will allocate the case to the appropriate level of the judiciary and consider making the directions set out in COP Rules, r 85. If P is joined as a party, a direction will be given for him/her to be represented by a litigation friend. The court will also set a timetable for the filing of evidence, disclosure and give directions as to the attendance of witnesses at the final hearing and fix a trial window or, in the case of urgency, it will list the case for a final hearing.

---

[37]   COP Rules 2007, Part 10 and PD 10A and 10B.
[38]   COP Rules 2007, r 72.
[39]   PD 9C, para 33.
[40]   PD 9C, para 4.
[41]   COP Rules 2007, r 75 and PD 9C, para 5.

5.15 POWERS OF THE COURT OF PROTECTION IN MEDICAL TREATMENT CASES

Section 15 of the Act empowers the Court to make declaratory orders as the High Court has done and continues to do when exercising its inherent jurisdiction as to:

- Whether a person has or lacks capacity to make a particular decision specified in the declaration.

- Whether a person has or lacks capacity to make decisions on the matters described in the declaration.

- The lawfulness or otherwise of any act done or yet to be done in relation to that person.

The court may also appoint a deputy to make decision on behalf of the patient (see further under Chapter) although a decision of the Court is to be preferred and the appointment of a deputy for welfare issues will not be made routinely as in the case of property and affairs.

An 'act' in this context is defined as including an omission and a course of conduct.

5.16 COSTS

See under Chapter 2, at **2.8**.

5.17 APPEALS

Section 53(1) of the Act provides that an appeal lies to the Court of Appeal from any decision of the Court but s 53(2) enables the COP Rules to provide that an appeal from the district judge or circuit judge lies to a prescribed higher judge of the Court of Protection. COP Rules, Part 20 sets out the detailed provision relating to Appeals as follows:

(1) appeals from the decision of a district judge will lie to a nominated circuit judge;

(2) from the decision of the circuit judge to a High Court judge who is nominated to sit in the Court of Protection including the President and the Chancellor of the Chancery Division;

(3) from the decision of the High Court to the Court of Appeal.

Permission to appeal will be required from the Court making the decision. Permission may be sought at the conclusion of the hearing, or by an appellant's notice to the first instance judge or to the appeal judge (see further under Chapter 12).

5.18 PROCEDURAL GUIDE FOR APPLICATIONS FOR URGENT TREATMENT

Permission to Apply	Required by everyone except by the person lacking capacity	MCA 2005 s 50 COP Rules 2007, Part 8
	If the person lacking capacity is under 18 anyone with parental responsibility	
	Donee of a LPA to which the application relates	
	Deputy appointed by the Court	
	A person named in an existing order	
	Official Solicitor/Public Guardian	
Applicant must file	Form **COP2** if permission is required	COP Rules 2007, Part 9
	Forms **COP1** and **COP1A**	PD 9A and
	Form **COP3**	COP Rules 2007, rr 62-64
	Form **COP4** where a deputy has been assigned	
Court Office	(1) Issues application and gives to the Applicant:	
	• Form **COP5**	
	• Forms **COP14** and **COP14A**	
	• Forms **COP15** and **COP15A**	
	• Form **COP20**	
	(2) Judge considers the application and decides whether to give directions or list for directions/disposal hearing	COP Rules 2007, r 9
	(3) May decide to make order without a hearing in which case order court will serve order on all the parties	
What the Applicant must do	(1) Serve on the respondent/s within 21 days Forms **COP1**, **COP1A**, **COP5**, **COP15** and **COP15A**	
	(2) Notify P on Forms **COP14**, **COP14A** and **COP5** of the application	COP Rules 2007, r 69
	(3) Notify any relevant party on Forms **COP15** and **COP15A**	COP Rules 2007, r 70
	(4) File certificate of service and notification in Form **COP20**	
	(5) If an urgent application is required, file Form **COP9**	COP Rules 2007, Part10 PD 10A ad 10B

What the Respondent must do	File an acknowledgement of service in Form **COP5**	PD 9C(3)
What the person notified must do	File an acknowledgement of notification in Form **COP5**	PD 9C(4)
Hearing	The court will consider the application give directions; allocate the case; set the time table and trial window or, if urgent, list for a disposal hearing; make any other appropriate orders	COP Rules 2007, r 85
Orders that the Court may make at the final hearing	(1) Declare whether a person lacks capacity to make a particular decision specified in the declaration (2) Declare whether the person lacks capacity on the matters set out in the declaration (3) The lawfulness or otherwise of any act done or yet to be done (4) Any other consequential or protective orders	MCA 2005, s 15

PRECEDENTS

PRECEDENT FOR A STATEMENT IN SUPPORT OF AN APPLICATION FOR URGENT TREATMENT

IN THE COURT OF PROTECTION   CASE NO ....

IN THE MATTER OF THE MENTAL CAPACITY ACT 2005

AND IN THE MATTER OF MELAINIS LOVE

BETWEEN

HELLENIC COUNTY   Applicant
COUNCIL

And

MELAINIS LOVE   Respondent

(By her Litigation friend the
Official Solicitor)

I, Hestia Goodlady of the Social Services Department of Hellenic County Council, Hogh Road Hellenic, Social Worker will state as follows:

1. I make this statement in support of the Applicant's application for leave to make the application for a declaration that the Respondent Melainis Love lacks capacity to make a decision relating to her medical treatment and that it would be lawful for the medical team at the Blackford Hospital Trust to perform a Caesarean operation on Melainis Love.

2. I have been the allocated social worker for Melainis Love since she came out of care at the age of 18 years. I graduated in social science in 1994 and then went on to an MSc and Diploma in social work completing my studies in 1998. Since then the focus of my career has been to work with those who have severe learning difficulties and have undertaken special training in this field.

3. Melainis Love suffers from severe learning difficulties and has been assessed as having the mental age of a 5 year old. She has from time to time also suffered from delusions.

4. For the past three years she has been living in a residential unit with other young people of her age and who also suffer from various disabilities. She has been having an emotional relationship with one of the residents. Although every effort has been taken to monitor them she became pregnant.

5. During the pregnancy every effort has been made by all the professionals involved to make her understand her condition. The pregnancy however has been a difficult one and has involved her being admitted to hospital for various complications.

6.   More recently I and the midwife have tried to explain to her what is involved in giving birth to a child. We were both under the impression, as were the doctors, that she understood what would happen.

7.   Yesterday she went into labour. She has now been in labour for 38 hours and with every hour that has passed Melainis has become more confused and now believes we are all out to take her baby away. Her condition and that of the baby is fast deteriorating and the consultant gynecologist now advises that the life of the baby is at risk unless a Caesarean operation is carried out. We have attempted to explain this to Melainis but she is now under the delusion that we are all trying to cut her open to take the baby away. She has refused to co operate and is utterly confused.

8.   The consultant psychiatrist at the hospital has assessed her and concluded that she is delusional and that she is totally unable to understand what is happening to her, or the advice that she is receiving on her treatment or the risk to her and her unborn child.

9.   I attach with this statement the report of Dr. Brilliant, the Consultant gynecologist and Dr Whizkid's assessment of Melainis' mental capacity. The Official Solicitor has been contacted and served with the medical reports and he has agreed to act as Melainis litigation friend. He has also consulted with the medical team. He is in agreement with this application being made.

10.   In the circumstances I apply for permission to make an application to the Court for a declaration on her capacity and for the Caesarean operation to be carried out as a matter of urgency.

PRECEDENT FOR A DRAFT ORDER

IN THE COURT OF PROTECTION   CASE NO ....

IN THE MATTER OF THE MENTAL CAPACITY ACT 2005

AND IN THE MATTER OF MELAINIS LOVE

BETWEEN

HELLENIC COUNTY   Applicant
COUNCIL

And

MELAINIS LOVE   Respondent

(By her Litigation friend the
Official Solicitor)

DRAFT ORDER

Made by

At

On ....

UPON hearing Counsel for the Applicant and Counsel for the PCT and Counsel instructed by the Official Solicitor

AND UPON reading the bundle prepared for this hearing, the letter from the Hellinic County Council (HCC) dated .... and considering the submissions made

IT IS DECLARED THAT:

1. ML lacks capacity to litigate.

2. By reason of her Severe Learning Disability and delusional condition ML does not have capacity to make decisions on the medical treatment advised and for a Caesarean operation which needs to be performed on her and to give her consent.

3. It is lawful and in ML's best interests for the medical practitioners having the responsibility for her care and treatment to sedate ML and to perform the proposed Caesarean operation and administer such medication and provide such nursing care as may be deemed necessary.

4.   It is lawful and in ML's best interests for her to remain an inpatient at the .... Hospital and to receive post operative care and treatment as may be deemed necessary.

5.   It is lawful and in ML's best interests that reasonable measures are taken to ensure that ML continues to remain at the hospital and if she leaves the hospital that reasonable and proportionate measures are taken to return her there.

6.   There be no order for costs save that one half of the Official Solicitor's costs be paid by the Applicant.

CHAPTER 6

SERIOUS MEDICAL TREATMENT

LAW AND PRACTICE

6.1 INTRODUCTION

The Act provides that the new Court of Protection now has jurisdiction to make declarations and issue orders that were previously made by the High Court. The jurisdiction includes cases of serious medical treatment and procedures. Previously the inherent jurisdiction of the High Court, which relates to its general jurisdiction as a superior court of record and as a trustee of the Crown's power towards its subject based on the principle of the Crown's duty to protect all its subjects, who owe allegiance to the Crown (*parens patriae*), extended to children as well as adults. Except where the jurisdiction had been specifically curtailed, restricted or taken away by statute or judicial decisions the Court's inherent jurisdiction was both unlimited and unrestricted.

When the Mental Health Acts 1959 and 1983 came into force there were some doubts as to whether the High Court could continue to exercise its inherent jurisdiction in respect of adults who lack capacity. The House of Lord's decision in *Re F (Mental Patient: Sterilisation)*[1] confirmed that the High Court continued to have jurisdiction to make declaratory orders in respect of an adult person who lacked capacity. Thereafter, the question of what medical treatment should or should not be provided to an adult who lacks capacity, and whether or not certain medical procedures should or should not be carried out on such a person, was referred to the Family Division of the High Court for determination. In many cases concerning the provision of medical treatment to and medical procedures on an incapacitated adult, the High Court developed the law on issues relating to the health, welfare and medical treatment of those lacking capacity. More significantly the test of capacity, the concept of 'best interests' and best practice guidelines when dealing with cases involving adults who lack capacity and on providing or withholding life-sustaining treatment were developed in these cases and formed the basis of the provisions which are now contained in the Mental Capacity Act 2005.

---

[1]   [1990] 2 AC 1.

The Act now provides a statutory framework supplemented by the procedural rules and practice directions for making these decisions. The President's Practice Direction 'Applications Relating to Serious Medical Treatment' defines the treatment that is classed as serious and specifically deals with the procedure to be followed when making an application in such cases.

It is unlikely, therefore, that in future the High Court's inherent jurisdiction will need to be invoked in the majority of cases which concern an incapacitated adult. The inherent jurisdiction may still be relied on in cases which concern a vulnerable adult or where the person's ability to consent is unclear or fluctuates, or where there is uncertainty regarding the vulnerable adult's capacity to decide all the issues relating to his health and welfare.[2] In such cases it is suggested that the application should be issued in the Court of Protection and transferred to the High Court to be determined by a nominated judge of the Family Division so that, if necessary, the Court can exercise dual jurisdiction under the Act and under its inherent jurisdiction.

6.2   DEFINITION OF 'SERIOUS MEDICAL TREATMENT' AND 'SERIOUS CONSEQUENCES'

Section 37(6) of the Act defines 'serious medical treatment' as treatment which involves providing, withholding or withdrawing treatment of the kind prescribed by regulations made by the appropriate authority. 'Treatment' includes a diagnostic or other procedure.[3]

The Mental Capacity Act 2005 (Independent Mental Capacity Advocates) (General) Regulations 2006[4] defines 'serious medical treatment' for the purposes of s 37 as treatment which involves providing, withdrawing or withholding treatment in circumstances where:

(a)   in a case where a single treatment is being proposed, there is a fine balance between its benefits to P (person lacking capacity) and the burdens and risks it is likely to entail for him;

(b)   in a case where there is a choice of treatments, a decision as to which one to use is finely balanced; or

(c)   what is proposed would be likely to involve serious consequences for P.

---

[2]   See *MM: Local Authority X v MM (by the Official Solicitor) and KM* [2009] 1 FLR 443.

[3]   MCA 2005, s 64.

[4]   SI 2006/1832.

'Serious consequences' are described as 'those which could have a serious impact on P, either from the effects of the treatment, procedure or investigation itself or its wider implications'. This may include treatments, procedures or investigations which:

(a)   cause, or may cause, serious prolonged pain, distress or side effects;

(b)   have potentially major consequences for P; or

(c)   have a serious impact on P's future life choices.

The President's Practice Direction (PD 9E) 'Applications relating to serious medical treatment' also provides that cases involving any of the following decisions should be regarded as serious medical treatment for the purposes of the Rules and the practice direction and should be brought to the Court:

(a)   decisions about the proposed withholding or withdrawal of artificial nutrition and hydration from a person in a permanent vegetative state or a minimally conscious state;

(b)   cases involving organ or bone marrow donation by a person who lacks capacity to consent; and

(c)   cases involving non-therapeutic sterilisation of a person who lacks capacity to consent.

The Practice Direction also lists some procedures and treatments which may be considered to be 'serious medical treatment. These are:

(a)   certain terminations of pregnancy in relation to a person who lacks capacity to consent to such a procedure;

(b)   a medical procedure performed on a person who lacks capacity to consent to it, where the procedure is for the purpose of a donation to another person;

(c)   a medical procedure or treatment to be carried out on a person who lacks capacity to consent to it, where that procedure or treatment must be carried out using a degree of force to restrain the person concerned;

(d)   an experimental or innovative treatment for the benefit of a person who lacks capacity to consent to such treatment; and

(e)   a case involving an ethical dilemma in an untested area.[5]

---

[5]   PD 9E, para 6.

There may be other procedures or treatments not contained in the list above which can be regarded as serious medical treatment. Whether or not a procedure is regarded as serious medical treatment will depend on the circumstances and the consequences for P.

Cases involving issues, treatments and procedures set out in the Practice Direction have been adjudicated upon by the High Court under its inherent jurisdiction. In future such cases should be commenced in the Court of Protection where P lacks capacity. Reference to the case law as developed by the High Court may provide a guide in future cases. Some of these are referred to below.

6.3   WITHHOLDING /WITHDRAWING ANH FROM A PERSON IN A PERSISTENT VEGETATIVE STATE (PVS) AND CASES OF CPR

In identifying the three categories of cases when the matter should be brought before the Court the Practice Direction follows the practice which has been developed by the High Court in case law.

The first of these categories includes all cases where the withholding or withdrawal of ANH is proposed for a P in PVS. It confirms, in accordance with *Airedale NHS Trust v Bland*[6], that it is 'good practice' where it is proposed to withdraw ANH from a P in PVS to bring the case before the Court. Prior sanction/opinion of the Court therefore should be sought in all cases as to the legality of any proposed discontinuance of life support of a PVS P (see PD 9E). The PD however does not set out any guidelines which apply in such cases. The guidelines and principles to be applied in cases of persistent vegetative state (PVS) set out in *Airedale NHS Trust v Bland*[7] and subsequently approved in *Frenchay Healthcare NHS Trust v S*[8] and *Re R (Adult: Medical Treatment)*[9] may thus be of assistance.

6.4   WHAT OF CASES WHERE THERE IS SOME AWARENESS IN P IN A PVS?

The guidelines issued by the Medical Ethics Committee of the British Medical Association on treatment decisions for Ps in PVS set out certain guidelines which were applied in cases before the High Court. Guidelines of the Royal College of Physicians state that there are three clinical requirements which must all be fulfilled for the diagnosis to be considered and three further clinical features must be present. Although the Court had followed these guidelines in the earlier cases of *An NHS Trust v M;*

---

[6]   [1993] 1 FLR 1026.
[7]   [1993] 1 FLR 1026.
[8]   [1994] 1 FLR 485.
[9]   [1996] 2 FLR 99.

An NHS Trust v H,[10] they were not followed in *NHS Trust A v H*.[11] In that case, P had some degree of visual tracking and of response to menace. Under the guidelines, one of the clinical features which must be present is that P should not have visual fixation, be able to track moving objects with the eyes or show a menace response. A paper by the International Working Party on the Vegetative State produced by the Royal Hospital for Neurodisability also set out various diagnostic signs which were not in complete accord with the Royal College's guidelines. In that paper, tracking eye movements was listed as a feature that may be present in a permanent vegetative state. The President, in *NHS Trust A v H* when granting the declaration, preferred the criteria set out in the Working Party's paper, at least in the circumstances that were present in the case before her. She took the view that the Royal College's guidelines were in need of clarification and since there had been no change in P's condition for 8 years the hospital could have sought a declaration earlier. The Court of Protection Practice Direction PD 9E specifically provides that decisions relating to ANH where the person is in a 'minimally conscious state' are to be regarded as 'serious medical treatment' and should be brought before the Court. Hence what was regarded as 'good practice' in *R (Burke) v General Medical Council and Others*[12] is now given legal force by the Practice Direction.

The Code of Practice at para 6.18 also confirms that the previous case-law requirement to seek a declaration from the Court in cases where it is proposed to withdraw or withhold life-sustaining treatment from a P in a persistent vegetative state is unaltered by the MCA 2005.

Other matters established in case law, which may be relevant, include the fact that a diagnosis of irreversible PVS should not be considered confirmed until P has been insentient for at least 12 months. Every effort should be made at rehabilitation. It has also been held that decisions concerning life and death should be left to the doctors. The function of the judges is to state the legal principles upon which the lawfulness of the actions of doctors depend.

A distinction may be drawn between:

(1)   cases in which, having regard to all the circumstances, it may be judged not to be in the *interest* of P to initiate or continue life-prolonging treatment; and

(2)   cases in which the treatment is of *no benefit* to P because he is totally unconscious and there is no prospect of any improvement in his condition.

---

10   [2001] 2 FLR 367.

11   [2001] 2 FLR 501.

12   [2005] EWCA 1003.

In both cases, the decision whether or not to withhold treatment should be made in the best interests of P. In the first class of case, however, the decision should be taken by weighing all the relevant considerations and allowing P to die peacefully and with dignity. The task of the Court will be to balance the advantages or disadvantages, benefits or lack of it to P in granting the declaration that it is not in P's best interests to receive resuscitation or other invasive treatment.[13] Where, however, P is totally unconscious and there is no prospect of improvement in his condition, it could be argued that there is no balancing exercise to be performed. Medical treatment is not appropriate or requisite simply to prolong P's life when such treatment has no therapeutic purpose, or where it is futile, because P is unconscious and there is no prospect of any improvement in his condition. Account should also be taken of the invasiveness of the treatment and of the indignity to which a person has to be subjected if his life is prolonged by artificial means, and the likelihood of the distress which would be caused to his family.[14]

In the case of *Re D (Medical Treatment)*[15] the principles set out above were applied where P remained in a coma and was wholly dependent upon artificial feeding and unaware of anything and anybody and where three consultant neurologists were of the view that P was in an irreversible vegetative state but one of the paragraphs of the Royal College of Physicians guidelines for determining PVS was not fulfilled. The court held that, since all the evidence established that there was no awareness and no meaningful life whatsoever and that P was suffering a living death, it was not in her best interest artificially to keep the body alive.

In *Re H (A Patient)*[16] where it was possible to obtain tracking movement of the eyes and P could be roused by clapping or by touch, the 'best interest' test was applied when permitting the withdrawal of treatment where P had no prospect of recovery and was wholly unaware of her environment. The application of the 'best interest' test has in the past raised considerable controversy particularly where the evidence does not suggest that P is suffering in any way (see [1996] Fam Law 535) but under the Act the 'best interest' is to be applied in every case.

Ever developing medicine has most recently discovered the possibility of limited communication in PVS patients by way of brain scanning. This will no doubt have implications for future decision making in this area by the courts.

---

[13]   See *NHS Trust v D and D* [2006] 1 FLR 638 and the review of the authorities in *Wyatt v Portsmouth NHS* [2006] 1 FLR 554, CA.

[14]   *Airedale NHS Trust v Bland* [1993] 1 FLR 1026 (per Lord Goff at p 1040). See also *Portsmouth NHS Trust v Wyatt and Wyatt Southampton NHS Intervening* [2004] EWHC 2247 (Fam), [2005] 1 FLR 21 and *Re L (Medical Treatment: Benefit* [2004] EWHC 2713 (Fam), [2005] 1 FLR 491.

[15]   [1998] 1 FLR 411.

[16]   [1998] 2 FLR 36.

6.5   CARDIO-PULMONARY RESUSCITATION (CPR)

A statement issued by the British Medical Association and the Royal
College of Nursing states that:

> 'Cardio-pulmonary resuscitation (CPR) can be attempted on any individual
> in whom cardiac or respiratory function ceases. Such events are inevitable as
> part of dying and thus CPR can theoretically be used on every individual
> prior to death. It is therefore essential to identify patients for whom
> cardio-pulmonary arrest represents a terminal event in their illness and in
> whom CPR is inappropriate.'

The publication provides guidelines as a framework within which
decisions may be formulated.

Unlike cases of PVS, where the Court is asked to approve a course aimed
at terminating life or accelerating death, in cases of CPR the Court will be
asked to consider and rule upon the circumstances in which steps should
not be taken to prolong life.

At common law the test applied in such cases is the same as in PVS, ie the
best interest of P. In *Re J (A Minor) (Wardship: Medical Treatment)*[17]
the Court of Appeal, when considering the issue of whether a child, who
was not terminally ill but who suffered from convulsions requiring
resuscitation, should not, in the event of further convulsions, be revived
by means of mechanical ventilation, held that the test in the case of a
child was the paramountcy of the child's best interest. Where a child was
not terminally ill, the Court in determining where the child's interest lay,
would take into account the pain and suffering to the child if
life-prolonging treatment were given and assess its effect from the child's
position were he able to make a sound judgment. If from this standpoint,
his future life might be regarded as intolerable to him the Court might
choose a course which did not prevent his death:

> 'the correct approach is for the Court to judge the quality of life the child
> would have to endure if given treatment, and decide whether in all the
> circumstances such a life would be so afflicted as to be intolerable to that
> child'

(per Taylor LCJ in *Re J (A Minor) (Wardship: Medical Treatment)*).[18]

In *Re C (Medical Treatment)*[19] the High Court applied the principles set
out in *Re J* (above) and exercised its inherent jurisdiction to approve the
recommended treatment, which involved the withdrawal of ventilation as
advised by the medical team, notwithstanding the objections of the

---

[17]   [1991] Fam 33, [1991] 1 FLR 366.
[18]   [1991] 1 FLR 366, at 383.
[19]   [1998] 1 FLR 384.

parents on the basis that the best interest of the child (who was 16 months old) required that she be prevented from suffering.

The same principle would be applied in the case of a handicapped incapacitated adult.

In cases where the issue is whether the administration of antibiotics should be withheld in the event of P developing a potentially life-threatening infection, the decision can only be taken at the time by P's responsible medical practitioners in the light of the prevailing circumstances and 'falls fairly and squarely within the clinical responsibility of the consultant treating the patient' (per Sir Stephen Brown P in *Re R (Adult: Medical Treatment)*[20]). Where the Court is satisfied that the medical team having responsibility for P's treatment have P's best interest in mind, the Court will leave the decision to them subject to conditions, for example that the medical practitioner and the consultant, having the responsibility at the time for P's treatment and care, advise the withholding of antibiotics.

6.6   CASES INVOLVING ORGAN OR BONE MARROW DONATION BY A PERSON WHO LACKS CAPACITY

The second category of cases referred to in Practice Direction 9E (para 5) is those where an organ or bone marrow donation by a person who lacks capacity is proposed. A declaration must be sought from the Court for an organ or bone marrow donation. In considering such an application, the Court will apply the best interests provision set out in s 4 and adopt an objective approach with an element of subjective factors set out in s 4(6), ie the wishes and feelings, beliefs and values that would be likely to influence the person concerned when making his decision. In *Re W Healthcare NHS Trust v KH*[21] where there was a conflict between the incapacitated person's views and the patient's 'best interests' as demonstrated by the views of the treating doctors, the Court overruled P's views and applying the best interests test permitted the doctor to provide life-sustaining treatment to P. (But see **6.13** under 'Advance decision'.)

At common law, cases involving organ and bone marrow donation require the sanction of the Court. For an example of a case where the Court approved bone marrow donation see *Re Y (Mental Patient: Bone Marrow)*.[22]

---

20   [1996] 2 FLR 99, at 109.
21   [2004] EWCA Civ 1324.
22   [1997] Fam 110.

6.7 NON-THERAPEUTIC STERILISATION

Non-therapeutic sterilisation cases are classified as 'serious medical treatment' and require a determination by the Court.[23] This reflects the common law position: see *GF (Medical Treatment)*[24] where the Court ruled that no declaration was needed regarding the lawful performance of a hysterectomy, which had the incidental effect of sterilisation on a woman who lacked capacity and was severely disabled and who suffered from excessively heavy periods which she was unable to deal with. Two medical practitioners were satisfied that the operation was necessary for therapeutic purposes; was in the best interests of P and there was no other less intrusive means of treating the condition. However, this decision turned on its facts and in a later case of *Re S (Sterilisation)*[25] it was said that the test set in *Re GF* (above) for bringing applications in sterilisation cases was expressed in broad terms and that if a particular case lay anywhere near the boundary line it should be referred to the Court. Sterilisation as a contraceptive procedure in the absence of gynecological pathology would in general not be justified. Consideration should also be given to whether or not other non-invasive or least invasive medical or surgical treatment was available which would resolve the problem. The possibility of pregnancy and its effect on P may also be relevant in assessing the best interests of the incapacitated person. In *Re S* on appeal the declaration that it was lawful to carry out the hysterectomy was overruled on the facts of the case.

6.8 OTHER CASES WHERE THE CASE SHOULD BE TREATED AS REQUIRING SERIOUS MEDICAL TREATMENT

Practice Direction 9E lists five specific examples but with the proviso that the list is not an exhaustive one and that there may be other procedures or treatment which can be regarded as serious medical treatment depending on the circumstances and the consequences for P. The general principle established at common law in *D v An NHS Trust (Medical Treatment: Consent)*[26] namely:

'In cases of controversy and cases involving momentous and irrevocable decisions, the courts have treated as justiciable any genuine question as to what the best interests of a patient require or justify...'.

remains the position under the Act. It will be up to the decision maker to decide, having had regard to all the circumstances of the individual case, whether to rely on the protection afforded by s 5 of the Act or to take the

---

[23]   PD 9E, para 5(c).
[24]   [1992] 1 FLR 293.
[25]   [2000] 2 FLR 389.
[26]   [2004] 1 FLR 1110.

safer option of seeking a declaration from the Court particularly where the case is one which may be regarded as borderline.

6.9   TERMINATION OF PREGNANCY

Where termination is carried out in accordance with the requirements of the Abortion Act 1967 and where the issues of capacity and best interests are clear and beyond doubt, an application is generally not necessary. If there is any doubt about capacity or best interests an application should be made. Where, it is a borderline case it should be referred to the Court in good time in particular where:

'(i)   there is a dispute as to capacity, or where there is a realistic prospect that P will regain capacity, following a response to treatment, within the period of her pregnancy or shortly thereafter;

(ii)   where there is a lack of unanimity amongst the medical professionals as to the best interests of P;

(iii)   where the procedures under s 1 of the Abortion Act 1967 have not been followed (ie where two medical practitioners have not provided a certificate);

(iv)   where P, members of her immediate family, or the foetus' father have opposed, or expressed views inconsistent with, a termination of the pregnancy; or

(v)   where there are exceptional circumstances (including where the termination may be the last chance to bear a child).'

(per Coleridge J in *D v NHS Trust (Medical Treatment: Consent: Termination)*[27]).

In *Re SS (Medical Treatment: Late Termination)*[28] a woman who had a history of schizophrenia, psychosis and who was detained under s 3 of the Mental Health Act 1983, applied for a declaration that it was in her best interest to have a termination of her pregnancy at 24 weeks. On assessing the competing risks the Court dismissed her application on the ground that the continuation of the pregnancy carried a lesser detriment to the applicant and thus concluded that termination of the pregnancy was not in the applicant's interests. The court observed that the delay in seeking a declaration in this case was unacceptable and suggested that each hospital should have a protocol to deal with possible termination of pregnancies of psychiatric Ps in good time, so that termination could be carried out at the earliest opportunity, and that the protocol should ensure P was referred to independent legal advice at an early stage.

---

[27]   [2004] 1 FLR 1110.
[28]   [2002] 1 FLR 445.

6.10 USE OF REASONABLE FORCE

In *Tameside and Glossop Acute Services Trust v CH*[29] Wall J left open the question whether the Court had power in common law to authorise the use of force on P. In *Norfolk and Norwich Healthcare Trust v W*,[30] *Rochdale Healthcare (NHS) Trust v C*[31] and *Re C (Detention: Medical Treatment)*[32], the Court held that it had jurisdiction at common law to grant a declaration that it would be lawful for reasonable force to be used in the course of treatment. In *Re MB* (above), the Court of Appeal, although confirming that, where a P is found to be incompetent to refuse treatment, it may become necessary to use force to give the necessary treatment, and stating that the extent of the force or compulsion which may become necessary will depend on the circumstances of each individual case and can be judged only by the professionals treating P, did not lay down any guidelines. The court left the question open.

The Act, in ss 5 and 6, sets out the circumstances when restraint and use of force may be permitted where it is necessary to carry out the act in order to prevent harm to P, provided the act is a proportionate response to the likelihood of P's suffering harm and the seriousness of that harm (see further Chapter 4). In such cases, it may become necessary for those treating P to carry out a balancing exercise between continuing treatment forcibly and deciding not to continue with it. It is submitted that in all cases where the doctor is doubtful about the use of force or the extent of force to be used, an application should be made to the Court for a declaration.

In any case where treatment may require the use of force, an application should be made to the Court for authorisation to do so before the urgency arises.

6.11 EXPERIMENTAL MEDICAL TREATMENT

Under the MCA 2005 experimental or innovative treatment for the benefit of a person who lacks capacity must be referred to the Court for approval, as has been the case under common law. In *JS v An NHS Trust; JA v An NHS Trust*,[33] two teenagers were at the advanced stages of variant Creutzfeldt-Jakob disease (vCJD). Both had sustained severe brain damage, were confined to their beds with a severely limited enjoyment of life and a limited extent of expressing their feelings. The court was asked to declare that both Ps had no capacity to consent to treatment and that it would be lawful to subject them to a new experimental treatment, which had not been tested on humans, involving

---

[29] [1996] 1 FLR 762.
[30] [1996] 2 FLR 613.
[31] [1997] 1 FCR 274.
[32] [1997] 2 FLR 180.
[33] [2002] EWHC 2734 (Fam), [2003] 1 FLR 879.

intraventricular administration of a drug. It was known that the treatment would only provide a slight chance of resulting in some benefit to Ps and the very best that could be hoped for was the possibility of slight neurological improvement in their condition, the temporary arresting of the disease's progress, or the prolongation of life but with risks involved to both Ps. The court held that both Ps lacked capacity to give consent to the treatment; that where there was a responsible body of relevant professional opinion which supported the innovative treatment, subject to the seriousness of the risks involved and the degree of benefit that might be achieved, the test in *Bolam v Friern Hospital Management Committee*[34] (the 'Bolam test') ought not to be allowed to inhibit medical progress and innovative work. Where there was no alternative treatment available and the disease was progressive and fatal, it was reasonable to consider experimental treatment with unknown risks but risks that did not seem to fall outside the bounds of responsible surgical and medical treatment so as to be unacceptable and without significant risk of increased suffering to P, but where there was a chance of benefit to P by way of some improvement in the present state of the illness. A P who was unable to consent to pioneering treatment ought not to be deprived of a chance in circumstances where he would have been likely to consent if he had been competent.

On the facts, the Court held that it was in the best interest of both Ps for the treatment to be carried out as both had lives worth preserving and any treatment that might be beneficial would be of value to them; that a reduced enjoyment of life even at quite a low level was to be respected and protected and even the prospect of a slightly longer life was a benefit worth having for these Ps. See also *Simms v Simms; A v A (A Child)*.[35]

The court will also protect P's privacy in such cases by granting an injunction. The terms of the injunction order granted in the above case are reproduced below as a guide to practitioners:

> 'IT IS ORDERED THAT:
> 1 No written or photographic material shall be published or broadcast in any form whatsoever to any person whether in writing or electronically which might lead directly or indirectly to any of the following being identified as being connected with these proceedings –
>   (a) ... JA (being a person suffering from variant Creutzfeldt-Jakob disease and for whom treatment with Pentosan Polysulphate (PPS) has been proposed).
>   (b) any member of her family.
>   (c) at any time before PPS treatment for JS or JA commences, any clinician, hospital or NHS trust (including the second defendant trust) as being a clinician, hospital or NHS trust which may be involved in treating either JS or JA.

---

[34] [1957] 2 All ER 118, [1957] 1 WLR 582.
[35] [2003] Fam 83.

(d)   at any time after PPS treatment for JS or JA has commenced, any clinician, hospital or NHS trust as being the clinician, hospital or NHS trust which is actually involved in treating either JS or JA.

(e)   any clinician, hospital or NHS trust that normally has clinical responsibility for JS or JA.

2   This order shall not prevent the reporting of any information contained in a judgment given in open court or any information already in the public domain (provided that information shall not be considered to be in the public domain on the ground only that it has been published outside the jurisdiction of this court).

3   This order shall remain in effect until the death of both JS and JA has occurred.

4   Copies of this order endorsed with a penal notice may be served by the parties to the proceedings:

(a)   on such newspapers and sound or television broadcasting or cable or satellite programme services as they may think fit in each case by facsimile transmission or pre-paid first class post addressed to the editor in the case of a newspaper or senior news editor in the case of a broadcasting or cable or satellite programme service; and

(b)   on such other persons as they may think fit in each case by personal service,

And the parties and any person affected by the injunction in paragraph 1 above are to be at liberty to apply on 24 hours notice to the parties. Such application to be listed before the President of the Family Division if available.'

6.12   EMERGENCY MEDICAL TREATMENT

Under the common law in a case of an emergency, pursuant to the doctrine of necessity, where the treatment is to preserve life or P's well-being and the doctor acts in accordance with the accepted practice in consultation with other medical opinion, he may administer treatment lawfully to such a P without his/her consent.

Where there is a responsible body of opinion against a proposed treatment it would be prudent to apply to the Court for a declaration. In such cases the opposition to the proposed treatment is a relevant factor which the Court will take into account when applying the best interests of P test and the medical necessity test. It should be noted, however, that where Art 3 of the European Convention is raised, the Court will apply the standard of proof with respect to medical necessity as set out in *Herczegfalvy v Austria*.[36] It must be 'convincingly' shown that treatment is necessary rather than that the particular treatment is a medical necessity on the balance of probability.[37] In cases where it is proposed to administer

---

[36]   (1993) EHRR 437.
[37]   *R(N) v Doctor M* [2002] EWCA Civ 1789, [2003] 1 FLR 667.

innovative experimental treatment the Court will take account of whether there is any alternative treatment available and weigh-up the risks involved, the degree of benefit that might be achieved and whether the treatment carries any significant risk of increased suffering to P. Subject to the particular circumstances of each individual case, the views of the patient's family is also a relevant factor and would carry considerable weight.[38]

Where P is incompetent to give consent or there appears to be doubt about his capacity, the assistance of the Court should be obtained; see *Re T (An Adult) (Consent to Medical Treatment)* above, where Lord Donaldson MR, at 474 said:

> 'In cases of doubt as to the effect of a purported refusal of treatment, where failure to treat threatens P's life or threatens irreparable damage to his health, doctors and health authorities should not hesitate to apply to the courts for assistance.'

In that case the Court declared treatment to be lawfully administered to an adult.

Similar principles apply under the Act which makes provision for an application to be made under s 15, for a declaration as to capacity and under s 48, which expressly confers powers on the Court to take steps 'pending' the determination of any question relating to capacity, and to make such orders as are expedient in the best interests of P. The court's interim jurisdiction under this section is something less than that required to justify the ultimate declaration. The 'gateway' test for the engagement of the Court's powers under s 48 is lower than that of evidence sufficient, in itself, to rebut the presumption of capacity. When determining such an application the Court in the first instance will consider whether there is evidence giving good cause for concern that the person might lack capacity in some relevant regard. Once that is raised as a serious possibility, the Court will decide what action, if any, it is in the person's best interests to take before a final determination of his or her capacity could be made. Where necessary, the Court will make such orders as may be appropriate to permit safeguarding steps to be undertaken with regard to P's health and as a matter of the emergency, depending on the individual facts of the case and the urgency of the decision in question, balanced against the person's right to autonomy and his best interests; see under **3.5** (interim order) and *Re F (Court of Protection)* HHJ Marshall QC, 28 May 2009.

---

[38]   *JS v An NHS Trust; JA v An NHS Trust* [2002] EWHC 2734 (Fam), [2003] 1 FLR 879.

6.13 ADVANCE DECISION – SS 24–26

Under the common law in cases where P, being an adult and of sound mind, in anticipation of becoming incapable and entering into a condition such as PVS, has given clear instruction, whether orally or in writing, with full understanding of the nature and consequences of his decision that in such an event he was not to be given medical care designed to keep him alive, his wishes should be respected and it would be unlawful to administer medical treatment. The principle of a competent adult's autonomy to make decisions for himself is determinative, provided that decision remains valid and unequivocal. This principle was followed in the case of *Re AK (Medical Treatment: Consent)*,[39] where a young man of 19, who had motor neurone disease and was reduced to eye movement only, had indicated clearly and independently that he no longer wished to be kept alive once his last means of communication had gone. The High Court granted the medical team who were treating the young man a declaration that they would not be acting unlawfully in withdrawing life support. The court found that the man was able to see, hear, think and understand. He was capable of making an informed decision and his wishes should be respected. The advance indication given by P who was of full capacity and sound of mind was effective. However, the Court held that care must be taken to ensure that such advance indications of wishes still represented the current wishes of P. Doctors will need to be satisfied that the patient is of full capacity to give consent and to examine carefully and critically the issue of consent, particularly where communication is difficult.

Where P's wish is clear, the continuation of invasive treatment without the consent of an adult P of sound mind will be unlawful. Where the directive is contained in a 'living will' the same principle applies.

In *Re B (Consent to Treatment: Capacity)*[40] the patient had made a living will in which she had indicated that if she were unable to give instructions she wished for treatment to be withdrawn if she was suffering from a life threatening condition, permanent mental impairment or if she became unconscious. The intensive care team treated her with a ventilator and she underwent surgery. P then asked for the ventilator to be switched off which was declined. Her application for a declaration that she had the mental capacity whether to accept or reject treatment and that the doctors had treated her unlawfully was granted.[41] In the absence of any such expressed intention or views, where the person is totally unconscious, it is the duty of doctors to apply the 'best interest' test, ie such treatment as in their informed opinion is in P's best interests bearing in mind that although the principle of the sanctity of human life forbids the taking of positive steps to cut short the life of the terminally ill P, it is not an

---

[39] [2001] 1 FLR 129.
[40] [2002] 1 FLR 1090.
[41] See also *HE v A Hospital NHS Trust* [2003] 2 FLR 408.

absolute principle and does not forbid the discontinuance of treatment which serves merely to keep alive a P who is terminally ill and to prolong his suffering. In such cases, the wishes of P's immediate family should also be given due weight. The best interest test is broad and flexible and allows room for the exercise of judgment by the doctors as to whether the relevant conditions exist which justify the discontinuance of life support.

This principle is now embodied in ss 24–26 of the Act with additional safeguards. The statutory provisions specifically address the issue of validity and when the decision may not be applicable. It also specifically imposes conditions in relation to advance decisions relating to life-sustaining treatment.

An advance consent will apply only if:

• the person has reached the age of 18 years;

• had capacity when he made the decision;

• the decision is that if, at a later date and in such circumstances as he may specify, a specified treatment is proposed to be carried out or continued by the health care provider and at that time he lacks capacity to consent to that treatment;

• the specified treatment is not to be carried out or continued;

• the advance directive has not been withdrawn by any means at any time when the person had capacity to do so.

The Act does not require that the advance decision should be made in any formal document. It may be expressed in 'layman's terms.[42] However the Code of Practice, para 9.19 sets out the information that should be included in a written advance decision. This includes the following:

• full details of the maker of the advance decision including the date of birth, home address and any distinguishing features (in case healthcare professionals need to identify an unconscious person, for example);

• the name and address of the person's GP and whether they have a copy of the document;

• a statement that the document should be used if the person ever lacks capacity to make treatment decisions;

• a clear statement of the decision, the treatment to be refused and the circumstances in which the decision will apply;

---

[42]   MCA 2005, s 24(1).

- the date the document was written (or reviewed);

- the person's signature (or the signature of someone the person has asked to sign on their behalf and in their presence);

- the signature of the person witnessing the signature, if there is one (or a statement directing somebody to sign on the person's behalf).

Although the signature of the maker of the advance decision is not essential, except where it relates to an advance decision to refuse life-sustaining treatment, if there is a witness it is advised that a description of the relationship between the witness and the person making the advance decision is given. In the case where the witness is a professional, who has assessed the person's capacity, the professional witness should also make a record of the assessment. In the case of a non professional witness the witness's role is not to certify the person's capacity and his/her signature does not prove that there has been an assessment of the maker of the advance decision.

In the case of a verbal advance decision the Code of Practice, para 9.23 advises healthcare professionals to make a record of the decision to refuse treatment in the person's healthcare record and to ensure that the record includes:

- a note that the decision should apply if the person lacks capacity to make treatment decisions in future;

- a clear note of the decision, the treatment to be refused and the circumstances in which the decision will apply;

- details of someone who was present when the oral advance decision was recorded and the role in which they were present (for example, healthcare professional or family member); and

- whether they heard the decision, took part in it or are just aware that it exists.

6.13.1   Validity of the decision

An advance decision will not be valid if P has:

- withdrawn the decision at any time when he had capacity to do so;

- under a lasting power of attorney created after the advance decision was made, conferred authority on the donee (or if more than one, any of them) to give or refuse consent to the treatment to which the advance decision relates, or

- done anything else clearly inconsistent with the advance decision remaining his fixed decision.[43]

An advance decision will not be applicable if:

- at the material time the person has capacity to give or refuse consent;

- that treatment is not the treatment specified in the advance decision;

- any circumstances specified in the advance treatment are absent; or

- there are reasonable grounds for believing that circumstances exist which the person did not anticipate at the time of the advance decision and which would have affected his decision had he anticipated them.

6.13.2   Conditions which must be satisfied for an effective advance decision relating to life-sustaining treatment

Any advance decision to refuse life-sustaining treatment must:

- be in writing;

- be signed by P (or under his direction and in his presence by another) and the signature must be made or acknowledged by P in the presence of a witness who must sign or acknowledge his signature in the presence of P.[44]

A personal welfare lasting power of attorney which authorises health care decisions cannot override a subsequent advance decision refusing treatment and does not prevent it from being regarded as valid and applicable.[45]

6.13.3   Effect of an advance decision

A valid and applicable advance decision has effect as if the person had capacity to make it at the time when the question arises whether the treatment should be carried out or continued.[46]

The person treating the person concerned will not incur any liability:

(a)   for providing the treatment or continuing the treatment, unless at the time he is satisfied that an advance decision exists which is valid and applicable; or

---

[43]   MCA 2005, s 25.
[44]   MCA 2005, s 25(6).
[45]   MCA 2005, s 25(7).
[46]   MCA 2005, s 25(1).

(b)   for the consequences of withholding or withdrawing treatment from the P concerned if, at the time, he reasonably believes that an advance decision exists which is valid and applicable to the treatment.

In the case of any doubt in relation to the existence of or the validity or applicability of an advance consent, or the capacity of the maker when he/she made the advance decision, an application should be made to the Court for a declaration. The Act, in s 26(5), provides that whilst a decision in respect of any relevant issue is sought the treatment provider is not prevented from providing life-sustaining treatment or doing any act he reasonably believes to be necessary to prevent a serious deterioration in that person's condition.[47]

6.14   INDEPENDENT MENTAL CAPACITY ADVOCATES SS 35–37

6.14.1   The purpose of the IMCA

The provision of an independent mental capacity advocate (IMCA) is a creation of the Act. The need to provide the service was identified by the Joint Parliamentary Committee because it considered that an independent advocacy service plays:

> 'an essential role in assisting people with capacity problems to make and communicate decisions; helping them to enforce their rights and guard against unwarranted intrusion into their lives; providing a focus on the views and wishes of an incapacitated person in the determination of their best interests; providing additional safeguards against abuse and exploitation; and assisting in the resolution of disputes.'

The Act, in s 35, carries this through by imposing a duty on the Secretary of State for Health in England (and the Welsh Assembly in Wales) to make such arrangements as it considers reasonable to enable independent mental capacity advocates to be available to represent and support persons to whom acts or decisions specified in ss 37–39 of the Act apply. It ensures that the objective of this provision is met by identifying in s 35(4) that in making the arrangements for an IMCA the Secretary of State:

> 'must have regard to the principle that a person to whom a proposed act or decision relates should, as far as practicable, be represented and supported by a person who is independent of any person who will be responsible for the act or decision.'

When serious medical treatment is provided or proposed by an NHS body, it imposes a duty on the NHS body to instruct an IMCA to

---

[47]   MCA 2005, s 26(5).

represent P, before it provides or secures the provision of serious medical treatment as defined in s 37(6) of the Act (see **5.1** above) for a P who lacks capacity to consent to treatment if it is satisfied that there is no person other than one engaged in providing care or treatment for P in a professional capacity or for remuneration, whom it would be appropriate to consult in determining what would be in P's best interests.[48] The only exception to this duty is where there is:

(a)   a person nominated by P (in whatever manner) as a person to be consulted on matters to which that duty relates;

(b)   a donee of a lasting power of attorney created by P who is authorised to make decisions in relation to those matters; or

(c)   a deputy appointed by the Court for P with power to make decisions in relation to those matters;[49] and

where the treatment needs to be provided as a matter of urgency. It does not apply to treatment under the Mental Health Act 1983.[50] Where emergency serious medical treatment is required it is more than likely that an application will be made to the Court and the Court will invite the Official Solicitor to act for P who lacks capacity.

Note however that a person appointed under Part 10 of Sch A1 to be P's representative is not by virtue of that appointment, a person nominated by P to be consulted in matters relating to this duty.[51]

Section 37(5) imposes a further duty on the NHS body in providing or securing the provision of treatment for P to take into account any information given, or submissions made by the IMCA.

6.14.2   Definition of clauses referred to above

The Mental Capacity Act 2005 (Independent Mental Capacity Advocates) (General) Regulations 2006[52] ('General Regulations') make the necessary provisions which inter alia relate to the provision of serious medical treatment stipulated in the Act and define the terms 'serious medical treatment' and 'NHS body' for this purpose. They also contain provisions as to who can be appointed to act as an IMCA and the IMCA's function when he has been instructed to represent a person who lacks capacity.

The General Regulations 2006 define 'serious medical treatment' for the purposes of s 37 as:

---

[48]   MCA 2005, s 37(1).
[49]   MCA 2005, s 40(1).
[50]   MCA 2005, s 37(4).
[51]   MCA 2005, s 40(2).
[52]   SI 2006/1832.

'treatment which involves providing, withdrawing or withholding treatment in circumstances where:

(a)   in a case where a single treatment is being proposed, there is a fine balance between its benefits to the patient and the burdens and risks it is likely to entail for him,

(b)   in a case where there is a choice of treatments, a decision as to which one to use is finely balanced, or

(c)   what is proposed would be likely to involve serious consequences for the patient.'

It defines an NHS body to mean:

(a)   a Strategic Health Authority which is established under s 8 of the National Health Service Act 1977;

(b)   an NHS foundation trust established under s 1 of the National Health Service and Community Care Act 1990;

(c)   a Primary Care Trust established under s 16A of the National Health Service Act 1977;

(d)   an NHS Trust established under s 5 of the National Health Service and Community Care Act 1990;

(e)   a Care Trust designated as a Care Trust under s 45 of the Health and Social Care Act 2001.

6.14.3   Functions of the IMCA

Section 36 of the Act gives powers to make regulations on the functions of the IMCA and specifically identifies the steps the IMCA must take for the purposes of discharging those functions. The IMCA is required to take such steps as he may be required for the purpose of:

(a)   providing support to the person whom he has instructed to represent (P) so that P may participate as fully as possible in any relevant decision;

(b)   obtaining and evaluating relevant information;

(c)   ascertaining what P's wishes and feelings would be likely to be, and the beliefs and values that would be likely to influence P if he had capacity;

(d)   ascertaining what alternative courses of action are available in relation to P;

(e)   obtaining a further medical opinion where treatment is proposed and the advocate thinks that one should be obtained;

(f)   the advocate may challenge or provide assistance for the purpose of challenging any relevant decision.

The General Regulations provide that the IMCA must determine in all the circumstances how best to represent and support P and in particular the IMCA must:

(a)   verify that the instructions were issued by an authorised person;

(b)   to the extent that it is practicable and appropriate to do so, interview P and examine the records relevant to P to which the IMCA has access under s 35(6) of the Act;

(c)   to the extent that it is practicable and appropriate to do so, consult persons engaged in providing care or treatment for P in a professional capacity or for remuneration, and other persons who may be in a position to comment on P's wishes, feelings, beliefs or values;

(d)   take all practicable steps to obtain such other information about P or the act or decision that is proposed in relation to P, as the IMCA considers necessary;

(e)   evaluate all the information he has obtained for the purpose of ascertaining the extent of the support provided to P to enable him to participate in making any decision about the matter in relation to which the IMCA has been instructed and what the patient's wishes and feeling are likely to be and the beliefs and values that would be likely to influence him/her if he/she had capacity in relation to the proposed act or decision and to consider what alternative courses of action are available and whether P is likely to benefit from a further medical opinion.

In accordance with the provisions of s 37(3) the IMCA is given the right to challenge the decision taken or proposed as if he were a person engaged in caring for P or interested in his welfare. In most cases this can be achieved by using the complaints procedure to resolve disputes but there may be circumstances where the IMCA may be obliged to apply to the Court of Protection for relief.

Regulation 5 of the General Regulations provides certain minimum requirements that a person must meet in order to be appointed as an IMCA. In order to act as an IMCA, a person must be approved by a local authority as meeting the appointment requirements, or he must be a member of a class which has been so approved. The appointment requirements are that:

•   he/she must have appropriate experience/training;

- he/she be a person of integrity and good character;

- he/she must be able to act independently of anyone who instructs him to act as an IMCA.

Regulation 5(3) further provides that a criminal record certificate or enhanced criminal record certificate must be obtained.

6.15 PRACTICE AND PROCEDURE

6.15.1 Allocation

The Central Registry for the Court of Protection is based in Archway Towers, Archway, London. Regional Courts are located in Birmingham, Bristol, Cardiff, Manchester, Newcastle and Preston. Cases will also be heard at the RCJ. The President of the Family Division is also the President of the Court of Protection. Sir Andrew Morritt, the Chancellor of the Chancery Division has been appointed Vice-President and Denzil Lush, the former Master of the Court of Protection, is the Senior Judge. A number of High Court judges, circuit and district judges have also been nominated to hear Court of Protection cases.

The COP Rules 2007, r 86 allows a practice direction to specify the types of application which may be dealt with only by the President, the Vice-President or one of the other judges nominated by virtue of s 46(2)(a) to (c) of the Act. Practice Directions PD 9E and PD 12A make provision for the allocation of serious medical cases as follows:

(1) An application involving the lawfulness of withholding or withdrawing artificial nutrition and hydration from a person in a permanent vegetative state, or minimally conscious state or a case involving an ethical dilemma in an untested area must be heard by the President of the Court of Protection or by a judge nominated by the President (including permission, the giving of any directions and any other hearing).[53]

(2) All other application in relation to serious medical treatment or where a declaration of compatibility pursuant to s 4 the Human Rights Act 1998 is sought (including permission, the giving of any directions, and any hearing) must be conducted by the President of the Family Division, the Chancellor or a puisne judge of the High Court.[54]

(3) Non-urgent cases: It will be for the Senior Judge of the Court of Protection or a judge nominated by him to determine whether the

---

[53] PD 9E, para 11 and PD 12A, para 2.
[54] PD 9E, para 12 and PD 12A, para 3.

case falls within the Practice Directions or is one which may properly be dealt with by a judge of the Court other than a designated High Court Judge.[55]

6.15.2   Steps to be taken pre-proceedings

Those seeking orders or declarations under the MCA 2005 must ensure that all the steps set out in ss 1–4 MCA and the relevant matters set out in the Code of Practice, particularly Chapters 4 and 5 (see above) have been undertaken. The Court of Protection Rules 2007, r 9, PD 9E specifically applies to cases of serious medical treatment (for definition, see above). Parts 8, 10, 12–16 set out the procedure which applies to all applications made to the Court of Protection under MCA 2005. Before an application is issued in relation to serious medical treatment, it is advisable to contact the Official Solicitor (family and medical lawyer) and discuss the issues. The Official Solicitor's offices are at 81, Chancery Lane, London WC2A 1DD; tel: 020 7922 7205; fax: 020 7911 7105; email enquiries@offsol.gsi.gov.uk. The applicant must seek permission to make the application, unless exempt from doing so (see below).

6.15.3   The application form

(1)   The application should be made in Form COP1. Where it relates to serious medical treatment it should be headed 'serious medical treatment' to draw the Court's attention to this fact. It should also be headed with the name of the person to whom the application relates unless an order dispensing with this requirement is obtained pursuant to r 19.

(2)   It should state the issues which the Court is asked to determine and the order sought. It is good practice to lodge a draft of the order with the application. Where a declaration is required PD 9E, para 17 requires that the order sought should be in the following or similar terms:

> '(a)   That P lacks capacity to make a decision in relation to the ... [*proposed medical treatment or procedure*]; or
> (b)   That P lacks capacity to make a decision in relation to sterilisation by vasectomy, and
> (c)   That having regard to the best interests of P, it is lawful for the ... [*proposed medical treatment or procedure*] to be carried out by ... [*the proposed healthcare provider*].'

Where the order sought is for withdrawal of life-sustaining treatment, the order should be in the following or similar terms:

> '(a)   That P lacks capacity to consent to continued life-sustaining treatment measures [*specify what these are*]; and

---

[55]   PD 12A, para 5.

(b)   That having regard to the best interests of P it is lawful for
      ... [*name of healthcare provider*] to withdraw the life-sustaining
      treatment from P.'[56]

It should state:

(a)   the name of the applicant and his/her address;
(b)   the name and address of P;
(c)   name and address of each respondent and details of his or her
      connection with P;
(d)   the name and addresses of each person whom the applicant
      intends to notify of the application and details of his or her
      connection with P.

(3)   The application form must be verified by a statement of truth if it
      contains evidence on which the applicant seeks to rely.

(4)   The application form must be supported by evidence relied on. If
      that is contained in a witness statement, the statement must be
      verified by a statement of truth.

(5)   Part 9, r 64 requires that the following documents must be filed with
      the application form:
      (a)   any evidence on which the applicant relies;
      (b)   copy of the order granting permission;
      (c)   an assessment of capacity form where this is required by the
            PD;
      (d)   any other document referred to in the application form; and
      (e)   any other information and material as may be set out in a PD.

(See further PD 9A, para 12.)

If an assessment of capacity has not been completed and filed, a witness
statement must be filed explaining why the assessment has not been
obtained; what attempts have been made to obtain it and the basis on
which it is believed that P lacks capacity to make the specific decision.

6.15.4   The applicant

The applicant will usually be the organisation which will be responsible
for providing the clinical or caring services to P but it could be P (see *Re C
(Refusal of Medical Treatment)*,[57] where a schizophrenic P exercised his
right to invoke the High Court's inherent jurisdiction in order to obtain a
ruling by way of injunction or declaration that he was capable of refusing
or consenting to medical treatment) or a family member, eg a parent.

---

[56]   PD 9E, para 18.
[57]   [1994] 1 FLR 31.

6.15.5   Permission to apply

An applicant will be required to obtain permission to start proceedings unless the applicant is:

(a)   P or if under 18, a person with parental responsibility for the patient;

(b)   a deputy for the person to whom the application relates;

(c)   a donor or donee of LPA to which the application relates;

(d)   a person named in an existing order if the application relates to the order;

(e)   the Official Solicitor or Public Guardian.

If permission is required the applicant must file the application for permission in Form COP2 and must file with it a draft of the application form (COP1) and an assessment of capacity using Form COP3. If the applicant is unable to complete an assessment of capacity form, the applicant should file a witness statement explaining the reasons for the same and why he believes that P lacks capacity.[58] There is no need for the applicant to file any of the annexes to the application form with the permission form.

Factors which the Court will take into account when dealing with an application for permission are set out in s 50(3):

(1)   the applicant's connection with the person who is the subject of the application;

(2)   the reasons for the application;

(3)   whether there is any benefit to the person to whom the application relates if the proposed order or directions were given; and

(4)   whether there are other ways of achieving the same beneficial results for the person concerned.

Within 14 days of the application for permission being filed the Court is obliged to:

(a)   grant the application in whole or part or on condition and the Court may give directions;

---

[58]   PD 8A, para 7.

(b)   refuse the application or fix a date for the hearing.[59]

It is submitted that where the Court refuses the application without a hearing it should provide that if the applicant disagrees with the Court's decision he/she should apply within a specified period to have the order revoked or varied.

Where the Court fixes a hearing it will notify the applicant and others who it considers should be informed (see PD 9B for those who should be notified) and serve a form for acknowledging the notification. Any person who is notified and who wants to take part in the proceedings must, within 21 days of notice of the application, file the acknowledgement notification. If the person served with the acknowledgment notification form does not file it with the information required in r 57(4) within 21 days he will not be permitted to take part in the proceedings.

6.15.6   Court fees

On issuing the application the applicant will be required to pay the Court fee for the application.

The Court of Protection Fees Order 2007[60] applies to applications issued in the Court of Protection. The fee payable for an application is £400 (art 4) and for a hearing £500 (art 6). Article 8 makes provision for exemptions from payment of these fees. A fee is not payable by a person who is in receipt of:

(a)   income support;

(b)   working tax credit, provided that:
   (i)   child tax credit is being paid to the person, or to a couple (as defined in s 3(5)(A) of the Tax Credit Act 2002) which includes the person; or
   (ii)   there is a disability element or severe disability element (or both) to the tax credit received by the person;

(c)   income-based jobseeker's allowance under the Job Seekers Act 1995;

(d)   guarantee credit under the State Pensions Credit Act 2002;

(e)   council tax benefit under the Social Security Contributions and Benefits Act 1992; and

(f)   housing benefit.

---

[59]   COP Rules 2007, Part 8, r 55.
[60]   SI 2007/1745 (L 13).

Article 9 also provides that where it appears to the Lord Chancellor that the payment of any fee prescribed by the order would, owing to the exceptional circumstances of the particular case, involve undue hardship, he may reduce or remit the fee in that case. A person earning up to £11,500 will be fee exempt. A person earning up to £13,000 will be entitled to a remission of 75% of the fee; between £13,001 and £14,500 to a remission of 50% and £14,5001 to £16,000 a remission of 25% of the fee. Form OPG506A needs to be completed in order to apply for a remission and sent to the Court with supporting documents.

6.15.7   Urgent applications

(1)   Where possible, urgent applications should be issued and dealt with within court hours by attendance at the Court. In really serious medical treatment cases which are urgent it may be expedient to go directly to the Clerk of the Rules at the Royal Courts of Justice Family Division to seek an urgent hearing before the first available nominated judge on an undertaking to issue the proceedings at the Court of Protection within a specified perioed (eg 24 hours or the next working day).

(2)   Cases of extreme urgency may also be dealt with by telephone at the Court during court hours on 084 5330 2900.

(3)   When it is not possible to apply during court hours, contact should be made with the security office at the RCJ on 020 7497 6000[61] without filing the application form at the Court of Protection. However, the Court will require an undertaking that the application form be issued at the Court of Protection on the next working day after the emergency hearing or as the Court directs.[62] Where a case is extremely urgent application may be made directly to the High Court without filing an application form in COP1. If an application form has already been filed and an emergency arises, the applicant should where possible file and serve an application notice in form COP9. In an exceptionally urgent case an application may be made without notice and the notice served later.[63] However, it would be prudent to give any interested party notice by telephone or by other electronic means eg text message, e-mail, fax.[64]

NB where an urgent application has been made outside court hours, if the judge dealing with the application considers that the application could have been made within court hours he/she may require the applicant or the applicant's representative to attend to provide an explanation for the delay.

---

[61]   PD 10B, para3.
[62]   PD 10B, para 9.
[63]   PD 10B, para 8.
[64]   PD 10B, para 8.

Where the application is not so urgent the applicant should contact the listing officer at the Court of Protection to ensure that the case is placed before one of the district judges immediately for consideration on whether it should be transferred to the High Court.

6.15.8 Parties to the application

The applicant and the respondent/s who filed the acknowledgment notification in Form COP5 are parties. P is not a party unless the Court otherwise directs[65] but he must be notified (see further Part 7, rr 42–45). The court however, has a discretion to hear P even if he is not a party.

6.15.9 Respondent to the application

Where, the organisation, which is to provide the treatment etc is not the applicant, it should be made a respondent.[66] Part 9, r 73 provides that unless the Court orders otherwise, P should not be named as a respondent to any proceedings. However, since the rules require that P should be named, the Official Solicitor should be invited to act for him/her, or steps must be taken to ensure he/she is represented by an advocate or litigation friend.

Any other person, who the applicant reasonably believes to have an interest should be made a respondent. The court may direct a person to be joined as a party to the proceedings if it considers that it is desirable to do so for the purpose of dealing with the application.[67] Any other person who has a connection or interest in P may apply to be joined as a party to the proceedings. (See Part 9, r 75 for the procedure for such application.)

6.15.10 Persons (although not respondents) who should be notified

The applicant must attempt to identify at least three persons who are likely to have an interest in being notified. The members of P's close family will be the most likely to have an interest in him or her. PD 9B, para 7 gives a suggested list of the members of the family who are presumed to have an interest in P. Notice must be sent out to these individuals in Form COP15.[68]

---

[65] COP Rules 2007, Part 9, r 73(4).
[66] PD 9E, para 9.
[67] COP Rules 2007, Part 9, r 73(2).
[68] PD 9B, para 12.

6.15.11   Steps that the respondent/s need to take (PD 9C)

A person who wishes to take part in the proceedings must file an acknowledgment of service within 21 days of service of the application form. The acknowledgement of service must state whether the respondent:

(a)   consents to the order/s sought;

(b)   opposes the application and if so, set out the grounds for so doing;

(c)   seeks alternative orders and give particulars of the order/s sought;

(d)   files a statement and/or report upon which he intends to rely (but see Part 15, r 120 which restricts the filing of experts' reports unless the Court directs);

(e)   if not already a party, states whether he/she wishes to be joined as a party, giving details of the reasons and identifying his interest in the proceedings or connection with P.

6.15.12   First directions

Save in the case where the matter needs to be disposed of urgently, the Court will list the application for a directions hearing. At the hearing the Court will give such directions as it considers appropriate. PD 9E requires the Court to consider whether to give directions on any or all of the following matters at the first hearing:

(a)   decide whether P should be joined as a party to the proceedings and give directions to that effect;

(b)   if P is joined as a party to the proceedings, decide whether the Official Solicitor should be invited to act as a litigation friend or whether some other person should be appointed as a litigation friend;

(c)   identify anyone else who has been notified of the proceedings and who has filed an acknowledgement and applied to be joined as a party to the proceedings, and consider that application; and

(d)   set a timetable for the proceedings including where possible, a date for the final hearing.[69]

---

[69]   PD 9E, para 14.

The court should also consider what if any of the direction listed in r 85(2) should be given;[70] see under **5.14.6** (Urgent Medical Treatment).

6.15.13 Form of draft order

Precedents of possible orders are set out under **6.15.3**. It is suggested that the precedents of orders in cases of PVS, CPR, use of force, reporting restrictions etc. set out in *Emergency Remedies in the Family Courts* may also be a useful guide. These orders were developed by the High Court in cases of serious medical treatment and can be adapted for use in applications before the Court of Protection.

It is also suggested that when seeking the sanction of the Court in such cases, the procedure set out in *Practice Note of 1 May 2001 (Official Solicitor: Declaratory Proceedings: Medical and Welfare Decisions for Adults who Lack Capacity)* [2001] 2 FLR 158 should be used as a guide in conjunction with the procedure set out in PD 9E to the Court of Protection Rules.

---

[70] PD 9E, para 15.

6.16   PROCEDURAL GUIDE FOR AN APPLICATION IN CASES OF SERIOUS MEDICAL TREATMENT

The Applicant	Will usually be the organisation which will be providing the treatment	
Permission to Apply	Required by everyone except by the person lacking capacity	MCA 2005, s 50 COP Rules 2007, Part 8
	If the person lacking capacity is under 18 anyone with parental responsibility	
	Donee of a LPA to which the application relates	
	Deputy appointed by the Court	
	A person named in an existing order	
	Official Solicitor/Public Guardian	
Applicant must file	Form **COP2** if permission is required	COP Rules 2007, Part 9
	Forms **COP1** and **COP1B** Form **COP1** should be headed '**Urgent medical treatment**'	PD 9E and COP Rules, rr 62-64
	Form **COP24** (witness statement) setting out reasons connection with P and reasons for the application and benefit to P	
	Statement must be verified by a statement of truth	
	Form **COP3**	
	Form **COP4** where a deputy has been assigned	
	Copy of a Lasting Power of Attorney if relevant	
	Any other evidence relied on	
Applicant must pay Court Fees	£400	COP Fees Order 2007, art 4
Urgent applications	Apply directly to the Clerk of the Rules High Court Family Division to attend before a nominated Judge	PD 10B
Extreme Urgency	May be dealt with by telephone 084 5330 2900 (Office hours) 020 7497 6000 (out of hours)	
Respondents	Organisation that will provide treatment (if not the applicant) The O/S as litigation friend Any other person having an interest Any other person directed by the Court	
Court Office	(1) Issues application and gives to the Applicant:	

		• Form **COP5**	
		• Forms **COP14** and **COP14A**	
		• Forms **COP15** and **COP15A**	
		• Form **COP20**	
	(2)	Judge considers the application and decide whether to give directions or list for directions/disposal hearing	COP Rules 2007, r 89
	(3)	May decide to make order without a hearing in which case order court will serve order on all the parties	
What the Applicant must do	(1)	Serve on the respondent/s within 21 days Forms **COP1,COP1A, COP5, COP15** and **COP15A**	
	(2)	Notify P on Forms **COP14, COP14A** and **COP5** of the application	COP Rules 2007, r 69
	(3)	Notify any relevant party on Forms **COP15** and **COP15A**	COP Rules 2007, r 70
	(4)	File certificate of service and notification in Form **COP20**	
	(5)	If an urgent application is required file Form **COP9**	COP Rules 2007, Part 10 PD 10A and 10B
What the Respondent must do		File an acknowledgement of service in Form **COP5** indicating whether R	
	(a)	consents	
	(b)	opposes a the application	
	(c)	seeks alternative remedy	
		File evidence intended to be relied on	
What the person notified must do		File an acknowledgement of notification in Form **COP5** and indicate whether wants to be joined as a party and file Form **COP10**	PD 9C(4)
Hearing		The court will consider the application	
		Give directions	COP Rules 2007, r 85
		Allocate the case	
		Set the time table and trial window or if urgent list for a disposal hearing	
		Make any other appropriate orders	
Orders that the Court may make at the interim hearing	(1)	Declare whether a person lacks capacity to make a particular decision specified in the declaration	MCA 2005, s 15

And at the final hearing (for which fee of £500 is payable)	(2)	Declare whether the person lacks capacity on the matters set out in the declaration
	(3)	Declare the lawfulness or otherwise of any act done or yet to be done
	(4)	Authorise deprivation of liberty in certain circumstances
	(5)	Specify where P should live
	(6)	Define the extent of contact between P and others
	(7)	Grant injunctions
	(8)	Appoint a deputy where appropriate
	(9)	Any other consequential or protective orders

PRECEDENTS

PRECEDENT FOR A DRAFT ORDER SEEKING AUTHORITY TO WITHHOLD CARDIO-PULMONARY RESUSCITATION AND ADMINISTRATION OF ANTIBIOTICS, TO WITHDRAW GASTRO/NASAL FEEDING AND/OR OTHER FORMS OF LIFE SUSTAINING TREATMENT

IN THE COURT OF PROTECTION   CASE NO ....

IN THE MATTER OF THE MENTAL CAPACITY ACT 2005

AND IN THE MATTER OF JOSIE SMITH

BETWEEN

HELLINIC COUNTY COUNCIL   Applicant

And

BLACKFORD HOSPITAL TRUST   1st Respondent

And

JOHN SMITH   2nd Respondent
(by his litigation friend the Official Solicitor)

DRAFT ORDER

Made by ....

At the Royal Courts of Justice Strand

On ....

UPON hearing counsel for all parties

AND UPON reading the bundle of documents filed in the proceedings

AND UPON hearing the oral evidence of ....

IT IS DECLARED THAT:

1.   P lacks capacity to make a decision in relation to his medical condition.

2.   P lacks capacity to make a decision in relation to the proposal to withhold cardio-pulmonary resuscitation and administration of antibiotics [*or other forms of life sustaining treatment – set these out*].

3.   Having regard to the best interests of P it shall be lawful for the Blackford NHS Trust and responsible medical practitioners having responsibility at the time for the patient's treatment and care:

   (a)   to perform the proposed .... [*set out the details of the surgical operation if appropriate*];

   (b)   to withhold cardio-pulmonary resuscitation of P;

   (c)   to withhold the administration of antibiotics in the event of P developing a potentially life-threatening infection which would otherwise call for the administration of antibiotics, but only if immediately before withholding the same;

      (i)   the Applicant is so advised by both the medical practitioner and by the consultant neurologist/psychiatrist [*or as the case may be*] having the responsibility at the time for the treatment and care of P; and

      (ii)   [*set out any other condition that may be appropriate*];

   (d)   to discontinue treatment and/or nourishment thereafter not to furnish medical treatment except for the sole purpose of enabling her to end her life and to die peacefully with the greatest of dignity and least distress; or

   (e)   to furnish such treatment and nursing care as may from time to time be appropriate to ensure that P suffers the least distress and retains the greatest dignity.

4.   An order that in the event of a material change in the existing circumstances occurring before the withholding of treatment any party shall have permission to apply for such further or other declaration or order as may be just.

5.   An injunction forbidding until further order, any person whether by himself or by encouraging or instructing any other person, or in the case of a company whether by its directors or officers, servants, agents or otherwise from:

   (a)   publishing the name and address or otherwise identifying:

      (i)   The Applicant;

       (ii)   P;

       (iii)   any hospital at which P is receiving treatment or has been treated;

       (iv)   any medical practitioner or nurse or any other person who has had the care of P;

(b)   soliciting any information relating to P [*identify any other person to whom the order relates*], any staff at any hospital where P is being treated or has been treated or any other person who may have had the care of P.

6.   Such further or other consequential orders and direction as may be necessary.

7.   That the costs of this application be provided for.

PRECEDENT FOR A DRAFT ORDER FOR DISCONTINUING LIFE-SUSTAINING TREATMENT

IN THE COURT OF PROTECTION   CASE NO ....

IN THE MATTER OF THE MENTAL CAPACITY ACT 2005

AND IN THE MATTER OF JOSIE SMITH

BETWEEN

HELLINIC COUNTY   Applicant
COUNCIL

And

BLACKFORD HOSPITAL   1st Respondent
TRUST

And

JOHN SMITH   2nd Respondent
(by his litigation friend the
Official Solicitor)

DRAFT ORDER

Made by ....

At the Royal Courts of Justice Strand

On ....

UPON hearing counsel for all parties

AND UPON reading the bundle of documents filed in the proceedings

AND UPON hearing the oral evidence of ....

IT IS DECLARED THAT:

1.   P lacks capacity to consent to continued life-sustaining treatment measures [*specify what these are*].

2.   Having regard to the best interests of P it shall be lawful for the responsible medical practitioners [*or the name of the health provider*]:

      (a)   to discontinue/withdraw all life-sustaining treatment and medical support measures designed to keep P alive in her existing [persistent vegetative] state including the termination of ventilation, nutrition and hydration by artificial means; and

(b)   to discontinue and thereafter need not furnish medical treatment/or nourishment to P except for the purpose of enabling her to end her life and to die with the greatest dignity and least distress.

3.   An order that in the event of a material change in the existing circumstances occurring before the withdrawal of artificial feeding and hydration any party shall have permission to apply for such further or other declaration or order as may be just.

IT IS FURTHER ORDERED THAT:

4.   Until further order, it is forbidden for any person whether by himself or by encouraging or instructing any other person, or in the case of a company whether by its directors or officers, servants, agents or otherwise from:

(a)   publishing the name and address or otherwise identifying:

(i)   the Applicant;

(ii)   P;

(iii)   any hospital at which P is receiving treatment or has been treated;

(iv)   any medical practitioner or nurse or any other person who has had the care of P;

(b)   soliciting any information relating to P or her parents, any staff at any hospital where P is being treated or has been treated or any other person who may have had the care of P.

5.   Such further or other consequential orders and direction as may be necessary.

6.   That the costs of this application be provided for.

PART III

PROPERTY AND AFFAIRS

CHAPTER 7

SUSPENSION AND REVOCATION OF DEPUTY APPOINTMENT

LAW AND PRACTICE

7.1 BACKGROUND

Where a person (P) lacks capacity in relation to decisions concerning his or her personal welfare or property and affairs, the Court of Protection is given wide powers under s 16(2) of the Act either to make an order, make the decision(s) on P's behalf or appoint a person (a deputy formerly a receiver) to make such decisions. The court's power, however, is subject to the principles set out in s 1 and the best interests provisions set out in s 4 (for a detailed discussion of best interests see Chapter 2). When deciding whether it is in P's best interests to appoint a deputy the Court must have regard to P's best interests, to the principle that a decision by the Court is to be preferred to the appointment of a deputy to make a decision, and that powers conferred on a deputy should be as limited in scope and duration as is reasonably practicable in the circumstances.[1]

When deciding to appoint a deputy the Court may appoint one or more deputies to make all decisions or specify the decisions that may be undertaken by the deputy/deputies which may relate only to personal welfare or property and affairs or both. It may make restricted or unrestricted orders or one-off single orders.

7.2 THE COURT'S APPROACH WHEN APPOINTING A DEPUTY

On appointing a deputy the Court has wide powers to identify the duties and responsibilities of the deputy and to impose restrictions on the deputy's powers. The court may:

- Confer powers or impose duties on a deputy as it thinks necessary or expedient for giving effect to, or otherwise in connection with, an order or appointment made by it.[2]

---

[1]   MCA 2005, s 16(4).
[2]   MCA 2005, s 16(5).

- Make the order, give the directions or make the appointment on such terms as it considers are in P's best interests, even though an application is before the Court for an order, directions or an appointment on those terms.[3]

- Vary or discharge an order made by a subsequent order[4] but subject to the provisions of para 6 of Sch 2 to the Act.[5]

- Revoke the appointment of a deputy or vary the powers conferred on him/her.[6]

- Restrict the deputies powers[7] (see **7.7**).

7.3   COURT'S POWERS IN RELATION TO PERSONAL WELFARE

The court's powers in relation to personal affairs extend in particular to:

(a)   deciding where P is to live;

(b)   deciding what contact if any P is to have with any specified persons;

(c)   making an order prohibiting a named person from having contact with P;

(d)   giving or refusing consent to the carrying out or continuation of a treatment by a person providing health care for P;

(e)   giving direction that a person responsible for P's health care allow a different person to take over that responsibility.

A deputy may be given all these powers save the authority to prohibit a person from having contact with P or giving direction to a person who is responsible for P's care to allow a different person to take over that responsibility.[8]

---

3   MCA 2005, s 16(6).
4   MCA 2005, s 16(7).
5   MCA 2005, s 18(5).
6   MCA 2005, s 16(8).
7   MCA 2005, s 20.
8   MCA 2005, s 20(2).

7.4 COURT'S POWERS IN RELATION TO PROPERTY AND AFFAIRS

The Court's powers in relation to property and affairs include:

(a) the control and management of P's property;

(b) the sale, exchange, charging, gift or other disposition of P's property;

(c) the acquisition of property in P's name or on P's behalf;

(d) the carrying on, on P's behalf, of any profession, trade or business;

(e) the taking of a decision which will have the effect of dissolving a partnership of which P is a member;

(f) the carrying out of any contract entered into by P;

(g) the discharge of P's debts and of any of P's obligations, whether legally enforceable or not;

(h) the settlement of any of P's property, whether for P's benefit or for the benefit of others and such other consequential vesting or other orders as the case may require including in the exercise of such a power, any order which could have been made in such a case under Part 4 of the Trustee Act 1925.[9] If a settlement has been made, the Court may by order vary or it if the settlement makes provision for its variation or revocation, the Court is satisfied that a material fact was not disclosed when the settlement was made or if it is satisfied that there has been a substantial change of circumstances;[10]

(i) the execution for P of a will;

(j) the exercise of any power (including a power to consent) vested in P whether beneficially or as trustee or otherwise;

(k) the conduct of legal proceedings in P's name or on P's behalf.

A deputy may be given all these powers save in relation to the settlement of any of P's property ((h) above) the execution of a will on P's behalf ((i) above) or the exercise of any power (including the power of consent) vested in P whether beneficially or as trustee or otherwise.[11] The court may also confer on a deputy powers to take possession or control of all or

---

9   MCA 2005, Sch 2, para 5.
10   MCA 2005, Sch 2, para 6.
11   MCA 2005, s 20.

any specified part of P's property and to exercise all or any specified powers in respect of it, including such powers of investment as the Court may determine.[12]

These powers may be exercised even though P has not reached 16 years of age, if the Court considers it likely that P will still lack capacity to make decisions in respect of that matter when he or she reaches 18 subject to the usual restrictions which apply to deputies.

7.5   WHO CAN BE A DEPUTY?

A deputy appointed by the Court in relation to P's welfare must be an individual who has reached the age of 18. In relation to matters of property and affairs a deputy may be an individual who has reached the age of 18 or a trust corporation.[13] The consent of the individual to be appointed must be obtained.[14]

The court may appoint two or more deputies to act jointly, jointly and severally or jointly in respect of some matters and jointly and severally in respect of others.[15] Provision may also be made for one or more other person to succeed the existing deputy/deputies in such circumstances or on the happening of such events, as may be specified in the order or for such period as may be so specified.[16]

7.6   COSTS

A deputy is entitled to be reimbursed out of P's property for his reasonable expenses for discharging his function and the Court when making the appointment may also direct that the deputy's remuneration for discharging his function be paid out of P's property.[17] Where a court appoints a solicitor to act as a deputy for P, the fixed rates of remuneration will apply.[18]

The court may require a deputy to give to the Public Guardian such security as the Court thinks fit for the due discharge of his functions before any action is taken by the deputy[19] and to submit to the Public Guardian such reports at such times or at such intervals as the Court may direct.[20] The court will almost invariably require a deputy who is being replaced or suspended to submit such a report.

---

[12]   MCA 2005, s 19(8).
[13]   MCA 2005, s 19(1).
[14]   MCA 2005, s 19(3).
[15]   MCA 2005, s 19(4).
[16]   MCA 2005, s 19(5).
[17]   MCA 2005, s 19(7).
[18]   See PD 19B – Fixed Costs in the Court of Protection.
[19]   COP Rules 2007, r 200.
[20]   MCA 2005, s 19(9).

7.7 RESTRICTIONS ON DEPUTIES

In addition to the restrictions referred to above the following further restrictions apply to a deputy appointed by the Court:

- He/she may not make a decision on behalf of P in relation to a matter if he knows or has reasonable grounds for believing that P has capacity in relation to the matter.[21]

- He/she may not refuse life sustaining treatment on P's behalf.[22]

- His/her authority is subject to the principles embodied in s 1 and the best interests as defined in s 4 of the Act.

- He/she may not do any act which is inconsistent with a decision made under a lasting power of attorney conferred by P.

- He/she may not do any act that is intended to restrain P unless the 4 conditions set out in s 20(8)-(11) are met namely:
  (i) in doing the act, the deputy is acting within the scope of an authority expressly conferred on him/her by the Court;
  (ii) the deputy must reasonably believe that P lacks capacity in relation to the matter in question;
  (iii) the deputy reasonably believes that it is necessary to do the act in order to prevent harm to P;
  (iv) the act must be a proportionate response to the likelihood of P's suffering harm and the seriousness of that harm.

'Restrain' is defined in s 6(4) of the Act and may take many forms. It may be verbal eg shouting or physical eg forcibly holding P down or restraining P by means of a restraint device such as a belt or by locking the person in a confined area. A deputy will be treated as restraining P if he/she uses, or threatens to use, force to secure the doing of an act which P resists or restricts P's liberty of movement, whether or not P resists, or if he authorises another person to do any of those things.[23] A deputy will be regarded as doing more than restraining P if he/she deprives P of his or her liberty within the meaning of Art 5(1) of the Human Rights Convention (whether or not the deputy is a public authority)[24] (see Chapter 4 and **4.3**).

---

[21] MCA 2005, s 20(1).
[22] MCA 2005, s 20(5).
[23] MCA 2005, s 20(12).
[24] MCA 2005, s 20(13).

7.8   REVOCATION/VARIATION OF APPOINTMENT

It is unfortunately the case that despite the rigours of the application some deputies are unable to carry out their duties. Some are simply dishonest. In those circumstances the Court has the power to remove their authority or alternatively to restrict their influence.

By virtue of s 16(8) the Court may revoke the appointment of a deputy or vary the powers conferred on him/her if it is satisfied that the deputy:

(a)   has behaved, or is behaving, in a way that contravenes the authority conferred on him by the Court or is not in P's best interests; or

(b)   proposes to behave in a way that would contravene that authority or would not be in P's interests.

Hence if the deputy is found to contravene any of the directions or orders specified in the order appointing him/ her or if he/she is failing to comply with the order, or it is found or reasonably believed that the deputy is misappropriating P's property or mismanaging P's affairs it would be a ground for seeking his/her replacement. In such cases the circumstances may be such that an urgent application needs to be made to the Court and dealt with expeditiously.

7.9   HOW TO MAKE THE APPLICATION FOR REVOCATION/SUSPENSION

7.9.1   Is permission required

Permission to make the application will be required unless it is made by:

(a)   P;

(b)   if P has not reached the age of 18 years, by anyone with parental responsibility for him/her;

(c)   by the donor or a donee of a lasting power of attorney to which the application relates;

(d)   by a deputy appointed by the Court;

(e)   by a person named in an existing order of the Court if the application relates to the order;[25]

(f)   by the Official Solicitor;[26]

---

[25]   MCA 2005, s 50.

[26]   COP Rules 2007, r 51(1)(a).

(g)   by the Public Guardian;[27]

(h)   where the application concerns P's property and affairs, unless the application is of a kind specified in COP Rules, r 52 or a lasting power of attorney which is or purports to be created under the Act or an instrument which is or purports to be an enduring power of attorney.

7.9.2   How to apply

If permission is required the application for permission should be made in Form COP2 and filed with the substantive application in Form COP1. In addition the following accompanying forms should be filed namely Form COP1A (ie all the supporting information). Form COP3 to confirm that P continues to lack capacity should also be filed.

The Court fee of £400 will have to be paid when the application is issued.

7.9.3   Urgent application

If the matter is urgent the applicant must file an application in Form COP9 with a draft of the orders sought and if possible a disc of the order.

7.9.4   The Court

Where permission is required the Court is required to deal with the application within 14 days. It may grant or refuse the application or list the application for a hearing and give directions including specifying who should be given notice of the hearing.[28] If a hearing is listed a person who is notified of the hearing should file an acknowledgement of service in Form COP5.

If permission is given the substantive application will be issued by the Court. The applicant will receive from the Court Form COP5 (the acknowledgement of service), Form COP14 (the notice of proceedings to P) with the guidance notes in Form COP14A, notice in Form COP15 and guidance notes of the issue of the application and the certificate of service Form COP20. The Court in an emergency may make an interim order suspending the deputy pending the final hearing. This may be done at a hearing, on notice or without notice or on the papers depending on the urgency. It is important to specify in the forms what order is required and when. If an order is made without notice, the Court may give directions for a reply from the deputy and fix an interim directions hearing. It may

---

[27]   COP Rules 2007, r 51(1)(b).
[28]   See COP Rules 2007, rr 55, 56 and 89.

be necessary to apply at the same time in the same application form for a freezing order or an injunction to protect P's assets in the interim (see Chapter 11 below).

7.9.5   Service

It is the duty of the applicant to:

*   Serve all the necessary documents and Forms on the respondents within 21 days.

*   Serve P with Forms COP14 and 14A and COP5.

*   Notify any other relevant person of the application in Forms COP15 and COP5.

*   File the certificate of service within 7 days of service in Form COP20.

7.9.6   The respondent/s to the application

Every respondent and any person who wishes to take part in the proceedings must file the acknowledgment of service within 21 days. The Court will then either give directions without a hearing or list the matter for a directions hearing.

7.10 PROCEDURAL GUIDE FOR SUSPENSION/REMOVAL OF DEPUTY

Permission to Apply	Required by everyone except by the person lacking capacity	MCA 2005 s 50 COP Rules, Part 8
	If the person lacking capacity is under 18 anyone with parental responsibility	
	Donee of a LPA to which the application relates	
	Deputy appointed by the Court	
	A person named in an existing order	
	Official Solicitor/Public Guardian	
Applicant must file	Form **COP2** if permission is required	COP Rules, Part 9 PD 9A and COP Rules, rr 62-64
	Forms **COP1, COP1A, COP1B, COP3**	
	Form **COP4** where a deputy has been assigned	
	Copy of a Lasting Power of attorney if relevant	
	If the application is urgent Form **COP9** and draft of order and disc	
Court Office	(1) Issues application and gives to the Applicant:	
	• Form **COP5**	
	• Forms **COP14** and **COP14A**	
	• Forms **COP15** and **COP15A**	
	• Form **COP20**	
	(2) Judge considers the application and decides whether to give directions or list for directions/disposal hearing	COP Rules, r 89
	(3) May decide to make order without a hearing in which case order court will serve order on all the parties and direct the deputy to file a reply and consider an application for a freezing order if made	
What the Applicant must do	(1) Serve on the respondent/s within 21 days Forms **COP1, COP1A, COP5, COP15** and **COP15A**	

	(2)	Notify P on Forms **COP14**, **COP14A** and **COP5** of the application	COP Rules, r 69
	(3)	Notify any relevant party on Forms **COP15** and **COP15A**	
	(4)	File certificate of service and notification in Form **COP20**	
	(5)	If an urgent application is required file Form **COP9**	COP Rules, Part10 PD 10A and 10B
What the Respondent must do		File an acknowledgement of service in Form **COP5** within 21 days or such shorter period as may be directed	PD 9C(3)
What the person notified must do		File an acknowledgement of notification in Form **COP5**	PD 9C(4)
Hearing		The court will consider the application	
		Give directions	COP Rules, r 85
		Allocate the case	
		Set the time table and trial window or if urgent list for a disposal hearing	
		Make any other appropriate orders	
Orders that the Court may make at the interim hearing	(1)	Declare whether a person lacks capacity to make a particular decision specified in the declaration	MCA 2005, s 15
And at the final hearing	(2)	Declare whether the person lacks capacity on the matters set out in the declaration	
	(3)	Declare the lawfulness or otherwise of any act done or yet to be done	
	(4)	Any other consequential or protective orders	

PRECEDENTS

STATEMENT IN SUPPORT OF APPLICATION
TO DISCHARGE A DEPUTY

IN THE COURT OF PROTECTION   CASE NO ....

IN THE MATTER OF THE MENTAL CAPACITY ACT 2005

AND IN THE MATTER OF P [*insert forename and surname*]

BETWEEN

HELLINIC COUNTY   Applicant
COUNCIL

And

GREEDY SCROUGE   1st Respondent

And

PATIENCE FRAIL   2nd Respondent

(by her litigation friend the
Official Solicitor)

STATEMENT OF RUBY JOLLY IN SUPPORT OF AN
APPLICATION FOR
THE REMOVAL OF A DEPUTY

I, RUBY JOLLY of Bright House in the County of Hellinic will state as follows:

1.   I am a care manager employed by the Hellenic County Council. My Qualifications are as follows: [*set these out*]

2.   I have been the allocated care manager for the Second Respondent since she was placed at Bright House by her son Greedy Scrouge in January 2004. On 6 June 2004 he was appointed receiver to manage the property and affairs of his mother by the Court. He became a deputy by operation of law on 1 October 2007.

3.   I make this statement in support of the Applicant's application for the removal of the First Respondent as a Deputy for the Second Respondent.

4.   Since her placement at Bright House I have observed the First

Respondent's behaviour towards his mother on every occasion that he has visited her. I have heard him speak to her in a very harsh and aggressive way and seen her being quite intimidated by him. On many occasions I have had to intervene and those occasions he has been aggressive and abusive towards me and other members of staff at Bright Home.

5.   More recently he has insisted on seeing his mother in her room and on some of those occasions she has been heard to cry out in distress.

6.   I have recently observed him getting the First Respondent to sign what appeared to me to be legal documents. When he has left the Second Respondent has appeared very withdrawn. Last week when I was assisting her to get ready for bed she disclosed to me that she was concerned and confused about some documents that her son had got her to sign.

7.   I reported the incident to my employers. I understand that they reported the matter to the Public Guardian who confirmed that his office had been sent a report alleging that Greedy Scrouge the Second Respondent's son has mortgaged his mother's property and that he has also withdrawn a large sum of money from her building society account at Prudence Provident Society.

8.   An investigation has been lodged by the Public Guardian. The investigation has revealed some inappropriate dealings with the Second Respondent's assets and more particularly that the First Respondent has not filed any returns since his appointment.

9.   It is therefore in the best interests of the Second Respondent that an independent person be appointed to manage her financial and personal affairs pending a full investigation in order to protect the Second Respondent and to prevent her assets being dissipated dishonestly by the First Respondent.

PRECEDENT FOR A DRAFT ORDER
ON THE SUSPENSION OF A DEPUTY

IN THE COURT OF PROTECTION   CASE NO ....

IN THE MATTER OF THE MENTAL CAPACITY ACT 2005

AND IN THE MATTER OF P [*insert forename and surname*]

BETWEEN

HELLINIC COUNTY   Applicant
COUNCIL

And

GREEDY SCROUGE   1st Respondent

And

PATIENCE FRAIL   2nd Respondent

(by her litigation friend the
Official Solicitor)

DRAFT ORDER

Made by District Judge Wise

At ....

On 21 December 2009

UPON hearing Counsel for the Applicant and the Respondents

AND UPON reading the trial bundle and hearing the sworn oral evidence of Greedy Scrouge the First Respondent

IT IS ORDERED THAT:

1.   [*If it is an interim order*] The First Respondent Greedy Scrouge be suspended as deputy for the property and affairs of the Second Respondent on an interim basis pending the final hearing or [*if a final order*] The First Respondent be removed as a deputy for the property and affairs of the Second Respondent.

2.   A member of the panel maintained by the Office of the Public Guardian be appointed as deputy (The Deputy) in accordance with the procedure set out in Schedule 1 to this Order, to make decisions on behalf of the Second Respondent that she is unable to

make for herself in relation to her personal welfare and property and affairs subject to any conditions or restrictions set out in this order.

3. The court confers general authority on the deputy to take possession or control of the property and affairs of the Second Respondent and to exercise the same powers of management and investment as she has as the beneficial owner, subject to the terms and conditions set out in this order (see also separate order of the same date).

4. The deputy may make provision for the needs of anyone who is related to or connected with the Second Respondent if she provided for or might be expected to provide for that person's needs, by doing whatever she did or might reasonably be expected to do to meet those needs.

5. The Deputy may (without obtaining any further authority from the Court) dispose of the money or property of the Second Respondent by way of gift to any charity to which she made or might have been expected to make such gifts and on customary occasions to persons who are related to or connected with her, provided that the value of each such gift is not unreasonable having regard to all the circumstances and, in particular, the size of her estate.

6. For the purposes of giving effect to any decision the Deputy may execute or sign any necessary deeds or documents.

7. The Deputy is required to investigate (for the avoidance of doubt in a way that is proportionate as described in paragraph 14 below).

    (a) the current assets, liabilities, income and expenditure of the Second Respondent;

    (b) the Second Respondent's income savings and expenditure from 1 January 2004 to the present. The First Respondent and the Official Solicitor and any other person shall disclose to the Deputy their knowledge of any bank accounts, sources of income, expenditure or testamentary document executed by the Second Respondent, with documents in support of the same including bank statements and any other accounts provided to third parties to be disclosed to the Deputy within 14 days of his/her request of the same.

8. The Deputy is required to keep statements, vouchers, receipts and other financial records.

9. The Deputy must complete an annual report in a form to be

determined by the Public Guardian and, if requested to do so, file the report with the Public Guardian within a month of the anniversary of this Order.

10. The Deputy is required to obtain and have regard to advice from an investment adviser regulated by the Financial Services Authority in relation to the investment of the Second Respondent's assets. The report to be filed within two months of the sale of property with the Public Guardian.

11. The Deputy is to provide to the Public Guardian with such documents or evidence that the Public Guardian may require in connection with the investment of the Second Respondent's assets.

12. The Deputy is authorised to pay from the Second Respondent's estate any reasonable expenses incurred in obtaining such proper advice.

13. The Deputy is entitled to be reimbursed for reasonable expenses incurred provided they are in proportion to the size of the estate of the Second Respondent and the functions performed by the Deputy.

14. The Deputy is authorised to pay solicitors' fixed costs for this application, or where the amount exceeds the fixed costs allowed, the Deputy is authorised to agree the costs for making this application and to pay them from the funds belonging to the Second Respondent. In default of agreement, or if the Deputy or solicitors would prefer the costs to be assessed, this order is to be treated as authority to the Supreme Court Cost Office to carry out a detailed assessment on the standard basis.

15. The Deputy is required, upon appointment, to obtain and maintain security in the sum determined by the Office of the Public Guardian in accordance with the standard requirements as to the giving of security.

16. The First Respondent shall by 30 January 2010 provide to the Public Guardian and the Deputy financial returns from 1 January 2004 until the present and account for all the income received and expenditure incurred; the title deeds of all property, share certificates and other documentary evidence of all the assets and liabilities the Second Respondent.

17. The First Respondent is forbidden whether by himself or by instructing encouraging or suggesting to another to dispose of, transfer, charge or in any other way deal with any of the Second Respondent's assets and in particular the following: [*set these out*]

Residence and Contact

18. The First Respondent shall not remove or seek to remove the

Second Respondent from Bright House or from any other place of residence where the Second Respondent may reside for any reason or encourage any other person to do so. For the avoidance of doubt this does not prevent the First Respondent from discussing the continuing suitability of Bright House for the Second Respondent in accordance with the terms of this Order.

19.   The First Respondent shall have face to face contact (or supervised contact as the case may be) at Bright House not more than once per week.

20.   Face to face Contact between the First and Second Respondent at Bright House shall be supervised but the supervisor shall not take notes during contact.

21.   The First Respondent shall give Bright House no less than ... days written notice of his proposed visits for contact and Bright House shall respond to such requests no less than 24 hours before the proposed visit and may refuse such visit if there is good reason or the Second Respondent declines the visit.

22.   The First Respondent must not arrange for anyone to visit the Second Respondent at Bright House without the permission of the Applicant, such permission not be unreasonably withheld. The First Respondent may have social visits from friends and or family.

23.   The First Respondent shall not bring food or drink for the Second Respondent when he visits except with the permission of Bright House, such permission not to be unreasonably withheld.

24.   The First Respondent shall not remove any items from the Second Respondent's room without the prior consent of Bright House.

25.   The First Respondent shall not behave in an aggressive or threatening manner towards the staff at Bright House or towards any employee of the Applicant or to the Deputy appointed in accordance with this Order.

26.   The First Respondent shall make any complaint or raise any concern with regard to the Second Respondent's welfare or the care she is (or is not) receiving in writing by letter addressed to the Applicant's Legal Department at ....

27.   Bright House and/or the Applicant shall inform the First Respondent (in writing or by telephone as appropriate) of any incident of ill health requiring any immediate medical treatment for or hospitalisation of the Second Respondent as soon as reasonably practicable and in any event within .... hours.

28.   No Order as to costs save for detailed assessment of the Second Respondent's publicly funded costs.

Dated .... December 2009

PRECEDENT OF DRAFT ORDER WHERE A RECEIVER/DEPUTY HAS DIED OR WISHES TO RETIRE

IN THE COURT OF PROTECTION   CASE NO ....

IN THE MATTER OF THE MENTAL CAPACITY ACT 2005

AND IN THE MATTER OF P [*insert forename and surname*]

BETWEEN

HELLINIC COUNTY   Applicant
COUNCIL

And

GREEDY SCROUGE   1st Respondent

And

PATIENCE FRAIL   2nd Respondent

(by her litigation friend the
Official Solicitor)

DRAFT ORDER

Made by District Judge Wise

At ....

On 21 December 2009

[if the order is made without a hearing]

WHEREAS

1.   By an order dated .... [*insert date*] .... [*insert name/s of Receiver/Deputy*] was appointed Receiver/Deputy [*as the case may be*] and has died/ and now wishes to retire [*as the case may be*]

2.   An application has been made for an order under the Mental Health Act 2005 by .... [*insert the name of the applicant*].

3.   The Court is satisfied that P's [*insert name of person under capacity*] property and affairs cannot be as effectively managed in a manner less restrictive of his/her rights and freedom of action than by an appointment of a deputy.

[*If the order is made after a hearing state as below*]

UPON hearing Counsel for the Applicant and the Respondents

UPON reading the trial bundle and hearing the sworn oral evidence of the ....

IT IS DECLARED THAT:

1.   By an order dated .... [*insert date*] .... [*insert name/s of Receiver/Deputy*] was appointed Receiver/Deputy [*as the case may be*] and has died/ and now wishes to retire [*as the case may be*].

2.   An application has been made for an order under the Mental Health Act 2005 by .... [*insert the name of the applicant*].

3.   P [*insert name of person lacking capacity*] lacks capacity to make decision about his/her residence, care/contact and property and affairs.

4.   The Court is satisfied that P's [*insert name of person under capacity*] property and affairs cannot be as effectively managed in a manner less restrictive of his/her rights and freedom of action than by an appointment of a deputy.

IT IS ORDERED THAT:

[*if previous receiver/deputy has died*]

1.   The Receiver [*insert name*] *or* Deputy [*insert name*] be discharged forthwith and his/her account be dispensed with and security cancelled.

[*if previous receiver/deputy retires*]

The Receiver [*insert name*] or Deputy [*insert name*] be discharged from the Receivership/deputyship [*as the case may be*] and is to render to the Court a final account and is to pay any balance due thereon to the deputy hereinafter appointed and his/her security is discharged.

APPOINTMENT OF A NEW DEPUTY

[see also precedent orders above/below and Chapter 3]

IN THE COURT OF PROTECTION   CASE NO ....

IN THE MATTER OF THE MENTAL CAPACITY ACT 2005

AND IN THE MATTER OF P [*insert forename and surname*]

BETWEEN

HELLINIC COUNTY
COUNCIL

Applicant

And

GREEDY SCROUGE

1st Respondent

And

PATIENCE FRAIL

(by her litigation friend the
Official Solicitor)

2nd Respondent

**DRAFT ORDER APPOINTING A DEPUTY
FOR PROPERTY AND AFFAIRS**

Made by ....

At Archway Tower, 2 Junction Road, London, N19 5SZ

On .... [*insert date*]

WHEREAS

(1)   An application has been made for an order under the Mental Capacity Act 2005.

(2)   The court is satisfied that P [*forename and surname*] is unable to make various decisions for himself in relation to a matter or matters concerning his property and affairs because of an impairment of, or a disturbance in the functioning of, his mind or brain.

(3)   The court is satisfied that the purpose for which the order is needed cannot be as effectively achieved in a way that is less restrictive of his rights and freedom of action.

IT IS ORDERED that:

1. Appointment of deputy

(a)   Deputy [*insert full name* of] .... [*insert address*] is appointed as deputy ("the deputy") to make decisions on behalf of P [*insert forename and surname*] that he is unable to make for himself in relation to his property and affairs subject to any conditions or restrictions set out in this order.

(b)   The appointment will last until further order.

(c)   The deputy must apply the principles set out in section 1 of the Mental Capacity Act 2005 and have regard to the guidance in the Code of Practice to the Act.

2. Authority of deputy

(a)   The court confers general authority on the deputy to take possession or control of the property and affairs of P [*insert forename and surname*] and to exercise the same powers of management and investment as he has as beneficial owner, subject to the terms and conditions set out in this order.

(b)   The deputy may make provision for the needs of anyone who is related to or connected with P [*insert forename and surname*], if he provided for or might be expected to provide for that person's needs, by doing whatever he did or might reasonably be expected to do to meet those needs.

(c)   The deputy may (without obtaining any further authority from the Court) dispose of money or property of P [*insert forename and surname*] by way of gift to any charity to which he made or might have been expected to make gifts and on customary occasions to persons who are related to or connected with him, provided that the value of each such gift is not unreasonable having regard to all the circumstances and, in particular, the size of his estate.

(d)   The deputy is authorised to sell the property of P [*insert forename and surname*] known as .... [*insert address of property with postcode*] on the best possible terms and after payment of legal fees and other professional charges to invest the net proceeds for his benefit.

(e)   For the purpose of giving effect to any decision the deputy may execute or sign any necessary deeds or documents.

(f)   The deputy/applicant is directed to investigate and report to the Court of Protection by .... [*insert date*] as to P's [*insert forename and surname*] assets, liabilities and property.

3. Letting property

The *applicant/deputy* is authorised to manage and let the property known as .... [*insert address*] belonging to P [*insert forename and surname*] on an assured shorthold tenancy for a period of not less than six months but not exceeding twelve months with authority to extend any tenancy of less than twelve months up to a total of twelve months and to pay all proper outgoings in respect thereof and the *applicant/deputy* is authorised to institute Court proceedings to determine the tenancy on behalf of P [*insert forename and surname*].

Sell/let property (if undecided)

The *applicant/deputy* is authorised to

i.   sell .... [*insert property address and post code*] on the best possible terms and after payment of legal fees and other professional charges to invest the net proceeds for the benefit of P [*insert forename and surname*]; or

ii.   manage and let the property known as .... [*insert property address and post code*] belonging to P [*insert forename and surname*] on an assured shorthold tenancy for a period of not less than six months but not exceeding twelve months with authority to extend any tenancy of less than twelve months up to a total of twelve months and to pay all proper outgoings in respect thereof and the *applicant/deputy* is authorised to institute Court proceedings to determine the tenancy on behalf of P [*insert forename and surname*].

To determine/enter into a tenancy agreement

The *applicant/deputy* is authorised on behalf of P [*insert forename and surname*] to take such steps as may be necessary to determine the tenancy of .... [*insert property address and post code*] upon the best terms that can be obtained.

or

The *applicant/deputy* is authorised on behalf of P (*insert forename and surname*) to enter into a tenancy agreement upon the best possible terms that can be obtained.

To buy property

The *applicant/deputy* is authorised to purchase in P's (*insert forename and surname*) .... [*insert address of property*] at a price of no more than £ .... [*insert amount*] including legal fees, other professional charges and costs of moving.

(And if required)

and the *applicant/deputy* is authorised to withdraw that amount held in P's name [*insert forename and surname*] at the Court Funds Office.

(And if required)

The *applicant/deputy* is not authorised to sell the property without first obtaining the permission of the court and a restriction to this effect shall be entered on the register.

Restriction of annual funds (claims cases) (if required)

The deputy is authorised to withdraw £ .... [*insert amount*] per annum to meet P's [*insert name*] outgoings. **OR**

The deputy may withdraw £ .... [*insert amount*] per annum to meet P's [*insert name*] expenses and the deputy is also authorised to instruct the Courts Funds Office to release capital funds for investment by a financial adviser who must remit the capital funds directly to the deputy without prior approval by the Court.

4.   Powers of Investment

(a)   The deputy must exercise such care and skill as is reasonable in the circumstances when investing the assets of P [*insert forename and surname*].

(b)   The deputy may make any kind of investment that the person absolutely entitled to those assets could make.

(c)   This general power of investment includes investment in land and investment in assets outside England and Wales.

(d)   In exercising the power of investment, the deputy must have regard to the standard investment criteria namely the suitability of the investments and the need for diversification in so far as is appropriate to the circumstances of P [*insert forename and surname*].

(e)   The deputy must from time to time review the investments, and consider whether, having regard to the standard investment criteria, they should be varied.

(f)   Unless the deputy reasonably concludes that in all the circumstances it is unnecessary or inappropriate to do so, before exercising any power of investment, the deputy must obtain and consider proper advice about the way in which, having regard to the standard investment criteria, the power should be exercised.

(g)   'Proper advice' is the advice of a person who the deputy reasonably believes to be qualified to give it by their ability in and practical experience of financial and other matters relating to the proposed investment.

The deputy is further authorised in accordance with advice, obtained pursuant to paragraph 3 below, the original advice having been exhibited to the Court Funds Office and copied to the Public Guardian, to withdraw further funds as recommended for investment purposes without prior approval from the Court of Protection.

OR

(a)   The deputy is required, within three months of the date of this order, to obtain and have regard to advice from an investment adviser regulated by the Financial Services Authority in relation to the investment of P's [*insert forename and surname*] assets.

(b)   The deputy is to provide the Public Guardian with such documents or evidence that the Public Guardian may require in connection with the investment of P's (*insert forename and surname*) assets.

(c)   The deputy is authorised to pay from P's [*insert forename and surname*] estate any reasonable expenses incurred in obtaining such proper advice.

5. Reports

(a)   The deputy is required to keep statements, vouchers, receipts and other financial records.

(b)   The deputy must submit a report to the Public Guardian as and when required.

6. Costs and Expenses

(a)   The deputy is entitled to be reimbursed for reasonable expenses incurred provided they are in proportion to the size of the estate of P [*insert forename and surname*] and the functions performed by the deputy.

(b)   The deputy is authorised to pay Messrs .... [*insert name of solicitors*] fixed costs for this application, or where the amount exceeds the fixed costs allowed, the deputy is authorised to agree the costs for making this application and to pay them from the funds belonging to P [*insert forename and surname*]. In default of agreement, or if the deputy or the solicitors would prefer the costs to be assessed, this order is to be treated as authority to the Senior Court Costs Office to carry out a detailed assessment on the standard basis.

(c)   The deputy is entitled to receive fixed costs in relation to this application and to receive fixed costs for the general management of the affairs of P [*insert name and forename*]. If the deputy would prefer the costs to be assessed, this order is to be treated as authority to the Senior Court Costs Office to carry out a detailed assessment on the standard basis.

7. Security

(a)   The deputy is required forthwith to obtain and maintain security in the sum of £ .... [*insert amount*] in accordance with the standard requirements as to the giving of security.

(b)   To enable the deputy to give security, this order becomes effective one calendar month from the date it was made.

(c)   The deputy must not discharge any functions until the security is in place.

8. Letting property

The *applicant/deputy* is authorised to manage and let the property known as .... [*insert address and post code*] belonging to P [*insert forename and surname*] on an assured shorthold tenancy for a period of not less than six months but not exceeding twelve months with authority to extend any tenancy of less than twelve months up to a total of twelve months and to pay all proper outgoings in respect thereof and the *applicant/deputy* is authorised to institute Court proceedings to determine the tenancy on behalf of P [*insert forename and surname*].

****

Sell/let property (if undecided)

The *applicant/deputy* is authorised to:

i.   sell .... [*insert property address and post code*] on the best possible terms and after payment of legal fees and other professional charges to invest the net proceeds for the benefit of P (*insert forename and surname*); or

ii.   manage and let the property known as .... [*insert address and post code*] belonging to P (*insert forename and surname*) on an assured shorthold tenancy for a period of not less than six months but not exceeding twelve months with authority to extend any tenancy of less than twelve months up to a total of twelve months and to pay all proper outgoings in respect thereof and the *applicant/deputy* is authorised to institute Court proceedings to determine the tenancy on behalf of P [*insert forename and surname*]

****

To determine/enter into a tenancy agreement

The *applicant/deputy* is authorised on behalf of P (*insert forename and surname*) to take such steps as may be necessary to determine the tenancy of .... [*insert address*]upon the best terms that can be obtained.

OR

The *applicant/deputy* is authorised on behalf of P [*insert forename and surname*] to enter into a tenancy agreement upon the best possible terms that can be obtained.

****

PRECEDENT FOR ORDER APPOINTING JOINT DEPUTIES FOR PROPERTY AND AFFAIRS

IN THE COURT OF PROTECTION   CASE NO ....

IN THE MATTER OF THE MENTAL CAPACITY ACT 2005

AND IN THE MATTER OF P [*insert forename and surname*]

BETWEEN

HELLINIC COUNTY COUNCIL   Applicant

And

GREEDY SCROUGE   1st Respondent

And

PATIENCE FRAIL   2nd Respondent

(by her litigation friend the Official Solicitor)

ORDER APPOINTING JOINT DEPUTIES FOR PROPERTY AND AFFAIRS

Made by ....

At Archway Tower, 2 Junction Road, London, N19 5SZ

On ....

WHEREAS

(1) An application has been made for an order under the Mental Capacity Act 2005.

(2) The court is satisfied that P [*insert forename and surname*] is unable to make various decisions for himself in relation to a matter or matters concerning his property and affairs because of an impairment of, or a disturbance in the functioning of, his mind or brain.

(3) The court is satisfied that the purpose for which the order is needed cannot be as effectively achieved in a way that is less restrictive of his rights and freedom of action.

IT IS ORDERED that:

1.   Appointment of joint deputies

(a)   First Deputy [*insert name*] of .... [*insert full address with post code*] and .... [*insert second deputy's name*] of [*insert address and postcode*] are appointed as joint deputies ("the joint deputies") to make decisions on behalf of P [*insert forename and surname*] that he is unable to make for himself in relation to his property and affairs subject to any conditions or restrictions set out in this order.

(b)   The appointment will last until further order.

(c)   The joint deputies must apply the principles set out in section 1 of the Mental Capacity Act 2005 and have regard to the guidance in the Code of Practice to the Act.

2.   Authority of joint deputies

(a)   The court confers general authority on the joint deputies to take possession or control of the property and affairs of P [*insert forename and surname*] and to exercise the same powers of management and investment as he has as beneficial owner, subject to the terms and conditions set out in this order.

(b)   The joint deputies may make provision for the needs of anyone who is related to or connected with, P [*insert forename and surname*] if he provided for or might be expected to provide for that person's needs, by doing whatever he did or might reasonably be expected to do to meet those needs.

(c)   The joint deputies may (without obtaining any further authority from the Court) dispose of money or property of P [*insert forename and surname*] by way of gift to any charity to which he made or might have been expected to make gifts and on customary occasions to persons who are related to or connected with him, provided that the value of each such gift is not unreasonable having regard to all the circumstances and, in particular, the size of his estate.

(d)   The joint deputies are authorised to sell the property of P [*insert forename and surname*] known as .... [*insert address with postcode*] on the best possible terms and after payment of legal fees and other professional charges to invest the net proceeds for his benefit.

(e)   For the purpose of giving effect to any decision the joint deputies may execute or sign any necessary deeds or documents.

3. Reports

(a) The joint deputies are required to keep statements, vouchers, receipts and other financial records.

(b) The joint deputies must submit a report to the Public Guardian as and when required.

4. Costs and Expenses

(a) The joint deputies are entitled to be reimbursed for reasonable expenses incurred provided they are in proportion to the size of the estate of P [*insert forename and surname*] and the functions performed by the joint deputies.

(b) The joint deputies are authorised to pay Messrs .... [*insert name and address of solicitors*] fixed costs for this application, or where the amount exceeds the fixed costs allowed, the joint deputies are authorised to agree the costs for making this application and to pay them from the funds belonging to P [*insert forename and surname*]. In default of agreement, or if the joint deputies or the solicitors would prefer the costs to be assessed, this order is to be treated as authority to the Senior Court Costs Office to carry out a detailed assessment on the standard basis.

(c) Any professional deputy is entitled to receive fixed costs in relation to this application and to receive fixed costs for the general management of the affairs of P [*insert forename and surname*]. If the professional deputy would prefer the costs to be assessed, this order is to be treated as authority to the Senior Court Costs Office to carry out a detailed assessment on the standard basis.

5. Security

(a) The joint deputies are required forthwith to obtain and maintain security in the sum of £ .... [*insert amount*] in accordance with the standard requirements as to the giving of security.

(b) To enable the joint deputies to give security, this order becomes effective one calendar month from the date it was made.

(c) The joint deputies must not discharge any functions until the security is in place.

PRECEDENT FOR AN ORDER APPOINTING JOINT AND SEVERAL DEPUTIES FOR PROPERTY AND AFFAIRS

IN THE COURT OF PROTECTION   CASE NO ....

IN THE MATTER OF THE MENTAL CAPACITY ACT 2005

AND IN THE MATTER OF P [*insert forename and surname*]

BETWEEN

HELLINIC COUNTY   Applicant
COUNCIL

And

GREEDY SCROUGE   1st Respondent

And

PATIENCE FRAIL   2nd Respondent

(by her litigation friend the
Official Solicitor)

ORDER APPOINTING JOINT AND SEVERAL DEPUTIES FOR PROPERTY AND AFFAIRS

Made by ....

At Archway Tower, 2 Junction Road, London, N19 5SZ

On ....

WHEREAS

(1)   An application has been made for an order under the Mental Capacity Act 2005.

(2)   The court is satisfied that P [*insert forename and surname*] is unable to make various decisions for himself in relation to a matter or matters concerning his property and affairs because of an impairment of, or a disturbance in the functioning of, his mind or brain.

(3)   The court is satisfied that the purpose for which the order is needed cannot be as effectively achieved in a way that is less restrictive of his rights and freedom of action.

IT IS ORDERED that:

1.   Appointment of joint & several deputies

(a)   .... [*insert name of first deputy*] of .... [*insert address and postcode*] and .... [*insert name of second deputy*] of .... [*insert address of second deputy*] are appointed jointly and severally as deputies to make decisions on behalf of P [*insert forename and surname*] that he is unable to make for himself in relation to his property and affairs subject to any conditions or restrictions set out in this order.

(b)   The appointment will last until further order.

(c)   The deputies must jointly & severally apply the principles set out in section 1 of the Mental Capacity Act 2005 and have regard to the guidance in the Code of Practice to the Act.

2.   Authority of joint & several deputies

(a)   The court confers general authority on the deputies jointly and severally to take possession or control of the property and affairs of P [*insert forename and surname*] and to exercise the same powers of management and investment as he has as beneficial owner, subject to the terms and conditions set out in this order.

(b)   The deputies may jointly and severally make provision for the needs of anyone who is related to or connected with P [*insert forename and surname*] if he provided for or might be expected to provide for that person's needs, by doing whatever he did or might reasonably be expected to do to meet those needs.

(c)   The deputies may jointly and severally (without obtaining any further authority from the Court) dispose of money or property of P [*insert forename and surname*] by way of gift to any charity to which he made or might have been expected to make gifts and on customary occasions to persons who are related to or connected with him, provided that the value of each such gift is not unreasonable having regard to all the circumstances and, in particular, the size of his estate.

(d)   The deputies are jointly and severally authorised to sell the property of P [*insert forename and surname*] known as .... [*insert address and postcode of property*] on the best possible terms and after payment of legal fees and other professional charges to invest the net proceeds for his benefit.

(e)   For the purpose of giving effect to any decision the joint deputies may jointly and severally execute or sign any necessary deeds or documents.

3.   Reports

(a)   The joint deputies are required to keep statements, vouchers, receipts and other financial records.

(b)   The joint deputies must submit a report to the Public Guardian as and when required.

4.   Costs and Expenses

(a)   The deputies are jointly and severally entitled to be reimbursed for reasonable expenses incurred provided they are in proportion to the size of the estate of P [*insert forename and surname*] and the functions performed by the joint deputies.

(b)   The deputies are jointly and severally authorised to pay Messrs [*insert details of solicitors*] fixed costs for this application, or where the amount exceeds the fixed costs allowed, the deputies are jointly and severally authorised to agree the costs for making this application to pay them from funds belonging to P [*insert forename and surname*]. In default of agreement, or if the deputies jointly and severally or the solicitors would prefer the costs to be assessed, this order is to be treated as authority to the Senior Court Costs Office to carry out a detailed assessment on the standard basis.

(c)   Any professional deputy is entitled to receive fixed costs in relation to this application and to receive fixed costs for the general management of the affairs of P [*insert forename and surname*]. If the professional deputy would prefer the costs to be assessed, this order is to be treated as authority to the Senior Court Costs Office to carry out a detailed assessment on the standard basis.

5.   Security

(a)   The deputies are jointly required forthwith to obtain and maintain security in the sum of £ .... [*insert amount*] in accordance with the standard requirements as to the giving of security.

(b)   To enable the deputies jointly to give security, this order becomes effective one calendar month from the date it was made.

(c)   The deputies jointly and severally must not discharge any functions until the security is in place.

CHAPTER 8

ENDURING POWERS OF ATTORNEY

LAW AND PRACTICE

8.1 BACKGROUND

The Enduring Powers of Attorney ('EPAs') are creatures of statute ie the Enduring Powers of Attorney Act 1985 which came into force on 1 March 1986. EPAs differ from ordinary powers of attorney because they endure beyond the onset of incapacity (subject to the requirement of registration). They also enable the attorney to make gifts and make provision for someone whom the donor might have provided for or been responsible for. They are limited in scope in that it relates only to the donor's property and affairs. The attorney does not have any powers in relation to the donor's personal welfare such as residence, care, contact and health. By reason of the fact that they are based on the donor's autonomy to choose the person he wished to manage his affairs, they were open to abuse because of the limited degree of supervision and intervention available to protect the donor when he was unable to make decisions on his own behalf through lack of capacity.

The Mental Capacity Act 2005, s 66 abolished the Enduring Powers of Attorney Act 1985. No EPAs can be made after 1 October 2007.[1] However, all existing EPAs will continue to remain effective, subject to the provision of Sch 4 to the Mental Capacity Act 2005, which in effect incorporates the provisions of the 1985 into the new Act and thus the safeguards introduced by the 1985 Act are preserved. EPAs have been replaced by Lasting Powers of Attorney (LPAs), see Chapter 9.

8.2 CHARACTERISTIC OF EPAS

To be valid the EPA:

- Must be made in the prescribed form.

- Must be executed in the prescribed manner by the donor and the attorney or attorneys if more than one.

---

[1] MCA, s 66(2).

- Must incorporate at the time of execution by the donor the prescribed explanatory information.

- Must not appoint an individual as an attorney who has not reached the age of 18 unless it is a trust corporation, and the individual appointed must not be bankrupt.

- Must not give the attorney the right to appoint substitute or successor.

The instrument which creates the EPA will be presumed to have been appropriately executed unless the contrary is proved. An immaterial difference in the form and mode of expression than that which is prescribed will not render the instrument ineffective.[2]

In addition, to the above requirements, the statutory provisions impose a duty on the attorney to register the EPA with the Court of Protection in the prescribed form with the prescribed supporting statement, when he/she believes that the donor is or is becoming incapable of managing his property and affairs. Before making the application the attorney is required to notify the donor personally and at least three relatives in a prescribed order of classes of relatives[3] and any other attorney appointed of his/her intention to do so.

8.3   CONTENTS OF THE NOTICE

The notice to the donor must:

- be in the prescribed form;

- state that the attorney proposes to make an application for registration of the instrument creating the EPA in question; and

- inform the donor that, while the instrument remains registered, any revocation of the power by him/her will be ineffective unless and until the revocation is confirmed by the Court.[4]

The notice to the relatives and to other attorneys (if more than one) must:

- be in the prescribed form;

- state that the attorney intends to register the EPA;

---

[2]   MCA, Sch 4, para 2(4).
[3]   MCA, Sch 4, paras 5–7.
[4]   MCA, Sch 4, para 10.

- inform the person concerned that he has a right to object to the registration within 5 weeks of the date of the notice; and

- specify the grounds set out in para 13(9) on which an objection to registration may be made.[5]

8.4 GROUNDS OF OBJECTIONS

Schedule 4, para 13(9) sets out five specific grounds on which objection may be made to the registration of the EPA namely:

(a) that the power purported to have been created by the instrument was not valid as an EPA;

(b) that the power created by the instrument no longer subsists;

(c) that the application is premature because the donor has not yet becoming mentally incapable;

(d) that fraud or undue pressure was used to induce the donor to create the power; and

(e) that having regard to all the circumstances and in particular the attorney's relationship to or connection with the donor, the attorney is unsuitable to be the donor's attorney.

8.5 REVOCATION

An EPA is revoked if:

- The donor or the attorney becomes bankrupt.

- The court exercises it powers to make decisions in respect of P concerning his/her personal welfare and or property and affairs and its powers to appoint deputies under ss 16–20 of the MCA 2005 and directs that the EPA is revoked.

In addition, if the Court is satisfied that any of the grounds set out in para 13(9) above is established it must direct the Public Guardian not to register the instrument. If the Court is satisfied that fraud or undue pressure was used to induce the donor to create the power or that having regard to the all the circumstances and in particular the attorney's

---

[5]   MCA, Sch 4, para 9.

relationship or connection with the donor, the attorney is unsuitable to be the donor's attorney, the Court must revoke the power created by the instrument.[6]

If the Court directs the Public Guardian not to register the instrument on any of the grounds set out in para 13(9) the instrument must be delivered up and be cancelled unless the objection has been established on the ground that the application is premature or the Court otherwise directs[7] (see below for the Court's power).

8.6   LEGAL EFFECT OF REGISTRATION

Once registered:

- Any revocation of the power by the donor will be invalid unless and until the Court confirms the revocation.

- Any disclaimer of the power by the attorney is not valid until the attorney gives notice of the disclaimer to the Public Guardian.

- The donor cannot extend or restrict the scope of the authority conferred by the instrument.

- No instruction or consent given by the donor after registration confers any right or imposes or confers any obligation or right on or creates any liability of the attorney or other persons having notice of the instruction or consent.

Registration of an instrument is evidence of the contents of the instrument and of its registration.[8]

8.7   COURT'S POWERS

Where an instrument has been registered the Court has the following functions with respect to the power:

The Court may:

(a) determine any question as to the meaning or effect of the instrument;

(b) give directions with respect to the management or disposal by the attorney of the property and affairs of the donor; the rendering of accounts by the attorney and the production of the records kept by

---

6   MCA, Sch 4, para 13(11).
7   MCA, Sch 4, para 13(12).
8   MCA, Sch 4, para 15.

him for the purpose and the remuneration or expenses of the attorney, whether or not in default or in accordance with any provision made by the instrument, including directions for the repayment of excessive or the payment of additional remuneration;

(c) require the attorney to supply information or produce documents or things in his possession as attorney;

(d) give any consent or authorisation to act which the attorney would have to obtain from the mentally capable donor;

(e) authorise the attorney to act so as to benefit himself or other persons than the donor otherwise than in accordance with para 16(2) and (3) (but subject to any conditions or restrictions contained in the instrument);

(f) relieve the attorney wholly or partly from any liability which he has or may have incurred on account of a breach of his duties as attorney.

8.7.1 The court's power to confirm revocation on application by the donor

On an application made for the purpose by or on behalf of the donor, the Court must confirm the revocation of the power if it is satisfied that the donor:

(a) has done whatever is necessary in law to effect an express revocation of the power; and

(b) was mentally capable of revoking a power of attorney when he did so (whether or not he is so when the Court considers the application).[9]

8.7.2 The court's power to direct cancellation of a registered instrument

The Court must direct the Public Guardian to cancel the registration of an instrument in the following circumstances:

(a) on confirming the revocation of the power (see above under **8.7.1**);

(b) on directing (see above under **8.7.1(b)**);

(c) on being satisfied that the donor is and is likely to remain mentally capable;

---

[9]   MCA, Sch 4, para 16(3).

(d)   on being satisfied that the power has expired or has been revoked by the mental incapacity of the attorney;

(e)   on being satisfied that the power was not a valid and subsisting enduring power when registration was effected;

(f)   on being satisfied that fraud or undue pressure was used to induce the donor to create the power;

(g)   on being satisfied that, having regard to all the circumstances and in particular the attorney's relationship to or connection with the donor, the donor is unsuitable to be the donor's attorney.[10]

8.8   CANCELLATION OF REGISTRATION BY PUBLIC GUARDIAN

The Public Guardian must cancel the registration of an instrument creating an enduring power of attorney in the following circumstances:

(a)   on receipt of a disclaimer signed by the attorney;

(b)   if satisfied that the power has been revoked by the death or bankruptcy of the donor or attorney or, if the attorney is a body corporate, by its winding up or dissolution;

(c)   on receipt of notification from the Court that it has revoked the power;

(d)   on confirmation from the Court that the donor has revoked the power.

8.9   PRACTICE AND PROCEDURE

Practice Direction 9H (PD 9H) applies where any person entitled to be given notice of the application to register an instrument wishes to apply to the Court for direction that the instrument should or should not be registered.

8.9.1   How to apply

The application must be made on Form COP8. The application form must state:

(a)   what direction the applicant is seeking;

---

[10]   MCA, Sch 4, para 16(4).

(b)   if the applicant objects to the registration, the grounds on which he does so; or

(c)   if the applicant is seeking registration, his reasons for doing so.[11]

The application form must be supported by evidence. This may be contained in either the application form, provided it is verified by a statement of truth, or in a witness statement which must also be verified by a statement of truth.

8.9.2   Service

As soon as practicable after issue, but in any event within 21 days of the application form being issued, the applicant must serve a copy of the application form together with the acknowledgment of service in Form COP5:

(a)   unless the applicant is the donor or an attorney, on the donor of the power and every attorney under the power;

(b)   if he/she is the donor, on every attorney under the power; or

(c)   if he/she is an attorney, on the donor and any other attorney under the power;

(d)   where the applicant knows or has reasonably grounds to believe that, the donor of the power lacks capacity to make a decision in relation to the matter that is the subject of the application, he must notify the donor of the application in accordance with COP Rules, r 40 and PD 7A. The applicant in this case must, unless the Court otherwise directs, explain to P who the applicant is; what the application is about; what will happen if the Court makes an order or direction that has been applied for and that P may seek advice and assistance in relation to any matter of which he is notified. This information must be provided to P in a way that is appropriate to P's circumstances (for example using simple language, visual aids or any other appropriate means). The information must be provided to P personally. Every effort should be made to inform P in a way that he/she will understand. The notification should be given on COP14 with COP14A which gives guidance on how to complete Form COP14. P must also be provided with the acknowledgment of notification Form COP5.

---

[11]   PD 9H, para 7.

8.9.3   Certificate of notification

Once the relevant persons have been notified, the applicant must file the certificate of notification in Form COP20. Where it is apparent that P is unable to act on the notification notice the Court should be informed that P is unlikely to return the acknowledgment form or do anything with it. The applicant is obliged to file the COP20 within 7 days of effecting service. If the applicant has difficulty in serving the documents he/she should apply on Form COP9 to the Court for direction for substituted service or service to be dispensed with.

8.9.4   The Court

The court when required to act in an emergency may:

- make orders on the papers without a hearing;

- make orders at a hearing without notice;

- abridge time for service.

Where an order is made without notice to the attorney the Court will make directions fixing a directions appointment or hearing and give directions for a reply by the attorney.

In cases where there is concern for the misuse of P's assets, application may also be made at the same time for freezing orders or injunctions to protect the position.[12]

An urgent hearing may take place by telephone (PD 9B, para 11) and in an exceptional case an oral application may be made without issue of an application notice (PD 9B, para 9). If the order sought is unusually long a disc should be provided for the Court's use.[13]

---

[12]   See COP Rules 2007, r 82 and chapter 11 Enforcement.
[13]   PD 9B, para 7.

8.10 PROCEDURAL GUIDE FOR REGISTRATION OF ENDURING POWER OF ATTORNEY AND OBJECTING TO REGISTRATION AND CANCELLATION OF THE POWER

Attorney	Files application to register in Form **EP2G**	MCA 2005, Sch 3, Part 3 Regulations 2007, reg 23 and Sch 7
Attorney notifies donor and relevant relatives	Notice of registration in Form **EP1G**	Regulations 2007, reg 23 and Sch 4, Part 3
Public Guardian	Sends notice of receipt to P and any other attorney and to the attorney if notice of registration is made by P	Regulations 2007, reg 11
Registration	If there are no grounds for Refusing the registration and no objections received within 35 days Public Guardian registers the EPA	MCA 2005, Sch 4
Donor and other relevant persons' objections to the Court by application	Must be made within 5 weeks on prescribed grounds (see **9.4**) on Form **COP8** or **COP1** if the applicant is not entitled to be notified of registration	MCA2005, Sch 4 COP Rules 2007 PD 9H (6)-(10)
Application to the Court		
Applicant		
Donor (P) Attorney/s Relevant relatives	Form **COP8** and Form **COP24** with a witness statement and supporting evidence and draft order sought	COP Rules 2007 PD 9H PD 9A
Any other person	Form **COP1**	
Service within 21 days on P and other relevant persons	Donor/attorney of Forms **COP14** and **COP14A** and **COP5**	COP Rules 2007 PD 9H(9)
Applicant files	Certificate of notification on Form **COP20** Within 7 days of service	PD 9H
Acknowledgement by persons served	On Form **COP5**	COP Rules, r 72 PD 9H
Orders that court may make	see **8.7**	

PRECEDENTS

See under Chapter 9.

CHAPTER 9

REVOCATION OF LASTING POWERS OF ATTORNEY

LAW AND PRACTICE

9.1 BACKGROUND

A lasting power of attorney (LPA) is a power of attorney which allows the donor (P) to confer on the donee/s authority to make decisions about all or any matters relating to the personal welfare or specified matters concerning P's welfare and P's property and affairs or specified matters relating to P's property and affairs. Its importance is that it includes authority to make such decisions in circumstances where P no longer has capacity.[1] It follows from its nature that it is made by the donor when he/she has capacity and presumes the principles contained in ss 1 and 2 of the Act (see Chapter 2), ie that whilst the donor has capacity to make a decision he/she makes that decision himself/herself. In order to prevent abuse, the power of an attorney will be restricted by the terms of the power so that it is exercised only in relation to the specified matters and in certain circumstances identified in the document. The Act also imposes restrictions on this power which are discussed below. The common law restrictions such as the duty of care to P and the duty owed by a person in a fiduciary position to another not to misappropriate P's property or to obtain a gain will also apply. The Court of Protection is now given wide powers which are aimed at preventing abuse of the attorney's powers. The LPA replaces the Enduring Power of Attorney (EPA). No new EPAs can now be created since the MCA 2005 came into force. Those created prior to the new Act remain valid so long as they are lawfully created (see Chapter 8).

9.1.1 Conditions and restrictions

Section 9(2) provides that a lasting power of attorney is not created unless:

(a) section 10 is complied with;

---

[1] MCA 2005, s 9.

(b)   an instrument conferring authority of the kind mentioned in subsection 1 is made and registered in accordance with Sch 1; and

(c)   at the time when P executes the instrument, P has reached 18 and has capacity to execute it.

The lasting power of attorney must be in the prescribed form and must be registered before it can take effect. Section 9(4) also provides that the authority conferred by a lasting power of attorney is subject to the provisions of the Act and, in particular, the principles set out in ss 1 and 4 of the Act and any conditions or restrictions specified in the instrument.

A lasting power of attorney does not authorise the donee/s to do an act that is intended to restrain P unless three conditions are met, namely:

(a)   that P lacks capacity or the donee reasonably believes that P lacks capacity in relation to the matter in question;

(b)   that the donee reasonably believes that it is necessary to do the act in order to prevent harm to P;

(c)   that the act is a proportionate response to the likelihood of P's suffering harm and the seriousness of that harm.

A donee will be treated as using restraint on P if he/she uses, or threatens to use, force to secure the doing of an act which P resists or restricts P's liberty of movements, whether or not P resists or if he/she authorises another person to do any of those things.[2] The donee/s will be treated as doing more than merely restraining P if he deprives P of his liberty within the meaning of Art 5(1) of the Human Rights Convention[3] (see Chapter 4 and **4.3**).

In relation to any authority given in the instrument relating to decisions about P's personal welfare, s 11(7) and (8) impose the following restrictions, namely, the authority:

(a)   does not extend to making such decisions in circumstances other than those where P lacks capacity, or the donee reasonably believes that P lacks capacity;

(b)   is subject to ss 24–26 (advance decisions to refuse treatment; see above under **6.13**).

The power in relation to welfare decisions will extend to giving or refusing consent to the carrying out or continuation of a treatment by a person providing health care for P but it does not authorise the giving or refusing

---

2   MCA 2005, s 11(1)–(5).
3   MCA 2005, s 11(6).

of consent to the carrying out or continuation of life-sustaining treatment, unless the instrument contains express provision to that effect and in such a case it will be subject to any conditions or restriction set out in the instrument.

Where a lasting power confers authority to make decisions about P's property and affairs, s 12 provides that this does not authorise the attorney/s to dispose of P's property by making gifts except to the extent permitted by subsection (2). Subject to any conditions or restrictions contained in the instrument, the attorney may make gifts on customary occasions (including himself) to those who are related to or connected with P or to any charity to whom P made or might have been expected to make gifts.[4] Customary occasion means the occasion or anniversary of a birth, or marriage or the formation of a civil partnership or any other occasion on which presents are customarily given within families or among friends or associates.

9.1.2 Registration of the Lasting Power of Attorney

A Lasting Power of Attorney is ineffective until it is registered. An application to register is made to the Public Guardian in a prescribed form – Form LPA002. It must be accompanied with the original instrument and the appropriate fee. The applicant must also give notice in Form LPA001 to any person named in the instrument. If the applicant is the attorney, the Public Guardian is required to give notice of the application to the donor. Where the application for registration is made by the donor the Public Guardian is required to give notice to the attorney/s and if an application is made by one of two attorneys to the other attorney. The Public Guardian must register the LPA unless one or more of the circumstances set out in Sch 1, paras 13–14 to the Act apply. If the Public Guardian has no grounds for refusing to register or he has not received any objections to the registration within 5 weeks of the notice being given and not less than 6 weeks after notice was given by the Pubic Guardian, he must register the instrument as a lasting power of attorney.

The grounds on which the Public Guardian may refuse to register the LPA are:

(1) If it appears that the lasting power of attorney is not valid.

(2) If it appears to the Public Guardian that an instrument accompanying the application is apparently defective or contains ineffective provisions in which case the Public Guardian must not register the power unless the Court of Protection directs him to do so. Where the instrument contains a provision which is ineffective or would prevent the instrument from operating as a valid lasting

---

4   MCA 2005, s 12(2).

power of attorney the Public Guardian must apply to the Court for it to determine the matter under s 23(1) of the Act.

(3)   If it appears to the Public Guardian that the Court has already appointed a deputy for P and the powers conferred on the deputy by the Court would conflict with the powers of the attorney. In this case the instrument cannot be registered unless the Court directs the Public Guardian to do so.

(4)   If notice is given by an attorney or a named person of an objection to the registration on one or more of the specified grounds in s 13(3) or (6)(a)–(d) which has had the effect of revoking the instrument and the Public Guardian is satisfied that the ground for making the objection is established, unless the Court on the application of the person applying for the registration is satisfied that the ground is established and directs the Public Guardian to register the instrument.

(5)   If the Court of Protection receives a notice of objection from an attorney or a named person on a prescribed ground and notifies the Public Guardian of the application.

(6)   If the donor on receiving the application for registration gives notice to the Public Guardian of an objection to the registration the Public Guardian must not register the instrument unless the Court on the application of the attorney/s is satisfied that P lacks capacity to object to the registration and directs the Public Guardian to register the instrument.

9.1.3   Grounds of objection

The grounds on which a person named in the instrument or an attorney can object are set out in s 13(3) and (6) and s 22(3). The grounds under s 13 are:

(a)   P has revoked the power;

(b)   it is alleged that P lacked capacity when he executed the instrument;

(c)   P's bankruptcy revokes the power so far as it relates to P's property and affairs;

(d)   the death or bankruptcy of the attorney or if the attorney is a trust corporation its winding up or dissolution;

(e)   the LPA has been disclaimed by the attorney;

(f)   P has died;

(g)   the marriage or civil partnership between P and the attorney has been dissolved;

(h)   the attorney lacks capacity.

The grounds prescribed under s 22(3) are:

(a)   fraud or undue pressure has been used to induce P to create the LPA;

(b)   the attorney has behaved, or is behaving in a way that contravenes his authority or is not in P's best interests; or

(c)   the attorney proposes to behave in a way that would contravene his authority or would not be in P's best interests.

9.2   THE COURT'S POWERS TO REVOKE AND CANCEL

Inevitably, as has been described in Chapter 7 regarding deputies, some attorneys will fail to carry out their responsibilities properly. This may be as a result of their own incapacity or dishonesty. In those circumstances an application may need to be made to the Court for the revocation of the instrument creating the power and cancellation of its registration.

The court's powers to determine issues relating to the validity or operation of a lasting power of attorney are set out in ss 22 and 23 of the Act. The court has the following specific powers:

* Where P has executed or purported to execute an instrument with a view to creating a lasting power of attorney or an instrument has been registered as a lasting power of attorney conferred by P, the Court is empowered to determine whether one or more of the requirements for the creation of a lasting power of attorney have been met and whether the power has been revoked or has otherwise come to an end.

* The court also has power to direct that an instrument purporting to create a lasting power of attorney is not registered, or if P lacks capacity to do so, revoke the instrument or the lasting power of attorney if the Court is satisfied:
    (a)   that fraud or undue duress was used to induce P to execute an instrument for the purpose of creating a lasting power of attorney or to create a lasting power of attorney; or
    (b)   that the attorney/s of a lasting power of attorney has behaved, or is behaving in or proposes to behave in a way that would contravene his/her authority or would not be in P's best interests.

Where there is more than one attorney the Court may revoke the instrument or the lasting power of attorney so far as it relates to any of them.

- The court may determine any question as to the meaning or effect of a lasting power of attorney or an instrument purporting to create one.

- The court may give directions with respect to decisions which the attorney of a lasting power of attorney has authority to make and which P lacks capacity to make.

- The court may give any consent or authorisation to act which the attorney would have to obtain from P if P had capacity to give.

- The court may authorise the making of gifts which are not within s 12(2) (see above at chapter 7).

- The court may if P lacks capacity:
  (a) give directions to the attorney with respect to the rendering by him of reports or accounts and the production of records kept by him for that purpose;
  (b) require the attorney to provide information or produce documents or things in his possession as an attorney;
  (c) give directions with respect to the remuneration or expenses of the attorney;
  (d) relieve the attorney wholly or partly from any liability which he has or may have incurred on account of a breach of his duties as an attorney.

The court when required to act in an emergency may:

- make orders on the papers without a hearing;

- make orders at a hearing without notice;

- abridge time for service.

Where an order is made without notice to the attorney the Court will make directions fixing a directions appointment or hearing and give directions for a reply by the attorney.

In cases where there is concern for the misuse of P's assets, application may also be made at the same time for freezing orders or injunctions to protect the position (see Chapter 11).

9.3   HOW TO APPLY

A person wishing to object to the registration under one or more of the above grounds must do so by making an application to the Court of Protection in Form COP7 and support the application with a witness statement and other supporting evidence of the objections made. The person making the objections must also inform the Public Guardian of the application to the Court in Form LPA007.

Where the application objecting to the registration is made by a person other than P or an attorney or person named in the instrument, the application must be made in Form COP1.

In the case of an application being made after the lasting power of attorney has been registered any application for the cancellation of the registration or any other directions or order of the Court should be made in Form COP1.

9.4 PROCEDURAL GUIDE FOR REGISTRATION OF LASTING POWER OF ATTORNEY AND OBJECTING TO REGISTRATION AND CANCELLATION OF THE POWER

Attorney	Files application to register in Form **LPA002**	Regulations 2007, reg 11 and Sch 3
Attorney serves person named P in the LPA	Notice of registration in Form **LPA001**	Regulations 2007, reg 10 and Sch 2
Public Guardian	Sends notice of receipt to P and any other attorney and to the attorney if notice of registration is made by P	Regulations 2007, reg 11
Registration	If there are no grounds for Refusing the registration and no objections received within 6 weeks Public Guardian registers the LAP in Form **LPA004**	Regulations 2007, reg 12 and 17
Objections to the Public Guardian	On factual grounds within 5 weeks on Form **LPA001**	Regulations 2007, reg 14(2) and 15(3)
Objections to the Court	On prescribed grounds **(see 9.1.3, s 22)** within 5 weeks on Form **COP7**	
Application to the Court		
Applicant		
Applicant Donor (P) Attorney/s Person named in the LPA	Form **COP7** and Form **COP24** with a witness statement and supporting evidence and draft order sought	COP Rules 2007, rr 51(2)(b) and 64 PD 9A
Orders that court may make	see **9.2**	

PRECEDENTS

WITNESS STATEMENT IN SUPPORT OF AN APPLICATION FOR THE REMOVAL OF AN ATTORNEY

IN THE COURT OF PROTECTION

IN THE MATTER OF THE MENTAL CAPACITY ACT 2005

AND IN THE MATTER OF FREDA FRUMP (D.O.B. 01.12.1917)

BETWEEN

RUM COUNTY COUNCIL   Applicant
SOCIAL AND
COMMUNITY SERVICES
DEPARTMENT

And

FREDA FRUMP   1st Respondent

(By her litigation friend the
Public Guardian)

And

BETSY FRUMP   2nd Respondent

WITNESS STATEMENT OF MELANIS LOVE

I, Melanis Love of Rum County Council Social and Community Services Department, of 22 Acropolis Street, Rum will state as follows:

1.   I am a care manager employed by Rum County Council Social and Community Services Department in the Adults' Services Team. I am the allocated care manager for Freda Frump, currently of The Good Samaritan Residential Home in Rum.

2.   I qualified as a Social Worker in 1990 with an MSc and Certificate of Qualification in Social Work (CQSW).

3.   I have been employed by the Rum County Council since 2003. I had initially worked as a field social worker for different local authorities and in day care and residential units for the elderly. For a period of about 10 years before commencing my employment

with Rum County Council I was employed as a social worker for the elderly by Hellinic Borough Council.

4.   I make this statement in support of an application for authorisation for Freda Frump to be placed in residential care at the Good Samaritan Residential Home on a permanent basis subject to the standard residential placement reviewing system and for Betsy Frump to be discharged as Freda Frump's attorney and to appoint a panel deputy to manage the property and affairs of both Freda and Betsy Frump. I make this statement based on my personal knowledge and from information contained on Freda Frump's file. I have also been responsible for Freda's care since her admission to the residential care home and in that capacity have had to discuss the plans for Freda with the medical experts and the Mental Health Team.

5.   Freda and Betsy are sisters. Freda is 92 years of age and Betsy is 95. Neither of them married and have no other siblings or relatives.

6.   Until June 2009 the sisters lived together in their family home. I am aware that they have both executed mutual wills and hold an enduring power of attorney for each other.

7.   In about 2007 Freda was diagnosed with dementia. Her health deteriorated and it became difficult for Betsy to care for her. On 15 June 2009 Freda fell down the stairs at their home. Fortunately she had minor injuries but she lost all confidence and it became necessary to place her in the residential home. Betsy then registered the EPA with the Public Guardian and took over the responsibility for Freda's finances.

8.   Since then it has become apparent that Betsy is becoming disorientated and it appears that she too may be losing capacity.

9.   The local authority's plan for Freda is that she should remain living in and be cared for at the residential home. This plan has been discussed with Betsy but she has refused to co operate and has failed to discharge the fees for the residential care home. She has also refused to pay for the necessary expenses relating to Freda's personal care.

10.   Betsy had been visiting her sister at the care home but more recently she has not done so. Attempts made to engage with her at her home have proved unsuccessful and concerns have been expressed by those who have visited her that she is extremely disorientated. There is now produced and shown to me marked 'ML1' the reports of the assessments carried out on Betsy.

11.   Before making the decision to make this application, I made one last attempt to discuss Freda's care with Betsy but she appeared not to comprehend even the simplest of matters relating to her sister. I too am concerned about Betsy welfare and capacity.

12.   There is now produced and shown to me marked 'ML2' a report of Dr Wise a consultant psychiatrist for Older Adults and her colleague Dr. Brilliant who have both diagnosed Freda with unspecified dementia.

12.   In those circumstances the local authority applies to the Court of Protection to cancel registration and revoke the EPA made by Freda appointing her sister Betsy as her attorney and to appoint a panel deputy to manage the property and affairs of both sisters.

13.   The facts stated in this witness statement are true.

Signed

Name ....

Dated ....

ORDER FOR THE REVOCATION OF AN EPA AND REPLACEMENT OF AN ATTORNEY

IN THE COURT OF PROTECTION

IN THE MATTER OF THE MENTAL CAPACITY ACT 2005

AND IN THE MATTER OF .... [*insert P's forename and surname*]

BETWEEN

<table>
<tr><td>RUM COUNTY COUNCIL
SOCIAL AND
COMMUNITY SERVICES
DEPARTMENT</td><td>Applicant</td></tr>
</table>

And

<table>
<tr><td>FREDA FRUMP
(By her litigation friend the
Public Guardian)</td><td>1st Respondent</td></tr>
</table>

And

<table>
<tr><td>BETSY FRUMP</td><td>2nd Respondent</td></tr>
</table>

DRAFT ORDER

Made by District Judge Felicity Sharp

At ....

On 21 December 2009

UPON hearing Counsel for the Applicant and Solicitor for the Public Guardian and for BF Respondents

AND UPON considering the trial bundle

WHERAS THE COURT IS SATISFIED [*or See the deputy order and delete para 1-3*]

1.   FF lacks capacity to make decisions about her residence and property and affairs.

2.   It is lawful in FF's best interests for her to continue to reside at the Good Samaritans Residential Home until further order.

3.   It is lawful, being in FF's best interests for the Applicant to arrange contact between FF and her sister BF.

IT IS ORDERED THAT:

1.   The Applicant Local Authority do have permission to make the application for the cancellation of registration and revocation of an EPA

2.   FF is joined as First Respondent and BF is joined as a Second Respondent and subject to his consent the O/S is appointed to act for FF OR

3.   **[in the case where the attorney has died]** It is noted that the attorney .... [*insert name*] appointed by P [*insert name*] by instrument dated [*insert date*] and registered on .... [*insert date of registration*] has died and the instrument is accordingly cancelled.

AND IT IS FURTHER DIRECTED THAT

1   This application and the evidence filed be served on the First and Second Respondent by the ... day of .... [*service having been abridged*].

2.   The parties do by .... file and serve all the evidence upon which they intend to rely at the hearing.

3.   The hearing be listed on the .... with a T/E of 2 hours.

4.   Pursuant to the Court of Protection Rules 2007 rule 4 the parties shall co operate to agree a trial bundle to be provided to the Court and all parties by the Applicant by 12 noon on .... 2010. The parties agreeing the contents by .... skeleton arguments to be filed at Court by ....

5.   BF as attorney for FF shall disclose to the Court all accounts, shares holdings, bonds state benefits and pensions and other investments of FF by ....

6.   BF shall cause the sum of £ .... to be paid from the account of FF with the Prudent bank to be paid into Court Funds Office by ....

8.   BF is forbidden to withdraw, transfer dispose of or in any other way deal with the funds held in the name of FF in the Prudent Bank and any other assets belonging to FF until further order.

[Final Order]

1.   The EPA dated .... appointing BF as attorney for FF shall be discharged/revoked and BF shall forthwith cease to be FF's attorney.

2.   A member of the panel maintained by the Office of the Public guardian be appointed deputy in accordance with the procedure set out in the Schedule to this order, to make decisions on behalf of FF that she is unable to make for herself in relation to her property and affairs subject to any conditions or restrictions set out in this order.

3.   (See Precedent in Chapter 7 under Deputies).

4.   No order as to costs save detailed assessment of FF's publicly funded costs/ or make an order that costs be paid out P's assets.

CHAPTER 10

STATUTORY WILLS

LAW AND PRACTICE

10.1 INTRODUCTION

Anyone who is 18 years of age or over and who has testamentary capacity can make a valid will. The presumption is that the testator has testamentary capacity unless proved otherwise but he/she must have the mental capacity to do so, both at the time of giving instructions or making the will. If he/she has capacity both at the time of giving instruction and executing the will, then his/her wishes however bizarre or eccentric should be respected.

Before the Act came into force on 1 October 2007 the Court of Protection's powers were limited to all issues relating to an incapacitated person's property and financial affairs. Various Mental Health Acts gave the Court of Protection authority to do everything necessary or expedient for the maintenance or other benefit of an incapacitated person and in relation to his property and affairs and 'for making provision for other persons or purposes for whom or which he might be expected to provide if he were not mentally disordered'.[1] Section 103 of the MHA 1959 empowered the Court to direct the making of settlements. With effect from January 1970, following amendments made to the MHA 1959 by the Administration of Justice Act 1969, the Court was given power to order the execution of a statutory will for a person whom it had reason to believe lacked testamentary capacity. The court's powers were however limited by the statutory direction that it had to make a decision on the basis of what the 'patient might be expected to provide if he were not mentally disordered', often referred to as the 'substituted judgment approach'. It was not until the case of *Re D(J)*[2] and the decision of Sir Robert Megarry V-C that a framework of the principles on which the Court should act was developed to assist those preparing statutory wills and the Court. These principles can be summarised as follows:

(i)   it is to be assumed that the incapacitated person is having a brief lucid interval at the time when the will is made;

---

[1]   MHA 1959, s 102(1).
[2]   [1982] Ch 237.

(ii)   during the notional lucid interval the incapacitated person has a full knowledge of the past, and a full realisation that as soon as the will is executed he or she will relapse into the actual mental state that previously existed with the prognosis as it actually is;

(iii) in this lucid interval it is the actual incapacitated person who has to be considered not a hypothetical incapacitated person;

(iv)   the Court should assume that during the hypothetical lucid interval the incapacitated person has had the benefit of being advised by competent solicitors;

(v)   in all normal cases the Court should assume that the incapacitated person would take a broad brush to the claims on his bounty, rather than an accountant's pen.

These guidelines acknowledged the Court's limitations and introduced an objective element into the approach to be adopted.

The Mental Health Act 1983 contained similar provision in s 95 and the approach set out in *Re D(J)* (above) continued to be applied until the Act came into force on 1 October 2007. In *Re C (A Patient)*[3] the incapacitated person had never enjoyed a rational mind and there was no other information from which the Court could construct a subjective assessment of what she would have wanted to do. The court assumed that she would have been a normal decent person and acted in accordance with contemporary standards of morality. In *Re S (Gifts of Mental Patient)*[4] although the decision turned on its particular facts Ferris J applying the guidelines said:

> 'it seems to me that I ought not to authorise the making of dispositions to charity except to the extent that I have a reasonable degree of confidence that not only is it objectively reasonable but that it is something which the patient herself would have wished to be done if she were of full capacity and aware of the circumstances.'

The approach under the Act has radically changed the way in which decisions are made and acts done on behalf of an incapacitated person and the way he is treated. The Act has introduced the six key principles which must be applied when making any decision relating to an incapacitated person his welfare, property or affairs with the emphasis being on what is in the 'best interest' of the person (see Chapter 2). Section 4 sets out a check list of factors which must be considered in deciding what is in the person's best interest.

---

[3]   [1992] 1 FLR 51.
[4]   [1997] 1 FLR 96.

10.2 POSITION UNDER THE ACT

The Court of Protection is empowered to make a will on behalf of P by virtue of ss 16(2)(a) and 18(1)(i). Section 16(2)(a) provides that the Court may by making an order, make the decision or decisions on P's behalf in relation to the matters and s 18 extends the Court's powers to make such orders which includes the execution for P of a will. The approach the Court must take under the new Act was fully considered in *Re P*.[5] Lewison J considered the past guidance of *Re D(J)*[6] and set out the way in which the Act now requires the Court to interpret the 'best interest' test which the Act requires must be applied in all decisions made on behalf of P. He said that 'the overarching principle is that any decision made on behalf of P must be in P's best interests. This is not necessarily the same as inquiring what P would have decided if he or she had had capacity'. The earlier cases therefore are no longer relevant.

> 'The Act does not require the counter-factual assumption that P is not mentally disordered. The facts must be taken as they are. It is not therefore necessary to go through the mental gymnastics of imagining that P has a brief lucid interval and then relapse into his former state …. The goal of the inquiry is not what P "might be expected" to have done; but what is in P's best interests. This is more akin to the "balance sheet" approach than to the "substituted judgment" approach.'

The Code of Practice makes this clear. All the relevant circumstances must be taken into consideration in deciding what was in the person's best interest. The Act provides a structured decision making process and:

> 'expressly directs the decision maker to take a number of steps before reaching a decision. These include encouraging P to participate in the decision. He must also "consider" P's past and present wishes and his beliefs and values and must " take into account" the views of third parties as to what would be in P's best interests.

> Having gone through these steps, the decision maker must then form a value judgment of his own giving effect to the paramount statutory instruction that any decision must be made in P's best interests.'

10.2.1 Best interest and P's wishes

The Act requires any decision made or act done to be one which is in the best interest of the incapacitated person and in determining what is in P's best interests the decision maker is required to consider, so far as is ascertainable, P's past and present wishes and feelings and, in particular, any relevant written statement made by him when he had capacity; the beliefs and values that would be likely to influence his decision if had capacity and the other factors that he would be likely to consider if he

---

[5]   [2009] EWHC 163 (Ch).

[6]   [1982] 2 All ER 37.

were able to do so. In addition the views of those who are engaged in caring for P, or interested in his welfare, and any donee of a lasting power of attorney or a deputy appointed by the Court or anyone named by P, must also be taken into account.[7] However, P's wishes and feelings are not paramount. It is only one of the matters that the Court is required to take account of. Thus, it does not necessarily follow that the person's wishes will in all instances be followed notwithstanding the principle of adult autonomy and that a person has the freedom to dispose of his property as he wishes. Levinson J acknowledged that that was:

> 'part of the overall picture, and an important one ... but what will live on after P's death is his memory; and for many people it is in their best interests that they be remembered with affection by their family and as having done "the right thing" by their will. In my judgment the decision maker is entitled to take into account, in assessing what is in P's best interests, how he will be remembered after his death.'

However, when dealing with the issue of P's wishes at para 40 of his judgment Levinson J said that Ps wishes should not be 'lightly overridden'. On the contrary, the Act expressly requires them to be considered; and for particular consideration to be given to wishes expressed by P when he had capacity. He referred with approval to the decision of HHJ Hazel Marshall QC in *Re S and S (Protected Persons)*[8] (an appeal from a district judge of the CoP) and her conclusion on the issue of P's wishes when she had said that 'the views and wishes of P in regard to decisions made on his behalf are to carry great weight' and whilst accepting that the Act does not say that P's wishes are to be paramount she expressed that by giving prominence to the best interests of P the Act in her judgment recognised that having his views and wishes taken into account and respected is a very significant aspect of P's best interests. Due regard should therefore be paid when doing the weighing exercise of determining what is in P's best interests.

> 'And ... in my judgment where P can and does express a wish or view which is not irrational (in the sense of being a wish which a person of full capacity might reasonably have), is not impractical as far as its physical implementation is concerned, and is not irresponsible having regard to the extent of P's resources ... then that situation carries great weight, and effectively gives rise to a presumption in favour of implementing those wishes, unless there is some potential sufficiently detrimental effect for P of doing so which outweighs this.'

Levinson J agreed with the broad thrust of this but thought that HHJ Marshall QC may have slightly overstated the importance to be given to P's wishes because firstly:

---

7   MCA 2005, s 4(6) and (7).
8   Lawtel Case No AC0119248.

'section 1(6) is not a statutory direction that one "must achieve" any desired objective by the least restrictive route. Section 1(6) only requires that before a decision is made "*regard* must be had" to that question. It is an important question, to be sure, but it is not determinative. The only imperative is that the decision must be made in P's best interests, Second, although P's wishes must be given weight, if, as I think Parliament has endorsed the "balance sheet" approach they are only one part of the balance. I agree those wishes are to be given great weight, but I would prefer not to speak in terms of presumption. Third, any attempt to test a decision by reference to what P would hypothetically have done or wanted runs the risk of amounting to a 'substituted judgment' rather than a decision of what would be in Ps best interests ....The decision maker must consider the beliefs and values that would be likely to influence P's decision if he had capacity and also the other factors that P would be likely to consider if he were able to do so.'

Levinson J also pointed out the need for a third party when making a decision on behalf of P to take legal or other advice if appropriate, and to the fact that the decision maker is entitled to take into account, in assessing what is in P's best interests, how he will be remembered after his death.

The decision in *Re P* clearly demonstrates that in future the Court is likely to balance P's known wishes with other objective considerations in determining what is in his best interests. This will include for instance the Court considering any possible claims for proprietary estoppel and claims under the Inheritance (Provision for Family and Dependants) Act 1975 for financial provision and reducing inheritance tax where appropriate. It will be of interest how the Court in future cases applies the principles set out in *Re P*.

10.3 CAPACITY

The Act affirms in s 1(1) the common law presumption that a person must be assumed to have capacity unless it is established that he lacks capacity. In order for P to have testamentary capacity, it is not necessary that the he/she is able to follow all the provisions relating to the making of the will. It will suffice if at the time of executing the will he/she has an understanding and appreciation that he/she is executing a will. The observations made by Cockburn CJ in his judgment in *Banks v Goodfellow*[9] are often relied on as providing a test of testamentary capacity:

'It is essential that a testator shall understand the nature of the act and its effects, shall understand the extent of the property of which he is disposing, shall be able to comprehend and appreciate the claims to which he ought to give effect; and with a view to the latter object, that no disorder of the mind shall poison his affections, pervert his sense of right, or prevent the exercise of his natural faculties – that no insane delusion shall influence his will in

---

[9]   (1870) LR 5 QB 549, 39 LJQB 237.

disposing of his property and bring about a disposal of it which, if the mind had been sound, would not have been made.'

Section 42(4) of the Act imposes a legal duty on any person to have regard to any relevant code, if he is acting in relation to a person who lacks capacity and is doing so in one or more of the following ways:

(a)   as the donee of a lasting power of attorney;

(b)   as a deputy appointed by the Court;

(c)   as a person carrying out research in reliance on any provision made by or under the Act;[10]

(d)   as an independent mental capacity advocate;

(e)   in a professional capacity;

(f)   for remuneration.

In addition s 1 sets out six fundamental principles which must be applied in every case (see further **2.3**). The Act also sets out the statutory definition or test of incapacity which must be applied and the criteria for assessing what is in the 'best interest' of the person concerned (see **2.4** and **2.5**). It is only if, having applied these principles and criteria, the medical advice establishes that P lacks testamentary capacity that an application will be entertained by the Court of Protection for an order that a Statutory Will be executed for P.

10.4   FACTORS TO BE CONSIDERED BEFORE MAKING AN APPLICATION

On the basis of the decision in *Re P* details of the incapacitated person's life, interests, relationships, moral obligations, and values which were important to him/her when he/she had capacity will be relevant factors. Before an application to the Court is issued it is important to establish whether P has executed a valid Will when he was competent. If such a Will exists an application to the Court for a statutory will to be executed on behalf of P is unlikely to succeed unless it is established that P's circumstances have changed so drastically that the earlier Will is no longer in P's best interests and needs to be reviewed and reconsidered. Changes relating to P's personal and marital status, family structure and financial assets may constitute significant reasons to justify a review particularly where it is established that it does not reflect the testator's current wishes. An application may be justified, where P's marriage has been dissolved or where he/she has remarried, or where grandchildren have been born since

---

[10]   See MCA 2005, ss 30–34.

the earlier Will was executed. It may also be justified where a significant beneficiary has died or a previous amicable relationship with a relative or friend has broken down and the wishes of P have therefore changed. It may also be justified where there is doubt regarding the validity of the Will purported to have been executed by P or doubts about P's testamentary capacity when he/she made the earlier Will. In *Re C (A Patient)*[11] it was shown that P never had testamentary capacity and was therefore unable to make a valid Will. Another example is where it can be shown that P executed a will under undue influence or duress where in similar circumstances a testator with capacity would not have done so and that it is in his best interests to make a new Will. The application is likely to be received sympathetically in cases where P has not made a valid Will particularly if the operation of the intestacy rules would result in the benefit of the estate passing to less deserving persons than those with whom P has a good and caring relationship or worst if it is shown that there are no persons who would inherit in the case of an intestacy and the estate would pass to the Crown as *bona vacantia*.

In a nutshell therefore, the Court is unlikely to accede to an application for a statutory will to be executed on behalf of P unless a significantly good reason is shown for doing so.

When considering whether to make an application for a statutory will to be executed the Court will of course have regard to:

- the key principles which underpin the Act and the requirement that any act done or decision made on behalf of P must be done or made in his best interest; and

- the factors set out in s 4 of the Act – the best interest test (see **2.4** and **2.5**).

10.5   PROCEDURE

The procedure to be followed when making an application for a statutory will is set out in the Court of Protection Rules 2007, Part 9 and Practice Direction 9F.

10.5.1   Who may apply for a statutory will

Section 50 of the Act and the CoP Rules 2007, rr 51(1) and 52(2) set out the list of persons who are eligible to apply for a statutory will without first seeking the permission of the Court. They are:

(a)   the patient;

---

[11]   [1991] All ER 866.

(b)   a deputy appointed by the Court for the patient;

(c)   the Official Solicitor;

(d)   the Public Guardian;

(e)   a person who has made an application for the appointment of a deputy;

(f)   a person who under any known Will of the patient or under his intestacy may become entitled to any property of the patient or any interest in it;

(g)   a person who is an attorney under an Enduring Power of Attorney which has been registered at the Office of the Public Guardian;

(h)   a person who is a donee under a Lasting Power of Attorney which has been registered at the Office of the Public Guardian;

(i)   any person for whom the patient might be expected to provide if had capacity to do so.

Persons not included in the above list must apply for permission to issue an application for an order for a statutory will to be made.

10.5.2   Respondents to an application for a statutory will – PD 9F(9)

The following persons must be joined as respondents to any application for a statutory will:

(a)   any beneficiary under an existing Will or Codicil who is likely to be materially or adversely affected by the application;

(b)   any beneficiary under a proposal or Codicil who is likely to be materially or adversely affected by the application;

(c)   any prospective beneficiary under the patient's intestacy where the patient has not made a will.

10.5.3   Person who must be notified of the application

Rule 70 of the COP Rules 2007 requires the applicant within 21 days of the issue of the application to notify the persons specified in the relevant practice direction that the application has been issued and whether it relates to the exercise of the Court's jurisdiction in relation to the patient's property and affairs or his personal welfare or to both and the orders sought. The notice must be accompanied with a form for acknowledging notification. The applicant is also required to file a certificate of notification within 7 days of service of the notice.[12]

Practice Direction 9B requires notice in Form COP15 to be given to the person listed in PD 9B but acknowledges that the persons who should be notified will vary according to the nature of the application. In relation to an application for a statutory will the applicant must notify at least three people who may have an interest in being notified. These will include members of P's family who are likely to have an interest. The PD specifies the relatives who may have such an interest and should be notified according to the presumed closeness in terms of relationship to P. They should be notified in descending order (as appropriate to the patient's circumstances). They are:

(a)   spouse or civil partner

(b)   person who is not a spouse or civil partner but who has been living with P as if they were;

(c)   parent or guardian;

(d)   child;

(e)   brother or sister;

(f)   grandparent or grandchild;

(g)   aunt or uncle;

(h)   child of a brother or sister;

(i)   step-parent; and

(j)   half brother or half-sister.

It may well be the case that some of the above relatives would in any event be made respondents to the application and it would be advisable to notify those (if their whereabouts are known) who are not made respondents to the application in any event.

Any deputy appointed by the Court, an attorney appointed under an enduring power of attorney or a donee of the lasting power of attorney (where that person has power to make decisions on behalf of P in regard to his property and affairs) should also be notified.[13]

---

[12]   COP Rules 2007, r 70.
[13]   PD 9B, para 10(c).

10.5.4   The application form

The application must be made in Form COP1 with supporting evidence and evidence of the P's incapacity in Form COP3 completed by a medical practitioner who has examined P and who can certify that he has applied the legal test for testamentary capacity. A fee of £400 is payable on issue.

In the case of urgency it would be desirable to make a telephone call to the Judicial Support Unit at the Court (Tel: 020 7664 7178) and inform the Court of the urgency. Consideration should be given to provide for the will to be executed by someone who is available to act on the making of an order eg the Official Solicitor.

10.5.5   Information to be provided with the application form – PD 9F(6)

The Practice Direction sets out the evidence information and documents which must be filed with the application form. These are:

(a)   a copy of the draft will or codicil with a copy;

(b)   copy of any existing will or codicil;

(c)   any consents to act by the proposed executors;

(d)   details of P's family preferably in the form of a family tree, including details of the full name and date of birth of each person included in the family tree;

(e)   a schedule showing details of P's current assets, with up to date valuation;

(f)   a schedule showing the estimated net yearly income and spending of P;

(g)   a statement showing P's needs both current and future estimates, and his general circumstances;

(h)   if P is living in NHS accommodation, information on whether he may be discharged to local authority accommodation or to other fee paying accommodation or to his own home;

(i)   if the applicant considers it relevant, full details of the resources of any proposed beneficiary, and details of any likely changes if the application is successful;

(j)   details of any capital gains tax, inheritance tax, or income tax which may be chargeable in respect of the subject matter of the application;

(k) an explanation of the effect, if any, that the proposed changes will have on P's circumstances, preferably in the form of a 'before and after' schedule of assets and income;

(l) if appropriate, a statement of whether any land would be affected by the proposed will or settlement and if so, details of its location and title number, if applicable;

(m) where the application is for a settlement of property or for variation of an existing settlement or trust, a draft of the proposed deed, plus one copy;

(n) a copy of any registered enduring power of attorney or lasting power of attorney;

(o) confirmation that P is a resident of England and Wales; and

(p) an up to date report of P's present medical condition, life expectancy, likelihood of requiring increased expenditure in the foreseeable, and testamentary capacity.

A copy of any existing will

This will inform the Court what the wishes of P were then and how it has changed over the years. It may also identify those persons who have had a meaningful relationship with P and those with whom he has broken all ties. Where there are significant changes or a number of testamentary documents which set out the wishes of P it would be good practice to prepare a schedule to enable a comparison to be made at a glance.

Any consents to act as proposed executors

It is important to provide as much detail as possible relating to those who are prepared to act as executors so that the Court can scrutinise the persons ability and suitability to act as an executor particularly where P's estate is likely to be substantial or complex and difficult to administer or where there is a likelihood of disputes arising or future claims being made against the estate eg under the Inheritance (Provision for Family and Dependants) Act 1975. Consideration should also be given to appointing an existing deputy to act as an executor with others.

Details of family members

It is important to provide the Court with as much information as is possible about the relatives in order for the Court to carry out an informed assessment of the relationship between them and P. Of particular relevance will be information relating to any conflicts and rejection.

Valuation of assets

A professional and comprehensive valuation will only become necessary where the assets are substantial or complex or there is a any hint that the valuations will be disputed.

A schedule of the patient's current and future needs

This document will need to be carefully prepared. It is suggested that this document should reflect the information which is often set out in the schedule of special damages in personal injury cases, particularly where P may require special care over a long period or where P is young. A schedule of assets and income and expenditure, such as the schedule prepared in applications for ancillary relief in matrimonial cases, may also be considered as a way of showing the issues at a glance and to assist the Court.

Details of any capital gains tax etc

The most significant of the taxes listed is of course the inheritance tax liability. An estimate of the liability and evidence of the impact of the liability on the estate will assist those who represent P to present his case and seek professional advice where appropriate on how best to manage and reduce the liability. It will also enable the Court to make an informed decision on what is in the best interest of P.

An explanation of the effect if any, that the proposed changes will have on the patient's circumstances, preferably in the form of 'before and after' schedule of assets and income

Re G (Patients)[14] is a recent example of the significance of this information.

10.6   EVIDENCE REQUIRED

The court will require evidence that P lacks capacity to make a valid will for himself/herself. In most cases the Court will require recent evidence as to lack of testamentary capacity.

Where a will for P already exists, a copy of that will should be exhibited to the statement filed in support of the application. The statement in support must set out the need for the execution of a further will or codicil.

---

[14]   [2007] EWHC 1861 (Ch).

In the case of a new will, where the draft of the will names the executors, the consent of the executors named in the draft will should be filed with the supporting evidence.

10.7 PROVISION THAT MAY BE MADE IN A WILL

Further provisions which may be included in an order for the making of a statutory will are set out in Sch 2 to the Act. Paragraph 2 of the Act provides that the will may make any provisions (whether by disposing of property or exercising a power or otherwise) which could be made by a will executed by P if he or she had capacity to make it.

10.7.1 Requirements relating to execution

If a court makes an order under s 16 of the Act or gives directions requiring or authorising a person ('an authorised person') to execute a will on behalf of P the will must:

- state that it is signed by P acting by the authorised person;

- be signed by the authorised person with the name of P and his own name, in the presence of two or more witnesses present at the same time;

- be attested and subscribed by those witnesses in the presence of the authorised person, and

- be sealed with the official seal of the Court.

10.7.2 Effect of execution

Where the will is executed on behalf of P in accordance with the above requirements it has the same effect for all purposes as if P had had capacity to make a valid will and the will had been executed by him in the manner required by the Wills Act 1837 except:

(a) in so far as it disposes of immovable property outside England and Wales; or

(b) in so far as it relates to any other property or matter if, when the will is executed, P is domiciled outside England and Wales and under the law of P's domicile any questions of his testamentary capacity would fall to be determined in accordance with the law of the place outside England and Wales.[15]

---

[15] MCA 2005, Sch 2, para 4(3)–(5).

10.7.3   Procedure on execution of a statutory will

Once a will has been executed on behalf of P, the applicant must send the original and two copies of the will to the Court of Protection for sealing. On receipt of the documents the Court must seal the original and the copy and return both documents to the applicant.[16]

---

[16]   MCA 2005, Sch 2, paras 11 and 12.

10.8   PROCEDURAL GUIDE

Applicant who may apply without permission	(1) P	
	(2) A deputy appointed by the Court	
	(3) The Official Solicitor	COP Rules 2007, r 51(1)
	(4) The Public Guardian	
	(5) A person who has made an application for the appointment of a deputy	COP Rules 2007, r 51(4)
	(6) A person who, under any known will of P or under his intestacy may be entitled to any property of P or any interest in it	COP Rules 2007, r 51(4)(b)
	(7) An attorney appointed under an EPA which has been registered in accordance the Act and the regulations referred to in Sch 4 to the Act	COP Rules 2007, r 51(4)(c)
	(8) Any beneficiary under an existing will or Codicil who is likely to be affected	COP Rules 2007, r 51(4)(d)
	(9) A person for whom P might be expected to provide if he had capacity to do so	COP Rules 2007, r 51(4)(e)
Respondents	(1) Any beneficiary under an existing will or Codicil who is likely to be affected	PD9F, para 9
	(2) Any person who is likely to be a beneficiary under P's intestacy	
	(3) Any beneficiary under a proposed will or codicil who is likely to be affected by the application	
Applicant must file	Form **COP2** (if permission to apply is (required)	COP Rules 2007, r 54 PD8A, para 1
	Forms **COP1** and **COP1A**	
	Written statement in support and providing relevant information	COP Rules 2007, r 64 PD9A, paras 2–9 PD9F para 6-9
	Form **COP3** (assessment of capacity)	COP Rules 2007, r 64(c) PD9A, para 12
	Form **COP4** (deputy's declaration)	
	Copy of EPA or LAP(if applicable)	
Court Fee	£400	

Court	Within 14 days must deal with application for permission to apply	COP Rules 2007, r 55
	Judge will either grant or refuse application or fix a hearing and notify any person of the hearing	
	If permission is granted or not required Court will issue application and give the Applicant:	
	Form **COP5**	
	Form **COP 14** and **COP14A**	
	Form **COP15** and **COP15A**	
	Form **COP20**	
Service		
The applicant must within 21 days serve Respondents	Form **COP1** and **COP1A** and any other supporting documents Forms **COP5, COP15** and **COP15A**	COP Rules 2007, r 66
Notify and serve P	Forms **COP14, COP14A** and **COP5**	COP Rules 2007, r 69
Notify and serve any other relevant person	Forms **COP5, COP15** and **COP15A**	COP Rules 2007, r 70
Within 7 days of service Applicant must file	Form **COP20**	COP Rules 2007, rr 68(4) and 70(3)
Respondent must if he wishes to respond to the application within 21 days of service file	Form **COP5**	COP Rules 2007, r 72 PD9C, para 3
Persons notified must if they wish to take part within 21 days of notification file	Form **COP5**	COP Rules 2007, r 72 PD9C, para 4
Persons not notified of application who wish to be joined as parties must file	Form **COP9**	COP Rules 2007, r 75 PD10A, para 1
Court must as soon as practicable deal with the application	Court may deal with the application without notice, give directions, fix a direction hearing and give directions and fix final hearing	COP Rules 2007, rr 84 and 85
Orders	On a direction hearing the Court may give any of the orders set out in r 85	COP Rules 2007, r 85
	At a final hearing the Court may authorise the making of Statutory will and direct the terms of the will and its execution and safe custody	

What the applicant must do	File the original executed will with two copies for sealing	PD9F, para 11
	Execution of the will must comply with the requirement of MCA 2005 Sch 2 para3(2)	PD9F, para 12
Sealing of the will	Court must seal the original will and copy and return both documents to the applicant	

PRECEDENTS

PRECEDENT OF STATEMENT IN SUPPORT OF AN APPLICATION FOR AN ORDER FOR A STATUTORY WILL

IN THE COURT OF PROTECTION   No ....

IN THE MATTER OF THE MENTAL CAPACITY ACT 2005

AND IN THE MATTER OF AB [*insert forename and surname*]

BETWEEN

LUSH COUNTY   Applicant
COUNCIL'S SOCIAL AND
COMMUNITY SERVICES
DEPARTMENT

And

STEPHEN BROWN   1st Respondent

And

JESEBEL BROWN   2nd Respondent

And

AB   3rd Respondent

(by his litigation friend the
Official Solicitor)

I, Alice Goodfellow of Lush County Council will say as follows:

1.   The Lush County Council's Social and Community Services Department was appointed deputy for AB who lacks capacity. A copy of the order is now shown to me marked AG1.

2.   AB is 21-years-old. His parents were violent and neglectful. When he was 6 AB suffered brain damage when he was assaulted repeatedly about the head by his father. He has global developmental delay; functions mentally at about a chronological age of 8 and has limited mobility. An assessment of capacity is now shown to me marked AG2.

3.   Lush County Council took care proceedings in relation to AB and he was made the subject of a care order under s 31 Children Act 1989 when he was 7. He was placed in long term foster care with professional paid carers.

4. The care plan is for him to remain placed with them. He has a life expectancy of 35 years old and is unlikely to survive his carers.

5. AB's parents were convicted of criminal offences in relation to their treatment of him. They both received a custodial sentence but have now been released from prison.

6. AB received an award from CICA of £500,000 2 years ago and the Director of Social Services of Lush CC applied and was appointed deputy for his property and affairs.

7. Unless a will is executed AB's parents will inherit under the rules of intestacy.

8. AB loves horses. Despite his mobility problems AB has learned to ride with supervision and attends a stables specialising in horse riding for disabled people. His home with his carer is the only one he remembers. He has no grandparents alive but has an older sister with children of her own who visits regularly and takes him out.

9. The deputy now seeks an order of the Court.

    (a)   For authority to execute a will on AB's behalf urgently.

    (b)   To dispense with service on both parents.

Signed ....

Note:

Papers required

*   COP 1

*   COP3 (from social worker from the learning disability team of Lush CC)

*   Draft will (dividing assets into 2 halves, 50% to sister and after her, her children. 50% to be divided between Carers and stables)

*   Family tree

PRECEDENT OF STATEMENT IN SUPPORT OF AN
APPLICATION FOR AN ORDER FOR A STATUTORY WILL

IN THE COURT OF PROTECTION   No ....

IN THE MATTER OF THE MENTAL CAPACITY ACT 2005

AND IN THE MATTER OF XY [*insert forename and surname*]

BETWEEN

JULIUS ALPHONSO   Applicant

And

JACOBI GODDFELLOW   1st Respondent

And

XY   2nd Respondent

(by his litigation friend the
Official Solicitor)

I, Julius Alphono of 1 Crooked Lane in the County of Barset make oath and say as follows:

1.   I have known XY, who is now 92 years of age, for about 50 years when he and his wife moved to live next door to me at 3 Crooked Lane. We became good friends. He was a solicitor and extremely active.

2.   When his wife died he granted me an Enduring Power of Attorney.

3.   On .... 12 January 2000 he suffered a stroke and suffered brain damage and became partially paralysed. He lost all confidence. He was unable to take care of himself and would not co operate with the daily carers who initially came to take care of his daily needs.

4.   He had to be placed in residential care. His condition has gradually deteriorated. He now has to be helped with feeding toileting washing and dressing. Form COP3 completed by the geriatrician responsible for the care home confirms that XY lacks capacity.

5.   When XY lost capacity I applied to register the enduring power of attorney. A copy of the EPA is now shown to me marked 'JA1'.

6.   XY's home was sold to pay for his care and during the course of clearing the property I was unable to find a will.

7.   Enquiries of Sue & Co produced a copy of XY's will made 25 years previously. It disclosed that XY had left his entire estate to his brother who died three months ago. There is now produced and shown to me marked 'JA2' a certified copy of the death certificate and XY's family tree. There is also now shown to me marked 'JA3' a Schedule setting out XY's assets.

8.   XY did not have any other siblings.

9.   Inquiries have revealed that XY's uncle on his father's side is known to have family. A great nephew survives and lives in Australia. He has never met XY and during the 50 years that I have known XY he never mentioned the existence of any relatives in Australia.

10.   I contacted the great nephew when XY was placed in a residential home but he showed no interest. I have notified him that having regard to XY's deteriorating health it is my intention to apply for a statutory will to be executed. He has made it clear that he would object to any such application.

11.   XY had a companionship with his former housekeeper for 10 years prior to his stroke. Although they did not live together they would go on holiday several times a year birdwatching and spend Xmas and other seasonal holidays together. She visits him 3 times per week in his care home.

12.   In his retirement XY did a lot for the solicitor's benevolent association. His bank accounts also reveal regular standing orders for donations to three charities namely, the NSPCC, The Homeless Centre in Barset and the Barset Hospice.

13.   A draft will is now produced and shown to me marked 'JA3'. It is proposed that that the three charities should receive legacies and the residue of XY's estate be divided between his housekeeper and the RSPB.

14.   As his attorney I apply to the Court for authority to execute a will on behalf of XY. This has now become urgent because XY has suffered a bout of pneumonia and there are concerns that he may not recover.

15.   In view of the urgency and the objections raised by the great nephew I respectfully ask that the Court considers the application as soon as possible at a telephone hearing or by video link.

Signed ....

Signed ....

Papers to be filed

- COP1

- COP3 (completed by geriatrician responsible for the care home)

- Draft will (legacies to three charities and neighbour. Residue divided between housekeeper and RSPB)

- Family tree

- COP20

- COP5 (from the nephew in Canada objecting to his exclusion)

Court convenes urgent hearing with evidence from the nephew by telephone.

PRECEDENT FOR AN ORDER TO EXECUTE A STATUTORY WILL

IN THE COURT OF PROTECTION   No ......

IN THE MATTER OF THE MENTAL CAPACITY ACT 2005

AND IN THE MATTER OF XY [*insert initials of P's forenames and surname*]

BETWEEN

JULIUS ALPHONSO   Applicant

And

JACOBI GOODFELLOW   1st Respondent

And

XY   2nd Respondent

(by his litigation friend the
Official Solicitor)

DRAFT ORDER TO EXECUTE A STATUTORY WILL

Made by District Judge Wise

At ....

On 21 December 2009

UPON READING the draft of a will proposed to be executed for Cassandra Fragile

(initialled by District Judge Wise for the purpose of identification)

IT IS ORDERED THAT:

1.   The applicant .... [*insert name*] is authorised to execute a will on behalf of XY [*insert P's initials*] in the terms of the draft approved by the Court.

2.   The will when executed is to be held in safe custody in the name of XY [*insert P's initials*] by Messrs Sharp and Swift (the solicitors for

the applicant) and is to remain so held subject (during the lifetime of XY [*insert P's initials*]) to the directions of the Court.

3.   A detailed assessment of the costs of and incidental to this application of the Applicant and the Official Solicitor be carried out on the standard basis and the applicant is to pay the certified amounts thereof from the estate of XY [*insert P's initials*].

To: Messrs Sharp and Swift

The Official Solicitor

PRECEDENT FOR EXECUTION OF A STATUTORY CODICIL

IN THE COURT OF PROTECTION No ....

IN THE MATTER OF THE MENTAL CAPACITY ACT 2005

AND IN THE MATTER OF XY [*insert initials of P's forenames and surname*]

BETWEEN

JULIUS ALPHONSO Applicant

And

JACOBI GOODFELLOW 1st Respondent

And

XY 2nd Respondent
(by his litigation friend the Official Solicitor)

DRAFT ORDER TO EXECUTE A STATUTORY CODICIL

Made by District Judge Wise

At ....

On ....

UPON READING the draft of a statutory codicil proposed to be executed for Cassandra Fragile (initialled by District Judge Wise for the purpose of identification)

IT IS ORDERED THAT:

1. The applicant .... [*insert name*] is authorised in the name of and on behalf of XY [*insert P's initials*] to execute a statutory codicil in the terms of the draft approved by the Court.

2. The executed statutory codicil is to be held in safe custody in the name of XY [*insert P's initials*] by Messrs Sharp and Swift (the solicitors for the applicant) and is to remain so held subject (during the lifetime of XY [*insert P's initials*]) to the directions of the Court.

3.   A detailed assessment of the costs of and incidental to this
         application of the Applicant and the Official Solicitor be carried
         out on the standard basis and the applicant is to pay the certified
         amounts thereof from the estate of XY [*insert P's initials*].

To: Messrs Sharp and Swift

The Official Solicitor

EXAMPLE OF A FORM OF STATUTORY WILL

THIS IS THE LAST WILL of me AB [*insert name of P*] of .... [*set out the address*] acting by CD the person authorised in that behalf by an Order dated the .... day of .... 2010 made under the Mental Health Act 2005.

I revoke all my former wills and codicils and declare this to by my last will.

1.   I appoint EF and GH to be executors and trustees o this my will.

2.   I give and bequeath .... [*set out the details*]

In witness of which this will be signed by me AB acting by CD under the order mention above on the .... [*insert date*]

SIGNED

By the said AB [*insert P's forenames and surname*] *by* CD [*insert forenames and surname of authorised person*] And by the said CD with his (or her) own name pursuant to the said order in our presence and attested by us in the presence of CD [*authorised person's name*]

AB [*P's forenames and surname*]

[*authorised person's forenames and surname*]

[*Name and Address of witnesses*]

Sealed with the official seal of the Court of Protection the .... day of .... 2010.

CHAPTER 11

ENFORCEMENT

LAW AND PRACTICE

11.1 BACKGROUND

It is a common misconception that the Court of Protection has an ongoing supervisory responsibility to investigate misuse and abuse of P's welfare, property and affairs. In fact the Court has no role in this respect beyond the reinforcement or enforcement of its own orders. If physical, emotional or financial abuse of those who lack capacity is suspected the most effective remedy is to report the matter to the police and to make a referral to the local social services authority for investigation under the Protection of Vulnerable Adults procedures.

However the Court is empowered to strengthen its orders by imposing restraints by way of freezing orders or injunctions and in the event of non-compliance may enforce in the last resort by committal for contempt.

The Court of Protection's powers to make restraining orders are very wide and not limited by any statutory provisions such as contained in the Family Law Act 1996 or under the Protection from Harassment Act 1997. The MCA 2005 s 47(1) provides that the Court of Protection has the 'same powers, rights, privileges and authority as the High Court'. The Court of Protection Rules 2007, rr 183–194 also make provisions for the application of the Civil Procedural Rules with appropriate modification to apply to the Court of Protection. PD 21A makes further supplementary provisions in relation to those rules. The court thus has all the powers available to the High Court and in particular relating to charging orders, freezing orders, stop orders and writ of fieri facias. The court may also enforce any non-compliance of its orders by way of a committal order provided that the order which has been breached was endorsed with a penal notice and was served personally or in such other manner directed by the Court.

11.2 PENAL NOTICE

Although the Court is empowered to direct that a penal notice be endorsed on an order such a notice is not automatically endorsed on mandatory or prohibitive injunction orders. The Court of Protection Rules 2007, r 192 provides that the Court may direct that a penal notice is to be endorsed to any order warning the person to whom the copy of the order is served that disobeying the order would be a contempt of court punishable by imprisonment or fine. Unless such a direction is given by the Court a penal notice may not be attached to any order.

In relation to restraint orders against family members concerning personal welfare issues of P, a penal notice would not normally be attached to such an order in the first instance as the Court's approach is to deal with such issues where possible by agreement and in a conciliatory manner. However in relation to issues concerning P's property and financial affairs such a direction may be necessary to protect and preserve P's assets, particularly if the order is directed to a third party or a deputy/attorney.

11.3   FREEZING ORDERS AND INJUNCTIONS

Where there has been actual or suspected financial irregularity with regard to the management of P's property and affairs resulting in the suspension or discharge of a deputy or attorney it may be necessary for orders to be made protecting P's assets or preventing debts being incurred.

Similarly protective orders may be required where the deputy or attorney are themselves unsuitable to continue to act or where those who have not been properly authorised with financial responsibility are misusing P's assets. Orders may also be appropriate to regulate P's own use of funds pending for instance a declaration regarding capacity.

Orders may be applied for in conjunction with applications to suspend or discharge a deputy or an attorney but may also be applied for as free standing applications.

In common with all other applications there must be evidence of P's incapacity or at the very least s 48 threshold must be met where orders are necessary without delay.

The courts powers are contained in ss 16 and 18.

Section 16 provides:

> '(1)   This section applies if a person (P) lacks capacity in relation to a matter or matters concerning
>   (a)   ...
>   (b)   P's property and affairs
> (2)   The court may
>   (a)   by making an order, make the decision or decisions on P's behalf in relation to the matter or matters.'

Section 18 provides:

> '(1) The powers under s 16 as respects P's property and affairs extend in particular to
> (a) the control and management of P's property.'

In making its decision the Court is obliged by virtue of s 16(3) to take account of the general principles established by the Act and to make any decision in P's best interests.

The court's powers are extended to empower it to make interim orders as a matter of urgency and in order to protect P and his property and affairs and where appropriate as a holding measure. The COP Rules 2007, r 82 empowers the Court to grant interim remedies by way of:

- An interim injunction;

- An interim declaration; or

- Any other interim order it considers appropriate.

Such orders may be made in pending proceedings or before an application has been issued.[1] An application for restraint orders may also be made without notice, (by telephone if necessary) and a hearing on notice will be directed to enable the person against whom the order is made to be heard and for the Court to consider the issues fully.[2]

Section 16(3):

> '(3) The powers of the Court under this section are subject to the provisions of this Act and, in particular to sections 1 (the principles) and 4 (best interests).'

Of particular importance in this area will be the empowerment of P to take decisions for himself and the recognition that the making of unwise decisions does not automatically render someone unable to make decisions for themselves.

Having established the need for the Court to make a decision it must be done taking account of the guidance in s 4 which has been set out in detail at Chapter 2. Section 4 only comes into play once it has been decided that P lacks capacity or the s 48 criteria are met. The court has to follow the steps which must be taken to determine what is in P's best interests as set out in the best interests checklist. The purpose is to identify those factors which are most relevant to the individual against the background of the decision the Court has to make. The check list is not exhaustive and

---

[1]   PD 10B.
[2]   PD 10B.

points to 'all relevant circumstances' being considered. So for instance in a high value money case where the Court needs to protect P's assets from misuse by a professional deputy, information may be needed from P's accountant or fund manager. By contrast in a case where P is of modest means the appropriate line of enquiry may be to seek views from a relative or care home. Moreover the Act recognises that it is not always possible to make all relevant enquiries which is particularly pertinent in an emergency where interim orders are to be made.

Section 4(3) qualifies the extent of investigation by defining relevant circumstances as those:

'(a)   of which the person making the determination is aware, and
(b)   which it would be reasonable to regard as relevant.'

Freezing orders place an embargo on dealings with assets whilst an injunction will restrict a person from so dealing. For example where there is misuse of funds from a particular bank account the Court may impose a freezing order in respect of any dealings. The order will take the form of a direction to the bank preventing all dealings with the account. On a practical point, caution needs to be exercised here. The court should avoid making an order which prevents proper payments to be made such as care home fees, especially in cases where there are limited funds paid into only one account. In these circumstances an injunction against named persons making withdrawals may be more effective in terms of managing P's finances. Injunctions are also more appropriate in the case of irregular land or share transactions and the Court can impose an injunction preventing a person signing a contract or transfer document on behalf of P. In a case where it is suspected that P is adversely influenced by a particular person an injunction may be termed so as to restrict their contact with P and in particular the giving of financial advice.

Injunctions are also a useful tool in managing P's welfare needs providing an effective way of regulating contact particularly in a climate of hostile family pressures. Nonetheless where injunctive remedies are sought in the context of domestic abuse, remedies under the Family Law Act 1996 are to be preferred. This is by reason of their more effective enforcement procedure, specifically the change in the law since 1 July 2007, by the Domestic Violence, Crime and Victims Act 2004, which amends the FLA 1996 to make a breach of a non-molestation order a criminal offence. Also in a case where an occupation order under s 33 of the FLA 1996 may be appropriate the Court when making such an order has a statutory power to attach a power of arrest not available to the Court of Protection

11.4   PROCEDURE

Applications for freezing orders and injunctions will usually be made in conjunction with a substantive application. In those circumstances the application should simply be included as one of the list of orders required so separate applications and permission applications are unnecessary. Where substantive proceedings have already been issued the application should be made on COP9.

For free standing orders the following applies:

11.4.1 Permission

Permission to make the application will be required unless it is made by:

(a) P;

(b) if P has not reached the age of 18 years, by anyone with parental responsibility for him/her;

(c) by the donor or a donee of a lasting power of attorney to which the application relates,

(d) by a deputy appointed by the Court;

(e) by a person named in an existing order of the Court if the application relates to the order;[3]

(f) by the Official Solicitor;[4]

(g) by the Public Guardian;[5]

(h) where the application concerns P's property and affairs, unless the application is of a kind specified in COP Rules, r 52 or a lasting power of attorney which is or purports to be created under the Act or an instrument which is or purports to be an enduring power of attorney.

11.4.2 How to apply

If permission is required the application for permission should be made in Form COP2 and filed with the substantive application in Form COP1. In addition the following accompanying forms should be filed namely Form COP1A (ie all the supporting information). Form COP3 to confirm that P lacks or continues to lack capacity should also be filed.

The Court fee of £400 will have to be paid when the application is issued.

---

3   MCA 2005, s 50.
4   COP Rules 2007, r 51(1)(a).
5   COP Rules 2007, r 51(1)(b).

11.4.3   Issue

Where permission is necessary the Court is required to deal with the application within 14 days. It may grant or refuse the application or list the application for a hearing and give directions including specifying who should be given notice of the hearing.[6] If a hearing is listed a person who is notified of the hearing should file an acknowledgement of service in Form COP5.

If permission is given the application will be issued by the Court. The applicant will receive from the Court Form COP5 (the acknowledgement of service), Form COP14 (the notice of proceedings to P) with the guidance notes in Form COP14A, notice in Form COP15 and guidance notes of the issue of the application and the certificate of service Form COP20.

In an emergency, the Court may also make immediate interim orders:[7]

- by dealing with the application before issue;

- by abridging time;

- by dispensing with service;

- by telephone;

- by making the order sought on the papers without notice and without a hearing.

In those circumstances the Court will fix a return date and give directions and a timetable for respondents to reply to the application.

11.4.4   Service

It is the duty of the applicant to:

- serve all the necessary documents and Forms on the respondents within 21 days;

- serve P with Forms COP14 and 14A and COP5;

- notify any other relevant person of the application in Forms COP 15 and COP 5;

- file the certificate of service within 7 days of service in Form COP20.

---

6   COP Rules 2007, rr 55, 56 and 89.
7   COP Rules 2007, r 82 and PD 10B.

11.4.5 The respondent/s to the application

Every respondent and any person who wishes to take part in the proceedings must file the acknowledgment of service within 21 days. The Court will then either give directions without a hearing or list the matter for a directions hearing. In urgent applications the Court will abridge the applicable time limits.[8]

11.4.6 Orders

The court has a wide ranging power to make protective/restraining orders to meet the circumstances of each individual case. For menus of orders see precedent in Chapter 3.

11.5 Committals

Applications for a committal order have been extremely rare in the Court of Protection, but that is not to imply that the remedy is ineffective or not to be considered as an appropriate means of ensuring compliance with orders made by the Court. Where a mandatory or prohibitive order made by the Court has not been complied with or has been disobeyed it can be enforced on an application made to a nominated judge of the Court of Protection. The court has the same powers of committal as any other civil court. The Court of Protection Rules 2007, rr 185–194 and the PD 21A specifically provide the procedure which must be followed.

Rule 192 empowers the Court to direct that a penal notice be attached to an order warning that the consequences of breach may result in imprisonment or a fine. The direction order is expressed as: '*You must obey this order. If you do not, you may be sent to prison for contempt of court*'. The application for a penal notice to be endorsed to an order must be made on Form COP9 with supporting evidence. If a mode of service other than personal service is required the application should seek a substituted order for service and set out the reasons for the same. It is also important to follow the correct procedure which applies to committals in every court.

Because proceedings for committal for contempt of court are quasi criminal in nature and concern the liberty of the subject the relevant rules must be complied with and the appropriate prescribed forms must be used unless the Court has otherwise directed. The CPR PD Committal, para 10 provides that any procedural defect in the commencement or conduct by the applicant of a committal application may be waived by the Court if satisfied that no injustice has been caused to the respondent by the defect. Lord Woolf in *Nicholls v Nicholls*[9] also stated that the requirements are

---

8 COP Rules 2007, r 26.
9 [1997] 1 FLR 649.

not 'mandatory, in the sense that any non-compliance with the rule means that a committal for contempt is irredeemably invalid'.

Lord Woolf also stated that:

(1)   As committal orders involve the liberty of the subject it is particularly important that the relevant rules are duly complied with. It remains the responsibility of the judge when signing the committal order to ensure that it is properly drawn and that it adequately particularises the breaches which have been proved and for which the sentence has been imposed.

(2)   As long as the contemnor has had a fair trial and the order has been made on valid grounds the existence of a defect whether in the application to commit or in the committal order served will not result in the order being set aside except insofar as the interests of justice require this to be done.

(3)   Interests of justice will not require an order to be set aside where there is no prejudice caused as the result of errors in the application to commit or in the order to commit. When necessary the order can be amended.

(4)   When considering whether to set aside an order, the Court should have regard to the interests of justice of any other party and the need to uphold the reputation of the justice system.

(5)   If there has been a procedural irregularity or some other defect in the conduct of the proceedings which has occasioned injustice, the Court will consider exercising its power to order a new trial unless there are circumstances which indicate that it would not be just to do so.

In a more recent as yet unreported case *S-C v H-C*[10] it was once again stressed by the Court of Appeal that the formalities of committal proceedings must be strictly observed. Where the order is unusual, where one of the parties is in person, and where one or more of the parties is not English and has little or no understanding of the English language it is extremely important for the formalities to be observed if it is sought to penalise the contemnor The order needs to be clear on its face as to precisely what it means, what it forbids and where the order requires a person to do something, the order should clearly state what it is that the person is required to do and the time frame within which what is required of him/her should be done. Where the order requires the person to abstain from doing an act the order must make it clear what the person is abstained from doing.

---

[10]   [2010] EWCA Civ 21.

11.5.1 Service of order to be enforced

Before an application for committal is made it is essential to ensure that a penal notice has been endorsed in an appropriate form on the order to be enforced and that the order with the penal notice endorsed on it has been served on the person against whom the committal order is sought. The court may direct some other form of service or in an appropriate case make an order dispensing with service but such an order must be made before a breach has occurred to make the breach enforceable through committal unless it is a restraining order and the Court is satisfied that the person concerned had knowledge of the terms of the order or that the terms of the order were brought to his attention for example by the person being present in court when the order was made.

Where the order requires the person to do an act (mandatory order) the order must give the person sufficient time to comply with the order and the order must be personally served on the person in reasonable time to enable the person to do the act within the time specified by the Court. The court may in an appropriate case or where the circumstances are exceptional direct for an alternative mode of service. (See *Couzens v Couzens*[11] where the sentence imposed was set aside because the Court form had not been served on the respondent.)

11.5.2 Use and content of prescribed forms and evidence in support

The Court of Protection Rules 2007, r 186 deals with applications for committal orders. The application must be made on Form COP9 and supported by an affidavit.[12] The application must set out the grounds on which the committal application is made. Form COP9, in section 2.2, specifically requires the applicant to set out the grounds for the application.[13] The form also, in section 2.3, requires the applicant to set out the grounds on which the committal order is sought. Thus the applicant is required to set out details of the order and the alleged breaches of its terms. The contents to be included in the affidavit are set out at PD 21A, paras 4, 5 and 6. Form COP 9, in section 2.3, states that if the Court requires the evidence to be given by affidavit the applicant needs to use the Form COP25 affidavit form. It is essential that the person against whom the committal order is sought is given sufficient details of the allegations.

---

[11] [2001] 2 FLR 701, CA.
[12] PD 21A, paras 2 and 3.
[13] See also *Harmsworth v Harmsworth* [1988] 1 FLR 349.

The content of the affidavit

The affidavit must contain:

(a)   the name and description of the person making the application;

(b)   the name address and description of the person sought to be committed;

(c)   the grounds on which committal is sought;

(d)   a description of each alleged act of contempt, identifying each act separately and numerically and if known, the date of each act; and

(e)   any additional information required by paras 5 and 6 of the PD;

(f)   if the allegation of contempt relates to prior proceedings the case number and date of those prior proceedings and the name of P;

(g)   the contents of any order, judgment or undertaking which it is alleged has been disobeyed or broken by the person sought to be committed, where the allegation of contempt is made on the grounds that:
  •   the person required by an order or judgment to do an act has refused or neglected to do it within the time fixed by the judgment or order or any subsequent order;
  •   a person has disobeyed a judgment or order requiring him to abstain from doing an act; or
  •   a person has breached the terms of an undertaking which he gave to the Court.

11.5.3   Service of the application for committal

Subject to the Court's power to dispense with service, the application, the affidavit in support and the notice of the date of the hearing of the application must be served personally on the person sought to be committed.[14] The court will only rely on the grounds set out in the application.

An order dispensing with service of the application for committal is exceptional. Dispensation of service may be granted where it is shown that the person concerned is deliberately evading service. Where a committal order is made without service on the person against whom the

---

[14]   COP Rules 2007, r 186(2).

order is made the order should provide that the person when arrested should be brought before the Court at the earliest opportunity after his/her arrest.[15]

11.5.4 Oral hearing

Rules 187 and 188 govern the hearing. The person sought to be committed is entitled to give oral evidence and must be given the opportunity to obtain legal representation. If he elects to give oral evidence he may be cross-examined.[16] The person to be committed must also be allowed to cross-examine the applicant and any witness called to give evidence on behalf of the applicant. PD 21A anticipates that the initial hearing may not proceed to determination and provides for directions to be granted for future disposal.

11.5.5 Burden and standard of proof

The burden of proof rests on the applicant to prove the allegations of contempt.

The standard of proof is that a breach must be proved beyond reasonable doubt and the breach must be wilful and deliberate.

11.5.6 Disposal of the committal application

The approach to be taken by the Court will vary in accordance with the background of the case. Where there is simple financial irregularity the approach will be in line with that taken in civil litigation generally. Where breaches are alleged in the context of complex and emotional welfare issues the Court's approach will be similar to that adopted in family cases. The overall aim is to achieve compliance and any punishment is likely to take into account the effect upon P, P's family and significant others.

Imprisonment will be considered in the most serious of cases. The court may make no order or adjourn the application if there is a likelihood of the order being complied with. It may impose a fine or suspend the committal order or consider other alternative options to achieve compliance with its order such as a writ of sequestration.[17]

11.5.7 Power of the Court to commit on its own initiative

The Court of Protection Rules 2007, r 194 empowers the Court to make an order for committal on its own initiative against a person who has disobeyed its order. Where a case is considering making an order in such

---

[15] *Lamb v Lamb* [1984] FLR 278.
[16] COP Rules 2007, r 186(10).
[17] See further *Hale v Tanner* [2000] 2 FLR 879.

circumstances it would be desirable to consider the following factors which were referred to by the Court of Appeal in *Re G (Contempt: Committal)*:[18]

- A committal order on the Court's own motion should only be made in exceptional circumstances.

- A committal order is a remedy of last resort to be made only in serious, or intentional or repeated contempts.

- In any event the person to be committed should be give an opportunity of an adjournment to enable him to seek advice and to be represented and to be informed of the acts which constitute the contempt.

- Committal proceedings should be held in public.

### 11.5.8	Discharge of person committed

A person who has been committed to prison for disobedience of an order of the Court should be given an opportunity to purge his contempt. Where a person has been committed for failing to comply with an order requiring him to deliver anything to some other person or to deposit it in court or elsewhere, and a writ of sequestration has also been issued to enforce that judgment or order, then if the thing is in the custody or power of the person committed, the commissioners appointed by the writ of sequestration may take possession of it as if it were the property of that person, and without prejudice to any application made by the contemnor to purge his contempt the Court may discharge him/her and may give such directions for dealing with the thing taken away by the commissioners as it thinks just.[19]

### 11.5.9	Form of committal order

There is no provision in the Court of Protection Rules or the Practice Direction for a committal form. Rule 188 provides that when making the committal order the Court must publicly identify the person committed and state in general terms the nature of the contempt in respect of which the order is made and the punishment imposed. It is submitted that the order should be drawn in the terms of Form N79 which is used in the county court (Form A85 is used in the High Court). A copy of Form N79 is provided under Precedent for guidance; Forms N78 (notice of an application to commit) and N80 (warrant for committal to prison) are also provided.

---

[18]	[2003] 2 FLR 58.
[19]	COP Rules, r 191.

11.6 PROCEDURAL GUIDE

Before the Application is issued	Obtain proof of service of the order endorsed with penal notice before the breach occurred	
Application	Form COP9 (must identify the provisions in the order alleged to have been breached and set out the ways in which it has been breached.)	
Affidavit in support with proof of service of the order	(1) Must identify the parties	PD 21A(4)-(6)
	(2) Must state the grounds, describe each act separately (with dates) and numerically	
	(3) Where appropriate give details of previous proceedings	
	(4) Set out in full details of the order allegedly breached	
Court Office	Fixes date of hearing and issues notice of hearing	PD 21A(7)
Service of application	Applicant must serve COP9, affidavit in Support and notice of hearing on the Contemnor unless otherwise directed	COP Rules 2007, r186(2)
Hearing	In open court	COP Rules 2007, r 188(3)
Orders	Committal order	COP Rules 2007, r 188
	Suspended committal order	COP Rules 2007, r 189
	Fine	COP Rules 2007, r 193
	Writ of sequestration	
	Provide security for good behaviour	
	No order	

PRECEDENT

EXAMPLES OF THE TERMS OF INJUCTIVE RELIEF
THAT MAY BE GRANTED

The Respondent/s .... [*insert name*] is/are forbidden whether by himself/herself themselves or by instructing, encouraging or suggesting to another person to do so.

(a)   To remove or attempt to remove JS from the .... Home/Hospital [*as the case may be*] or any other suitable hospital where JS may from time to time reside/or be admitted.

(b)   To remove or attempt to remove JS from the jurisdiction of this Court/England and Wales.

(c)   To obstruct or attempt to obstruct treatment and care while at the .... Hospital or any other suitable hospital where JS may from time to time reside.

(d)   To give or attempt to give any food or drink to JS other than that specified and agreed with the staff at the .... Hospital.

(e)   To administer or attempt to administer any medication to JS.

(f)   To interfere with the arrangements made by the Applicant for the care of JS at the Paradise Care Home or any hospital to which JS may be admitted.

(g)   To do or say anything calculated to interfere with the current or any future residence/placement of JS.

(h)   To enter or attempt to enter the Paradise Care Home or any hospital to which JS is admitted without the prior written agreement of the Applicant's social services department.

(i)   To see JS at the Paradise Care Home or any hospital to which JS is admitted.

(j)   To telephone the Paradise Care Home or any hospital to which JS may be admitted except at times set out in the schedule of contact attached to this order or times agreed in advance with the Applicant's Social Services Department.

(k)   To bring any food or drink for JS when he/she/they visit JS except with the permission of the Manager of the Paradise Care Home.

(l)   To remove any item from JS's room without prior agreement of the Manager or the Paradise Care Home.

(m)   To use or threaten violence or behave in an abusive or aggressive manner towards the staff at the Paradise Care Home/or any employee of the Applicant/or a deputy appointed by the Court.

(n)   To interfere in any manner whatsoever when the Applicant/social worker/etc has access to JS to assess him/her, speak with him/her or interview him/her.

(o)   To discuss these proceedings with JS.

(p)   To do any act calculated to interfere with JS's co-operation with any member of the HCC's employee or with the independent social worker or experts instructed in the proceedings.

(q)   To do any act which puts at risk the current care arrangements made for JS.

Orders relating to access to JS

The Second Respondent .... [*or as the case may be*] must allow a social worker of the HCC and the Team manager into the property at .... and to have access to JS alone to see and speak with him/her

Orders relating to passports

Immediately on receipt of this order or its terms being brought to his/her attention the Second Respondent [*or as the case may be and insert name of the person*] do hand over to .... the Team Manager JS's passport. Upon receipt of the passport .... the Team Manager shall hand over the same to the legal department of the HCC who will in turn ensure that the passport is delivered to the Official Solicitor for safe keeping until further order of the Court

FORMS

FORM 78

Notice to Show Good Reason why an Order for Your Committal to Prison should not be made

In the	
	County Court
Case No. *Always quote this*	

Between   Applicant

and   Respondent

To

of

On the   the Court made an order [*or* you gave an undertaking] as follows:

has applied for an order that you should be committed to prison. It is alleged that you have disobeyed the order [*or* broken the undertaking] by:

You must attend Court

at

on   at   o'clock to show good reason why you should not be sent to prison.

- If the Court is satisfied that any of the allegations are true, it may order that you be imprisoned for your contempt of this Court.
- **Important instructions about what you should do are set out overleaf.**

The applicant (Solicitor)
Name
Address

Ref

Tel

The court office at

is open between 10 am and 4 pm Monday to Friday. When corresponding with the court, please address forms or letters to the Court Manager and quote the claim number. Tel: Fax:

N78 Notice of an application to commit

Case No.

Important notes

- The Court has the power to send you to prison if it finds that any of the allegations made against you are true. Full details of the allegations are contained in the applicant's sworn statement (the affidavit).

- You must attend court on the date shown on the front of this form. It is in your own interest to do so. At the hearing, the person making this application will tell the Court why they believe you should be sent to prison. You will then have the opportunity to put your case. You should bring any witnesses and documents with you which you think will help you put your side of the case.

- If you need advice you should show this document at once to your solicitor or go to a Citizens' Advice Bureau. If you do not already have a solicitor acting for you the Court can give details of local solicitors. You may be entitled to help towards the cost of legal advice.

- Even if you do not seek advice, you can, if you wish, file a sworn statement at the Court setting out your side of the case. The Court Office can give you a form for this purpose and it can be sworn before a Court Officer. If you have disobeyed the order you can apologise for it on this form. You must still attend court on the date shown, however.

For Court use only

I certify that the notice, of which this is a true copy, was served by me on

(date)...

on   personally.

at the address stated in the notice, or at

Or *in accordance with an order for substituted service.*

Bailiff/Officer of the Court

Notice of Non – Service

I certify that this notice has not been served for the following reasons:

Bailiff/Officer of the Court

The court office at

is open between 10 am and 4 pm Monday to Friday. When corresponding with the court, please address forms or letters to the Court Manager and quote the claim number. Tel: Fax:

N78 Notice of an application to commit

FORM 79

Committal or Other Order upon Proof of Disobedience of a Court Order or Breach of an Undertaking

In the	
	County Court
Applicant Claimant Petitioner	

Between_____

Claim No. *Always quote this* _____

and _____ Respondent Defendant

Before His (Her) Honour Judge

Sitting at   on *(date)*

(seal)

1 **An application having been made by**[1]   for committal of[2]   to prison
   for disobeying the order [breach of the undertaking] dated   .The relevant terms of the order (undertaking)
   and the allegations made by the applicant are recited on the attached notice to show good reason.

   or

2 **Whereas**[2]   has been suspected of a breach of the attached order
   dated   and has been arrested by a constable and brought before the Judge under
   section 47(6) of the Family Law Act 1996.

   or

3 **Whereas**[2]   has been suspected of a breach of the attached order
   [undertaking] dated   and has been arrested under a warrant of arrest and brought before the Judge
   under [section 47(8) of the Family Law Act 1996] [section 3(3) of the Protection from Harassment Act 1997].

_____ IMMEDIATE CUSTODIAL ORDER _____

It is ordered that[2]   be committed for contempt to Her Majesty's Prison
(be detained under section 9(1) of the Criminal Justice Act 1982) at[3]   for a
(total) period of[4]   or until lawfully discharged if sooner, and that a warrant of arrest and
committal be issued forthwith.

And the contemnor can apply to the (court) (judge) to purge his contempt and ask for release.

[**And**, as the court by order dated   dispensed with service of the notice of application for a committal order,
It is ordered that the contemnor be brought before a judge of this court as soon as practicable.]

_____ ALTERNATIVE DISPOSAL _____

It is ordered that[2]   be committed for contempt to prison for a (total) period
of[4]

The order is suspended until   **20**   and will not be put in force if during that time the
contemnor[2]   complies with the following terms:

And it is further ordered that in the event of non compliance any application for issue of the warrant shall be made to a
judge (on notice to the contemnor)

It is ordered that[2]   be fined the sum of £   .
Such sum to be paid into the office of the court within 14 days of the date of this order.

It is ordered that consideration of the penalty for the contempts found proved be adjourned until   20
and may be restored for decision if during that time[2]   does not
comply with the following terms

_____ PROVISION FOR COSTS _____

And it is ordered that

Date

For record of service, hearing and contempts found proved, see next page

RECORD OF SERVICE, HEARING AND CONTEMPTS FOUND PROVED

At the hearing

(1)   [appeared personally] [was represented by solicitor/counsel] [did not attend]

(2)   [appeared personally] [was represented by solicitor/counsel] [did not attend]

The court read the affidavits of (Names)	Date affidavit(s) sworn

And the court heard oral evidence given by
Name(s)

And the court is satisfied having considered the facts disclosed by the evidence and/or admitted in court by him/her that(2)   has been guilty of contempt of this court by disobeying the order (breaking the undertaking) dated   by (and as set out in the attached schedule)

And for the particular contempt the court imposed the penalty of:

1.   1.

2.   2.

——————————— **RECORD OF SERVICE** ———————————

Service of Injunction Order with Penal Notice incorporated or indorsed	**Service of Notice to show good reason in form N78**	**Arrest under warrant of arrest**
(Order dated 20	(Order dated 20	Respondent arrested on
(for substituted) (dispensing with) service)	(for substituted) (dispensing with) service)	
Service proved by	Service proved by	by

☐ certificate of service
    dated   20
	☐ certificate of service
	    dated 20
		in accordance with a warrant of arrest issued on

☐ certificate of bailiff	☐ certificate of bailiff	
☐ oral evidence of	☐ oral evidence of	

Service of Immediate Custodial Order

I *(name of Officer)*   certify that I served the contemnor with a copy of this order by:

☐ delivery by hand to the contemnor before he was taken from the court building or other place of arrest to the place of detention

☐ delivery by hand to the contemnor at *(time)*   on *(date)*   20   at *(place)*

Where a suspended committal order is made, the applicant is responsible for service. (Rules of the Supreme Court Order 52 rule 7(2).)
Where there is suspended committal order or penalty is adjourned on terms, personal service is advisable.

The court office is open from 10 am to 4 pm Monday to Friday.

When corresponding with the court, please address forms and letters to the Court Manager and quote the case number.

Notes for completion of page 2
(RECORD OF SERVICE, HEARING AND CONTEMPTS FOUND PROVED)

—— **REPRESENTATION (At the hearing)** ——

Name the parties or their legal representative (advocate only).

—— **AFFIDAVIT EVIDENCE (The court read** the affidavits) ——

List only those affidavits which the judge has considered at the hearing. There is unlikely to be any affidavit evidence offered where the respondent has been brought to court under a power of arrest.

—— **ORAL EVIDENCE (And the court heard** oral evidence) ——

Give the names of only those witnesses sworn and examined.

—— **CONTEMPTS FOUND PROVED (And the court is satisfied)** ——

List and give exact details of only those allegations of contempt which the judge has found proved.

If separate penalties are imposed for each contempt found proved these are to be recorded in the right-hand column showing whether or not periods of detention are to run consecutively or concurrently.

If necessary, annex additional page and continue list on it. If an additional page is not used, delete the words *(and as set out in the attached schedule)*.

—— **JUDGE'S APPROVAL** ——

The Judge must be asked to initial the order indicated by the dotted line.

—— **RECORD OF SERVICE** ——

Enter details of certificates of service.

Record of delivery of an undertaking need not be made on this document as it can be found on the form of undertaking.

A sealed copy of the approved order must be served on the contemnor.

Order 29 rule 1(5) CCR states:

If a committal order is made, the order shall be for the issue of a warrant of committal and unless the judge otherwise orders:-

(a) a copy of the order shall be served on the person to be committed either before or at the time of the execution of the warrant; or

(b) where the warrant has been signed by the Judge, the order for issue of the warrant may be served on the person to be committed at any time within 36 hours after execution of the warrant.

Where the respondent is brought before the court under a power of arrest delete record of service of form N78.

Where the respondent is brought before the court under a warrant of arrest delete record of service of form N78 and complete record of service of warrant of arrest.

Terms or names that may be used more than once in the order are numbered in brackets as follows:

(1) Person making application for committal

(2) Person against whom the committal order is made (contemnor)

(3) Name of prison or young offender institution

(4) Period of detention

Notes for Guidance on completion of form N79
(Disobedience of a Court Order or Breach of an Undertaking)

The Court Officer responsible for the forms completion should note the following:

• **Where the respondent is brought before the court after being arrested under a power of arrest** (Section 47(6) of the Family Law Act 1996) a sealed copy of the injunction order giving the power of arrest (not Power of Arrest form FL406) with penal notice indorsed becomes part of form N79 and must be attached to the approved order.

• **Where the respondent is brought before the court after being arrested under a warrant of arrest** (section 47(8) of the Family Law Act 1996) (section 3(3) of the Protection from Harassment Act 1997) a sealed copy of the injunction order becomes part of form N79 and must be attached to the approved order.

• **In all other cases** Form N78 (notice to show good reason why an order for committal should not be made) becomes part of form N79 and a sealed copy of N78 must be attached to the approved order.

• In all cases the warrant is in form N80.

• **When the form has been fully completed it must be passed to the judge for approval.** If the judge is available he/she should be asked to approve and initial or sign the final (typed) version. If this is not possible the judge must be asked to initial or sign the final hand-written draft. In either case the document endorsed by the judge **must be retained on the court file.**

• Before the order is served it must also be checked by an officer of no less than HEO grade.

• Before the order is served these notes should be detached, they are for the guidance of Court Staff only.

When an immediate custodial order is made:

• A copy of N79 (with attached N78 or injunction) must be sent to the Office of the Official Solicitor.

• A sealed copy of the approved order must be served on the contemnor. Order 29 rule 1(5) CCR.

Notes for completion of page 1

Terms or names that may be used more than once in the order are numbered in brackets as follows:

(1) Person making application for committal

(2) Person against whom the committal order is made (contemnor)

(3) Name of prison or young offender institution

(4) Period of detention

—— CLAUSES 1 TO 3 ——————————————————————————

If the respondent has been brought before the court under a power of arrest (Family Law Act 1996) delete 1 and 3.

If the respondent has been brought before the court under a warrant of arrest (Family Law Act 1996 or Protection from Harassment Act 1997) delete 1 and 2.

In all other cases delete 2 and 3.

Enter the date of order (with penal notice incorporated or indorsed) or undertaking.

Date of form N78 Notice to show good reason (applies to 1 only).

Date of the warrant of arrest (applies to 3 only).

Note: A warrant of arrest cannot be issued on an undertaking under the Protection from Harassment Act 1997.

—— IMMEDIATE CUSTODIAL ORDER ——————————————————————

Complete this section if an immediate custodial order is made otherwise delete and complete section below

Section 9(1) of CJA is for persons aged less than 21 and at least 18.

The total period of detention must be specified by the Judge. The maximum period for contempt of court (including a county court) is 2 years.

If the offence is failure to do a specific act and the judge decides that the application may be made to a district judge upon proof that the act has been done delete (judge) otherwise delete (court).

Complete only if order dispensing with service of notice of application was granted otherwise delete.

—— ALTERNATIVE DISPOSAL ——————————————————————

Delete this section if an immediate custodial order is made otherwise delete alternatives not selected by judge.

Enter the exact terms of any suspended committal order or adjournment of penalty.

There are further possible alternative disposals, eg under sections 35, 37 and 38 of the Mental Health Act and sequestration.

—— COSTS ——————————————————————————————

Enter any order for costs here or show that no order for costs has been made if applicable.

Give the date of the order.

FORM 80

Warrant of Committal to prison

In the	
	County Court
Claim No.	
Warrant No.	

Between

_____ **Applicant**
Petitioner

and

_____ **Respondent**
Defendant

(Seal)

To   ●   **the District Judge and Bailiffs of the Court**

     ●   **every constable within his jurisdiction**

(1) Name of Prison   ●   **the Governor (of Her Majesty's Prison at)**[(1)]

(2) Name and
(3) address of
person to be
committed.

On the   **day of**   [19][20]   ,
(enter name of judge) has ordered that [(2)]

of [(3)]

(4) Where the
person to
be committed is
aged less than
21 years and
at least 18 delete
all references
to prison
otherwise
delete
reference to
Sec 9(1)CJA

should be committed to Prison [(4)] (detained under Section 9(1) Criminal Justice Act 1982) for
a period of [(5)]

You the District Judge and Bailiff are therefore required forthwith to arrest and deliver
[(2)]

to (Her Majesty's Prison at) [(1)]

(5) State term of
imprisonment

And you, the Governor, are required to receive and keep [(2)]
safely (in prison) from the arrest under this warrant for a period of [(5)]   or until
lawfully discharged, if sooner.

(6) Add if so
ordered
otherwise
delete

[[(6)] **And**, as the court by order dated   dispensed with service of the notice of
application for a committal order,
It is ordered that you, the Governor, bring [(2)]
before a judge of this court at such time and place as the court shall specify and afterwards,
return him to the prison unless the court orders his discharge.]

Date

I arrested the person named in this warrant on (date)
and delivered him into the custody of the Governor (of Her Majesty's Prison) at [(1)]
on *(date)*

                                               Bailiff of the County Court

The Court Office is open from 10am to 4pm Monday to Friday

Address all communications to the Court Manager and quote the above claim number.

N80 Warrant for committal to prison (4.99)   *Printed on behalf of The Court Service*

CHAPTER 12

APPEALS

LAW AND PRACTICE

12.1 INTRODUCTION

The provisions relating to appeals are set out in s 53 of the Act. Subsection (1) states that an appeal lies to the Court of Appeal from any decision of the Court but subsection (2) states that the Court of Protection Rules may provide that where a decision of the Court is made by a person exercising the jurisdiction of the Court by virtue of rules made under s 51(2)(d) (ie an officer of the Court) or a district or a circuit judge, an appeal from that decision lies to a prescribed higher judge of the Court and not to the Court of Appeal.

'Higher judge of the Court' is defined as follows; in relation to an officer, a circuit judge or a district judge; in relation to a district judge, a circuit judge, or a nominated judge.

The COP Rules, Part 20 make provisions relating to whether permission to appeal is required and if required to whom the application should be made and the grounds on which such application can be made and the consideration to be taken into account in relation to granting or refusing permission to appeal.

12.2 AVENUES OF APPEAL

Appeals from a district judge lie to a circuit judge.

Appeals from a decision of a judge which was itself made on appeal (ie second appeal) will be to the Court of Appeal.[1]

Appeals from a circuit judge lies to a High Court Judge nominated to sit in the Court of Protection.

Appeals from the President, Vice Chancellor or a High Court Judge, lie to the Court of Appeal.

---

[1]   COP Rules 2007, r 182.

12.3   GROUNDS FOR ALLOWING AN APPEAL

The appeal court will allow an appeal where the decision of the first
instance court was:

(a)   wrong; or

(b)   unjust, because of a serious or procedural or other irregularity in the
      proceedings before the fist instance judge.[2]

The decision below was 'wrong'

It will be for the appellant to establish, particularly if an interim remedy is
sought pending the full appeal, that there is merit in the appeal. It may
therefore be helpful to refer to decisions in the civil jurisdiction on what is
meant by 'wrong'.

The term 'wrong' in this context implies that the Court at first instance
erred: (i) in law; or (ii) on its assessment of the facts; or (iii) in the exercise
of its discretion but the basis on which an appeal is most likely to be
allowed is that the decision of the Court was wrong in law. The appeal is
not a rehearing but only a review and the appeal court's review of the
facts will be a cautious one because the judge at first instance heard the
evidence and had the advantage of assessing the demeanour of the
witnesses and their credibility. Baroness Hale in *Re J (Child Returned
Abroad: Convention Rights)*[3] at para 12 said that in the exercise of a
discretion in which various factors were relevant, the evaluation and
balancing of those factors was a matter for the trial judge. Only if his
decision was so plainly wrong that he must have given far too much
weight to a particular factor was the appellate court entitled to interfere.
If trial judges were led to believe that, even if they directed themselves
impeccably on the law, make findings of fact which were open to them on
the evidence and were careful in their evaluation and weighing of the
relevant factors, their decisions were liable to be overturned unless they
reached a particular conclusion, they will come to believe that they do not
in fact have any choice or discretion in the matter.

Similar observations were made by Lord Hoffman in *Piglowski v
Piglowski*[4] that an appellate court had to be very cautious in giving leave
and in granting appeals. The appellate court had to bear in mind that the
first instance judge had the advantage of seeing the parties and the other
witnesses. This is well understood on questions of credibility and findings
of primary facts including the evaluation of those facts. Given the
exigencies of daily courtroom life the reasons for judgment ought to be

---

2   PD 20A, para 179(3).
3   [2005] 2 FLR 802.
4   [1999] 2 FLR 763.

read on the assumption that unless the judge had demonstrated the contrary he knew how he should perform his functions and which matter he should take into account.[5]

As in cases involving children, the decision made in cases involving persons who lack capacity will be very much dependent on the factual evidence before the Court and the evaluation of that evidence. Where the decision involves the exercise of discretion unless it can be shown that the 'judge has either erred in principle in his approach or has left out of account or has taken into account some feature that he should, or should not, have considered' which throws doubt on the analysis and the basis of the decision it is unlikely that the appeal court will interfere with the decision.[6]) Butler Sloss LJ in *Re M and R (Child abuse: Evidence)*[7] succinctly put it:

> 'It is the function of the appellate court to make sure that the judge has correctly directed himself to and applied the correct law, has properly approached his task in deciding disputed facts and has not erred in principle. The appellate court then has to stand back and consider whether his decision is plainly wrong. If it is not, it is not for the appellate court to intervene.'

Guidance on the approach which the appellate court should adopt where errors of fact is alleged was given in *Assicurazioni Generali Spa v Arab Insurance Group*[8] at [6]-[23] by Clarke LJ and at [193]-[197] by Ward LJ but in such cases much will depend on the circumstances of the case and the nature of challenge made against the decision of the judge at first instance. However, the appellate court cannot substitute its own assessment of the evidence for that made by the trial judge.[9]

In relation to the issue of serious procedural or other irregularity the challenge raised must show that the irregularity was a serious one and it must have led to injustice.[10] The issues are likely to relate to the conduct of the proceedings and in particular to issues concerning the Art 6 rights eg refusal to allow a party to call a witness or adduce evidence, or to be heard, and whether the judge at first instance had taken into account matters which were irrelevant or ignored matters which were relevant or arrived at a conclusion which was plainly wrong (see *Breeze v Ahmed*[11] where the Court of Appeal allowed an appeal because the effect of two technical documents had been misrepresented to the Court).

---

[5]   See also *Assicurazioni Generali Spa v Arab Insurance Group* [2002] EWCA Civ 1642, [2003] 1 WLR 577.
[6]   *AEI Rediffusion Music Ltd v Phonographic Performance Ltd* [1999] 1 WLR 1507.
[7]   [1996] 2 FLR 195.
[8]   [2002] EWCA Civ 1642.
[9]   See *Designers Guild Ltd v Russell Williams (Textiles) Ltd* [2000] 1 WLR 2416, HL.
[10] See *Storer v British Gas Plc* [2000] 1 WLR 1237.
[11] [2005] EWCA Civ 192.

A review by the appeal court will necessarily involve the Court going through the process before the judge at first instance to determine whether or not there was any error in the steps undertaken before him or in the analysis of the evidence.

In relation to error in the exercise of discretion *G v G (Minors: Custody Appeal)*[12] Lord Fraser summarised the principles which the Court will apply as follows:

> '... the appellate court should only interfere when they consider that the judge of first instance has not merely preferred an imperfect solution which is different from an alternative imperfect solution which the Court of Appeal might or would have adopted, but has exceeded the generous ambit within which a reasonable disagreement is possible.'[13]

Before embarking on an appeal, and in particular seeking any interim relief, the grounds of the appeal will need to identify precisely how it is alleged that the judge at first instance was 'wrong' in matters of law or matters of fact or the exercise of his discretion.

12.4   PERMISSION TO APPEAL

Save in the case of an appeal against an order for committal to prison permission to appeal is required against any decision of the Court. The application for permission may be made to the trial judge or the appeal judge. Where an application for permission is refused by the trial judge a further application may be made as follows:

- Where the decision sought to be appealed is a decision of a district judge permission may be granted or refused by the President, the Vice President, a puisne judge of the High Court or a circuit judge.[14]

- Where the decision sought to be appealed is a decision of a circuit judge permission may be granted or refused by the President, Vice President or a puisne judge of the High Court.

- Where the appeal is from a decision of a judge which was itself made on appeal from a judge of the Court, permission will be required from the Court of Appeal.[15]

---

12   [1985] FLR 894.
13   Followed in *Tanfern Ltd v Cameron MacDonald* [2000] 1 WLR and see *AEI Rediffusion Music Ltd v Phonographic Performance Ltd* above and *Price v Price (t/a Popyland Headware)* [2003] EWCA Civ 888.
14   COP Rules 2007, r 172.
15   COP Rules 2007, r 182(2).

12.5 MATTERS TO BE TAKEN INTO CONSIDERATION WHEN CONSIDERING AN APPLICATION FOR PERMISSION

Permission to appeal will only be granted where:

(a) the Court considers that the appeal would have a real prospect of success; or

(b) there is some other compelling reason why the appeal should be heard[16] eg serious medical treatment involving life sustaining or withdrawal of treatment.

Where the application for permission is in relation to a second appeal and which must be made to the Court of Appeal, the Court of Appeal will not give permission unless it considers that:

(a) the appeal would raise an important point of principle or practice; or

(b) there is some other compelling reason for the Court of appeal to hear it.[17]

12.6 APPELLANT'S NOTICE

Where permission to appeal is being sought from the appeal court, it must be requested in the appellant's notice in Form COP35. The notice, with a copy for the Court, must be filed within such period as directed or specified in the order of the trial judge or where no such direction is given within 21 days after the date of the decision being appealed.[18]

The appellant must serve a sealed copy of the Appeal Notice on each respondent and such other person as the Court directs as soon as practicable and in any event within 21 days of the date on which it is issued. Where permission to appeal has been granted by the trial judge the appellant must also serve a skeleton argument on each respondent.[19] Once service is effected the appellant must file a certificate of service in Form COP20 within 7 days of service.[20]

---

[16] COP Rules 2007, r 173.
[17] COP Rules 2007, r 182(3).
[18] COP Rules 2007, r 175.
[19] PD 20A, para 4.
[20] PD 20A, para 7.

Where the appellant seeks a remedy incidental to the appeal eg an interim remedy under r 82 the appellant may include this application in the appellant's notice or in an application notice in Form COP9 and must attach this to the appellant's notice.

12.7   EXTENSION OF TIME

Where the time for filing the appellant's notice has expired an application for an extension of time may be made to the appeal judge by filing the appellant's notice in Form COP35 and include an application for an extension of time. The appellant's notice should include the reasons for the delay and any steps that have been taken prior to the application being made. The respondent has a right to be heard on an application for an extension of time.[21]

12.8   DOCUMENTS TO BE FILED WITH THE APPELLANT'S NOTICE

(a)   Skeleton Arguments

The appellant's notice must be accompanied by a skeleton argument using or attached to, a skeleton argument in Form COP37. Where the appellant is unable to provide a skeleton argument with the appellant's notice it must be filed and served on each respondent within 21 days of filing of the notice.[22]

The skeleton must contain a concise and numbered list of points which the party wishes to make. These should define and confine the areas of controversy. Each numbered point must also identify the document on which the appellant relies.

If a legal authority is cited the skeleton argument must state the proposition of law that the authority demonstrates and the parts of the authority (identified by page or paragraph references) that support the proposition. If more than one authority is relied upon the skeleton argument must state the reasons, the relevance of the authority or authorities to the argument and that the citation is necessary for the proper presentation of that argument.

(b)   Suitable record of the judgment

Where the judgment was recorded an approved transcript should accompany the appellant's notice. If there is no officially recorded judgment, but the Court handed down a written judgment, the Court will accept a written copy of the judgment endorsed with the judge's signature. If the judgment was not recorded or given in writing an agreed note of the judgment should be submitted for approval to the trial judge. If agreement cannot be reached, both parties should submit their respective note to the trial judge. Where

---

[21]   PD 20A, para 8.
[22]   PD 20A, paras 16 and 17.

permission to appeal is sought the note need not be approved by the respondent or the trial judge for approval.[23] Where the appellant was not represented but the respondent was, it is the duty of the respondent's advocate to make a note of the judgment and provide a copy to the appellant without charge if the judgment was not recorded or handed down in writing.

If permission to appeal is granted a transcript of the evidence should be obtained if the evidence was recorded. If not, a typed version of the judge's note should be obtained. Where the appellant's financial circumstances are such that the cost of the transcript would cause an excessive burden on him, the Court may direct that the transcript be obtained at public expense provided it is satisfied that there are reasonable grounds for appeal.[24]

(c)   A sealed copy of the order being appealed.

(d)   A copy of any order giving or refusing permission to appeal together with a copy of the judge's reasons for allowing or refusing permission to appeal.

(e)   Any witness statements or affidavits in support of any application included in the appellant's notice.

(f)   The application form and any application notice or response (where relevant to the subject of the appeal).

(g)   Any other documents which the appellant reasonably considers necessary to enable the Court to reach its decision on the hearing of the application or appeal.

(h)   Such other documents as the Court may direct.[25]

(i)   A list of persons who feature in the case, a glossary of technical terms and a chronology of relevant events should also be filed.

If it is not possible to file all the above documents with the appellant's notice, the appellant should identify which documents have not been filed and the reasons for the same and the time estimate within which the missing documents can be filed. The appellant must file the missing documents as soon as reasonably practicable.

---

[23]   PD 20A, para 24.
[24]   PD 20A, paras 26–29.
[25]   PD 20A, para 11.

12.9   RESPONDENT'S NOTICE

A respondent who wishes to cross appeal must seek permission to do so in accordance with r 172 (see above). If the respondent wishes to appeal or wishes to ask the appeal judge to uphold the order for reasons different from or additional to those given by the trial judge the respondent must file a respondent's notice. If he fails to do so he will not be entitled to rely on any reasons for upholding the decision unless the appeal court gives him permission.

The respondent who seeks permission to appeal or wishes to ask the appeal court to uphold the decision of the trial judge for reasons different from or additional to those given by the trial judge must file his notice in Form COP36 with his skeleton arguments in Form COP37 within the time specified by the trial judge or in any event within 21 days beginning with the date which is the soonest of:

(a)   the date on which the respondent is served with the appellant's notice where permission to appeal was given by the trial judge or permission to appeal is not required;

(b)   the date on which the respondent is served with notification that the appeal judge has given the appellant permission to appeal; or

(c)   the date on which the respondent is served with the notification that the application for permission to appeal and the appeal itself are to be heard together.

12.10   DOCUMENTS TO BE FILED WITH THE RESPONDENT'S NOTICE

The respondent to the appeal must file the following documents:

(a)   a copy of his skeleton argument which must conform to the requirement set out under **12.8**(a);

(b)   a sealed copy of the order being appealed;

(c)   a copy of any order giving or refusing permission to appeal together with a copy of the judge's reasons for allowing or refusing permission to appeal;

(d)   any witness statements or affidavits in support of any application included in the appellant's notice;

(e) any other documents which the respondent reasonably considers necessary to enable the Court to reach its decision on the hearing of the application or appeal;

(f) such other documents as the Court may direct;[26]

(g) a list of persons who feature in the case, a glossary of technical terms and a chronology of relevant events should also be filed.

The respondent's notice and the accompanying documents must be served on the appellant and any other respondent.[27]

12.11 SERVICE

The respondent must serve the respondent's notice on the appellant and any other respondent and on such other parties as the Court may direct, as soon as practicable and in any event within 21 days of the date on which it is issued unless the Court directs otherwise. Within 7 days of service of the respondent's notice the respondent must file a certificate of service in Form COP20.

12.12 POWER OF THE APPEAL JUDGE ON APPEAL

The appeal judge has all the powers of the trial judge whose decision is being appealed and may exercise his powers in relation to the whole or part of an order made by the trial judge. The appeal judge also has the power to:

• affirm, set aside or vary any order made by the trial judge;

• refer any claim or issue to that judge for determination;

• order a new hearing;

• make an order for costs.

12.13 DETERMINATION OF APPEALS

• An appeal is limited to a review of the decision of the trial judge unless the appeal judge considers that in the circumstances of the appeal it would be in the interest of justice to hold a re-hearing.

---

26 PD 20A, para 40.
27 PD 20A, para 43.

- The appeal judge will not receive any oral evidence or evidence which was not before the trial judge unless the Court otherwise directs.

- The appeal will only be allowed if the appeal judge considers that the decision at first instance was wrong; or unjust because of a serious procedural or other irregularity in the proceedings before the trial judge.

- The appeal judge will not allow a party to rely on a matter not contained in the appellant's or respondent's notice unless the appeal judge gives permission.

These powers are similar to those that apply in civil proceedings to which the Civil Procedure Rules 1998 apply and the grounds on which the appeal court may allow the appeal are identical to those set out in CPR 1998, r 52.11(3). This provides a uniform approach across appeals from all jurisdictions and to all appeal courts.

PART IV

FORMS

COURT OF PROTECTION FORMS

LASTING POWERS OF ATTORNEY FORMS

ENDURING POWERS OF ATTORNEY FORMS

DEPRIVATION OF LIBERTY FORMS

COURT OF PROTECTION FORMS

COP 1
03.10

Court of Protection

Application form

For office use only
Date received
Case no.
Date issued

Full name of person to whom the application relates
(this is the name of the person who lacks, or is alleged to lack, capacity)

SEAL

Please read first

- If you wish to apply to start proceedings in the Court of Protection you must complete this form and file it with the court.

- If your application is made in the course of existing proceedings then you need to complete a different form – the COP9 application notice for applications within proceedings.

- If you are appealing a Court of Protection decision then you need to complete the COP35 appellant's notice.

- You must pay a fee when you file an application. Please refer to the fees leaflet for details.

- You may need to pay for any costs you incur during proceedings. If the court considers that you have acted unreasonably you can be ordered to pay the costs incurred by other parties.

- Please continue on a separate sheet of paper if you need more space to answer a question. Write your name, the name and date of birth of the person to whom the application relates, and number of the question you are answering on each separate sheet.

- There are additional guidance notes at the end of this form.

- If you need help completing this form please check the website, www.hmcourts-service.gov.uk or www.direct.gov.uk, for further guidance or information, or contact Court Enquiry Service on 0300 456 4600 or courtofprotectionenquiries@hmcourts-service.gsi.gov.uk

- Court of Protection staff cannot give legal advice. If you need legal advice please contact a solicitor.

Section 1 - Your details (the applicant)

1.1   Your details   ☐ Mr.   ☐ Mrs.   ☐ Miss   ☐ Ms.   ☐ Other _____

First name

Middle name(s)

Last name

1.2   Address (including postcode)

Telephone no.   Daytime

Evening

Mobile

E-mail address

1.3   Is a solicitor representing you?   ☐ Yes   ☐ No

If Yes, please give the solicitor's details.

Name

Address (including postcode)

Telephone no.   Fax no.

DX no.

E-mail address

1.4   Which address should official documentation be sent to?

☐ Your address

☐ Solicitor's address

☐ Other address (please provide details)

2

1.5   Are you the person to whom this application relates?   ☐ Yes   ☐ No

If No, what is your relationship or connection to the person to whom the application relates?

[ ]

1.6   If you are applying in a respresentative capacity, please state what that capacity is.

[ ]

Section 2 - The person to whom this application relates

2.1   ☐ Mr.   ☐ Mrs.   ☐ Miss   ☐ Ms.   ☐ Other _____

First name [ ]

Middle name(s) [ ]

Last name [ ]

2.2   Address (including postcode) [ ]

Telephone no.   Daytime [ ]

Evening [ ]

Mobile [ ]

E-mail address [ ]

2.3   Date of birth   [D D M M Y Y Y Y]   ☐ Male   ☐ Female

Section 3 - Permission to apply

3.1   Do you need the court's permission to make this application? **(See note 1)**   ☐ Yes   ☐ No

If Yes, you also need to complete a COP2 permission form.

Section 4 - People to be served with/notified of this application

4.1   Please give details of all respondents. **(See note 2)**

Full name including title	Full address including postcode	Connection to the person to whom the application relates

4.2   Please give details of other people whom you will be notifying. **(See note 3)**

Full name including title	Full address including postcode	Connection to the person to whom the application relates

Section 5 - Order you are asking the court to make

5.1   Please state the matter you want the court to decide? **(See note 4)**

5.2   Please state the order you are asking the court to make? **(See note 5)**

5.3   How would the order benefit the person to whom the application relates? **(See note 6)**

5.4 Are you aware of any previous application(s) to the Court of Protection regarding the person to whom this application relates? ☐Yes ☐No

> If Yes, please give as much of the following information as you can. If there has been more than one previous application please attach the information about other previous applications on a separate sheet of paper.
>
> The name of the applicant
>
> [ ]
>
> The date of the order
>
> | D | D | M | M | Y | Y | Y | Y |
>
> Case number
>
> [ ]
>
> Please attach a copy of the order(s), if available.
>
> ☐ Copy attached ☐ Not available

Section 6 - Attending court hearings

6.1 If the court requires you to attend a hearing do you need any special assistance or facilities? **(See note 7)** ☐Yes ☐No

> If Yes, please say what your requirements are. If necessary, court staff may contact you about your requirements.
>
> [ ]

Section 7 - Statement of truth

The statement of truth is to be signed by you, your solicitor or your litigation friend.

*(I believe) (The applicant believes) that the facts stated in this application form and its annex(es) are true.

Signed

*Applicant('s litigation friend)('s solicitor)

Name

Date

Name of firm

Position or office held

* Please delete the options in brackets that do not apply.

Now read note 8 about what you need to do next.

Guidance notes

Note   1

Permission to apply

In some cases you will need the court's permission to make an application.

a) You **do not** need the court's permission if the application:

- is made by a person who lacks or is alleged to lack capacity (or, if the person is under 18 years, by anyone with parental responsibility);

- is made by the Official Solicitor, the Public Guardian, or a court appointed deputy;

- concerns a lasting power of attorney or an enduring power of attorney; or

- is about an existing court order and is made by a person named in that order.

b) You **may not** need the court's permission if the application concerns the property and affairs of the person to whom the application relates.

In most cases you will not need permission. There are some exceptions – you **do** need permission where:

- your application relates to the exercise of the jurisdiction of the court under section 54(2) of the Trustee Act 1925, and you are not:

  – person who has made an application for the appointment of a deputy;

  – a continuing trustee; or

  – any other person who, according to the practice of the Chancery Division, would have been entitled to make the application if it has been made in the High Court.

- your application is under section 36(9) of the Trustee Act 1925 for leave to appoint a new trustee in place of the person to whom the application relates, and you are not

  – a co-trustee; or

  – another person with the power to appoint a new trustee.

- your application is seeking the exercise of the court's jurisdiction under section 18(1)(b) (where this relates to the making a gift of the property of the person to whom the application relates), (h) or (i) of the Mental Capacity Act 2005 (the Act), and you are not:

  – a person who has made an application for the appointment of a deputy;

  – a person who, under any known will of the person to whom the application relates or under their intestacy, may become entitled to any property or any interest in it;

  – a person who is an attorney appointed under an enduring power of attorney which has been registered in accordance with the Act or the regulations referred to in Schedule 4 to the Act;

  – a person who is a donee of a lasting power of attorney which has been registered in accordance with the Act; or

  – a person for whom the person to whom the application relates might be expected to provide if they had capacity to do so.

- your application is under section 20 of the Trusts of Land and Appointment of Trustees Act 1996, and you are not a beneficiary under the trust or if there is more than one, by both or all of them.

c) You **do** need the court's permission for all other applications.

Where part of the application concerns a matter that requires permission, and part of it does not, you need the court's permission only for that part of it which requires permission.

Note   2

Respondents

You must provide the details of any person who you reasonably believe has an interest which means they ought to be heard by the court in relation to the application. Respondents have the opportunity to be joined as parties to the proceedings if they wish to participate in the hearing.

You must serve respondents with copies of all documents relating to your application when the court has issued your application form, in order to allow them the opportunity to support or oppose your application.

Note 3

Other people to be notified

You must provide the details of other people who are likely to have an interest in being notified of your application. You must notify these people when the court has issued your application form. They have the opportunity to apply to the court to be joined as parties to the proceedings if they wish to participate.

You should seek to identify at least three people to be notified of your application. If you have not already named the following close family members as respondents, they should be notified in descending order as appropriate to the circumstances of the person to whom the application relates:

a) spouse or civil partner

b) person who is not a spouse or a civil partner but who has been living with the person to whom the application relates as if they were

c) parent or guardian

d) child

e) brother or sister

f) grandparent or grandchild

g) aunt or uncle

h) niece or nephew

i) step-parent

j) half-brother or half-sister

Where you think that a person listed in one of the categories ought to be notified, and there are other people in that category (e.g. the person has four siblings) you should provide the details of all of the people falling within that category – unless there is good reason not to do so

You do not need to provide the details for a close family member who has little or no involvement with the person to whom the application relates, or if there is another good reason why they should not be notified.

In some cases, the person to whom the application relates may be closer to people who are not relatives and if so, it will be appropriate to provide their details instead of close family members.

In addition to the above list, you should also provide the details (if applicable) of:

- any person with parental responsibility, if the person to whom the application relates is under 18;

- any legal or natural person who is likely to be affected by the outcome of the application (e.g. a local authority or primary care trust);

- any person who has the authority to act as an attorney or deputy in relation to the matter to which the application relates;

- any other person you consider to have an interest in being notified (e.g. a close friend who provides care on an informal basis).

Note 4

Matter you want the court to decide

In each case, the court needs to decide whether or not the person to whom the application relates is capable of making a decision about the matter to which the application relates. You therefore need to state the matter you are asking the court to decide (i.e. the matter that you feel the person to whom the application relates cannot decide for himself or herself).

For example, if your application relates to personal welfare you may want the court to decide if the person to whom the application relates is capable of deciding where they live. If your application relates to property and financial affairs, you may want the court to decide whether the person is able to make decisions about the management of their investments.

Note 5

Order you are asking the court to make

You need to state the order you are asking the court to make. Please be specific about what you are asking the court to do.

For example, you may want the court to order that the person to whom the application relates moves to a particular residence, or that a particular investment is made. In each of the examples you would need to provide the particular details of the residence or investment.

Note 6

Benefit to the person to whom the application relates

You need to explain how the order you are asking for will benefit the person to whom the application relates. If you are asking the court to appoint a deputy, please explain why you think this is necessary and why the court should not make the decision on behalf of the person to whom the application relates.

Note 7

Attending court hearings

If you need special assistance or special facilities for a disability or impairment, please set out your requirements in full. It is important that you make the court aware of your needs to avoid causing any delays.

The court staff will need to know, for example, whether you want documents to be supplied in an alternative format, such as Braille or large print. They will also
need to know about any specific requirements should there be a hearing, such as wheelchair access, a hearing loop or a sign language interpreter.

Note 8

What you need to do next

When you have completed this application form you need to consider which other forms you need to complete. If you are in doubt please contact customer services.

Type of application	Forms to be completed
You need permission **and** Your application relates to property and affairs	You must complete the following forms now: • **COP2 Permission form** • **COP3 Assessment of capacity** You must complete the following form, but you can choose to do it now, or wait until permission is granted: • **COP1A Supporting information for property and affairs applications** If you are applying to be appointed as a deputy, then you must complete the following form, but you can choose to do it now or wait until permission is granted: • **COP4 Deputy's declaration**
You need permission **and** Your application relates to personal welfare	You must complete the following forms now: • **COP2 Permission form** • **COP3 Assessment of capacity** You must complete the following form, but you can choose to do it now, or wait until permission is granted: • **COP1B Supporting information for personal welfare applications** If you are applying to be appointed as a deputy then you must complete the following form, but you can choose to do it now or wait until permission is granted: • **COP4 Deputy's declaration**
You need permission **and** Your application relates to property and affairs and personal welfare	You must complete the following forms now: • **COP2 Permission form** • **COP3 Assessment of capacity** You must complete the following forms, but you can choose to do it now, or wait until permission is granted: • **COP1A Supporting information for property and affairs applications** • **COP1B Supporting information for personal welfare applications** If you are applying to be appointed as a deputy then you must complete the following form, but you can choose to do it now or wait until permission is granted: • **COP4 Deputy's declaration**

Type of application	Forms to be completed
You do not need permission **and** Your application relates to property and affairs	You must complete the following forms now: • **COP3 Assessment of capacity** • **COP1A Supporting information for property and affairs applications** If you are applying to be appointed as a deputy then you must also complete the following form now: • **COP4 Deputy's declaration**
You do not need permission **and** Your application relates to personal welfare	You must complete the following forms now: • **COP3 Assessment of capacity** • **COP1B Supporting information for personal welfare applications** If you are applying to be appointed as a deputy then you must also complete the following form now: • **COP4 Deputy's declaration**
You do not need permission **and** Your application relates to property and affairs and personal welfare	You must complete the following forms now: • **COP3 Assessment of capacity** • **COP1A Supporting information for property and affairs applications** • **COP1B Supporting information for personal welfare applications** If you are applying to be appointed as a deputy then you must also complete the following form now: • **COP4 Deputy's declaration**

If you are unable to provide the COP3 assessment of capacity form

If you are unable to provide the COP3 assessment of capacity (for example, because the person to whom the application relates refuses to undergo an assessment) then you need to complete and file a COP24 witness statement with the application form explaining:

- why you are not able to provide an assessment of capacity;
- what attempts (if any) you have made to obtain an assessment of capacity; and
- why you know or believe that the person to whom the application relates lacks capacity to make a decision in relation to the matter you want the court to decide.

Other documents to be filed

The following documents must also be filed with the application form, if applicable:

- if permission has already been granted, a copy of the court order granting permission;
- the order appointing a deputy, where the application relates to or is made by a deputy;
- the order appointing a litigation friend, where the application is made by, or where the application relates to the appointment of a litigation friend;
- the order of the Court of Protection, where the application relates to the order;
- the order of another court, where the application relates to the order;
- any written evidence on which you intend to rely (in accordance with the relevant practice direction) using the COP24 witness statement form;
- any other documents you refer to in the application form; and
- any other information and material as may be set out in a practice direction that supplements the Court of Protection Rules 2007.

The court requires two copies (i.e. the original plus one copy) of each form and document you file.

Please return the original completed forms, documents and copies to:

Court of Protection
Archway Tower
2 Junction Road
London N19 5SZ

Note   8

What happens next?

If you need permission to apply

The court will notify you when permission is granted, refused or if a date has been fixed for a hearing of the application for permission.

If permission is granted then you will need to file any other forms you need to complete, if you have chosen not to file these with the permission form.

If permission is granted and the court has received the correct completed forms, the court will issue your application form and legal proceedings will start. The court will notify you when your application form has been issued and will return a sealed copy of the application form. You will need to serve a copy on each respondent and notify the person to whom the application relates and the other people you have named in section 4.2 of this form.

If you do not need permission to apply

When the court has received the correct completed forms, it will issue your application form and legal proceedings will start. The court will notify you when your application form has been issued and will return a sealed copy of the application form. You will need to serve a copy on each respondent and notify the person to whom the application relates and the other people you have named in section 4.2 of this form.

 Court of Protection

Annex A
Supporting information for
property and affairs applications

For office use only
Date received
Case no.

Full name of person to whom the application relates
(this is the person who lacks, or is alleged to lack, capacity)

Please read first

- You need to complete and file this form if your application relates to property and affairs (which includes financial matters).

- If your application relates to personal welfare (which includes health matters) then you need to complete COP1B.

- Please continue on a separate sheet of paper if you need more space to answer a question. Write your name, the name and date of birth of the person to whom the application relates, and the number of the question you are answering on each separate sheet.

- If you need help completing this form please check the website, www.hmcourts-service.gov.uk or www.direct.gov.uk, for further guidance or information, or contact Court Enquiry Service on 0300 456 4600 or courtofprotectionenquiries@hmcourts-service.gsi.gov.uk

- Court of Protection staff cannot give legal advice. If you need legal advice please contact a solicitor.

Section 1 - Your details (the applicant)

1.1   Full name

Address
(including
postcode)

Telephone no.

Section 2 - Information about the person to whom the application relates

2.1   What is the address of the person to whom the application relates?

2.2   What is their date of birth?

| D | D | M | M | Y | Y | Y | Y |

2.3   What type of accommodation is the person to whom the application relates living in?

☐ Own home

☐ Family member/friend's home (including spouse/civil partner)

☐ Private rented home

☐ Council rented home

☐ Housing Association rented home

☐ Supported housing e.g. provided by organisation such as YMCA

☐ Local Authority nursing home or residential home

☐ Private nursing home or residential home

☐ NHS accommodation e.g. hospital, hostel

☐ Private hospital

☐ Other (please give details)

2.4   When did he or she move to this accommodation (if known)?

2.5 If he or she lives in private accommodation, do they share accommodation with anyone else? ☐Yes ☐No

If Yes, please give the name of the other person(s) and state their connection to the person to whom the application relates.

2.6 Is the person to whom the application relates:

☐ Married or in a civil partnership

☐ In a relationship with a person who is not a spouse or civil partner, but living together as if they were

☐ Separated

☐ Divorced or their civil partnership has dissolved

Date of divorce/dissolution _____

☐ Widowed or a surviving civil partner

Date of death of spouse/civil partner _____

☐ Single

2.7 Do you personally visit the person to whom the application relates? ☐Yes ☐No

If Yes, how frequently? _____

2.8 Does anyone else visit the person to whom the application relates? ☐Yes ☐No

If Yes, please provide details of the most frequent visitors.

Name	Connection to the person to whom the application relates	Frequency of visits

3

2.9   Where the person to whom the application relates lives in his or her own home, please provide brief details of the arrangements made for domestic assistance and care and details of any proposed changes.

2.10   Is a social worker or care manager involved with the person to whom the application relates?

☐ Yes   ☐ No

If Yes, please give details (if known).

Full name

Address
(including
postcode)

Telephone no.

2.11   Please provide the name and contact details for any GP or practitioner of the person to whom the application relates.

Full name

Address
(including
postcode)

Telephone no.

Section 3 – Powers granted/arrangements already made

Guardianship

3.1   Have powers of guardianship under the Mental Health Act 1983 been conferred   ☐ Yes   ☐ No
      on the Social Services Department of the Local Authority or some other approved
      person in relation to the welfare of the person to whom the application relates?

      If Yes, please give the full name, address and telephone number of the guardian or
      name of the Local Authority.

Name of
guardian or   [   ]
Local Authority

Address
(including   [   ]
postcode)

Telephone no.   [   ]

Will

3.2   Has the person to whom the application relates made a will?   ☐ Yes

                                                                       ☐ No **(Go to Section 3.5)**

                                                                       ☐ Not known **(Go to Section 3.5)**

      If Yes, have you attached a copy of the will?   ☐ Yes   ☐ No

3.3   If you cannot obtain a copy of the will but you know who holds a copy, please give
      their name and contact details.

      [   ]

3.4   If known, please provide the names of the executor(s) of the will.

      [   ]

                                    5

Power of attorney, enduring power of attorney and lasting power of attorney

3.5   Has the person to whom the application relates granted a power of   ☐Yes   ☐No
       attorney, enduring power of attorney or lasting power of attorney?
                                                                                  ☐Don't know

                 If Yes, please state which type(s) and the date granted (if known).

                        ☐ Power of attorney   [   ]

                        ☐ Enduring power of attorney   [   ]

                        ☐ Lasting power of attorney for property and affairs [   ]

                        ☐ Lasting power of attorney for personal welfare [   ]

3.6   Has any enduring power of attorney or lasting power of attorney been   ☐Yes   ☐No
       registered with the Public Guardian?
                                                                                  ☐Don't know

                 If Yes, please state the date(s) of registration

                        Enduring power of attorney   [   ]

                        Lasting power of attorney   [   ]

3.7   Has there been any unsuccessful applications to register an enduring power or   ☐Yes   ☐No
       attorney or a lasting power of attorney with the Public Guardian?
                                                                                  ☐Don't know

3.8   Please state the name(s) and address(es) of the attorney(s) who act (or have acted) for the person to
       whom the application relates.

       [   ]
       [   ]
       [   ]
       [   ]
       [   ]
       [   ]
       [   ]

Section 4 – Income, assets and expenditure

Social security benefits

4.1 Does the person to whom the application relates receive any
     social security benefits?

☐ Yes

☐ No **(Go to Section 4.4)**

4.2 What is the national insurance number of the person to whom the application relates?

☐☐ ☐☐ ☐☐ ☐☐ ☐

4.3 Please give details below of all social security benefits the person to whom the application relates is
     entitled and state who is currently receiving these. Please also list any benefits that have been claimed
     for the person to whom the application relates but are not yet being received.

Social security benefit	Weekly amount	Received by
State retirement pension		
Attendance allowance		
Severe disablement allowance		
Disability living allowance		
Incapacity benefit		
Income support		
Council tax benefit		
Child benefit		
Other type of benefit (please give details)		

Occupational/company pensions and annuities

4.4   Does the person to whom the application relates receive any   ☐ Yes
       occupational/company pensions or annuities?
                                                                            ☐ No **(Go to Section 4.5)**

       If Yes, please give the following details for each occupational/company
       pension or annuity:

Name, address and reference of the company/payer	Amount received (indicate whether gross or net)	Frequency of payments

Trusts

4.5   Is the person to whom the application relates entitled to any income,   ☐ Yes
       property or capital from a trust?
                                                                              ☐ No **(Go to Section 4.6)**

       If Yes, please give details of any interest in a trust or similar to which
       the person to whom the application relates is entitled or to which
       they may become entitled. Please give the circumstances under
       which he/she will become entitled, together with details of the
       property and particulars of the will or settlement and the names of
       the present trustees.

Interest in a deceased's estate

4.6   Does the person to whom the application relates have any interest in   ☐ Yes
       the estate of someone who has died (or is he/she likely to become
       entitled to such an interest shortly)?   ☐ No **(Go to Section 4.7)**

       Please give full details of any interests to which the person to whom the application relates has become
       entitled (or may become entitled) under a will or intestacy.

       ┌──┐
       │   │
       │   │
       │   │
       │   │
       │   │
       └──┘

       Please provide the name, address and telephone number of the person dealing with the administration of
       the estate.

       ┌──┐
       │   │
       │   │
       │   │
       │   │
       │   │
       └──┘

Damages and criminal injuries compensation

4.7   Has the person to whom the application relates recently received a damages   ☐ Yes   ☐ No
       award (for example, following a road accident or medical negligence) or is he/
       she expected to receive a damages award?

       If Yes, please give details, including the name and address of solicitors involved
       in the case and the present position with regard to the litigation. Is a settlement/
       trial imminent?

       ┌──┐
       │   │
       │   │
       │   │
       │   │
       │   │
       └──┘

4.8   Has the person to whom the application relates made a claim to the Criminal   ☐ Yes   ☐ No
         Injuries Compensation Authority?

         If Yes, please give the name and address of solicitors involved in the case
         and details of any awards or interim payments, including the amount.

Income from employment

4.9   Please give details of any income the person to whom the application relates receives from employment.

Miscellaneous income

4.10   Please list any income to which the person to whom the application relates is (or may become)
         entitled which has not been mentioned elsewhere in this form. If there is none, please say so.

Money held in bank accounts

4.11   Does the person to whom the application relates have any money held in bank or building society accounts (or similar)?

☐ Yes

☐ No **(Go to Section 4.12)**

If Yes, please give the following details:

	Account 1	Account 2	Account 3
Name and full postal address of the bank/ building society branch where the account is held			
Name of the account			
Sort code			
Account number			
Type of account (e.g. current, deposit, high interest)			
How much is in the account?			
If the account is a joint account, please give the name and address of the co-holder			
If the account is a joint account, please give a brief explanation of the circumstances in which the monies came to be held in a joint account			

Please provide the above information for any additional accounts on a separate sheet of paper.

4.12   Does any other person or organisation (other than those already mentioned)   ☐Yes   ☐No
        hold money for the person to whom the application relates?

        If Yes, please give full details including the name and address of those involved,
        the amount held and the reason for holding the money.

        ┌───┐
        │   │
        │   │
        │   │
        │   │
        │   │
        └───┘

Investments

4.13   Does the person to whom the application relates own or have an interest in   ☐Yes   ☐No
        any investments such as stocks and shares, unit trusts, bonds etc?

        If Yes, please give a full list of the investments of the person to whom the   ☐Valuation
        application relates. Alternatively, please provide a valuation from the fund   attached
        manager.

        ┌───┐
        │   │
        │   │
        │   │
        │   │
        │   │
        │   │
        │   │
        │   │
        │   │
        └───┘

Life assurance policies

4.14   Does the person to whom the application relates have any life assurance policies?   ☐Yes   ☐No

If Yes, please give full details of any policies, the premiums payable and whether
you wish to continue to keep the policies going.

```

```

Land and property

4.15   Does the person to whom the application relates own any land or
property?

☐ Yes

☐ No (Go to Section 4.21)

If Yes, please enter the address(es) and state whether the land or
property is freehold, leasehold or commonhold property.

```

```

4.16   If leasehold, please give details (if known) of the length of the lease, any rent or service
charges payable and any restriction on the sale of the property.

```

```

13

4.17   Please state the approximate value of each property.

4.18   If any land or property is owned jointly, please give details of the other joint owner(s) and state what share of the property is held by the person to whom the application relates.

4.19   If any property has a mortgage owing, please give details including the names of the people who have taken out the mortgage, the mortgage provider and the outstanding balance.

4.20   Please give information on any recent or proposed sale of parts of the client's property or possessions (e.g. their home).

Personal possessions

4.21   Please provide here an estimate of the overall value of the belongings of the person to whom the application relates.

4.22   Please list any items which are thought to be particularly valuable and give an indication of the value.

Business

4.23   Does the person to whom the application relates own or have any interest in a business?   ☐ Yes   ☐ No

If Yes, please provide the name and details of the business, who is running the business, and the role/interest of the person to whom the application relates.

15

Debts and money owed

4.24 Does the person to whom the application relates have any outstanding debts? ☐ Yes ☐ No

If Yes, please give details of any debts of the person to whom the application relates including the name(s) of any creditors and the amount of the debt.

4.25 Does anyone owe the person to whom the application relates money? ☐ Yes ☐ No

If Yes, please give details including who owes the money and the amount.

Miscellaneous assets and investments

4.26 Please use this section to list any other property or other assets which the person to whom the application relates may own or have an interest in which have not been mentioned elsewhere in this form. If there are none, please say so.

Expenditure

4.27 If the person to whom the application relates is in a nursing or residential home or some other type of accommodation that is charged for, please state the cost of the accommodation and whether the amount is the annual, quarterly, monthly or weekly cost.

4.28 Has the person to whom the application relates been assessed by the Local Authority to pay a contribution towards their accommodation costs? ☐ Yes ☐ No

4.29 Please give information about any regular gifts and regular charitable donations made by the person to whom the application relates.

4.30 Please give information on any recent significant expenditure made on behalf of the person to whom the application relates, either using his/her funds or funds provided by someone else.

Section 5 – Other information

5.1   Please provide any additional background information about the person to whom the application relates that is relevant to your application (such as key dates and facts).

Signed	

Name	

Date	

Name of firm	

Position or office held	

Now read note 8 of the COP1 application form about what you need to do next.

Court of Protection

Annex B
Supporting information for
personal welfare applications

For office use only
Date received
Case no.

Full name of person to whom the application relates
(this is the person who lacks, or is alleged to lack, capacity)

Please read first

- You need to complete and file this form if your application relates to personal welfare (which includes health matters).

- If your application relates to property and affairs (which includes financial matters) then you need to complete COP1A.

- Please continue on a separate sheet of paper if you need more space to answer a question. Write your name, the name and date of birth of the person to whom the application relates, and the number of the question you are answering on each separate sheet.

- If you need help completing this form please check the website, www.hmcourts-service.gov.uk or www.direct.gov.uk, for further guidance or information, or contact Court Enquiry Service on 0300 456 4600 or courtofprotectionenquiries@hmcourts-service.gsi.gov.uk.

- Court of Protection staff cannot give legal advice. If you need legal advice please contact a solicitor.

Section 1 - Your details (the applicant)

1.1   Full name

Address
(including
postcode)

Telephone no.

Section 2 - Information about the person to whom the application relates

2.1   What is the address of the person to whom the application relates?

2.2   What is their date of birth?

D	D	M	M	Y	Y	Y	Y

2.3   What type of accommodation is the person to whom the application relates living in?

☐ Own home

☐ Family member/friend's home (including spouse/civil partner)

☐ Private rented home

☐ Council rented home

☐ Housing Association rented home

☐ Supported housing e.g. provided by organisation such as YMCA

☐ Local Authority nursing home or residential home

☐ Private nursing home or residential home

☐ NHS accommodation e.g. hospital, hostel

☐ Private hospital

☐ Other (please give details)

2.4   When did he or she move to this accommodation (if known)?

2.5   If he or she lives in private accommodation, do they share accommodation with anyone else?   ☐ Yes   ☐ No

If Yes, please give the name of the other person(s) and state their connection to the person to whom the application relates

2.6   Is the person to whom the application relates:

☐ Married or in a civil partnership

☐ In a relationship with a person who is not a spouse or civil partner, but living together as if they were

☐ Separated

☐ Divorced or their civil partnership has dissolved

Date of divorce/dissolution

☐ Widowed or a surviving civil partner

Date of death of spouse/civil partner

☐ Single

2.7   Do you personally visit the person to whom the application relates?   ☐ Yes   ☐ No

If Yes, how frequently?

2.8   Does anyone else visit the person to whom the application relates?   ☐ Yes   ☐ No

If Yes, please provide details of the most frequent visitors.

Name	Connection to the person to whom the application relates	Frequency of visits

2.9   Where the person to whom the application relates lives in his or her own home, please provide brief details of the arrangements made for domestic assistance and care, and details of any proposed changes.

2.10   Is a social worker or care manager involved with the person to whom the application relates.   ☐ Yes   ☐ No

        If Yes, please give details (if known).

        Full name

        Address
        (including
        postcode)

        Telephone no.

2.11   Please provide the name and contact details for any GP or practitioner of the person to whom the application relates.

        Full name

        Address
        (including
        postcode)

        Telephone no.

Section 3 – Powers granted/arrangements already made

Guardianship

3.1   Have powers of guardianship under the Mental Health Act 1983 been conferred ☐ Yes   ☐ No
on the Social Services Department of the Local Authority or some other approved
person in relation to the welfare of the person to whom the application relates?

If Yes, please give the full name, address and telephone number of the guardian or
name of the Local Authority.

Name of
guardian or
Local Authority

Address
(including
postcode)

Telephone no.

Will

3.2   Has the person to whom the application relates made a will?   ☐ Yes

☐ No **(Go to Section 3.5)**

☐ Not known **(Go to Section 3.5)**

If Yes, have you attached a copy of the will?   ☐ Yes   ☐ No

3.3   If you cannot obtain a copy of the will but you know who holds a copy, please give
their name and contact details.

3.4   If known, please provide the names of the executor(s) of the will.

Power of attorney, enduring power of attorney and lasting power of attorney

3.5   Has the person to whom the application relates granted a power of   ☐ Yes   ☐ No
      attorney, enduring power of attorney or lasting power of attorney?
                                                                                ☐ Don't know

              If Yes, please state which type(s) and the date granted (if known)

              ☐ Power of attorney   [   ]

              ☐ Enduring power of attorney   [   ]

              ☐ Lasting power of attorney for property and affairs   [   ]

              ☐ Lasting power of attorney for personal welfare   [   ]

3.6   Has any enduring power of attorney or lasting power of attorney been   ☐ Yes   ☐ No
      registered with the Public Guardian?
                                                                                ☐ Don't know

              If Yes, please state the date(s) of registration

                  Enduring power of attorney   [   ]

                  Lasting power of attorney   [   ]

3.7   Has there been any unsuccessful applications to register an enduring power or   ☐ Yes   ☐ No
      attorney or a lasting power of attorney with the Public Guardian?
                                                                                ☐ Don't know

3.8   Please state the name(s) and address(es) of the attorney(s) who act (or have acted) for the person to
      whom the application relates.

      [   ]
      [   ]
      [   ]
      [   ]
      [   ]
      [   ]
      [   ]

Section 4 – Other information

4.1 Please provide any additional background information about the person to whom the application relates that is relevant to your application (such as key dates and facts).

Section 5 – Signature

Signed

Name

Date

Name of firm

Position or office held

Now read note 8 of the COP1 application form about what you need to do next.

COP
2
03.10
Court of Protection
Permission form

Full name of person to whom the application relates
(this is the name of the person who lacks, or is alleged to lack, capacity)

Please read first

- You must complete and file this form if you need permission to make an application to start proceedings.

- Some of the questions in section 3 of this form are the same as questions in section 5 of the COP1 application form. You need to answer the questions on both forms. Where the questions are the same you should copy the answers you provide on the application form.

- In deciding whether to grant permission to start proceedings the court will consider:

  – your connection with the person to whom the application relates;

  – the reasons for the application;

  – the benefit to the person to whom the application relates; and

  – whether the benefit can be achieved any other way.

- Please continue on a separate sheet of paper if you need more space to answer a question. Write your name, the name and date of birth of the person to whom the application relates, and the number of the question you are answering on each separate sheet.

- If you need help completing this form please check the website, www.hmcourts-service.gov.uk or www.direct.gov.uk, for further guidance or information, or contact Court Enquiry Service on 0300 456 4600 or courtofprotectionenquiries@ hmcourts-service.gsi.gov.uk.

- Court of Protection staff cannot give legal advice. If you need legal advice please contact a solicitor.

Section 1 - Your details (the applicant)

1.1 Your details

☐ Mr. ☐ Mrs. ☐ Miss ☐ Ms. ☐ Other _____

First name

Middle name(s)

Last name

Section 2 - Your application for permission

2.1 What is your relationship or connection to the person to whom this application relates?

2.2 What are your reasons for making the application?

2.3 How would the order you have set out in Section 5 of the COP1 application form benefit the person to whom the application relates?

2.4   Is there any other way this benefit could be achieved?

┌───┐
│   │
│   │
│   │
│   │
│   │
│   │
└───┘

2.5   Are you seeking any directions from the court at the permission hearing?   ☐Yes   ☐No

         If Yes, please give details.

┌───┐
│   │
│   │
│   │
│   │
│   │
│   │
└───┘

3

Section 3 - Statement of truth

The statement of truth is to be signed by you, your solicitor or your litigation friend.

*(I believe) (The applicant believes) that the facts stated in this permission form and are true.

Signed

*Applicant('s litigation friend)('s solicitor)

Name

Date

Name of firm

Position or office held

* Please delete the options in brackets that do not apply.

Now read note 8 of the COP1 application form about what you need to do next.

4

COP 3
03.10
Court of Protection

Assessment of capacity

For office use only
Date received
Case no.

Full name of person to whom the application relates
(this is the name of the person who lacks, or is alleged to lack, capacity)

Please read first

- If you are applying to start proceedings with the court you must file this form with your COP1 application form. The assessment must contain current information.

- You must complete Part A of this form.

- You then need to provide the form to the practitioner who will complete Part B.
  The practitioner will return the form to you or your solicitor for filing with the court.

- The practitioner may charge a fee for completing the form. Please ask the practitioner about the amount they will charge.

- The practitioner may be a registered medical practitioner, psychologist or psychiatrist who has examined and assessed the capacity of the person to whom the application relates.
  In some circumstances it might be appropriate for a registered therapist, such as a speech therapist or occupational therapist, to complete the form.

- When the form has been completed, its contents will be confidential to the court and those authorised by the court to see it, such as parties to the proceedings.

- Please continue on a separate sheet of paper if you need more space to answer a question. Write your name, the name and date of birth of the person to whom the application relates, and number of the question you are answering on each separate sheet.

- There are additional guidance notes at the end of this form.

- If you need help completing this form please check the website, www.hmcourts-service.gov.uk or www.direct.gov.uk, for further guidance or information, or contact Court Enquiry Service on 0300 456 4600 or courtofprotectionenquiries@ hmcourts-service.gsi.gov.uk

- Court of Protection staff cannot give legal advice. If you need legal advice please contact a solicitor.

- This form has been prepared in consultation with the British Medical Association, the Royal College of Physicians and the Royal College of Psychiatrists.

Part A - To be completed by the applicant

Section 1 - Your details (the applicant)

1.1 Your details ☐ Mr. ☐ Mrs. ☐ Miss ☐ Ms. ☐ Other _____

First name

Middle name(s)

Last name

1.2 Address (including postcode)

Telephone no.

Daytime	
Evening	
Mobile	

E-mail address

1.3 Is a solicitor representing you? ☐ Yes ☐ No

If Yes, please give the solicitor's details.

Name

Address (including postcode)

Telephone no.		Fax no.	
DX no.			
E-mail address			

1.4 To which address should the practitioner return the form when they have completed Section 2?

☐ Your address

☐ Solicitor's address

☐ Other address (please provide details)

2

Section 2 - The person to whom the application relates (the person to be assessed by the practitioner)

2.1   ☐ Mr.   ☐ Mrs.   ☐ Miss   ☐ Ms.   ☐ Other _____

First name

Middle name(s)

Last name

Address
(including
postcode)

Telephone no.

Date of birth   ☐ Male   ☐ Female

Section 3 - About the application

3.1   Please state the matter you are asking the court to decide. **(see note 1)**

3.2   What order are you asking the court to make?

3.3   How would the order benefit the person to whom the application relates?

3.4   What is your relationship or connection to the person to whom the application relates?

3

Section 4 - Further information

Please provide any further information about the circumstances of the person to whom the application relates that would be useful to the practitioner in assessing his or her capacity to make any decision(s) that is the subject of your application. **(see note 2)**

Now read note 3 about what you need to do next.

Part B - To be completed by the practitioner

Section 5 - Your details (the practitioner)

5.1   ☐ Mr.   ☐ Mrs.   ☐ Miss   ☐ Ms.   ☐ Dr.   ☐ Other _____

First name

Middle name(s)

Last name

Address (including postcode)

Telephone no.

E-mail address

5.2   Nature of your professional relationship with the person to whom the application relates (e.g. general practitioner, psychiatrist or other)

5.3   Professional qualifications

Section 6 – Sensitive information

If there is information that you do not wish to provide in this form because of its sensitive nature you can provide the information directly to the court.

6.1 Are you providing any sensitive information separately to the court? ☐ Yes ☐ No

Please provide it in writing to:
Court of Protection
Archway Tower
2 Junction Road
London N19 5SZ

Please include your name and contact details, and the name, address and date of birth of the person to whom the application relates on any information you provide separately to the court.

Section 7 - Assessment of capacity

7.1 The person to whom the application relates has the following impairment of, or disturbance in the functioning of, the mind or brain: **(see note 4)**

This has lasted since:

As a result, the person is unable to make a decision for themselves in relation to the following matter(s) in question:

6

7.2   The person to whom the application relates is unable to make a decision in relation to the relevant matter because: **(see note 5)**

☐ he or she is unable to understand the following relevant information (please give details);

```



```

and/or

☐ he or she is unable to retain the following relevant information (please give details);

```



```

and/or

☐ he or she is unable to use or weigh the following relevant information as part of the process of making the decision(s) (please give details);

```



```

or

☐ for cases where he or she can in fact understand, retain and use/weigh the information but is unable to communicate his or her decision(s) by any means at all (please give details).

```



```

7.3 My opinion is based on the following evidence of a lack of capacity:

```



```

7.4 Please answer either (a) **or** (b).

(a) I have acted as a practitioner for the person to whom the application

relates since ☐☐☐☐☐☐☐☐ and last assessed

him or her on ☐☐☐☐☐☐☐☐

(b) I assessed the person to whom the application

relates on ☐☐☐☐☐☐☐☐

following a referral from:

```



```

7.5   Has the person to whom this application relates made you aware of any views they   ☐ Yes   ☐ No
have in relation to the relevant matter?

If Yes, please give details.

7.6   Do you consider there is a prospect that the person to whom the application relates might regain or acquire capacity in the future in respect of the decision to which the application relates? **(see note 6)**

        ☐ Yes – please state why and give an indication of when this might happen.

        ☐ No – please state why.

7.7   Are you aware of anyone who holds a different view regarding the capacity of the   ☐ Yes   ☐ No
person to whom the application relates?

If Yes, please give details.

7.8 Do you, your family or friends have any interest (financial or otherwise) in any matter concerning the person to whom the application relates? ☐ Yes ☐ No

If Yes, please give details.

7.9 Do you have any general comments or any other recommendations for future care? **(see note 7)**

Signed

Name   **Date**

Now read note 8 about what you need to do next.

Guidance notes

Note 1

About the application

These questions are repeated on the COP1 application form. Please copy your answers from the COP1 form so that the information on both forms is the same.

Note 2

Further information

Please provide any further information about the circumstances of the person to whom the application relates that would be relevant in assessing their capacity. For example, if your application relates to property and financial affairs, it would be useful for the practitioner to know the general financial circumstances of the person concerned. This information will help the practitioner evaluate the decision-making responsibility of the person to whom the application relates and may help to inform the practitioner's view on whether that person can make the decision(s) in question.

Note 3

What you need to do next

Please provide this form to the practitioner who will complete Part B.

The practitioner will return the form to you or your solicitor when they have completed Part B. You will then need to file the form with the court together with the COP1 application form and any other information the court requires. See note 8 on the COP1 form for further information.

Note 4

Assessing capacity

For the purpose of the Mental Capacity Act 2005 a person lacks capacity if, at the time a decision needs to be made, he or she is unable to make or communicate the decision because of an impairment of, or a disturbance in the functioning of, the mind or brain.

The Act contains a two-stage test of capacity:

1. Is there an impairment of, or disturbance in the functioning of, the person's mind or brain?

2. If so, is the impairment or disturbance sufficient that the person lacks the capacity to make a decision in relation to the matter in question?

Please refer to Part A of this form where the applicant has set out details of the application and relevant information about the circumstances of the person to whom the application relates. In particular, section 3.1 sets out the matter the applicant is asking the court to decide.

The assessment of capacity must be based on the person's ability to make a decision in relation to the relevant matter, and not their ability to make decisions in general. It does not matter therefore if the lack of capacity is temporary, if the person retains the capacity to make other decisions, or if the person's capacity fluctuates.

Under the Act, a person is regarded as being unable to make a decision if they cannot:

- understand information about the decision to be made;

- retain that information;

- use or weigh the information as part of the decision-making process; or

- communicate the decision (by any means).

A lack of capacity cannot be established merely by reference to a person's age or appearance or to a particular condition or an aspect of behaviour. A person is not to be treated as being unable to make a decision merely because they have made an unwise decision.

The test of capacity is not the same as the test for detention and treatment under the Mental Health Act 1983. Many people covered by the Mental Health Act have the capacity to make decisions for themselves. On the other hand, most people who lack capacity to make decisions will never be affected by the Mental Health Act.

Practitioners are required to have regard to the Mental Capacity Act 2005 Code of Practice. The Code of Practice is available online at www.publicguardian.gov.uk. Hard copies are available from The Stationery Office (TSO), for a fee, by:

- phoning 0870 600 5522;

- emailing customerservices@tso.co.uk; or

- ordering online at www.tsoshop.co.uk.

For further advice please see (for example):

- Making Decisions: A guide for people who work in health and social care (2nd edition), Mental Capacity Implementation Programme, 2007.

- Assessment of Mental Capacity: Guidance for Doctors and Lawyers (2nd edition), British Medical Association and Law Society (London: BMJ Books, 2004)

Note 5

Capacity to make the decision in question

Please give your opinion of the nature of the lack of capacity and the grounds on which this is based. This requires a diagnosis and a statement giving clear evidence that the person to whom the application relates lacks capacity to make the decision(s) relevant to the application. It is important that the evidence of lack of capacity shows how this prevents the person concerned from being able to take decision(s).

Note 6

Prospect of regaining or acquiring capacity

When reaching any decision the court must apply the principles set out in the Act and in particular must make a determination that is in the best interests of the person to whom the application relates. It would therefore assist the court if you could indicate whether the person to whom the application relates is likely to regain or acquire capacity sufficiently to be able to make decisions in relation to the relevant matter.

Note 7

General comments

The court may make any order it considers appropriate even if that order is not specified in the application form. Where possible, the court will make a one-off decision rather than appointing a deputy with on-going decision making power. If you think that an order other than the one being sought by the applicant would be in the best interests of the person to whom the application relates, please give details including your reasons.

Note 8

What you need to do next

Please return the completed form to the applicant or their solicitor, as specified in section 1.4. You are advised to keep a copy for your records.

	For office use only

COP 4   Court of Protection
03.10   **Deputy's declaration**

For office use only
Date received
Case no.

Full name of person to whom the application relates
(this is the name of the person who lacks, or is alleged to lack, capacity)

Please read first

- If you are applying to be appointed as a deputy then you need to complete this form and file it with the court.

- The court will use the information you provide in the declaration to assess your suitability to be a deputy.

- If you are appointed as a deputy you must have regard to the Mental Capacity Act 2005 Code of Practice. The Code of Practice has information about the duties and responsibilities that you have to take on as a deputy.

- The Code of Practice is available online at www.publicguardian.gov.uk. Hardcopies are available from The Stationery Office (TSO), for a fee, by:

  – phoning 0870 600 5522;

  – emailing customerservices@tso.co.uk; or

  – ordering online at www.tso.shop.co.uk.

- Please continue on a separate sheet of paper if you need more space to answer a question. Write your name, the name and date of birth of person to whom the application relates, and number of the question you are answering on each separate sheet.

- If you need help completing this form please check the website, www.hmcourts-service.gov.uk or www.direct.gov.uk, for further guidance or information, or contact Court Enquiry Service on 0300 456 4600 or courtofprotectionenquiries@ hmcourts-service.gsi.gov.uk.

- Court of Protection staff cannot give legal advice. If you need legal advice please contact a solicitor.

Section 1 - Your details (the person applying to be appointed as a deputy)

1.1 Your details ☐ Mr. ☐ Mrs. ☐ Miss ☐ Ms. ☐ Other _____

First name

Middle name(s)

Last name

1.2 Address (including postcode)

Telephone no. | Daytime
 | Evening
 | Mobile

E-mail address

1.3 What is your connection to the person to whom the application relates?

Details of the person to whom the application relates

1.4 Full name

Address (including postcode)

Date of birth | D | D | M | M | Y | Y | Y | Y

2

Section 2 - Your personal circumstances

2.1   What is your current occupation?
       If you are not in paid employment, please give details of your current circumstances.

       _____

2.2   How long have you worked in your current occupation?

       [   ] Years   [   ] Months

2.3   Have you ever been appointed to act as a deputy or attorney for anyone else?   ☐ Yes   ☐ No

       If Yes, please give the name(s) of the person(s) and (if known) the court reference(s).

       _____

2.4   Have you ever been convicted of a criminal offence?   ☐ Yes   ☐ No
       (Do not include convictions spent under the Rehabilitation of Offenders Act 1974).

       If Yes, please provide details of the offence, including the date of conviction.

       _____

2.5   Are there any circumstances (personal or otherwise) which would interfere with your   ☐ Yes   ☐ No
       ability to carry out the duties of a deputy effectively? (e.g. ill health or business/family
       commitments).

       If Yes, please provide details.

       _____

2.6   If you are not appointed as a deputy or become unable to take up an appointment,   ☐ Yes   ☐ No
       are you aware of any other person (or officer holder) who might wish to be
       considered as a deputy?

       If Yes, please provide details.

       _____

Section 3 - Your financial circumstances

Please complete this section if you are applying to be appointed as a property and affairs deputy.

3.1 Do you have a personal bank or building society current/deposit account? ☐Yes ☐No

3.2 Have you ever been refused credit? (e.g. having a personal loan application refused) ☐Yes ☐No

If Yes, please provide details.

3.3 Do you have any outstanding judgment debts? ☐Yes ☐No

If Yes, please provide details.

3.4 Have you personally ever been declared bankrupt or the debtor under an Individual Voluntary Arrangement under Part VIII of the Insolvency Act 1986? ☐Yes ☐No

If Yes, please provide details.

3.5 Are you currently an undischarged bankrupt or the debtor under an Individual Voluntary Arrangement? ☐Yes ☐No

If Yes, please give provide details.

3.6 Has any business that you have been involved with (whether a company, partnership or otherwise) been subject to a recognised insolvency regime (e.g. voluntary arrangement, winding-up, administration, receivership, administrative receivership)? ☐Yes ☐No

If Yes, please provide details.

4

3.7   Have you been the subject of a declaration under section 213 (fraudulent trading)   ☐ Yes   ☐ No
or section 214 (wrongful trading) of the Insolvency Act 1986?

If Yes, please provide details.

```
┌────────────────────────────────────────────────────────────────────┐
│                                                                      │
│                                                                      │
│                                                                      │
│                                                                      │
└────────────────────────────────────────────────────────────────────┘
```

3.8   Have you been the subject of a bankruptcy restrictions order under section 281A   ☐ Yes   ☐ No
or Schedule 4A of the Insolvency Act 1986, or a disqualification order under
section 1 of the Company Directors (Disqualification) Act 1986?

If Yes, please provide details.

```
┌────────────────────────────────────────────────────────────────────┐
│                                                                      │
│                                                                      │
│                                                                      │
│                                                                      │
└────────────────────────────────────────────────────────────────────┘
```

3.9   Are you aware of any matter in which your financial interests may conflict with those   ☐ Yes   ☐ No
of the person to whom the application relates? (e.g. occupation of a property which
the person owns, any interest under the terms of their will)

If Yes, please provide details.

```
┌────────────────────────────────────────────────────────────────────┐
│                                                                      │
│                                                                      │
│                                                                      │
│                                                                      │
│                                                                      │
│                                                                      │
│                                                                      │
│                                                                      │
│                                                                      │
│                                                                      │
│                                                                      │
└────────────────────────────────────────────────────────────────────┘
```

Section 4 - Your personal undertakings to the person to whom the application relates

Becoming a deputy means that you have to take on a number of duties and responsibilities and have to act in accordance with certain standards. If you are appointed as a deputy, the court order will set out the exact powers conferred on you.

The main duties and responsibilities you may have to take on are set out below. Please review each one and tick 'Yes' if you give your undertaking to act in accordance with the duty or responsibility. You can use the 'Comments' section to support your undertakings. Please mention if you have a particular professional skill, life experience, public duty or role that you think is relevant.

If you do not give your undertaking and tick 'No', please use the 'Comments' section to explain your reasons. It may be because you do not yet have experience in the particular duty, or think you might not have the skills needed. It will not necessarily prevent your appointment as deputy.

Not all of the undertakings set out below will be relevant to every deputy. If you think this is the case, tick 'No' and explain in the 'Comments' section that the undertaking would be irrelevant to your appointment.

	Undertaking	Yes or No	Comments
1	I will have regard to the Mental Capacity Act 2005 Code of Practice and I will apply the principles of the Act when making a decision. In particular I will act in the best interests of the person to whom the application relates and I will only make those decisions that the person cannot make themselves.	☐ Yes ☐ No	
2	I will act within the scope of the powers conferred on me by the court as set out in the order of appointment and will apply to the court if I feel additional powers are needed.	☐ Yes ☐ No	
3	I will act with due care, skill and diligence, as I would do in making my own decisions and conducting my own affairs. Where I undertake my duties as a deputy in the course of my professional work (if relevant), I will abide by professional rules and standards.	☐ Yes ☐ No	
4	I will make decisions on behalf of the person to whom the application relates as required under the court order appointing me. I will not delegate any of my powers as a deputy unless this is expressly permitted in the court order appointing me.	☐ Yes ☐ No	
5	I will ensure that my personal interests do not conflict with my duties as a deputy, and I will not use my position for any personal benefit.	☐ Yes ☐ No	
6	I will act with honesty and integrity, and will take any decisions made by the person to whom the application relates while they still had capacity, into account when determing their best interests.	☐ Yes ☐ No	
7	I will keep the person's financial and personal information confidential (unless there is a good reason that requires me to disclose it).	☐ Yes ☐ No	

6

		Yes or No	Comments
8	I will comply with any directions of the court or reasonable requests made by the Public Guardian, including requests for reports to be submitted.	☐ Yes ☐ No	
9	I will visit the person to whom the application relates as regularly as is appropriate and take an interest in their welfare.	☐ Yes ☐ No	
10	I will work with the person to whom the application relates and any carer(s) to achieve the best quality of life for him or her within the funds available.	☐ Yes ☐ No	
11	I will co-operate with any representative of the court or the Public Guardian who might wish to meet me or the person to whom the application relates to check that the deputyship arrangements are working.	☐ Yes ☐ No	
12	I will immediately inform the court and the Public Guardian if I have any reason to believe that the person to whom the application relates no longer lacks capacity and may be able to manage his or her own affairs.	☐ Yes ☐ No	

	Further undertakings if you are applying to be appointed as a property and affairs deputy	**Yes or No**	**Comments**
13	I understand that I may be required to provide security for my actions as deputy. If I am required to purchase insurance, such as a guarantee bond, I undertake to pay premiums promptly from the funds of the person to whom the application relates.	☐ Yes ☐ No	
14	I will keep accounts of dealings and transactions taken on behalf of the person to whom the application relates.	☐ Yes ☐ No	
15	I will keep the money and property of the person to whom the application relates separate from my own.	☐ Yes ☐ No	
16	I will ensure so far as is reasonable that the person to whom the application relates receives all benefits and other income to which they are entitled, that their bills are paid and that a tax return for them is completed annually.	☐ Yes ☐ No	
17	I will take reasonable steps to maintain the property of the person to whom the application relates (if applicable), for example arranging for insurance, repairs or improvements. If necessary I will arrange and oversee a sale or letting of property with appropriate legal advice.	☐ Yes ☐ No	

Section 5 - Personal statement to the court

Please state why you wish to be the deputy of the person to whom the application relates.

Section 6 - Statement of truth

The statement of truth is to be signed by the person applying to be appointed as a deputy.

I believe that the facts stated in this declaration are true.

Signed

Name   **Date**

Now read note 8 of the COP1 application form about what you need to do next.

8

Court of Protection

Acknowledgment of service/notification

Case no.

Full name of person to whom the application relates
(this is the name of the person who lacks, or is alleged to lack, capacity)

Please read first

- You need to complete this form and file it with the court if you:

    - have been given notice of an application for permission and you wish to take part in the permission hearing;

    - have been served with a COP1, COP7 or COP8 application form and you wish to take part in the proceedings;

    - have received a COP14 notice about proceedings about you in Court of Protection and you wish to be joined as a party to the proceedings;

    - have received a COP15 notice that an application form has been issued by the court and you wish to be joined as a party to the proceedings.

- As a party you will be able to participate in the proceedings. You may need to pay for any costs you incur during proceedings. If the court considers that you have acted unreasonably you can be ordered to pay the costs incurred by other parties.

- You have 21 days from the day you are served/provided with notice to complete this form and file it with the court.

- You do not need to complete and file this form if you do not wish to be joined as a party to proceedings. You can still apply for a copy of any order of the court in respect of the proceedings by filing a COP9 application notice.

- Please continue on a separate sheet of paper if you need more space to answer a question. Write the case number, your name, the name of the person to whom the application relates, and the number of the question you are answering on each separate sheet.

- There are additional guidance notes at the end of this form.

- If you need help completing this form please check the website, www.hmcourts-service.gov.uk or www.direct.gov.uk, for further guidance or information, or contact Court Enquiry Service on 0300 456 4600 or courtofprotectionenquiries@hmcourts-service.gsi.gov.uk

- Court of Protection staff cannot give legal advice. If you need legal advice please contact a solicitor.

Section 1 - Your details (the person served/notified)

1.1   Your details   ☐ Mr.   ☐ Mrs.   ☐ Miss   ☐ Ms.   ☐ Other _____

        First name

        Middle name(s)

        Last name

1.2   Address (including postcode)

        Telephone no.   Daytime

                           Evening

                           Mobile

        E-mail address

1.3   Is a solicitor representing you?   ☐ Yes   ☐ No

        If Yes, please give the solicitor's details.

        Name

        Address (including postcode)

        Telephone no.   Fax no.

        DX no.

        E-mail address

1.4   Which address should official documentation be sent to?

                  ☐ Your address

                  ☐ Solicitor's address

                  ☐ Other address (please provide details)

2

1.5   What is your role in these proceedings?

☐ Person to whom the application/appeal relates

☐ Respondent*

☐ Person notified that the application form has been issued

☐ Person notified that the permission form has been issued

*You are a respondent if you have been served with a copy of the COP1 application form.

Section 2 – Application to be joined as a party

Please do not complete this section if:

- you have been given notice of an application for permission; or
- you are a respondent.

You will be able to take part in the permission hearing/proceedings upon return of this acknowledgment form. **Please go to section 3.**

You must complete this section if you are the person to whom the application relates or a person notified that the application form has been issued and you wish to apply to be joined as a party.

2.1   Do you wish to be joined as a party to proceedings? **(see note 1)**   ☐Yes   ☐No

2.2   If Yes, Please state your interest in the proceedings. **(see note 2)**

2.3   Evidence of your interest in the proceedings must be filed with this   ☐ Evidence
acknowledgment. If you are attaching any written evidence please use the   attached
COP24 witness statement form.

Section 3 – Acknowledgment of service/notification

3.1 Do you consent to the application? ☐Yes ☐No

If Yes, **go to Section 3.5**

3.2 Do you oppose the application? ☐Yes ☐No

If Yes, please set out your grounds for doing so.

```
```

3.3 Do you propose that a different order should be made? ☐Yes ☐No

If Yes, please set out what that order is.

```
```

3.4 If you oppose the order, or purpose a different order, any evidence on which you intend to rely must be filed with this acknowledgment. If you are attaching any written evidence please use the COP24 witness statement form. ☐ Evidence attached

3.5 Are you seeking any directions from the court? ☐Yes ☐No

If Yes, please give details.

```
```

Section 4 – Attending court hearings

4.1   If the court requires you to attend a hearing do you need any special
assistance or facilities? **(see note 3)**   ☐Yes   ☐No

If Yes, please say what your requirements are. If necessary, court staff may
contact you about your requirements.

Section 5 – Signature

Signed

*Person served/notified('s solicitor)('s litigation friend)

Name

Date

**Name
of firm**

**Position or
office held**   * Please delete the options in
brackets that do not apply.

Now read note 4 about what you need to do next.

5

Guidance notes

Note 1

Application to be joined as a party

If you have been notified that an application has been issued and you wish to participate in the proceedings then you need to apply to be joined as a party.

If you have applied to be joined as a party the court will consider your application to be joined and if it decides to do so, will make an order to that effect.

Note 2

Your interest in the proceedings

You need to provide the court with information that will be useful in considering your application to be joined as a party. This could include what your connection is to the person to whom the application relates, how long you have known them and any other information that explains why you have an interest in the proceedings.

Note 3

Attending the court

If you need special assistance or special facilities for a disability or impairment, please set out your requirements in full. It is important that you make the court aware of your needs to avoid causing delays.

The court will need to know for example, whether you want documents to be supplied in any alternative format, such as Braille or large print. They will also need to know about any specific requirements should there be a hearing, such as wheelchair access, a hearing loop, or a sign language interpreter.

Note 4

What you need to do next

Please return the completed acknowledgment to:

Court of Protection
Archway Tower
2 Junction Road
London N19 5SZ

Note 5

What happens next?

The court will serve the acknowledgment and any other documents you file with it on the applicant and other parties to the proceedings.

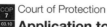 Court of Protection

Application to object to the registration of a lasting power of attorney (LPA)

For office use only
Date received
Case no.
Date issued

Name of the donor of the LPA (this is the person who made the LPA)

SEAL

Please read first

- You can only object using this form if you are an intended attorney or a named person who received an LPA001 notice of intention to apply for registration of a lasting power of attorney.

- There is no fee for filing this form with the court.

- An application to object must be made within five weeks from the day on which you received the LPA001 notice.

- If you are not one of the people who received the LPA001 notice but you wish to object, you can still do so but you need to file a COP1 application form and pay the specified fee. You need to notify the Public Guardian of your application. See note 1 at the end of this form for information on notifying the Public Guardian.

- An objection should be made to the Public Guardian (instead of the court) in the following circumstances:

    – if you are the donor, by using the form LPA006 objection by the donor to the registration of a lasting power of attorney;

    or

    – if you object on certain specified factual grounds, by using the form LPA007 objection to the Office of the Public Guardian of a proposed registration of a lasting power of attorney on factual grounds.

- You may need to pay for any costs you incur during the proceedings. If the court considers that you have acted unreasonably you can be ordered to pay the costs incurred by other parties.

- Please continue on a separate sheet of paper if you need more space to answer a question. Write your name, the name and date of birth of the person to whom the application relates, and the number of the question you are answering on each separate sheet.

- If you need help completing this form please check the website, www.hmcourts-service.gov.uk or www.direct.gov.uk, for further guidance or information, or contact Court Enquiry Service on 0300 456 4600 or courtofprotectionenquiries@hmcourts-service.gsi.gov.uk.

- Court of Protection staff cannot give legal advice. If you need legal advice please contact a solicitor.

© Crown Copyright 2010

Section 1 - Your details (the applicant)

1.1 Your details ☐ Mr. ☐ Mrs. ☐ Miss ☐ Ms. ☐ Other _____

First name

Middle name(s)

Last name

1.2 Address (including postcode)

Telephone no.	Daytime	
	Evening	
	Mobile	

E-mail address

1.3 Is a solicitor representing you? ☐ Yes ☐ No

If Yes, please give the solicitor's details.

Name

Address (including postcode)

| Telephone no. | | Fax no. | |

DX no.

E-mail address

2

1.4   To which address should all official documentation be sent?

☐ Your address

☐ Solicitor's address

☐ Other address (please provide details)

1.5   Your description

☐ Attorney

☐ Other person entitled to be notified of the application to register the LPA

Section 2 - Objection to the registration of an LPA

2.1   Full name of the donor

☐ Mr.   ☐ Mrs.   ☐ Miss   ☐ Ms.   ☐ Other _____

First name

Middle name(s)

Last name

2.2   Full name of intended attorney(s)

☐ Mr.   ☐ Mrs.   ☐ Ms.   ☐ Miss   ☐ Other _____

First name

Last name

☐ Mr.   ☐ Mrs.   ☐ Ms.   ☐ Miss   ☐ Other _____

First name

Last name

2.3   Date donor signed the LPA

D	D	M	M	Y	Y	Y	Y

2.4   Date you were given notice of the application to register the LPA

D	D	M	M	Y	Y	Y	Y

2.5   You can only object to the court against the registration of the LPA on grounds which are prescribed in regulations under the Mental Capacity Act 2005.

Please indicate your grounds for objecting to the proposed registration:

☐ The power purported to be created by the instrument* is not valid as a LPA. (e.g. the donor did not have capacity to make an LPA).

☐ The power created by the instrument no longer exists (e.g. the donor revoked it at a time when he or she had capacity to do so)

☐ Fraud or undue pressure was used to induce the donor to make the power.

☐ The attorney proposes to behave in a way that would contravene his authority or would not be in the donor's best interests.

The instrument means the LPA made by the donor.

2.6   Any evidence in support of your application must be filed with this application form. If you are attaching any written evidence please use the COP24 witness statement form.   ☐ Evidence attached

2.7   You must have notified the Public Guardian of your intention to apply to the court to object to the registration of the LPA. **(See note 1)**   ☐ I confirm that I have notified the Public Guardian

Section 3 - Attending court hearings

3.1   If the court requires you to attend a hearing do you need any special assistance or facilities? **(See note 2)**   ☐ Yes   ☐ No

If Yes, please say what your requirements are. If necessary, court staff may contact you about your requirements.

Section 4 – Statement of truth

The statement of truth is to be signed by you, your solicitor or your litigation friend.

*(I believe) (The applicant believes) that the facts stated in this application form are true.

Signed

*Applicant('s litigation friend)('s solicitor)

Name

Date

Name
of firm

Position or
office held

* Please delete the option in
  brackets that do not apply.

Now read note 3 about what you need to do next.

Court of Protection

Application relating to the registration of an enduring power of attorney (EPA)

For office use only
Date received
Case no.
Date issued

Name of the donor of the EPA (this is the person who made the EPA)

SEAL

Please read first

- You need to complete and file this application form if you are the donor, an intended attorney or a relative of the donor entitled by Schedule 4 of the Mental Capacity Act 2005 (the Act) to be notified of the application to register the EPA and:

    – you wish to object to the registration of the EPA; or

    – you wish to seek the registration of the EPA where you have been notified that the registration has been suspended.

- If you are entitled to be notified then either you will have received an EP1PG notice of intention to apply for registration, or the Public Guardian will have notified you that the registration has been suspended.

- There is no fee for filing this form with the court.

- Schedule 4 of the Act provides for the court to dispense with the requirement to give notice. If you are one of the people entitled by the Act to be notified then you can object to the court using this form even if you have not received an EP1PG notice but you find out about the application through other means.

- If you wish to apply to object to the registration of the EPA then you should do so as soon as reasonably possible after receiving the EP1PG notice. You should notify the Public Guardian of your application. If you do not make an application, the Public Guardian will ask for the court's directions on registration. See note 1 at the end of this form for information on notifying the Public Guardian.

- You may need to pay for any costs you incur during the proceedings. If the court considers that you have acted unreasonably you can be ordered to pay the costs incurred by other parties.

- If you are not one of the people entitled by the Act to be notified of the application to register the EPA but you wish to object you can still do so but you need to file a COP1 application form and pay the specified fee. You should notify the Public Guardian of your application. See note 1 in the separate guidance for information on notifying the Public Guardian.

- Please continue on a separate sheet of paper if you need more space to answer a question. Write your name, the name and date of birth of the donor, and the number of the question you are answering on each separate sheet.

- If you need help completing this form please check the website, www.hmcourts-service.gov.uk or www.direct.gov.uk, for further guidance or information, or contact Court Enquiry Service on 0300 456 4600 or courtofprotectionenquiries@hmcourts-service.gsi.gov.uk.

- Court of Protection staff cannot give legal advice. If you need legal advice please contact a solicitor.

Section 1 - Your details (the applicant)

1.1   Your details   ☐ Mr.   ☐ Mrs.   ☐ Miss   ☐ Ms.   ☐ Other _____

First name

Middle name(s)

Last name

1.2   Address
(including
postcode)

Telephone no.   Daytime

Evening

Mobile

E-mail address

1.3   Is a solicitor representing you?   ☐ Yes   ☐ No

If Yes, please give the solicitor's details.

Name

Address
(including
postcode)

Telephone no.   Fax no.

DX no.

E-mail address

1.4   Which address should official documentation be sent to?

☐ Your address

☐ Solicitor's address

☐ Other address (please provide details)

1.5   Your description

☐ Donor (person making the EPA)

☐ Attorney

☐ Other person entitled to be notified of the application to register the EPA

Section 2 - Details of the EPA

2.1   Full name of the donor (if you are not the donor)

☐ Mr.   ☐ Mrs.   ☐ Miss   ☐ Ms.   ☐ Other _____

First name	
Middle name(s)	
Last name	

2.2   Donor's address and telephone number (if you are not the donor)

Address (including postcode)	

Telephone no.	Daytime	
	Evening	
	Mobile	

E-mail address	

2.3   Donor's date of birth   D D M M Y Y Y Y

2.4 Full name of intended attorney(s)

☐ Mr. ☐ Mrs. ☐ Ms. ☐ Miss ☐ Other _____

First name

Last name

☐ Mr. ☐ Mrs. ☐ Ms. ☐ Miss ☐ Other _____

First name

Last name

☐ Mr. ☐ Mrs. ☐ Ms. ☐ Miss ☐ Other _____

First name

Last name

2.5 Date donor signed the EPA

D	D	M	M	Y	Y	Y	Y

2.6 Date you were given notice of the application to register the EPA

D	D	M	M	Y	Y	Y	Y

Section 3 - Your application

3.1 Please state the directions you are seeking.

3.2   If you object to the registration of the EPA you can only do so on grounds which are prescribed in the Mental Capacity Act 2005.

Please indicate your grounds for objecting to the proposed registration:

☐ The power purported to be created by the instrument* is not valid as an enduring power of attorney

☐ The power created by the instrument no longer subsists

☐ The application is premature because the donor is not yet becoming mentally incapable

☐ Fraud or undue pressure was used to induce the donor to make the power

☐ The attorney is unsuitable to be the donor's attorney (having regard to all the circumstances and in particular the attorney's relationship to or connection with the donor).

The instrument means the EPA made by the donor.

Please tick to confirm

3.3   I have notified the Public Guardian of my intention to apply to the court in relation to the registration of the EPA. **(See note 1)**   ☐ I confirm I have notified the Public Guardian

3.4   If you seek registration please state your reasons for doing so.

3.5   Any evidence in support of your application must be filed with this application form. If you are attaching any written evidence please use the COP24 witness statement form.   ☐ Evidence attached

Section 4 - Attending court hearings

4.1   If the court requires you to attend a hearing do you need any special assistance or facilities? **(See note 2)**   ☐ Yes   ☐ No

If Yes, please say what your requirements are. If necessary, court staff may contact you about your requirements

5

Section 5 – Statement of truth

The statement of truth is to be signed by you, your solicitor or your litigation friend.

*(I believe) (The applicant believes) that the facts stated in this application form are true.

Signed

*Applicant('s solicitor)('s litigation friend)

Name

Date

Name of firm

Position or office held

* Please delete the option in brackets that do not apply.

Now read note 3 about what you need to do next.

Guidance notes

Note 1

Notifying the Public Guardian

If you have not already done so, you should notify the Public Guardian of your objection within five weeks of receiving the EP1PG notice. Upon notification the Office of the Public Guardian will suspend the registration until the court provides further directions. If the Public Guardian is not notified there is a risk that the EPA will be registered.

You should also notify the Public Guardian of your application to the court.

You can notify the Public Guardian by writing to:

Customer Services
Archway Tower
2 Junction Road
London N19 5SZ

Note 2

Attending court hearings

If you need special assistance or special facilities for a disability or impairment, please set out your requirements in full. It is important that you make the court aware of your needs to avoid causing any delays.

The court staff will need to know, for example, whether you want documents to be supplied in an alternative format, such as Braille or large print.

They will also need to know about any specific requirements should there be a hearing, such as wheelchair access, a hearing loop or a sign language interpreter.

Note 3

What you need to do next

The court requires two copies (i.e. the original plus one copy) of the each form and document you file.

Please return the original completed forms, documents and copies to:

Court of Protection
Archway Tower
2 Junction Road
London N19 5SZ

Note 4

What happens next?

The court will notify you when your application form has been issued and the court will return a sealed copy of the application form. You will need to serve a copy on the donor and each attorney of the EPA.

COP 9
03.10 Court of Protection
Application notice

For office use only
Date received
Date issued

Case no.

Full name of person to whom the application relates
(this is the person who lacks, or is alleged, to lack capacity)

SEAL

Please read first

- This form can be used in a variety of circumstances and must be used for applications within proceedings. For further guidance on when this form is to be used please see the Court of Protection Rules 2007 and the Practice Directions accompanying the Rules or contact Customer Services at the number below.

- If you wish to apply to start proceedings please complete the COP1 application form.

- If you wish to apply to be joined as a party to the proceedings please complete the COP10 application notice for applications to be joined as a party.

- You may need to pay for any costs you incur during the proceedings. If the court considers that you have acted unreasonably you can be ordered to pay the costs incurred by other parties.

- Please continue on a separate sheet of paper if you need more space to answer a question. Write the case number, your name, the name of the person to whom the application relates, and number of the question you are answering on each separate sheet.

- If you need help completing this form please check the website, www.hmcourts-service.gov.uk or www.direct.gov.uk, for further guidance or information, or contact Court Enquiry Service on 0300 456 4600 or courtofprotectionenquiries@ hmcourts-service.gsi.gov.uk

- Court of Protection staff cannot give legal advice. If you need legal advice please contact a solicitor.

1

Section 1 - Your details

1.1　Your details　☐ Mr.　☐ Mrs.　☐ Miss　☐ Ms.　☐ Other _____

First name

Middle name(s)

Last name

1.2　Address
(including
postcode)

Telephone no.

Daytime	
Evening	
Mobile	

E-mail address

1.3　Is a solicitor representing you?　　　　　　　　　　☐Yes　　☐No

If Yes, please give the solicitor's details.

Name

Address
(Including
postcode)

Telephone no. | Fax no.

DX no.

E-mail address

1.4　Which address should official documentation be sent to?

☐ Your address

☐ Solicitor's address

☐ Other address (please provide details)

2

1.5   What is your role in the proceedings?

         ☐ Applicant (the person who filed the COP1 application form)

         ☐ Person to whom the application relates

         ☐ Other party to the proceedings

         ☐ Other (please give details)

Section 2 - Your application

2.1   What order or direction are you seeking from the court?

2.2   Please set out the grounds on which you are seeking the order or direction?

2.3   Any evidence in support of your application must be filed with this application notice. If you are attaching any written evidence please use the COP24 witness statement form.   ☐ Evidence attached

         If the court requires that evidence be given by affidavit then you need to use the COP25 affidavit form.

2.4   Please provide the details of any person who you reasonably believe has an interest which means they ought to be heard by the court in relation to this application notice and who is not already a party to the proceedings.

Full name including title	Full address including postcode	Connection to the person to whom the proceedings relate

Section 3 – Statement of truth

The statement of truth is to be signed by you, your solicitor or your litigation friend.

*(I believe) (The applicant believes) that the facts stated in this application notice are true.

Signed

*Applicant('s litigation friend)('s solicitor)

Name

Date

Name of firm

Position or office held

* Please delete the options in brackets that do not apply.

Now read note 1 about what you need to do next.

4

Guidance notes

Note 1

What you need to do next

The court requires two copies (i.e. the original plus one copy) of each form and document you file.

Please return the original completed forms, documents and copies to:

    Court of Protection
    Archway Tower
    2 Junction Road
    London N19 5SZ

Note 2

What happens next?

The court will notify you when your application notice has been issued. The court will return a sealed copy of the application notice. You may need to serve copies on:

- every other party to the proceedings;
- anyone who is named as a respondent in the application notice; and
- any other person as the court may direct.

COP 10
03.10

Court of Protection

Application notice for applications to be joined as a party

For office use only
Date received
Date issued

Case no.

Full name of person to whom the application relates
(this is the name of the person who lacks, or is alleged to lack, capacity)

SEAL

Please read first

- If you wish to apply to be joined as a party to the proceedings then you need to complete this application notice. You must be joined as a party to oppose an application or seek a different order.

- Do not complete this form if you have been served with a copy of COP1 application form or have received a COP15 notice that an application form has been issued. Instead you need to complete and file a COP5 acknowledgment of service/notification in order to be joined as a party.

- If your application relates to another matter and is made in the course of existing proceedings then you need to complete the COP9 application notice.

- You may need to pay for any costs you incur during the proceedings. If the court considers that you have acted unreasonably you can be ordered to pay the costs incurred by other parties.

- Please continue on a separate sheet of paper if you need more space to answer a question. Write the case number, your name and the name of the person to whom the application relates, and the number of the question you are answering on each separate sheet.

- If you need help completing this form please check the website, www.hmcourts-service.gov.uk or www.direct.gov.uk, for further guidance or information, or contact Court Enquiry Service on 0300 456 4600 or courtofprotectionenquiries@hmcourts-service.gsi.gov.uk

- Court of Protection staff cannot give legal advice. If you need legal advice please contact a solicitor.

Section 1 - Your details (the person applying to be joined as a party)

1.1   Your details   ☐ Mr.   ☐ Mrs.   ☐ Miss   ☐ Ms.   ☐ Other _____

First name

Middle name(s)

Last name

1.2   Address
(including
postcode)

Telephone no.

Daytime	
Evening	
Mobile	

E-mail address

1.3   Is a solicitor representing you?   ☐ Yes   ☐ No

If Yes, please give the solicitor's details.

Name

Address
(including
postcode)

Telephone no.		Fax no.	
DX no.			
E-mail address			

1.4   Which address should official documentation be sent to?

☐ Your address

☐ Solicitor's address

☐ Other address (please provide details)

2

Section 2 - Your application

2.1   What is your connection to the person to whom the application relates?

2.2   What is your interest in the proceedings?

2.3   Do you consent to the application?   ☐ Yes   ☐ No

2.4   Do you oppose the application?   ☐ Yes   ☐ No

     If Yes, please set out your grounds for doing so.

2.5   Do you propose that a different order should be made?   ☐ Yes   ☐ No

     If Yes, please set out what the order is.

2.6   Any evidence in support of your application must be filed with this application notice. If you are attaching any written evidence please use the COP24 witness statement form   ☐ Evidence attached

Section 3 – Attending court hearings

3.1   If the court requires you to attend a hearing do you need any special assistance or facilities? **(see note 1)**   ☐Yes   ☐No

If Yes, please say what your requirements are. If necessary, court staff may contact you about your requirements.

Section 4 - Statement of truth

The statement of truth is to be signed by you, or your solicitor or your litigation friend.

*(I believe) (The applicant believes) the facts stated in this application notice are true.

Signed

*Applicant('s litigation friend)('s solicitor)

Name

Date

Name of firm

Position or office held

* Please delete the options in brackets that do not apply.

Now read note 2 about what you need to do next.

Note `1`

Attending court hearings

If you need special assistance or special facilities for a disability or impairment, please set out your requirements in full. It is important that you make the court aware of your needs to avoid causing any delays.

The court staff will need to know, for example, whether you want documents to be supplied in an alternative format, such as Braille or large print. They will also need to know about any specific requirements should there be a hearing, such as wheelchair access, a hearing loop or a sign language Interpreter.

Note `2`

What you need to do next

The court requires a sufficient number of copies of this form to provide a copy to every party to the proceedings. Please contact Court Enquiry Service on 0300 456 4600 to find out how many copies you need to provide.

Please return the original completed form and copies to:
> Court of Protection
> Archway Tower
> 2 Junction Road
> London N19 5SZ

Note `3`

What happens next?

The court will serve the application notice and any accompanying documents on every party to the proceedings.

The court will consider your application to be joined and if it decides to do so, will make an order to that effect.

COP 12 **03.10** Court of Protection
Special undertaking by trustees

For office use only
Date received
Case no.

Full name of person to whom the application relates
(this is the name of the person who lacks, or is alleged to lack, capacity)

Please read first

- If your application relates to the appointment of a trustee then you need to complete this undertaking and file it with the court together with a COP1 application form and any other required forms and documents. All new and continuing trustees must sign the undertaking (not just the person making the application).

- For further information on applications relating to trustees please see Practice Direction G that supplements Part 9 of the Court of Protection Rules 2007.

- Please continue on a separate sheet of paper if you need more space to answer a question. Write your name, the name and date of birth of the person to whom the application relates, and the number of the question you are answering on each separate sheet.

- If you need help completing this form please check the website, www.hmcourts-service.gov.uk or www.direct.gov.uk, for further guidance or information, or contact Court Enquiry Service on 0300 456 4600 or courtofprotectionenquiries@ hmcourts-service.gsi.gov.uk

- Court of Protection staff cannot give legal advice. If you need legal advice please contact a solicitor.

Section 1 - Details of the person to whom the application relates

1.1   Full name

Address
(including
postcode)

Date of birth | D | D | M | M | Y | Y | Y | Y |

Section 2 - Special undertaking by trustees

2.1   Name of continuing trustee

Address
(including
postcode)

Name of second continuing trustee (if applicable)

Address
(including
postcode)

Name of new trustee (if applicable)

Address
(including
postcode)

2

Name of second new trustee (if applicable)

Address
(including
postcode)

2.2 Name of
property, will,
settlement, etc.

2.3 I/WE HEREBY UNDERTAKE that in the event of such appointment being approved and made, where the above named person lacks capacity in relation to the trust, to sell any land or property to the whole of any part of which the person is absolutely entitled in equity at such fair and reasonable price as can be obtained through a sale on the open market.

AND THAT in the event of the sale being effected where the above named person lacks capacity in relation to the trust we will deal with the proceeds of sale or with the person's undivided share thereof, as the case may be, in such manner as the court may direct but so that where the person is a joint tenant we will deal with the proceeds in such manner as the court (on behalf of the person) and the other joint tenant shall jointly direct and on severance of the joint tenancy we will deal with the person's share of the proceeds in such manner as the court may direct.

Section 5 – Signature

Signed

Name

Date

Signed

Name

Date

Signed

Name

Date

Signed

Name

Date

Now read note 8 of the COP1 application form about what you need to do next.

4

COP 14 Court of Protection
03.10 **Proceedings about you in the Court of Protection**

For office use only

To (enter name and address of person to whom the application relates)

Name

Address

This notice is to tell you of proceedings about you in the Court of Protection.

The court has powers to make decisions about the property and affairs and personal welfare of people who lack capacity to make such decisions.

If you have any questions or need further information about this notice you can:
- **ring Court Enquiry Service on 0300 456 4600;**
- **write to the Court of Protection, Archway Tower, 2 Junction Road, London N19 5SZ; or**
- **check the website, www.hmcourts-service.gov.uk or www.direct.gov.uk.**

The Court of Protection staff cannot give legal advice. If you need legal advice please contact a solicitor.

Details of the proceedings

Case number

Date the *(application)(appeal) was issued

D	D	M	M	Y	Y	Y	Y

Name of the *(applicant)(appellant)

The *(application)(appeal) relates to your:

☐ property and affairs

☐ personal welfare

☐ property and affairs and personal welfare.

* Please delete the options in
brackets that do not apply.

This notice is to tell you that

Signed

Name

Date

**Name
of firm**

**Position or
office held**

2

Court of Protection
Guidance notes on completing form COP14

The person to whom the application/appeal relates must be notified personally of certain matters.

You must also provide the person to whom the application/appeal relates with a COP14 notice which explains the matter for which notification is being provided. The box that begins "

This notice is to tell you that..." should be completed using simple, clear language as follows:

Nature of notification	Information to be included in the notice
Application has been issued by the court	Complete the sentence that starts "This notice is to tell you that..." with the following words – **an application about you will be considered by the Court of Protection.** Please add the following information: • the application raises the question of whether the person being notified lacks capacity in relation to a matter or matters and what that means; • what will happen if the court makes the order or direction that has been applied for; and • where the application contains a proposal for the appointment of a person to make decisions on behalf of the person to whom the application relates, details of who that person is.
The date when a hearing in relation to the application is to be held	Complete the sentence that starts "This notice is to tell you that..." with the following words – **a hearing of an application about you will be held at the Court of Protection on [insert the date and time] at [insert address].**
Application has been withdrawn	Complete the sentence that starts "This notice is to tell you that..." with the following words – an application about you has been withdrawn from the Court of Protection. Please add information about the consequence of the withdrawal.
Appellant's notice has been issued by the court	Complete the sentence that starts "This notice is to tell you that..." with the following words – **an appeal regarding a court decision about you will be considered by the Court of Protection.** Please add the following information: • the issues raised by the appeal; and • what will happen if the court makes the order or direction that has been applied for.
The date when a hearing in relation to the appeal is to be held	Complete the sentence that starts "This notice is to tell you that..." with the following words – **a hearing of an appeal regarding a court decision about you will be held at the Court of Protection on [insert the date and time] at [insert address].**
Appellant's notice has been withdrawn	Complete the sentence that starts "This notice is to tell you that..." with the following words – **an appeal regarding a court decision about you has been withdrawn from the Court of Protection.** Please add information about the consequence of the withdrawal.
Final order has been made by the court	Complete the sentence that starts "This notice is to tell you that..." with the following words – **a final order about you has been made by the Court of Protection.** Please add information about the effect of the order.
Any other matter as directed by the court	Complete the sentence that starts "This notice is to tell you that..." with information to briefly summarise the matter. Please add information about the matter as directed by the court.

Where the person is notified that an application form or appellant's notice has been issued then you must provide them with a COP5 acknowledgment of notification form.

You must complete a COP20 certificate of notification/non-notification and return it to the court within seven days of notification being provided.

 Court of Protection
Notice that an application form has been issued

To (enter name and address of person to be notified)

Name

Address

This notice is to tell you that an application form has been issued by the Court of Protection.

The court has powers to make decisions regarding the property and affairs and personal welfare of people who lack capacity to make such decisions.

If you wish to be involved in the proceedings, then you need to complete and file the COP5 acknowledgment of notification with the court and apply to be joined as a party.

If you have any questions or need further information about the application you can:

- ring Court Enquiry Service on 0300 456 4600;
- write to the Court of Protection, Archway Tower, 2 Junction Road, London N19 5SZ; or
- check the website, www.hmcourts-service.gov.uk or www.direct.gov.uk

Court of Protection staff cannot give legal advice. If you need legal advice please contact a solicitor.

Details of the application

Case number

Date the application was issued

D D M M Y Y Y Y

Name of the applicant

Name of the person to whom the application relates (this is the person who lacks, or is alleged to lack, capacity)

Applicant's connection to the person to whom the application relates

The application relates to the exercise of the court's jurisdiction in relation to the person's:

☐ property and affairs

☐ personal welfare

☐ property and affairs and personal welfare.

© Crown Copyright 2010

1

The matter the court has been asked to decide:

Order(s) the court has been asked to make:

Signed

Name

Date

Name of firm

Position or office held

COP 15A 10.07

Court of Protection
Guidance notes on completing form COP15

- You must notify the people who are likely to have an interest in being notified of your application within 21 days of the date on which your application form was issued by the court.

- These are the people whose details you provided in section 4.2 of the COP1 application form.

- You must also notify any other people that the court may direct.

- To notify people that your application has been issued by the court you provide each person to be notified with:

  - a COP15 notice that an application has been issued; and

  - a COP5 acknowledgment of notification.

- You must complete and sign the COP15 notice. Some of the questions are the same as those on the COP1 application form. Where the questions are the same you should copy the answers you provided on the application form.

- You can provide this information by:

  - delivering it to the person to be notified personally;

  - delivering it to their home address; or

  - posting it to their home address by first class post.

- You must complete a COP20 certificate of notification/non-notification and return it to the court within 7 days of notification being provided. You must complete a separate certificate for every person who is notified.

Court of Protection

Certificate of service/non-service

Certificate of notification/ non-notification

Case no.

Full name of person to whom the application relates
(this is the person who lacks, or is alleged to lack, capacity)

Please read first

- You need to complete and file this certificate when you:
  - serve a copy of a document;
  - provide notification that an application form has been issued by the court; or
  - provide notification to the person to whom the application/appeal relates of the issue or withdrawal of an application form or appellant's notice, the date fixed for a hearing, a final order of the court or any other matter as the court directs.

- You must complete a separate certificate for each person every time you serve a document or provide notification.

- You must file the certificate within 7 days beginning on the date on which you serve the document or provide notification.

- Please continue on a separate sheet of paper if you need more space to answer a question. Write the case number, your name, the name the of person to whom the application relates and the number of the question you are answering on each separate sheet.

- There are additional guidance notes at the end of this form.

- If you need help completing this form please check the website, www.hmcourts-service.gov.uk or www.direct.gov.uk, for further guidance or information, or contact Court Enquiry Service on 0300 456 4600 or courtofprotectionenquiries@hmcourts-service.gsi.gov.uk

- Court of Protection staff cannot give legal advice. If you need legal advice please contact a solicitor.

Section 1 - Your details and details of the person served/notified

1.1   Your name:

```

```

1.2   In what capacity are you serving/providing notice? **(See note 1)**

As the:

☐ Applicant   ☐ Respondent

☐ Applicant's solicitor   ☐ Respondent's solicitor

☐ Applicant's litigation friend   ☐ Respondent's litigation friend

☐ Applicant's agent   ☐ Respondent's agent

☐ Other (please give details)

```

```

1.3   Name of the person served/notified:

```

```

Being:

☐ a respondent/a party to the proceedings -
   complete Section 2 and Section 5 only

☐ a person notified that the application form has been issued -
   complete Section 3 and Section 5 only

☐ the person to whom the application/appeal relates -
   complete Section 4 and Section 5 only

2

Section 2 – Service

2.1   Please tick to confirm:

☐ the document was served   ☐ the document was not served

2.2   Title or description of the document (tick only one box)

☐ application form

☐ appellant's notice

☐ respondent's notice

☐ other (please give details)

```
┌──────────────────────────────────────────┐
│                                            │
│                                            │
│                                            │
└──────────────────────────────────────────┘
```

2.3   What is the address where you served or attempted to serve the document?

```
┌──────────────────────────────────────────┐
│                                            │
│                                            │
│                                            │
│                                            │
└──────────────────────────────────────────┘
```

2.4   Being the person's:

☐ residence

☐ last known residence

☐ place of business

☐ other (please specify)

```
┌──────────────────────────────────────────┐
│                                            │
│                                            │
│                                            │
└──────────────────────────────────────────┘
```

2.5 Method by which the document was served: (tick only one box)

☐ by first class post (or other service for next-day delivery)

☐ in person

☐ by document exchange

☐ by delivery of document to a permitted address

☐ by fax

☐ by other electronic means (please specify)

[ ]

☐ by the following alternative method permitted by the court (please specify)

[ ]

2.6 On what date was the document served? **(See note 2)** [D | D | M | M | Y | Y | Y | Y]

2.7 If service by some other means was permitted by the court, please give the details the court requires.

[ ]

Non-service

2.8 If you could not serve the document, please describe your attempt to do so, and explain the reasons why you were not able to serve it.

[ ]

4

Section 3 – Notification that the application form has been issued

3.1   Please tick to confirm:

☐ notification was provided   ☐ notification was not provided

3.2   What is the address where you provided or attempted to provide notification?

```
┌──────────────────────────────────────────────────────────────┐
│                                                                │
│                                                                │
│                                                                │
│                                                                │
└──────────────────────────────────────────────────────────────┘
```

3.3   Being the person's:

☐ residence

☐ last known residence

☐ place of business

☐ other (please specify)

```
┌──────────────────────────────────────────────────────────────┐
│                                                                │
│                                                                │
└──────────────────────────────────────────────────────────────┘
```

3.4   How was notification provided? (tick only one box)

☐ by first class post (or other service for next-day delivery)

☐ in person

☐ by document exchange

☐ by delivery of document to a permitted address

☐ by fax

☐ by other electronic means (please specify)

```
┌──────────────────────────────────────────────────────────────┐
└──────────────────────────────────────────────────────────────┘
```

☐ by the following alternative method permitted by the court (please specify)

```
┌──────────────────────────────────────────────────────────────┐
│                                                                │
│                                                                │
│                                                                │
│                                                                │
└──────────────────────────────────────────────────────────────┘
```

3.5   On what date was notification provided? **(See note 2)**   D D M M Y Y Y Y

3.6   If notification by some other means was permitted by the court, please give the details the court requires.

```



```

Non-notification

3.7   If you could not provide notification, please describe your attempt to do so, and explain the reasons why notification was not provided.

```



```

Section 4 – Notification to the person to whom the application/appeal relates

4.1   Please tick to confirm:

☐ notification was provided   ☐ notification was not provided

4.2   Nature of the notification:

☐ notification that an application form has been   ☐ issued   ☐ withdrawn

☐ notification that an appellant's notice has been   ☐ issued   ☐ withdrawn

☐ notification of the date on which a hearing is to be held

☐ notification of a final order of the court (please give details below)

☐ notification of another matter (please give details below)

```



```

4.3   What is the address where you provided or attempted to provide notification?

4.4   Being the person's:

☐ residence

☐ other (please specify)

4.5   On what date was notification provided?

D	D	M	M	Y	Y	Y	Y

Notification

4.6   Were you notifying the person to whom the application relates that an application form has been issued.   ☐ Yes   ☐ No

If Yes, please confirm that you explained to the person: ☐ I confirm that this
  • who the applicant is;   information has
  • that the application raises the question of whether they lack capacity   been provided.
    in relation to a matter or matters, and what that means;
  • what will happen if the court makes the order or direction that has
    been applied for;
  • where the application contains a proposal for the appointment of a
    person to make decisions on their behalf in relation to the matter to
    which the application relates, details of who that person is; and
  • that they may seek advice and assistance in relation to the application.

4.7   Were you notifying the person to whom the application relates that an application form has been withdrawn?   ☐ Yes   ☐ No

If Yes, please confirm that you explained to the person: ☐ I confirm that this
  • that the application form has been withdrawn;   information has
  • the consequence of the withdrawal; and   been provided.
  • that they may seek advice and assistance in relation to the
    application.

4.8   Were you notifying the person to whom the application relates that an appellant's notice has been issued?   ☐ Yes   ☐ No

If Yes, please confirm that you explained to the person: ☐ I confirm that this
  • who the appellant is;   information has
  • the issues raised by the appeal;   been provided.
  • what will happen if the court makes the order or direction applied for;
    and
  • that they may seek advice and assistance in relation to the appeal.

4.9   Were you notifying the person to whom the application relates that an   ☐ Yes   ☐ No
       appellant's notice has been withdrawn?

       If Yes, please confirm that you explained to the person: ☐ I confirm that this
       • that the notice has been withdrawn;   information has
       • the consequence of the withdrawal; and   been provided.
       • that they may seek advice and assistance in relation to the appeal.

4.10   Were you notifying the person to whom the application relates of a final   ☐ Yes   ☐ No
       order of the court.

       If Yes, please confirm that you explained to the person: ☐ I confirm that this
       • the effect of the order; and   information has
       • that they may seek advice and assistance in relation to the order.   been provided.

4.11   Were you notifying the person to whom the application relates of another   ☐ Yes   ☐ No
       matter as directed by the court?

       If Yes, please confirm that you explained to the person: ☐ I confirm that this
       • the matters directed by the court; and   information has
       • that they may seek advice and assistance in relation to the matter.   been provided.

Non-notification

4.12   If you could not provide notification, please describe your attempt to do so,
       and explain the reasons why notification was not provided.

Section 5 – Statement of truth

The statement of truth must be signed by the person who served/provided notification.

I believe that the facts stated in this certificate are true.

Signed

Name

Date

**Name
of firm**

**Position or
office held**

Now read note 3 about what you need to do next.

Guidance notes

 Note 1

Applicant's/respondent's agent

An agent can be any person who is appointed by the applicant to notify the person to whom the application/appeal relates.

 Note 2

Date notice was served/provided

The certificate must state the date set out in the following table depending on the method of delivery you use:

Method of delivery	Details to be certified
First class post (or other service for next-day delivery)	Date of posting
Personal	Date of personal service
Document exchange	Date when the document was left at the document exchange
Delivery of document to permitted address	Date when document was delivered to the permitted address
Fax	Date of transmission
Other electronic means	Date of transmission and the means used
Alternative method permitted by the court	As required by the court

If the court has permitted an alternative method of delivery it will specify the date or other details to be stated on the certificate of service.

 Note 3

What you need to do next

Please return the completed certificate to:

Court of Protection
Archway Tower
2 Junction Road
London N19 5SZ

COP
22
03.10
Court of Protection

Certificate of suitability of litigation friend

Case no.

Full name of person to whom the application relates
(this is the person who lacks, or is alleged to lack, capacity)

Please read first

- If you wish to act as a litigation friend for a party to the proceedings then you must complete this certificate and file it with the court.

- This does not apply if you wish to act as a litigation friend for the person to whom the application relates. You can apply for an order to be appointed as the litigation friend for the person to whom the application relates (where they are party to the proceedings) by filing a COP9 application notice.

- Please continue on a separate sheet of paper if you need more space to answer a question. Write the case number, your name, the name of the person to whom the application relates, and the number of the question you are answering on each separate sheet.

- If you need help completing this form please check the website, www.hmcourts-service.gov.uk or www.direct.gov.uk, for further guidance or information, or contact Court Enquiry Service on 0300 456 4600 or courtofprotectionenquiries@hmcourts-service.gsi.gov.uk

- Court of Protection staff cannot give legal advice. If you need legal advice please contact a solicitor.

Section 1 - Your details (the litigation friend)

1.1   Your full name   ☐ Mr.   ☐ Mrs.   ☐ Miss   ☐ Ms.   ☐ Other _____

First name

Middle name(s)

Last name

1.2   Address (including postcode)

Telephone no.   Daytime

     Evening

     Mobile

1.3   What is your relationship or connection to the person on whose behalf you wish to act as a litigation friend?

Section 2 - Details of the person on whose behalf you wish to act as a litigation friend

2.1   I consent to act as a litigation friend for:

Name

Address (including postcode)

Telephone no.

2

2.2　　Please tick to confirm:

☐　I know or believe that the person named in section 2.1 lacks capacity to conduct the proceedings on his or her own behalf.

The grounds for my belief are as follows:

If your belief is based upon medical opinion, please attach any relevant document and file it with the court. You are not required to serve the document on every other party to the proceedings (unless the court directs otherwise).　☐ Document(s) attached

Section 3 - Suitability to be a litigation friend

3.1　　Please tick to confirm:

☐　I am able to conduct proceedings on behalf of the person named in section 2.1 competently and fairly;

☐　I have no interests adverse to those of the person; and

☐　I have served a copy of this certificate on the relevant person specified in the table below and on every other person who is a party to the proceedings.

Nature of party	Person to be served
Child	• A person who has parental responsibility for the child within the meaning of the Children Act 1989; or • if there is no such person, a person with whom the child lives with or in whose care the child is.
Protected party (a person who lacks capacity to conduct proceedings, other than a child or the person to whom the application relates)	• The person who is authorised to conduct the proceedings in the protected party's name or on his or her behalf; • a person who is a duly appointed attorney or deputy of the protected party; or • if there is no such person, a person with whom the protected party lives or in whose care the latter is.

You must complete and file a COP20 certificate of service/non-service for every person served with a copy of this certificate.

Section 4 – Statement of truth

This statement of truth is to be signed by the person who wishes to become the litigation friend or their solicitor.

*(I believe)(The litigation friend believes) that the facts stated in this certificate are true.

Signed

*Litigation friend('s solicitor)

Name

Date

Name of firm

Position or office held

* Please delete the options in brackets that do not apply.

Please return the completed certificate to:
Court of Protection, Archway Tower, 2 Junction Road, London N19 5SZ

4

Court of Protection

Certificate of failure or refusal of witness to attend before an examiner

For office use only

Case no.

Full name of person to whom the application relates
(this is the person who lacks, or is alleged to lack, capacity)

Please read first

- If you required a deposition and the person ordered to attend before the examiner failed to attend or refused to be sworn, answer a question or produce a document, then you need to complete this certificate and file it with the court.

- You need to arrange for the examiner to complete and sign section 1 of this certificate.

- You may apply to the court for a further order in respect of the witness after this certificate has been filed.

- Please continue on a separate sheet of paper if you need more space to answer a question. Write the case number, your name, the name of the person to whom the application relates, and the number of the question you are answering on each separate sheet.

- If you need help completing this form please check the website, www.hmcourts-service.gov.uk or www.direct.gov.uk, for further guidance or information, or contact Court Enquiry Service on 0300 456 4600 or courtofprotectionenquiries@ hmcourts-service.gsi.gov.uk

- Court of Protection staff cannot give legal advice. If you need legal advice please contact a solicitor.

Section 1 - Failure or refusal of witness to attend before an examiner

This section is to be completed and signed by the examiner

1.1 What is the name of the witness?

1.2 What was the date of the order directing the examination?

D	D	M	M	Y	Y	Y	Y

1.3 On what day and at what time was the examination due to take place?

D	D	M	M	Y	Y	Y	Y

Time

1.4 Where was the examination due to take place?

1.5 The above named witness:

☐ failed to attend the examination

☐ refused to be sworn for the purpose of the examination

☐ refused to answer the following lawful question(s) at the examination (please specify)

☐ refused to produce the following document(s) at the examination (please specify)

1.6   Please provide any comments as to the conduct of the deponent or of any person attending
         the examination.

Signed | | Position or | |
                                                       office held

Name | | Date | |

Section 2 - Your details (party requiring the deposition)

This section is to be completed and signed by the party requiring the deposition

2.1 ☐ Mr.   ☐ Mrs.   ☐ Miss   ☐ Ms.   ☐ Other _____

First name

Middle name(s)

Last name

2.2 Address (including postcode)

Telephone no.

2.3 What is your role in these proceedings?

☐ Applicant (the person who filed the COP1 application form)

☐ Respondent

☐ Other (please provide details)

Section 3 – Signature

Signed

*(Applicant)(Respondent)('s litigation friend)('s solicitor)

Name

* Please delete the options in brackets that do not apply.

Date

Name of firm

Please return the completed certificate to:
Court of Protection, Archway Tower, 2 Junction Road, London N19 5SZ

Position or office held

4

COP 24 03.10 Court of Protection
Witness statement

Statement given by (name of witness)
Statement ☐ 1st   ☐ 2nd   ☐ 3rd   ☐ Other _____
Filed on behalf of (name of party)
Date statement was made

Case no.

[ ]

Full name of person to whom the application relates
(this is the person who lacks, or is alleged to lack capacity)

[ ]

Please read first

- If you are filing written evidence with the court then it should be included in or attached to this form.

- If the court requires that evidence be given by affidavit then you need to use the COP25 affidavit form.

- You must initial any alterations to the witness statement.

- A document referred to in a witness statement and provided to the court is known as an exhibit. Each exhibit must be identified in some way (e.g. 'Exhibit A'). The first page of the exhibit must contain all of the information provided in the box in the top-right corner of this page.

- Practice Direction A accompanying Part 14 of the Court of Protection Rules 2007 sets out more detailed requirements in relation to witness statements.

- Please continue on a separate sheet of paper if you need more space to provide your witness statement. Please mark each separate sheet with all of the information provided in the box in the top-right corner of this page.

- If you need help completing this form please check the website, www.hmcourts-service.gov.uk or www.direct.gov.uk, for further guidance or information, or contact Court Enquiry Service on 0300 456 4600 or courtofprotectionenquiries@ hmcourts-service.gsi.gov.uk

- Court of Protection staff cannot give legal advice. If you need legal advice please contact a solicitor.

1

Witness statement

1 Enter your full name

I, **1**

2 Enter your occupation or description

2

3 Enter your full address including postcode or, if making the statement in your professional, business or other occupational capacity, the position you hold, the name of your firm or employer and the address at which you work

of **3**

☐ am a party to the proceedings

☐ am employed by a party to the proceedings

and state that:

4 Set out in numbered paragraphs indicating:

- which of the statements are from your own knowledge and which are matters of information or belief, and

- the source for any matters of information or belief.

Where you refer to an exhibit, you should state the identifier you have used. For example, 'I refer to the (description of document) marked Exhibit A '

4

continued over

2

4

continued over

4

Statement of truth

The statement of truth is to be signed by the witness.

I believe that the facts stated in this witness statement are true.

Signed

Name **Date**

Please return the completed witness statement to:
Court of Protection, Archway Tower, 2 Junction Road, London N19 5SZ

COP
25
03.10
Court of Protection
Affidavit

Sworn by (name of deponent)
Affidavit ☐ 1st   ☐ 2nd   ☐ 3rd   ☐ Other ....
Filed on behalf of (name of party)
Date sworn

Case no.

Full name of person to whom the application relates
(this is the person who lacks, or is alleged to lack, capacity)

Please read first

- If the court requires that evidence be given by affidavit then it must be included in or attached to this form.
- Only the following may administer oaths:
  - Commissioners for Oaths;
  - practising solicitors;
  - other persons specified by statute;
  - certain officials of the Supreme Court;
  - a circuit judge or district judge;
  - any justice of the peace;
  - certain officials of the county court.
- Practice Direction A accompanying Part 14 of the Court of Protection Rules 2007 sets out more detailed requirements in relation to affidavits.

- Please continue on a separate sheet of paper if you need more space to provide the affidavit. Please mark each separate sheet with all of the information provided in the box in the top-right corner of this page.
- If you need help completing this form please check the website, www.hmcourts-service.gov.uk or www.direct.gov.uk, for further guidance or information, or contact Court Enquiry Service on 0300 456 4600 or courtofprotectionenquiries@hmcourts-service.gsi.gov.uk
- Court of Protection staff cannot give legal advice. If you need legal advice please contact a solicitor.

Affidavit

1 Enter full name of deponent	I, **1**	
2 Enter occupation or description	**2**	

3 Enter your full address including postcode or, if making the affidavit in your professional, business or other occuptional capacity, the position you hold, the name of your firm or employer and the address at which you work

of **3**

☐ am a party to the proceedings

☐ am employed by a party to the proceedings

and ☐ state on oath **or** ☐ do solemnly and sincerely affirm

4 Set out in numbered paragraphs indicating:
- which of the statements are from your own knowledge and which are matters of information or belief, and
- the source for any matters of information or belief.

Where you refer to an exhibit, you should state the identifier you have used. For example, 'I refer to the (description of document) marked Exhibit A...'

4

continued over

4

continued over

4

Sworn/affirmed by (signature)

before me (signature)

Full name

Qualifications

at (address)

On (date)

Please return the completed affidavit to:
Court of Protection, Archway Tower, 2 Junction Road, London N19 5SZ

Court of Protection

Notice of hearing for committal order

To (enter name and address of person to be notified)

Name

Address

This notice is to tell you that the hearing date for the following case has been fixed.

Details of the case

Case no.

Applicant

Details of the hearing

Date   Time

Location

Important notice

The court has the power to send you to prison and to fine you if it finds that any of the allegations made against you are true and amount to a contempt of court.

You must attend court on the date shown on this form. It is in your own interest to do so. You should bring with you any witnesses and documents which you think will help you put your side of the case.

If you consider the allegations are not true you must tell the court why. If it is established that they are true, you must tell the court of any good reason why they do not amount to a contempt of court, or, if they do, why you should not be punished.

If you have any questions or need further information about the hearing please check the website, www.hmcourts-service.gov.uk or www.direct.gov.uk or contact Court Enquiry Service on 0300 456 4600. Court of Protection staff cannot give legal advice. If you need legal advice please contact a solicitor.

If you need any special assistance or facilities to attend the hearing please contact Court Enquiry Service on the number above immediately so that arrangements can be made (if you have not done so already).

COP
30
03.10

Court of Protection

Notice of change of solicitor

Case no.

Full name of person to whom the application relates
(this is the person who lacks, or is alleged to lack, capacity)

Please read first

- You must complete this notice and file it with the court if you:

  – are changing the solicitor who is acting for you;

  – have been conducting the proceedings in person and are now appointing a solicitor to act on your behalf; or

  – have had a solicitor acting on your behalf and now intend to act in person.

- If you are applying for an order declaring that the solicitor acting for another party has ceased to act, then you need to use the COP9 application notice.

- You must provide a copy of this notice to every other party to the proceedings. If applicable, you must also provide a copy to the solicitor who is ceasing to act for you.

- The court will not consider that a change has occurred until you have filed this notice.

- Please continue on a separate sheet of paper if you need more space to answer a question. Write the case number, your name, the name of the person to whom the application relates, and the number of the question you are answering on each separate sheet.

- If you need help completing this form please check the website, www.hmcourts-service.gov.uk or www.direct.gov.uk, for further guidance or information, or contact Court Enquiry Service on 0300 456 4600 or courtofprotectionenquiries@hmcourts-service.gsi.gov.uk.

- Court of Protection staff cannot give legal advice. If you need legal advice please contact a solicitor.

1

Section 1 - Your details (party changing solicitor)

1.1   ☐ Mr.   ☐ Mrs.   ☐ Miss   ☐ Ms.   ☐ Other _____

First name

Middle name(s)

Last name

Address
(including
postcode)

Telephone no.

1.2   What is your role in these proceedings?

☐ Applicant (the person who filed the COP1 application form)

☐ Respondent

☐ Other (please provide details)

Section 2 - Change of solicitor

2.1   I give notice that:

☐ I am changing the solicitor who is acting for me.

☐ I have been conducting the proceedings in person but am now appointing
a solicitor to act on my behalf.

☐ I have had a solicitor acting on my behalf but now intend to act in person.

2.2 Details of solicitor being appointed (if applicable)

Name of solicitor	
Name of firm	
Address (including postcode)	

Telephone no.		Fax no.	
DX no.			
E-mail address			

2.3 Details of solicitor who will cease to act (if applicable)

2.4 Which address should official documentation be sent to?

☐ Your address

☐ Solicitor's address

☐ Other address (please provide details)

2.5 Please tick to confirm:

☐ I have provided a copy of this notice to every other party to the proceedings and to my former solicitor (if applicable).

Section 3 – Signature

Signed		**Name of firm**	
Name		**Position or office held**	
Date			

Please return the completed certificate to:
Court of Protection, Archway Tower, 2 Junction Road, London N19 5SZ

Court of Protection

Notice of intention to file evidence by deposition

For office use only

Case no.

Full name of person to whom the application relates
(this is the person who lacks, or is alleged to lack, capacity)

Please read first

- If you intend to use a deposition as evidence at a hearing then you must complete this notice to inform the court.

- You must file this notice at least 14 days before the date fixed for the hearing.

- You must provide a copy of this notice to every other party to the proceedings.

- The court may require the deponent (the person who was examined) to attend the hearing and give evidence in person.

- Please continue on a separate sheet of paper if you need more space to answer a question. Write the case number, your name, the name of the person to whom the application relates, and the number of the question you are answering on each separate sheet.

- If you need help completing this form please check the website, www.hmcourts-service.gov. uk or www.direct.gov.uk, for further guidance or information, or contact Court Enquiry Service on 0300 456 4600 or courtofprotectionenquiries@ hmcourts-service.gsi.gov.uk

- Court of Protection staff cannot give legal advice. If you need legal advice please contact a solicitor.

Section 1 - Your details (party intending to file evidence by deposition)

1.1 ☐ Mr. ☐ Mrs. ☐ Miss ☐ Ms. ☐ Other _____

Full name

1.2 Address (including postcode)

Telephone no.

1.3 What is your role in these proceedings?

☐ Applicant (the person who filed the COP1 application form)

☐ Respondent

☐ Other (please provide details)

Section 2 - Evidence by deposition

2.1 I intend to put a deposition in evidence at the hearing fixed to take place on

D	D	M	M	Y	Y	Y	Y

2.2 Full name of deponent (person who gave evidence by deposition)

Section 3 – Signature

Signed

Name of firm

Name

Position or office held

Date

Please return the completed certificate to:
Court of Protection, Archway Tower, 2 Junction Road, London N19 5SZ

2

COP 35 03.10 Court of Protection
Appellant's notice

For office use only
Date received
Appeal case no.
Date issued

Full name of person to whom the proceedings relate
(this is the person who lacks, or is alleged to lack, capacity)

SEAL

Please read first

- If you wish to appeal against a decision of the Court of Protection then you must complete this form and file it with the court.

- Do not use this form if you are appealing to the Court of Appeal. You need to follow the Court of Appeal procedures.

- The first person to appeal against any decision of the court is called the appellant. Any other party to the appeal is called a respondent.

- Respondents can apply for permission if they wish to make an additional, different appeal, or can apply to have the order of the first instance judge upheld on different or additional grounds by filing a COP36 respondent's notice.

- You have limited time to file your appellant's notice with the court. You must file it:

  – within the time limit set by the first instance judge; or

  – where the first instance judge did not set a time limit, within 21 days of the date of the decision you wish to appeal against.

- You must pay a fee when you file an appellant's notice. Please refer to the fees leaflet for details.

- You may need to pay for any costs you incur during proceedings. If the court considers that you have acted unreasonably you can be ordered to pay the costs incurred by other parties.

- Please continue on a separate sheet of paper if you need more space to answer a question. Write your name, the name and date of birth of the person to whom the application relates, and the number of the question you are answering on each separate sheet.

- There are additional guidance notes at the end of this form.

- If you need help completing this form please check the website, www.hmcourts-service.gov.uk or www.direct.gov.uk, for further guidance or information, or contact Court Enquiry Service on 0300 456 4600 or courtofprotectionenquiries@hmcourts-service.gsi.gov.uk

- Court of Protection staff cannot give legal advice. If you need legal advice please contact a solicitor.

Section 1 – Details of the decision you are appealing against

1.1   Case number

1.2   The name of the first instance judge (the judge whose decision you want to appeal)

1.3   Status of the first instance judge, if known

                    ☐ Circuit judge

                    ☐ District judge

1.4   Date of the decision you wish to appeal

        | D | D | M | M | Y | Y | Y | Y |

1.5   Address of the person to whom the proceedings relate

1.5   Date of birth of the person to whom the proceedings relate

        | D | D | M | M | Y | Y | Y | Y |

2

Section 2 – Details of appellant and respondent(s)

Your details (the appellant)

2.1   Your details   ☐ Mr.   ☐ Mrs.   ☐ Miss   ☐ Ms.   ☐ Other _____

     First name

     Middle name(s)

     Last name

2.2   Address (including postcode)

     Telephone no.   Daytime

                        Evening

                        Mobile

     E-mail address

2.3   Is a solicitor representing you?   ☐ Yes   ☐ No

     If Yes, please give the solicitor's details.

     Name

     Address (including postcode)

     Telephone no.   Fax no.

     DX no.

     E-mail address

2.5   Which address should official documentation be sent to?

☐ Your address

☐ Solicitor's address

☐ Other address (please provide details)

_____

Details of respondent(s) to the appeal (see note 1)

2.6

Full name including title	Full address including postcode

Section 3 – Application for permission to appeal

3.1   Do you need permission from the court to appeal? **(see note 2)**

☐ Yes

☐ No, I am appealing against an order for committal to prison

3.2   If Yes, has permission to appeal been granted?

☐ Yes

☐ No, I now seek permission to appeal

4

Section 4 - Details of appeal

4.1   Nature of decision you wish to appeal **(see note 3)**

☐ Case management decision

☐ Grant or refusal of an interim application

☐ Final decision

☐ Other (please give details)

```
[                                                    ]
[                                                    ]
[                                                    ]
[                                                    ]
```

4.2   What are you asking the appeal judge to do? **(see note 4)**

```
[                                                    ]
[                                                    ]
[                                                    ]
[                                                    ]
[                                                    ]
```

4.3   If you are asking the appeal judge to affirm, set aside or vary part of the order please specify which part

```
[                                                    ]
[                                                    ]
[                                                    ]
[                                                    ]
[                                                    ]
```

Section 5 – Grounds for appeal and skeleton argument

5.1   Please set out your grounds for appeal. **(see note 5)**

5.2   Please use the COP37 skeleton argument form for your arguments in support of your grounds for appeal.

A skeleton argument: (tick only one box)

☐ is filed with this notice; or

☐ will follow within 21 days of filing this notice.

6

Section 6 – Other applications

Please complete this section if you are asking for orders in addition to the order asked for in section 4.2. If you make other applications with your appellant's notice the court can either deal with these at any hearing which deals with your application for permission to appeal, or at another separate hearing before the hearing of your appeal.

6.1   Are you applying for a stay of execution of any order against you?   ☐ Yes   ☐ No

         If Yes, please state why you are applying for a stay of execution.

6.2   Are you applying for an extension of time for filing the appellant's notice? **(see note 6)**   ☐ Yes   ☐ No

         If Yes, please state the reasons for the delay.

6.3   Are you making any other applications to the court? **(see note 7)**   ☐ Yes   ☐ No

         If Yes, please state what order you are asking the court to make and
         state the reasons for your application.

Evidence in support

6.4   Any evidence in support of other applications must be filed with this   ☐ Evidence
         appellant's notice. If you are attaching any written evidence please use the   attached
         COP24 witness statement form.

Section 7 – Supporting documents

7.1   To support your appeal you should file all relevant documents listed below with this notice. To show which documents you are filing, please tick the appropriate boxes.

     ☐ Two copies of your appellant's notice for the court (i.e. the original plus one copy);

     ☐ One copy of your skeleton argument;

     ☐ A sealed (stamped by the court) copy of the order being appealed;

     ☐ A suitable record of the judgment of the first instance judge;

     ☐ A copy of any order giving or refusing permission to appeal, together with a copy of the judge's reasons for allowing or refusing permission to appeal;

     ☐ Any witness statements or affidavits in support of any other applications included in your appellant's notice;

     ☐ The application form and any application notice or response (where relevant to the subject of the appeal);

     ☐ In cases where the decision itself was made on appeal, the order of the first instance judge, the reasons given and the appellant's notice used to appeal from that order;

     ☐ Any other documents which you reasonably consider necessary to enable the court to reach its decision on the hearing of the application or appeal; and

     ☐ Such other documents as the court may direct.

7.2   If you have not been able to obtain any of the documents listed in 7.1 within the time allowed to file the appellant's notice please list the documents in the table and explain why you cannot provide them. You will still need to file the documents with the court – please give the date you expect to be able to do so.

Title of document	Reason not supplied	Date when it will be supplied

Section 8 - Statement of truth

The statement of truth is to be signed by you, your solicitor or your litigation friend.

*(I believe) (The appellant believes) that the facts stated in this appellant's notice are true.

Signed

*Appellant('s solicitor)('s litigation friend)

Name

Date

**Name
of firm**

**Position or
office held**

* Please delete the options in
brackets that do not apply.

Now read note 8 about what you need to do next.

Guidance notes

Note 1

Details of respondent(s) to the appeal

You must provide the details of the parties to the proceedings before the first instance judge who are affected by the appeal. You must serve respondents with copies of all documents relating to your appeal when the court has issued your appellant's notice in order to allow them the opportunity to respond.

Note 2

Application for permission to appeal

You do not need permission from the court to appeal if the order you are appealing against is an order for committal to prison.

You do need permission to appeal against any other order. Permission to appeal will be granted only where:

- the court considers that the appeal would have a real prospect of success; or
- there is some other compelling reason why the appeal should be heard.

Note 3

Details of appeal

Case management decisions include orders relating to:

- the timetable for hearing;
- the filing and exchange of information (of witnesses and experts);
- disclosure of documents; or
- adding a party to proceedings.

A grant or refusal of an interim application might include an injunction to prevent you from doing something or a declaration confirming an action is lawful.

Note 4

What are you asking the appeal judge to do?

You need to explain in section 4.3 what order you are asking the court to make. Please be specific about what you are asking the appeal judge to do. The appeal judge has the power to:

- affirm, set aside or vary any order made by the first instance judge;
- refer any claim or issue to that judge for determination;
- order a new hearing; or
- make a costs order.

Note 5

Grounds for appeal and arguments in support

An appeal must be based on relevant grounds (i.e. reasons for appealing). An appeal judge will only allow an appeal against a decision that is either wrong or unjust because of a serious procedural or other irregularity in the proceedings before the first instance judge.

Please set out briefly why you are appealing the judge's decision. Remember that you must not include any grounds for appeal that rely on new evidence (that is evidence that has become available since the order was made). You may not produce new evidence in your appeal unless the court allows you to do so (see section 6).

Note 6

Extension of time for filing the appellant's notice

If the time for filing your appellant's notice has expired then you need to file this notice and include an application for an extension of time. You need to state the reason(s) for the delay and the steps you have taken in attempting to avoid the delay.

Note 7

Other applications

If you wish to produce new evidence in your appeal you need to apply to the court to do so. You need to tell the court why the evidence was not available to the first instance judge and explain why you think it is necessary for the appeal.

Note 8

What you need to do next

Please return the appellant's notice and supporting documents to:

>   Court of Protection
>   Archway Tower
>   2 Junction Road
>   London N19 5SZ

If your skeleton argument will follow your appellant's notice, it must be filed within 21 days of the appellant's notice.

Any supporting documents that you cannot obtain in time to file with your appellant's notice must be filed with the court in such time as the court may direct, and in any case as soon as possible.

Note 9

What happens next?

If you need permission to appeal

The court will tell you if permission is granted, refused or if a date has been fixed for a hearing of the application for permission.

If permission is granted the court will issue your appellant's notice and will return a sealed copy. You will need to serve a copy on each respondent and notify the person to whom the proceedings relate.

If you already have permission, or do not need permission to appeal

The court will issue your appellant's notice and will return a sealed copy. You will need to serve a copy on each respondent and notify the person to whom the proceedings relate.

COP 36 03.10 Court of Protection

Respondent's notice

Appeal case no.

Full name of person to whom the proceedings relate
(this is the person who lacks, or is alleged to lack, capacity)

SEAL

Please read first

- You must file this respondent's notice if you are served with a COP35 appellant's notice and you wish to:
  - appeal on different grounds against the same order; or
  - ask the court to uphold the order of the first instance judge for reasons different from, or additional to, those given by the first instance judge.
- You do not need to file a respondent's notice if you:
  - agree with the original order and reasons given by the first instance judge; or
  - agree with the appellant and support the appeal.
- The first person to appeal against any decision of the court is called the appellant. Any other party to the appeal is a respondent.
- You must file your respondent's notice:
  - within the time limit set by the first instance judge; or
  - where the first instance judge has set no time limit, within 21 days beginning with the date you were served with:
    - the appellant's notice, where permission to appeal has been given or is not required; or
    - notification that permission has been granted; or
    - notification that the application for permission and the appeal are to be heard together.

- You may need to pay for any costs you incur during proceedings. If the court considers that you have acted unreasonably you can be ordered to pay the costs incurred by other parties.
- Please continue on a separate sheet of paper if you need more space to answer a question. Write the appeal case number, your name, the name of the person to whom the application relates, and the number of the question you are answering on each separate sheet.
- There are additional guidance notes at the end of this form.
- If you need help completing this form please check the website, www.hmcourts-service.gov.uk or www.direct.gov.uk, for further guidance or information, or contact Court Enquiry Service on 0300 456 4600 or courtofprotectionenquiries@ hmcourts-service.gsi.gov.uk
- Court of Protection staff cannot give legal advice. If you need legal advice please contact a solicitor.

1

Section 1 – Details of the case being appealed

1.1   Case number

            [   ]

Section 2 – Your details (the respondent)

2.1   ☐ Mr.   ☐ Mrs.   ☐ Miss   ☐ Ms.   ☐ Other _____

     First name   [   ]

     Middle name   [   ]

     Last name   [   ]

2.2   Address (including postcode)   [   ]

     Telephone no.

Daytime	
Evening	
Mobile	

     E-mail address   [   ]

2.3   Is a solicitor representing you?   ☐ Yes   ☐ No

     If Yes, please give the solicitor's details.

     Name   [   ]

     Address (including postcode)   [   ]

Telephone no.		Fax no.	
DX no.			
E-mail address			

2.4   To which address should all official documentation be sent?

☐ Your address

☐ Solicitor's address

☐ Other address (please provide details)

```



```

Section 3 – Application for permission to make a different appeal

If you wish only to ask that the appeal judge upholds the judgment or order of the first instance judge you do not require permission - please go to section 4.

3.1   Do you need permission from the court to appeal? **(see note 1)**

☐ Yes

☐ No, I am appealing an order for committal to prison

3.2   If Yes, has permission to appeal been granted?

☐ Yes

☐ No, I now seek permission to appeal

Section 4 - Details of response to appeal

4.1   Nature of decision you wish to appeal **(see note 2)**

☐ Case management decision

☐ Grant or refusal of an interim application

☐ Final decision

☐ Other (please give details)

```



```

3

4.2   What are you asking the appeal judge to do? **(see note 3)**

4.3   If you are asking the appeal judge to affirm, set aside or vary part of the order please specify which part.

4.4   If you are asking the appeal judge to uphold an order on different or additional grounds please specify those grounds.

Section 5 – Grounds for response to an appeal and skeleton argument

5.1   Please set out your grounds for appeal. **(see note 4)**

5.2   Please use the COP37 skeleton argument form for your arguments in support of your grounds for appeal.

A skeleton argument: (tick only one box)

☐ is filed with this notice; or

☐ will follow within 21 days of filing this notice.

Section 6 – Other applications

Please complete this section if you are asking for orders in addition to the order asked for in section 4.2. If you make other applications with your respondent's notice the court can either deal with these at any hearing which deals with your application for permission to appeal, or at another separate hearing before the hearing of your appeal.

6.1   Are you applying for a stay of execution of any order against you?   ☐ Yes   ☐ No

        If Yes, please state why you are applying for a stay of execution.

        ┌──┐
        │   │
        │   │
        │   │
        │   │
        └──┘

6.2   Are you applying for an extension of time for filing the respondent's notice?   ☐ Yes   ☐ No
        (see note 5)

        If Yes, please state the reasons for the delay.

        ┌──┐
        │   │
        │   │
        │   │
        │   │
        └──┘

6.3   Are you making any other applications to the court? **(see note 6)**   ☐ Yes   ☐ No

        If Yes, please state what order you are asking the court to make and
        state the reasons for your application.

        ┌──┐
        │   │
        │   │
        │   │
        │   │
        │   │
        │   │
        │   │
        └──┘

Evidence in support

6.4   Any evidence in support of other applications must be filed with this   ☐ Evidence
        respondent's notice. If you are attaching any written evidence please use   attached
        the COP24 witness statement form.

Section 7 – Supporting documents

7.1   To support your appeal you should file all relevant documents listed below with this notice. To show which documents you are filing, please tick the appropriate boxes.

☐ Two copies of your respondent's notice for the court (i.e. the original and one copy);

☐ One copy of your skeleton argument;

☐ A sealed copy of the order being appealed;

☐ A copy of any order giving or refusing permission to appeal, together with a copy of the judge's reasons for allowing or refusing permission to appeal;

☐ Any witness statements or affidavits in support of any other applications included in your respondent's notice;

☐ Any other documents which you reasonably consider necessary to enable the court to reach its decision on the hearing of your application or appeal; and

☐ Such other documents as the court may direct.

7.2   If you have not been able to obtain any of the documents listed in 7.1 within the time allowed to file the respondent's notice please list the documents in the table and explain why you cannot provide them. You will still need to file the documents with the court. Please give the date you expect to be able to do so.

Title of document	Reason not supplied	Date when it will be supplied

Section 8 - Statement of truth

The statement of truth is to be signed by you, your solicitor or your litigation friend.

*(I believe) (The respondent believes) that the facts stated in this respondent's notice are true.

Signed

*Respondent('s solicitor)('s litigation friend)

Name

Date

Name of firm

Position or office held

* Please delete the options in brackets that do not apply.

Now read note 7 about what you need to do next.

Guidance notes

Note 1

Application for permission to make a different appeal

You do not need permission from the court to appeal if the order you are appealing against is an order for committal to prison.

You do need permission to appeal against any other order. Permission to appeal will be granted only where:

- the court considers that the appeal would have a real prospect of success; or
- there is some other compelling reason why the appeal should be heard.

Note 2

Nature of the decision you want to appeal

Case management decisions include orders relating to:

- the timetable for hearing;
- the filing and exchange of information (of witnesses and experts);
- disclosure of documents; or
- adding a party to proceedings.

A grant or refusal of an interim application might include an injunction to prevent you from doing something or a declaration confirming an action is lawful.

Note 3

What are you asking the appeal judge to do?

You need to explain in section 4.2 what order you are asking the court to make. Please be specific about what you are asking the appeal judge to do. The appeal judge has the power to:

- affirm, set aside or vary any order made by the first instance judge;
- refer any claim or issue to that judge for determination;
- order a new hearing; or
- make a costs order.

Note 4

Grounds for response to appeal

Your response to an appeal must be based on relevant grounds. This applies if you wish to appeal the order, or if you wish the appeal judge to uphold the order on different or additional grounds. An appeal judge will only allow an appeal against a decision that is either wrong or unjust because of a serious procedural or other irregularity in the proceedings before the first instance judge.

Please set out briefly your grounds for appeal or for seeking to uphold the order. Remember that you must not include any grounds for appeal or for upholding the order that rely on new evidence (that is evidence that has become available since the order was made). You may not produce new evidence in your appeal unless the court allows you to do so (see section 6).

Note 5

Extension of time for filing the respondent's notice

Where the time for filing your respondent's notice has expired, you need to file this notice and include an application for an extension of time. You need to state the reason(s) for the delay and the steps you have taken in attempting to avoid the delay.

Note 6

Other applications

If you wish to produce new evidence in your appeal you need to apply to the court to do so. You need to tell the court why the evidence was not available to the first instance judge and explain why you think it is necessary for the appeal.

Note 7

What you need to do next

Please return the respondent's notice and supporting documents to:

> Court of Protection
> Archway Tower
> 2 Junction Road
> London N19 5SZ

If your skeleton argument will follow your respondent's notice, it must be filed within 21 days of the respondent's notice.

Any supporting documents that you cannot obtain in time to file with your respondent's notice must be filed with the court in such time as the court may direct, and in any case as soon as possible.

9

Note 8

What happens next?

If you need permission to appeal

The court will tell you if permission is granted, refused
or if a date has been fixed for a hearing of the
application for permission.

If permission is granted, the court will issue your
respondent's notice and will return a sealed copy.
You will need to serve a copy on the appellant and
any other respondents.

**If you already have permission, or do not need
permission to appeal**

The court will issue your respondent's notice and will
return a sealed copy. You will need to serve a copy on
the appellant and any other respondents.

 Court of Protection
Skeleton argument

For office use only
Date received
Date issued

Section 1 – Details of the case being appealed

Appeal case no.

Case no.

Full name of person to whom the application relates
(this is the name of the person who lacks, or is alleged to lack, capacity)

Section 2 – Your details

In the appeal, are you the:

☐ Appellant
☐ Respondent

☐ Mr.   ☐ Mrs.   ☐ Miss   ☐ Ms.   ☐ Other _____

First name

Last name

Address
(including
postcode)

Telephone no.

Daytime	
Mobile	

Section 3 – Skeleton argument

I *(the appellant)(the respondent) will rely on the following arguments at the hearing of the appeal.

Section 3 – Signature

Signed		Name of firm	

Name		Position or office held	

Date	

Now read note 2 about what you need to do next.

Guidance notes

Note 1

Skeleton argument

A skeleton argument must contain a numbered list of the points which you wish to make. These should both define and confine the areas of controversy. Each point should be stated as concisely as the nature of the case allows.

A numbered point must be followed by a reference to any document on which you wish to rely.

A skeleton argument must state, in respect of each authority cited:

a) the proposition of law that the authority demonstrates; and

b) the parts of the authority (identified by page or paragraph references) that support the proposition.

If more than one authority is cited in support of a given proposition, the skeleton argument must briefly state the reason for taking that course. This statement should not materially add to the length of the skeleton argument but should be sufficient to demonstrate, in the context of the argument:

a) the relevance of the authority or authorities to that argument; and

b) that the citation is necessary for a proper presentation of that argument.

Please continue on a separate sheet of paper if you need more space to provide your skeleton argument. Write your name, the name of the person to whom the proceedings relate and the case number of the case you are appealing against on each separate sheet.

Note 2

What you need to do next

The skeleton argument is to be filed with your appellant's/respondent's notice. Where you are unable to provide it with your appellant's / respondent's notice you must file it and serve it on all parties to the proceedings within 21 days of filing your appellant's / respondent's notice.

The court requires two copies (i.e. the original plus one copy) of the skeleton argument.

Please return the original completed form and copy to:

Court of Protection
Archway Tower
2 Junction Road
London N19 5SZ

LASTING POWERS OF ATTORNEY FORMS

Lasting power of attorney
Information sheet – the people involved

You are the person giving the lasting power of attorney. You are referred to as the Donor. To complete your lasting power of attorney, you need the following people involved:

- at least one person to act as your **attorney**
- at least one **certificate provider**
- at least one **person to be told** or a second certificate provider
- at least one **witness.**

Your attorney(s)	The people you want to make decisions for you. Attorneys do not have to have any legal knowledge or training.
	How many? You must have at least one attorney, and you can have as many as you like. (Note, however, that too many attorneys might make things difficult in practice.)
Your replacement attorney(s)	The people you want to make decisions for you when your attorney(s) cannot act for you any more.
	How many? You don't have to appoint any replacement attorneys, but you can have as many as you like.
The people to be told	Adults who know you well. Before your lasting power of attorney is registered, the 'people to be told' are given an opportunity to raise any concerns or objections.
	Your attorney(s) or replacement attorney(s) cannot also act as a person to be told.
	How many? You do not have to have any people to be told, but you can have up to five. If you don't have any, you must have two certificate providers.
A certificate provider	An independent person who is able to confirm that you understand the significance of your lasting power of attorney. They must have known you well for at least two years, or have relevant professional skills to enable them to confirm that you understand the significance of your lasting power of attorney (for example, your GP or solicitor). They also need to certify that no undue pressure or fraud is involved in the making of the lasting power of attorney.
	Your attorney(s) or replacement attorney(s) cannot also act as a certificate provider.
	A person to be told **can** act as a certificate provider.
	How many? You must have at least one certificate provider. If you decide not to have any people to be told, you must have two certificate providers.
Independent witnesses	The people who see your lasting power of attorney being signed, and who then sign themselves to confirm that it was signed in their presence.
	How many? When you sign at the end of part A your signature must be witnessed. Your certificate provider or person to be told **can** act as a witness. Your attorney(s) or replacement attorney(s) **cannot** act as a witness.
	When your attorney(s) sign part C their signature(s) must be witnessed. Another attorney, your replacement attorneys, or a certificate provider **can** also act as a witness to the attorney's signature.

Helpline
☏ **0300 456 0300**
🖱 **publicguardian.gov.uk**

LPA 10 09
© Crown copyright 2009

This lasting power of attorney is in three parts which must be filled in, signed, and dated in this order:

A You fill in, sign, and date part A.

- **You** fill in the details of who you want to act as your **attorney**(s) (and **replacement attorneys**, if any), and how you want them to make decisions for you.
- **You** fill in the details of any **people to be told** when your lasting power of attorney is registered.
- If you are completing a health and welfare power of attorney **you** and a **witness** sign to indicate your preference around **life sustaining treatment**.
- **You** and a **witness** sign at the end of part A (the date of signature on part A **must** be before or the same as the date of signature on parts B and C).

📄 **Continuation sheet?**
Your lasting power of attorney has space for two attorneys, one replacement attorney, and two people to be told. If you would like more attorneys or people to be told, fill in continuation sheet A1 where you see this symbol 📄.

📄 Use continuation sheet A2 if you require more space for joint decision making, restrictions, guidance or charges for services.

📄 Use continuation sheet A3 if you can't sign or make a mark.

📄 Fill in, sign and attach each continuation sheet **to the end of** your lasting power of attorney. Continuation sheets cannot be added after part A has been filled in and signed.

B Your certificate provider fills in, signs, and dates part B.

- If you decided not to have any people to be told when your lasting power of attorney is registered, your second certificate provider fills in continuation sheet B 📄.

C Your attorney(s) and any replacement attorney(s) sign part C.

- Your attorney(s), replacement attorney(s) and their **witness(es)** sign part C.
- If you have more than one attorney or replacement attorney, they should sign photocopies of part C 📄.
- If you are completing a property and financial affairs lasting power of attorney, and you are appointing a trust corporation as attorney or replacement attorney, the person signing on behalf of the trust corporation signs continuation sheet C 📄.

For OPG office use only

LPA PA
registered on

OPG reference
number

Office of the Public Guardian

Lasting power of attorney – property and financial affairs

About this lasting power of attorney

This lasting power of attorney allows you to choose people to act on your behalf (as an attorney) and make decisions about your **property and financial affairs,** when you are unable to make decisions for yourself.

If you also want someone to make decisions about your **health and welfare,** you will need a separate form (downloadable from our website or call 0300 456 0300).

Who can fill it in?

Anyone aged 18 or over, who has the mental capacity to do so.

Before you fill in the lasting power of attorney:

1. Please read the guidance available at **publicguardian.gov.uk** or by calling **0300 456 0300.** See, for example, the *Lasting power of attorney creation pack* or other relevant guidance booklets which are all available online or by post.

2. Make sure you understand the purpose of this lasting power of attorney and the extent of the authority you are giving your attorneys.

3. Read the separate **Information sheet** to understand all the people involved, and how the three parts of the form should be filled in.

4. Make sure you, your certificate provider(s), and your attorney(s) have read the section on page 2 called **Information you must read** before filling in their relevant part.

 This lasting power of attorney could be rejected at registration if it contains any errors.

Checklist

See the information sheet for guidance on all the people involved

Part A: about you, the attorneys you are appointing, and people to be told

How many **attorneys** are you appointing? *Write in words.*

How many **replacement attorneys** are you appointing? *Write in words or write 'None' if this does not apply.*

How many **people to be told** are you choosing? *Write in words from 'None' to 'five'. If 'None' you must have two certificate providers in part B.*

Part B: about your certificate providers

How many **certificate providers do you have?** *(Tick one box)*

☐ One   OR   ☐ Two

If you have used any continuation sheets each one must be signed and dated.

Attached to the back of this lasting power of attorney are: *(Write the number of each)*

continuation sheet A1	0
continuation sheet A2	0
continuation sheet A3:PFA	0
continuation sheet B	0
continuation sheet C	0
Total number of continuation sheets	0

LPA PA 10 09   © Crown copyright 2009

Helpline
☎ **0300 456 0300**
🖱 publicguardian.gov.uk

Valid only with Office of the Public Guardian stamp

2A About appointing a trust corporation as attorney or replacement attorney

About the trust corporation you are appointing *Please cross through this section if it does not apply.*

• A trust corporation cannot be going through winding-up proceedings.

Company name

Address

Are you appointing this trust corporation to act as an

☐ attorney, or

☐ replacement attorney?

Postcode

3   About appointing replacements if an attorney can no longer act

📋 *If you are appointing a trust corporation as replacement attorney, cross through this section.*
Your trust corporation should then fill in continuation sheet C →

Thinking about replacement attorneys

• Replacement attorneys will only act once your attorney can no longer act for you.

• You can appoint replacements to replace an attorney who does not want to act for you or who is permanently no longer able to act because they are dead, bankrupt, have disclaimed, lack mental capacity or if they were married to you or were your civil partner, and have now had the marriage or civil partnership annulled or dissolved.

• You do not have to appoint any replacements.

• If you appoint only one attorney and no replacements, this lasting power of attorney will end when your attorney can no longer act.

Your first or only replacement attorney   *Please cross through this section if it does not apply.*

Mr   Mrs   Ms   Miss Other title
☐   ☐   ☐   ☐

Date of birth of your first or only replacement

D D M M Y Y Y Y

First names of your first or only replacement

Address and postcode of your first or only replacement

Last name of your first or only replacement

Postcode

📋 *If you are appointing more than one replacement, use continuation sheet A1 to tell us about your other replacement attorneys.*

Other replacement attorneys you are appointing

Number of replacement attorneys named in continuation sheet **A1** attached to this lasting power of attorney

Cross through this box if this does not apply

Office of the Public Guardian

Lasting power of attorney – property and financial affairs

About this lasting power of attorney

This lasting power of attorney allows you to choose people to act on your behalf (as an attorney) and make decisions about your **property and financial affairs**, when you are unable to make decisions for yourself

If you also want someone to make decisions about your **health and welfare**, you will need a separate form (downloadable from our website or call 0300 456 0300).

Who can fill it in?

Anyone aged 18 or over, who has the mental capacity to do so.

Before you fill in the lasting power of attorney:

1. Please read the guidance available at **publicguardian.gov.uk** or by calling **0300 456 0300**. See, for example, the *Lasting power of attorney creation pack* or other relevant guidance booklets which are all available online or by post.

2. Make sure you understand the purpose of this lasting power of attorney and the extent of the authority you are giving your attorneys.

3. Read the separate **Information sheet** to understand all the people involved, and how the three parts of the form should be filled in.

4. Make sure you, your certificate provider(s), and your attorney(s) have read the section on page 2 called **Information you must read** before filling in their relevant part.

 This lasting power of attorney could be rejected at registration if it contains any errors.

Information you must read

This lasting power of attorney is a legal document.

Each person who signs parts A, B and C must read this information before signing.

Purpose of this lasting power of attorney

This lasting power of attorney gives your attorneys authority to make decisions about your property and financial affairs when you cannot make your own decisions. This can include running your bank accounts and savings accounts, decisions about making or selling investments and selling property, and spending your money.

When your attorneys can act for you

Your attorneys can use this lasting power of attorney only after it has been registered and stamped on every page by the Office of the Public Guardian. Your attorneys can make decisions for you as soon as this lasting power of attorney is registered – both when you have mental capacity and when you lack mental capacity, unless you put a restriction in this lasting power of attorney.

The Mental Capacity Act

Your attorneys cannot do whatever they like. They **must** follow the principles of the Mental Capacity Act 2005.

Guidance about these principles is in the Mental Capacity Act Code of Practice. Your attorneys must have regard to the Code of Practice. They can get a copy from The Stationery Office at **tso. co.uk** or read it online at **publicguardian.gov.uk**

Principles of the Act that your attorneys must follow

1. Your attorneys must assume that you can make your own decisions unless they establish that you cannot do so.

2. Your attorneys must help you to make as many of your own decisions as you can. They cannot treat you as unable to make the decision in question unless all practicable steps to help you to do so have been made without success.

3. Your attorneys must not treat you as unable to make the decision in question simply because you make an unwise decision.

4. Your attorneys must make decisions and act in your best interests when you are unable to make the decision in question.

5. Before your attorneys make the decision in question or act for you, they must consider whether they can make the decision or act in a way that is less restrictive of your rights and freedom but still achieves the purpose.

Your best interests

Your attorneys must act in your best interests in making decisions for you when you are unable to make the decision yourself. They must take into account all the relevant circumstances. This includes, if appropriate, consulting you and others who are interested in your welfare. Any guidance you add may assist your attorneys in identifying your views.

Cancelling this lasting power of attorney

You can cancel this lasting power of attorney at any time before or after it is registered as long as you have mental capacity to cancel it. Please read the guidance available at **publicguardian.gov.uk**

How to fill in this form

- Tick the boxes that apply like this

- Use black or blue ink and write clearly

- Cross through any boxes or sections that don't apply to you, like this:

> Any other names you are known by in financial documents or accounts
>
> ─────────────────────────────

- Don't use correction fluid – please cross out any mistakes and rewrite nearby. All corrections must be initialled by the person completing that section of the form (and their witness) like this:

> Any other names you are known by in financial documents or accounts
>
> WILLIAM EDWARD ~~SMITH~~
>
> *A.S.B / W.E.S.*   SMYTH

- Your application could be rejected if your intentions are not clear and explicit. If you are in any doubt, please start again on a new copy of the form.

What happens after you've filled it in?

The next step is to **register** it. You or your attorneys can do this at any time. The person applying will need to fill in a registration form and may need to pay a fee at that time. They will also need to send notices to the 'people to be told' named at part A when the application to register this lasting power of attorney is made. You can find out more and download the registration form at **publicguardian.gov.uk**

The 'people to be told' are given time to raise any concerns or objections. This means the earliest the Office of Public Guardian can register this lasting power of attorney is 6 weeks after they notify the donor or attorneys that an application to register has been received.

Your lasting power of attorney will **end** if it can no longer be used. For example, if a sole attorney dies or can no longer act for you and no replacement attorney has been named in this lasting power of attorney. Please read the guidance available at **publicguardian.gov.uk**

Helpline
0300 456 300
publicguardian.gov.uk

Valid only with Office of the Public Guardian stamp

Part A Declaration by the person who is giving this lasting power of attorney

Please write clearly using black or blue ink.

1 About the person who is giving this lasting power of attorney

Mr ☐ Mrs ☐ Ms ☐ Miss ☐ Other title ☐

First names

Last name

Date of birth
D D M M Y Y Y Y

Address and postcode

Postcode

Any other names you are known by in financial documents or accounts

2 About the attorneys you are appointing

📄 *If you are appointing a trust corporation alone, cross through this section and go to 2A →*

Thinking about your attorneys

- You can appoint more than one attorney if you want to. You do not have to appoint more than one attorney.
- Each attorney must be aged 18 or over. Choose people you know and trust to make decisions for you. You are recommended to read the separate guidance for people who want to make a lasting power of attorney for property and financial affairs.
- Your attorney must not be bankrupt.

Your first or only attorney

Mr ☐ Mrs ☐ Ms ☐ Miss ☐ Other title ☐

First names of your first or only attorney

Last name of your first or only attorney

Date of birth of your first or only attorney
D D M M Y Y Y Y

Address and postcode of your first or only attorney

Postcode

Your second attorney
Please cross through this section if it does not apply.

Mr ☐ Mrs ☐ Ms ☐ Miss ☐ Other title ☐

First names of your second attorney

Last name of your second attorney

Date of birth of your second attorney
D D M M Y Y Y Y

Address and postcode of your second attorney

Postcode

📄 *If you are appointing more than two attorneys, use continuation sheet A1 to tell us about your other attorneys.*

Other attorneys you are appointing

Number of attorneys named in continuation sheet **A1** attached to this lasting power of attorney

Cross through this box if this does not apply

Helpline
📞 **0300 456 0300**
🖱 publicguardian.gov.uk

Valid only with Office of the Public Guardian stamp

2A About appointing a trust corporation as attorney or replacement attorney

About the trust corporation you are appointing *Please cross through this section if it does not apply.*

• A trust corporation cannot be going through winding-up proceedings.

Company name

Address

Are you appointing this trust corporation to act as an

☐ attorney, or

☐ replacement attorney?

Postcode

3 About appointing replacements if an attorney can no longer act

If you are appointing a trust corporation as replacement attorney, cross through this section.
Your trust corporation should then fill in continuation sheet C →

Thinking about replacement attorneys

• Replacement attorneys will only act once your attorney can no longer act for you.

• You can appoint replacements to replace an attorney who does not want to act for you or who is permanently no longer able to act because they are dead, bankrupt, have disclaimed, lack mental capacity or if they were married to you or were your civil partner, and have now had the marriage or civil partnership annulled or dissolved.

• You do not have to appoint any replacements.

• If you appoint only one attorney and no replacements, this lasting power of attorney will end when your attorney can no longer act.

Your first or only replacement attorney *Please cross through this section if it does not apply.*

Mr　Mrs　Ms　Miss　Other title
☐　☐　☐　☐

Date of birth of your first or only replacement

D D M M Y Y Y Y

First names of your first or only replacement

Address and postcode of your first or only replacement

Last name of your first or only replacement

Postcode

If you are appointing more than one replacement, use continuation sheet A1 to tell us about your other replacement attorneys.

Other replacement attorneys you are appointing

Number of replacement attorneys named in continuation sheet **A1** attached to this lasting power of attorney

Cross through this box if this does not apply

Helpline
☎ **0300 456 0300**
🖱 **publicguardian.gov.uk**

Valid only with Office of the Public Guardian stamp

4   How you want your attorneys to make decisions

Thinking about how you want your attorneys to make decisions

🛈 **If you leave this section blank, your attorneys will be appointed to make all decisions jointly.**

- **Jointly**: this means that the attorneys must **make all decisions together**. → *For further information on appointing your attorneys jointly, see the separate guidance.*

- **Jointly and severally**: this means that attorneys can **make decisions together and separately**. This might be useful, for example, if one attorney is not available to make a decision at a certain time. If one attorney cannot act the remaining attorney is able to continue to make decisions.

- **Jointly for some decisions, and jointly and severally for other decisions**: this means that your attorneys **must make certain decisions together** and may make certain decisions separately. You will need to set out below how you want this to work in practice.

Choosing which decisions must be made together and which decisions may be made separately – how this will work in practice

- Please make your intentions clear about how your attorneys are to make decisions about running bank accounts and savings accounts, making or selling investments and selling property, and spending your money.

- Please check that your intentions will work in practice – it may not be possible to register or use this lasting power of attorney if, for example, a bank or building society account cannot be operated as you wish.

How you want your attorneys to make decisions

If you are appointing only one attorney and no replacement attorneys, now go to section 5 →

Jointly	☐	→ *Go to section 5 and cross through the box below*
Jointly and severally	☐	→ *Go to section 5 and cross through the box below*
Jointly for some decisions, and jointly and severally for other decisions	☐	

Only if you have ticked the last box above, now tell us in the space below which decisions your attorneys must make jointly and which decisions may be made jointly and severally

If you need more space, use continuation sheet A2

5   About restrictions and conditions

Putting restrictions and conditions into words

- You should read the separate guidance for examples of conditions and restrictions that will not work in practice.
- Your attorneys **must** follow any restrictions or conditions you put in place. But it may not be possible to register or use this lasting power of attorney if a condition is not workable.
- **Either**: give any restrictions and conditions about property and financial affairs here
- **Or**: if you would like your attorneys to make decisions with no restrictions or conditions, you should cross through this box.

Restrictions and conditions about property and financial affairs

If you need more space, use continuation sheet A2

6   About guidance to your attorneys

Putting guidance into words

- Any guidance you add may help your attorneys to identify your views. You do not have to add any.
- Your attorneys do not have to follow your guidance but it will help them to understand your wishes when they make decisions for you.
- **Either**: Give any guidance about property and financial affairs here
- **Or:** if you have no guidance to add, please cross through this box.

Guidance to your attorneys about property and financial affairs

If you need more space, use continuation sheet A2

7   About paying your attorneys

Professional charges

- Professional attorneys, such as solicitors and accountants, charge for their services. You can also choose to pay a non-professional person for their services. You **should** discuss payment with your attorneys and record any agreement made here to avoid any confusion later.
- You can choose to pay non-professional attorneys for their services, but if you do not record any agreement here they will only be able to recover reasonable out-of-pocket expenses

Charges for services

If you need more space, use continuation sheet A2

→ *For further information on paying attorneys, please see the separate guidance.*

Helpline
☎ **0300 456 0300**
🖱 publicguardian.gov.uk

Valid only with Office of the Public Guardian stamp

8 About people to be told when the application to register this lasting power of attorney is made

Thinking about people to be told

- For your protection you can choose up to **five people to be told** when your lasting power of attorney is being registered. This gives people who know you well an opportunity to raise any concerns or objections **before** this lasting power of attorney is registered and can be used.

> **!** • You do not have to choose anyone. But if you leave this section blank, you must choose two people to sign the certificate to confirm understanding at part B.

- The people to be told cannot be your attorney or replacement named at part A or in continuation sheets to part A.

The first or only person to be told
Please cross through this section if it does not apply.

Mr   Mrs   Ms   Miss   Other title

First names of first or only person to be told

Last name of first or only person to be told

Address and postcode of first or only person to be told

Postcode

The second person to be told
Please cross through this section if it does not apply.

Mr   Mrs   Ms   Miss   Other title

First names of second person to be told

Last name of second person to be told

Address and postcode of second person to be told

Postcode

Other people to be told
Please cross through this section if it does not apply

📄 Tell us about other people to be told on continuation sheet A1.

Number of other people to be told named in continuation sheet A1 attached to this lasting power of attorney

9   Declaration by the person who is giving this lasting power of attorney

Before signing please check that you have:

- filled in every answer that applies to you
- crossed through blank boxes that do not apply to you
- filled in any continuation sheets
- crossed through any mistakes you have made
- initialled any changes you have made.

No changes may be made to this lasting power of attorney and no continuation sheets may be added after part A has been filled in and signed. If any change appears to have been made, this lasting power of attorney will not be valid and will be rejected when an application is made to register it.

By signing (or marking) on this page, or by directing someone to sign continuation sheet A3:PFA, I confirm all of the following:

Statement of understanding

I have read or had read to me:

- the section called 'Information you must read' on page 2
- all information contained in part A and any continuation sheets to part A of this lasting power of attorney.

I appoint and give my attorneys authority to make decisions about my property and financial affairs, including when I cannot act for myself because I lack mental capacity, subject to the terms of this lasting power of attorney and to the provisions of the Mental Capacity Act 2005.

People to be told when the application to register this lasting power of attorney is made

I have chosen the people to be told, and have chosen **one** person to sign the certificate of understanding at part B.

OR

I do not want anyone to be told, and have chosen **two** people to sign certificates of understanding at part B.

If you cannot sign this lasting power of attorney you can make a mark instead.

If you cannot sign or make a mark use continuation sheet A3:PFA →

Signed (or marked) by the person giving this lasting power of attorney and delivered as a deed

Sign with usual signature

Date signed or marked

D D M M Y Y Y Y

! Sign (or mark) and date each continuation sheet at the same time as you sign (or mark) part A.

You must sign (or mark) and date part A here *before* parts B and C are signed and dated.

The witness should be independent of you and:

- Must be 18 or over.
- **Cannot** be an attorney or replacement attorney named at part A or any continuation sheets to this lasting power of attorney or the employee of any trust corporation named as an attorney or replacement attorney.
- Can be a certificate provider at part B.
- Can be a person to be told when the application to register this lasting power of attorney is made.
- Must initial any changes made in Part A.

Witnessed by

Signature of witness

Full names of witness

Address and postcode of witness

Postcode

Helpline

0300 456 0300

publicguardian.gov.uk

Valid only with Office of the Public Guardian stamp

Part B
Declaration by your first or only certificate provider: certificate to confirm understanding

Your certificate provider fills in, signs and dates this part.

Declaration by the person who is signing this certificate

Please refer to separate guidance for certificate providers. If the guidance is not followed, this lasting power of attorney may not be valid and could be rejected when an application is made to register it.

In part A (section 8) has the person giving this lasting power of attorney chosen at least one person to be told when the application to register this lasting power of attorney is made?

If yes = **one** certificate provider fills in this part

If no = the **first** certificate provider fills in this part and the **second** certificate provider must fill in continuation sheet **B** 📄.

The **donor** is the person who is giving this lasting power of attorney.

By signing below, I confirm:

My understanding of the role and responsibilities

I have read part A of this lasting power of attorney, including any continuation sheets.

I have read the section called '**Information you must read**' on page 2 of this lasting power of attorney.

I understand my role and responsibilities as a certificate provider.

Statement of acting independently

I confirm that I act independently of the attorneys and of the donor and I am aged 18 or over.

I am **not**:

- an attorney or replacement attorney named in this lasting power of attorney or any other lasting power of attorney or enduring power of attorney for the donor
- a family member related to the donor or any of their attorneys or replacements
- a business partner or paid employee of the donor or any of their attorneys or replacements
- the owner, director, manager or employee of a care home that the donor lives in, or a member of their family
- a director or employee of a trust corporation appointed as an attorney or replacement attorney in this lasting power of attorney.

How you formed your opinion

Before signing this certificate you must establish that the donor understands what it is, the authority they are giving their attorneys, and is not being pressurised into making it.

If someone challenges this lasting power of attorney, you may need to explain how you formed your opinion.

Statement of personal knowledge or relevant professional skills

Please cross through the box that does not apply.

EITHER

I have known the donor for at least two years and as more than an acquaintance. My personal knowledge of the donor is:

OR

I have **relevant professional skills**. (Please state your profession – for example, a GP or solicitor – and then the particular skills that are relevant to you forming your opinion – for example, a consultant specialising in geriatric care.)

My profession and particular skills are:

Continues over →

Part B – Declaration by the person who is signing this certificate (continued)

Things you certify

I certify that, in my opinion, at the time of signing part A:

- the donor understands the purpose of this lasting power of attorney and the scope of the authority conferred under it
- no fraud or undue pressure is being used to induce the donor to create this lasting power of attorney
- there is nothing else which would prevent this lasting power of attorney from being created by the completion of this form.

Your signature

Do not sign until part A of this lasting power of attorney has been filled in and signed.

Sign **as soon as possible** after part A is signed. If this part is signed before part A is signed, this lasting power of attorney will not be valid and will be rejected when an application is made to register it.

Signature of certificate provider

Date signed

D D M M Y Y Y Y

Name and address of the person who is signing this certificate

Mr   Mrs   Ms   Miss   Other title

First names of certificate provider

Last name of certificate provider

Address and postcode of certificate provider

Postcode

Valid only with Office of the Public Guardian stamp

Part C — Declaration by each attorney or replacement attorney
Your attorney(s) and replacement attorney(s) sign and date this part.

If you are appointing more than one attorney, including replacement attorneys: photocopy this sheet before it is filled in so that each attorney has a copy to fill in and sign.

Statement by the attorney or replacement attorney who is signing this declaration

- The attorney or replacement attorney must not be bankrupt.
- Before a replacement can act for you, they must get in touch with the Office of the Public Guardian and return the original lasting power of attorney form. They will get guidance at that time about what needs to happen next.

By signing below, I confirm all of the following:

Understanding of role and responsibilities

I have read the section called **'Information you must read'** on page 2 of this lasting power of attorney.

I understand my role and responsibilities under this lasting power of attorney, in particular:

- I have a duty to act based on the principles of the Mental Capacity Act 2005 and have regard to the Mental Capacity Act Code of Practice
- I can make decisions and act only when this lasting power of attorney has been registered
- I must make decisions and act in the best interests of the person who is giving this lasting power of attorney
- I can spend money to make gifts but only to charities or on customary occasions and for reasonable amounts
- I have a duty to keep accounts and financial records and produce them to the Office of the Public Guardian and/or to the Court of Protection on request.

Further statement of replacement attorney

If an original attorney's appointment is terminated, I will replace the original attorney if I am still eligible to act as an attorney.

I have the authority to act under this lasting power of attorney only after an original attorney's appointment is terminated and I have notified the Public Guardian of the event.

! For this lasting power of attorney to be valid and registered this part should not be signed before Part A or part B have been completed, **signed and dated.** Sign part C as soon as **possible** after part B is signed.

Signed or marked by the attorney or replacement attorney as a deed and delivered (or if to be signed at their direction refer to separate guidance)

Full name of [attorney] or [replacement attorney] *delete as appropriate*

Date signed or marked

The witness must be over 18 and can be:

- another attorney or replacement attorney named at part A or in continuation sheet A to this lasting power of attorney
- a certificate provider at part B of this lasting power of attorney.
- a person to be told when the application to register this lasting power of attorney is made.

The donor cannot be a witness.

The witness must see the attorney or replacement attorney sign or make a mark.

Signature of witness

Full name of witness

Address and postcode of witness

Postcode

Helpline
0300 456 0300
publicguardian.gov.uk

Valid only with Office of the Public Guardian stamp

Lasting power of attorney

Information sheet – the people involved

You are the person giving the lasting power of attorney. You are referred to as the Donor. To complete your lasting power of attorney, you need the following people involved:

- at least one person to act as your **attorney**
- at least one **certificate provider**
- at least one **person to be told** or a second certificate provider
- at least one **witness.**

Your attorney(s)	The people you want to make decisions for you. Attorneys do not have to have any legal knowledge or training.
	How many? You must have at least one attorney, and you can have as many as you like. (Note, however, that too many attorneys might make things difficult in practice.)
Your replacement attorney(s)	The people you want to make decisions for you when your attorney(s) cannot act for you any more.
	How many? You don't have to appoint any replacement attorneys, but you can have as many as you like.
The people to be told	Adults who know you well. Before your lasting power of attorney is registered, the 'people to be told' are given an opportunity to raise any concerns or objections.
	Your attorney(s) or replacement attorney(s) cannot also act as a person to be told.
	How many? You do not have to have any people to be told, but you can have up to five. If you don't have any, you must have two certificate providers.
A certificate provider	An independent person who is able to confirm that you understand the significance of your lasting power of attorney. They must have known you well for at least two years, or have relevant professional skills to enable them to confirm that you understand the significance of your lasting power of attorney (for example, your GP or solicitor). They also need to certify that no undue pressure or fraud is involved in the making of the lasting power of attorney.
	Your attorney(s) or replacement attorney(s) cannot also act as a certificate provider.
	A person to be told **can** act as a certificate provider.
	How many? You must have at least one certificate provider. If you decide not to have any people to be told, you must have two certificate providers.
Independent witnesses	The people who see your lasting power of attorney being signed, and who then sign themselves to confirm that it was signed in their presence.
	How many? When you sign at the end of part A your signature must be witnessed. Your certificate provider or person to be told **can** act as a witness. Your attorney(s) or replacement attorney(s) **cannot** act as a witness.
	When your attorney(s) sign part C their signature(s) must be witnessed. Another attorney, your replacement attorneys, or a certificate provider **can** also act as a witness to the attorney's signature.

Helpline
☎ **0300 456 0300**
🖱 publicguardian.gov.uk

LPA 10 09
© Crown copyright 2009

This lasting power of attorney is in three parts which must be filled in, signed, and dated in this order:

A   You fill in, sign, and date part A.

- **You** fill in the details of who you want to act as your **attorney**(s) (and **replacement attorneys**, if any), and how you want them to make decisions for you.
- **You** fill in the details of any **people to be told** when your lasting power of attorney is registered.
- If you are completing a health and welfare power of attorney **you** and a **witness** sign to indicate your preference around **life sustaining treatment**.
- **You** and a **witness** sign at the end of part A (the date of signature on part A **must** be before or the same as the date of signature on parts B and C).

Continuation sheet?
Your lasting power of attorney has space for two attorneys, one replacement attorney, and two people to be told. If you would like more attorneys or people to be told, fill in continuation sheet A1 where you see this symbol.

Use continuation sheet A2 if you require more space for joint decision making, restrictions, guidance or charges for services.

Use continuation sheet A3 if you can't sign or make a mark.

Fill in, sign and attach each continuation sheet **to the end of** your lasting power of attorney. Continuation sheets cannot be added after part A has been filled in and signed.

B   Your certificate provider fills in, signs, and dates part B.

- If you decided not to have any people to be told when your lasting power of attorney is registered, your second certificate provider fills in continuation sheet B.

C   Your attorney(s) and any replacement attorney(s) sign part C.

- Your attorney(s), replacement attorney(s) and their **witness(es)** sign part C.
- If you have more than one attorney or replacement attorney, they should sign photocopies of part C.
- If you are completing a property and financial affairs lasting power of attorney, and you are appointing a trust corporation as attorney or replacement attorney, the person signing on behalf of the trust corporation signs continuation sheet C.

Office of the Public Guardian

Lasting power of attorney for health and welfare

About this lasting power of attorney

This lasting power of attorney allows you to choose people to act on your behalf (as an attorney) and make decisions about your **health and personal welfare**, when you are unable to make decisions for yourself. This can include decisions about your healthcare and medical treatment, decisions about where you live and day-to-day decisions about your personal welfare, such as your diet, dress or daily routine.

If you also want someone to make decisions about your **property and financial affairs**, you will need a separate form (downloadable from our website or call 0300 456 0300).

Who can fill it in?

Anyone aged 18 or over, who has the mental capacity to do so.

Before you fill in the lasting power of attorney:

1. Please read the guidance available at **publicguardian.gov.uk** or by calling **0300 456 0300**. See, for example, the *Lasting power of attorney creation pack* or other relevant guidance booklets which are all available online or by post.

2. Make sure you understand the purpose of this lasting power of attorney and the extent of the authority you are giving your attorneys.

3. Read the separate **Information sheet** to understand all the people involved, and how the three parts of the form should be filled in.

4. Make sure you, your certificate provider(s), and your attorney(s) have read the section on page 2 called **Information you must read** before filling in their relevant part.

 This lasting power of attorney could be rejected at registration if it contains any errors.

Checklist

See the information sheet for guidance on all the people involved

Part A: about you, the attorneys you are appointing, and people to be told

How many **attorneys** are you appointing? *Write in words.*

[ ]

How many **replacement attorneys** are you appointing? *Write in words or write 'None' if this does not apply.*

[ ]

How many **people to be told** are you choosing? *Write in words from 'None' to 'five'. If 'None' you must have two certificate providers in part D.*

[ ]

Part B: about your certificate providers

How many **certificate providers** do you have? *(Tick one box)*

[ ] One   OR   [ ] Two

If you have used any continuation sheets each one must be signed and dated.

Attached to the back of this lasting power of attorney are:
(Write the number of each)

continuation sheet A1	0
continuation sheet A2	0
continuation sheet A3:HW *2 pages*	0
continuation sheet B	0
Total number of continuation sheets	0

Helpline
0300 456 0300
publicguardian.gov.uk

Valid only with Office of the Public Guardian stamp

Information you must read

This lasting power of attorney is a legal document.
Each person who signs parts A, B and C must read this information before signing.

Purpose of this lasting power of attorney

This lasting power of attorney gives your attorneys authority to make decisions about your health and welfare when you cannot make your own decisions. This can include where you live, who visits you and the type of care you receive.

When your attorneys can act for you

Your attorneys can use this lasting power of attorney only after it has been registered and stamped on every page by the Office of the Public Guardian. **Your attorneys can only act when you lack the capacity to make the decision in question.** You may have capacity to make some decisions about your personal health and welfare but not others.

The Mental Capacity Act

Your attorneys cannot do whatever they like. They **must** follow the principles of the Mental Capacity Act 2005.

Guidance about these principles is in the Mental Capacity Act Code of Practice. Your attorneys must have regard to the Code of Practice. They can get a copy from The Stationery Office at **tso. co.uk** or read it online at **publicguardian.gov.uk**

Principles of the Act that your attorneys must follow

1   Your attorneys must assume that you can make your own decisions unless they establish that you cannot do so.

2   Your attorneys must help you to make as many of your own decisions as you can. They cannot treat you as unable to make the decision in question unless all practicable steps to help you to do so have been made without success.

3   Your attorneys must not treat you as unable to make the decision in question simply because you make an unwise decision.

4   Your attorneys must make decisions and act in your best interests when you are unable to make the decision in question.

5   Before your attorneys make the decision in question or act for you, they must consider whether they can make the decision or act in a way that is less restrictive of your rights and freedom but still achieves the purpose.

Your best interests

Your attorneys must act in your best interests in making decisions for you when you are unable to make the decision in question yourself. They must take into account all the relevant circumstances. This includes, if appropriate, consulting you and others who are interested in your health and welfare. Any guidance you add may assist your attorneys in identifying your views.

Cancelling this lasting power of attorney

You can cancel this lasting power of attorney at any time before or after it is registered as long as you have mental capacity to cancel it. Please read the guidance available at **publicguardian.gov.uk**

How to fill in this form

• Tick the boxes that apply like this

• Use black or blue ink and write clearly

• Cross through any boxes or sections that don't apply to you, like this:

> Any other names you are known by in financial documents or accounts

• Don't use correction fluid – please cross out any mistakes and rewrite nearby. All corrections must be initialled by the person completing that section of the form (and their witness) like this:

> Any other names you are known by in financial documents or accounts
>
> *WILLIAM EDWARD SMITH*
> *A.S.B / W.E.S.   SMYTH*

• Your application could be rejected if your intentions are not clear and explicit. If you are in any doubt, please start again on a new copy of the form.

What happens after you've filled it in?

The next step is to **register** it. You or your attorneys can do this at any time. The person applying will need to fill in a registration form and may need to pay a fee at that time. They will also need to send notices to the 'people to be told' named at part A when the application to register this lasting power of attorney is made. You can find out more and download the registration form at **publicguardian.gov.uk**

The 'people to be told' are given time to raise any concerns or objections. This means the earliest the Office of Public Guardian can register this lasting power of attorney is 6 weeks after they notify the donor or attorneys that an application to register has been received.

Your lasting power of attorney will **end** if it can no longer be used. For example, if a sole attorney dies or can no longer act for you and no replacement attorney has been named in this lasting power of attorney. Please read the guidance available at **publicguardian.gov.uk**

Part A Declaration by the person who is giving this lasting power of attorney

Please write clearly using black or blue ink.

1 About the person who is giving this lasting power of attorney

Mr ☐ Mrs ☐ Ms ☐ Miss ☐ Other title ☐

First names ☐

Last name ☐

Date of birth D D M M Y Y Y Y

Address and postcode ☐

Postcode ☐

Any other names you are known by in medical records or welfare records ☐

2 About the attorneys you are appointing

Thinking about your attorneys

- You can appoint more than one attorney if you want to. You do not have to appoint more than one attorney

- Each attorney must be aged 18 or over. Choose people you know and trust to make decisions for you. You are recommended to read the separate guidance for people who want to make a lasting power of attorney for health and welfare.

Your first or only attorney

Mr ☐ Mrs ☐ Ms ☐ Miss ☐ Other title ☐

First names of your first or only attorney ☐

Last name of your first or only attorney ☐

Date of birth of your first or only attorney D D M M Y Y Y Y

Address and postcode of your first or only attorney ☐

Postcode ☐

Your second attorney
Please cross through this section if it does not apply.

Mr ☐ Mrs ☐ Ms ☐ Miss ☐ Other title ☐

First names of your second attorney ☐

Last name of your second attorney ☐

Date of birth of your second attorney D D M M Y Y Y Y

Address and postcode of your second attorney ☐

Postcode ☐

If you are appointing more than two attorneys, use continuation sheet A1 to tell us about your other attorneys.

Other attorneys you are appointing

Number of attorneys named in continuation sheet **A1** attached to this lasting power of attorney ☐

Cross through this box if this does not apply

Helpline
☎ **0300 456 0300**
🖱 publicguardian.gov.uk

Valid only with Office of the Public Guardian stamp

3   About appointing replacements if an attorney can no longer act

Thinking about replacement attorneys

- Replacement attorneys will only act once your attorney can no longer act for you.
- You can appoint replacements to replace an attorney who does not want to act for you or who is permanently no longer able to act because they are dead, have disclaimed, lack mental capacity or if they were married to you or were your civil partner, and have now had the marriage or civil partnership annulled or dissolved.
- You do not have to appoint any replacements.
- If you appoint only one attorney and no replacements, this lasting power of attorney will end when your attorney can no longer act.

Your first or only replacement attorney   *Please cross through this section if it does not apply.*

Mr   Mrs   Ms   Miss   Other title

☐   ☐   ☐   ☐   [_____]

First names of your first or only replacement

[_____]

Last name of your first or only replacement

[_____]

Date of birth of your first or only replacement

D D M M Y Y Y Y

Address and postcode of your first or only replacement

[_____]

Postcode [_____]

If you are appointing more than one replacement, use continuation sheet A1 to tell us about your other replacement attorneys.

Other replacement attorneys you are appointing

Number of replacement attorneys named in continuation sheet **A1** attached to this lasting power of attorney

[_____]   *Cross through this box if this does not apply*

4 How you want your attorneys to make decisions

Thinking about how you want your attorneys to make decisions

ⓘ **If you leave this section blank, your attorneys will be appointed to make all decisions jointly.**

- **Jointly**: this means that the attorneys must **make all decisions together**. → *For further information on appointing your attorneys jointly, see the separate guidance.*

- **Jointly and severally**: this means that attorneys can **make decisions together and separately**. This might be useful, for example, if one attorney is not available to make a decision at a certain time. If one attorney cannot act the remaining attorney is able to continue to make decisions.

- **Jointly for some decisions, and jointly and severally for other decisions**: this means that your attorneys **must make certain decisions together** and may make **certain decisions separately**. You will need to set out below how you want this to work in practice.

Choosing which decisions must be made together and which decisions may be made separately – how this will work in practice

- Please make your intentions clear about how your attorneys are to make the decision in question, for example about where you live, who visits you and the type of care you receive.

- Please check that your intentions will work in practice – it may not be possible to register or use this lasting power of attorney if they are not workable. Please read the separate guidance for examples that will not work in practice.

How you want your attorneys to make decisions

If you are appointing only one attorney and no replacement attorneys, now go to section 5 →

Jointly	☐	→ Go to section 5 and cross through the box below
Jointly and severally	☐	→ Go to section 5 and cross through the box below
Jointly for some decisions, and jointly and severally for other decisions	☐	

Only if you have ticked the last box above, now tell us in the space below which decisions your attorneys must make jointly and which decisions may be made jointly and severally

If you need more space, use continuation sheet A2

5   About life-sustaining treatment

Life-sustaining treatment means any treatment that a doctor considers necessary to keep you alive. Whether or not a treatment is life-sustaining will depend on the specific situation. Some treatments will be life-sustaining in some situations but not in others.

The decisions you authorise your attorneys to make for you in this lasting power of attorney take the place of any advance decision you have already made on the same subject.

You must be clear whether or not you want to give your attorneys this authority. This is very important so please be clear about the choice you are making. You might want to discuss this first with your attorneys or doctors and health professionals.

You must choose Option A OR Option B.

Your attorneys can **only** make decisions about life-sustaining treatment if you choose Option A. If you choose Option B, your doctors will take into account where it is practicable and appropriate the views of your attorneys and people who are interested in your welfare as well as any written statement you may have made.

When you make your choice and sign this section you **must** have a witness. If you cannot sign you can make a mark instead.

> *If you cannot sign or make a mark use continuation sheet A3:HW* →
> - someone else **must** sign for you at your direction.
> - they must sign in your presence **and** in the presence of **two witnesses.**

Option A
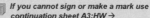 **Do not sign both boxes**

I want to give my attorneys authority to give or refuse consent to life-sustaining treatment on my behalf.

Signed in the presence of a witness by the person who is giving this lasting power of attorney

Your signature or mark

Date signed or marked

 D D M M Y Y Y Y

! The date you sign (or mark) here must be the same as the date you sign or mark section 10 Declaration.

Who can be a witness
- You must be 18 or over.
- You **cannot** be an attorney or replacement attorney named at part A or any continuation sheets A to this lasting power of attorney.
- If you have been asked to be the certificate provider at part B, you can be a witness at part A.
- A person to be told when the application to register this lasting power of attorney is made can be a witness.

Option B
! Do not sign both boxes

I do not want to give my attorneys authority to give or refuse consent to life-sustaining treatment on my behalf.

Signed in the presence of a witness by the person who is giving this lasting power of attorney

Your signature or mark

Date signed or marked

 D D M M Y Y Y Y

! The date you sign (or mark) here must be the same as the date you sign or mark section 10 Declaration.

Witnessed by

Signature of witness

Full names of witness

Address and postcode of witness

Postcode

Helpline
0300 456 0300
publicguardian.gov.uk

Valid only with Office of the Public Guardian stamp

6 About restrictions and conditions

Putting restrictions and conditions into words

- You should read the separate guidance for examples of conditions and restrictions that will not work in practice.
- Your attorneys **must** follow any restrictions or conditions you put in place. But it may not be possible to register or use this lasting power of attorney if a condition is not workable.
- **Either**: give any restrictions and conditions about health and welfare here
- **Or**: if you would like your attorneys to make decisions with no restrictions or conditions, you should cross through this box.

Restrictions and conditions about health and welfare

If you need more space, use continuation sheet A2

7 About guidance to your attorneys

Putting guidance into words

- Any guidance you add may help your attorneys to identify your views. You do not have to add any.
- Your attorneys do not have to follow your guidance but it will help them to understand your wishes when they make decisions for you.
- **Either**: Give any guidance about health and welfare here
- **Or:** if you have no guidance to add, please cross through this box.

Guidance to your attorneys about health and welfare

If you need more space, use continuation sheet A2

8 About paying your attorneys

Professional charges

- Professional attorneys, such as solicitors and accountants, charge for their services. You can also choose to pay a non-professional person for their services. You **should** discuss payment with your attorneys and record any agreement made here to avoid any confusion later.
- You can choose to pay non-professional attorneys for their services, but if you do not record any agreement here they will only be able to recover reasonable out-of-pocket expenses

Charges for services

If you need more space, use continuation sheet A2

→ *For further information on paying attorneys, please see the separate guidance.*

Helpline
J **0300 456 0300**
publicguardian.gov.uk

Valid only with Office of the Public Guardian stamp

9   About people to be told when the application to register this lasting power of attorney is made

Thinking about people to be told

- For your protection you can choose up to **five people to be told** when your lasting power of attorney is being registered. This gives people who know you well an opportunity to raise any concerns or objections **before** this lasting power of attorney is registered and can be used.

> ❗ • **You do not have to choose anyone. But if you leave this section blank, you must choose two people to sign the certificate to confirm understanding at part B.**

- The people to be told cannot be your attorney or replacement named at part A or in continuation sheets to part A.

The first or only person to be told	**The second person to be told**
Please cross through this section if it does not apply.	*Please cross through this section if it does not apply.*
Mr Mrs Ms Miss Other title	Mr Mrs Ms Miss Other title
First names of first or only person to be told	First names of second person to be told
Last name of first or only person to be told	Last name of second person to be told
Address and postcode of first or only person to be told	Address and postcode of second person to be told
Postcode	Postcode

Other people to be told

Please cross through this section if it does not apply

📄 *Tell us about other people to be told on continuation sheet A1.*

Number of other people to be told named in continuation sheet **A1** attached to this lasting power of attorney

10 Declaration by the person who is giving this lasting power of attorney

Before signing please check that you have:

- filled in every answer that applies to you
- crossed through blank boxes that do not apply to you
- filled in any continuation sheets
- crossed through any mistakes you have made
- initialled any changes you have made.

No changes may be made to this lasting power of attorney and no continuation sheets may be added after part A has been filled in and signed. If any change appears to have been made, this lasting power of attorney will not be valid and will be rejected when an application is made to register it.

By signing (or marking) on this page, or by directing someone to sign continuation sheet A3:HW, I confirm all of the following:

Statement of understanding

I have read or had read to me:

- the section called 'Information you must read' on page 2
- all information contained in part A and any continuation sheets to part A of this lasting power of attorney.

I appoint and give my attorneys authority to make decisions about my health and welfare, when I cannot act for myself because I lack mental capacity, subject to the terms of this lasting power of attorney and to the provisions of the Mental Capacity Act 2005.

Statement about life-sustaining treatment

I have chosen option A or option B about life-sustaining treatment in section 5 of this lasting power of attorney.

People to be told when the application to register this lasting power of attorney is made

I have chosen the people to be told, and have chosen **one** person to sign the certificate of understanding at part B.

OR

I do not want anyone to be told, and have chosen **two** people to sign certificates of understanding at part B.

If you cannot sign this lasting power of attorney you can make a mark instead.

If you cannot sign or make a mark use continuation sheet A3:HW →

Signed (or marked) by the person giving this lasting power of attorney and delivered as a deed

Date signed or marked

D D M M Y Y Y Y

❶ Sign (or mark) and date
- section 5 (Option A or Option B), and
- each continuation sheet
at the same time as you sign (or mark) part A here.

You must sign (or mark) and date part A here *before* parts B and C are signed and dated.

The witness should be independent of you and:

- Must be 18 or over.
- **Cannot** be an attorney or replacement attorney named at part A or any continuation sheets to this lasting power of attorney.
- Can be a certificate provider at part B.
- Can be a person to be told when the application to register this lasting power of attorney is made.
- Must initial any changes made in Part A.

❶ Sign section 5 (witnessing Option A or Option B) at the same time as you sign part A here.

Witnessed by

Signature of witness

Full names of witness

Address and postcode of witness

Postcode

Helpline
📞 **0300 456 0300**
🖱 **publicguardian.gov.uk**

Valid only with Office of the Public Guardian stamp

Part B — Declaration by your first or only certificate provider: certificate to confirm understanding

Your certificate provider fills in, signs and dates this part.

Declaration by the person who is signing this certificate

Please refer to separate guidance for certificate providers. If the guidance is not followed, this lasting power of attorney may not be valid and could be rejected when an application is made to register it.

In part A (section 9) has the person giving this lasting power of attorney chosen at least one person to be told when the application to register this lasting power of attorney is made?

If yes = **one** certificate provider fills in this part

If no = the **first** certificate provider fills in this part
          and the **second** certificate provider must fill
          in continuation sheet B .

The **donor** is the person who is giving this lasting power of attorney.

By signing below, I confirm:

My understanding of the role and responsibilities

I have read part A of this lasting power of attorney, including any continuation sheets.

I have read the section called '**Information you must read**' on page 2 of this lasting power of attorney.

I understand my role and responsibilities as a certificate provider.

Statement of acting independently

I confirm that I act independently of the attorneys and of the donor and I am aged 18 or over.

I am **not**:

- an attorney or replacement attorney named in this lasting power of attorney or any other lasting power of attorney or enduring power of attorney for the donor

- a family member related to the donor or any of their attorneys or replacements

- a business partner or paid employee of the donor or any of their attorneys or replacements

- the owner, director, manager or employee of a care home that the donor lives in, or a member of their family.

How you formed your opinion

Before signing this certificate you must establish that the donor understands what it is, the authority they are giving their attorneys, and is not being pressurised into making it.

If someone challenges this lasting power of attorney, you may need to explain how you formed your opinion.

Statement of personal knowledge or relevant professional skills

Please cross through the box that does not apply.

EITHER

I have **known** the donor for at least **two years** and as more than an acquaintance. My personal knowledge of the donor is:

OR

I have **relevant professional skills**. (Please state your profession – for example, a GP or solicitor – and then the particular skills that are relevant to you forming your opinion – for example, a consultant specialising in geriatric care.)

My profession and particular skills are:

Continues over →

Part B – Declaration by the person who is signing this certificate (continued)

Things you certify

I certify that, in my opinion, at the time of signing part A:

- the donor understands the purpose of this lasting power of attorney and the scope of the authority conferred under it
- no fraud or undue pressure is being used to induce the donor to create this lasting power of attorney
- there is nothing else which would prevent this lasting power of attorney from being created by the completion of this form.

Your signature

🛈 **Do not sign until part A of this lasting power of attorney has been filled in and signed.**

Sign **as soon as possible** after part A is signed. If this part is signed before part A is signed, this lasting power of attorney will not be valid and will be rejected when an application is made to register it.

Signature of certificate provider

Date signed

D D M M Y Y Y Y

Name and address of the person who is signing this certificate

Mr   Mrs   Ms   Miss   Other title

First names of certificate provider

Last name of certificate provider

Address and postcode of certificate provider

Postcode

Valid only with Office of the Public Guardian stamp

Part C
Declaration by each attorney or replacement attorney
Your attorney(s) and replacement attorney(s) sign and date this part.

If you are appointing more than one attorney, including replacement attorneys: photocopy this sheet before it is filled in so that each attorney has a copy to fill in and sign.

Statement by the attorney or replacement attorney who is signing this declaration

- Before a replacement can act for you, they must get in touch with the Office of the Public Guardian and return the original lasting power of attorney form. They will get guidance at that time about what needs to happen next.

By signing below, I confirm all of the following:

Understanding of role and responsibilities

I have read the section called **'Information you must read'** on page 2 of this lasting power of attorney.

I understand my role and responsibilities under this lasting power of attorney, in particular:

- I have a duty to act based on the principles of the Mental Capacity Act 2005 and have regard to the Mental Capacity Act Code of Practice
- I can make decisions and act only when this lasting power of attorney has been registered and when the person who is giving this lasting power of attorney lacks mental capacity
- I must make decisions and act in the best interests of the person who is giving this lasting power of attorney

Further statement of replacement attorney

If an original attorney's appointment is terminated, I will replace the original attorney if I am still eligible to act as an attorney.

I have the authority to act under this lasting power of attorney only after an original attorney's appointment is terminated and I have notified the Public Guardian of the event.

! For this lasting power of attorney to be valid and registered this part should not be signed before Part A or part B have been completed, signed and dated. Sign part C **as soon as possible** after part B is signed.

Signed or marked by the attorney or replacement attorney as a deed and delivered (or if to be signed at their direction refer to separate guidance)

Full name of [attorney] or [replacement attorney] (delete as appropriate)

Date signed or marked

D D M M Y Y Y Y

The witness must be over 18 and can be:

- another attorney or replacement attorney named at part A or in continuation sheet A to this lasting power of attorney
- a certificate provider at part B of this lasting power of attorney.
- a person to be told when the application to register this lasting power of attorney is made.

The donor cannot be a witness.

The witness must see the attorney or replacement attorney sign or make a mark.

Signature of witness

Full name of witness

Address and postcode of witness to the attorney's or replacement attorney's signature

Postcode

Helpline
0300 456 0300
publicguardian.gov.uk

Valid only with Office of the Public Guardian stamp

LPA 001 10.07

Notice of intention to apply for registration of a Lasting Power of Attorney

This notice must be sent to everyone named by the donor in the Lasting Power of Attorney as a person who should be notified of an application to register. Relatives are not entitled to notice unless named in the Lasting Power of Attorney.

The application to register may be made by the donor or the attorney(s).

Where attorneys are appointed to act together they all must apply to register.

Details of the named person

Name

Address

Telephone no.

Postcode

> **To the named person** - You have the right to object to the proposed registration of the Lasting Power of Attorney. You have **five weeks** from the day on which this notice is given to object. Details of how to object and the grounds for doing so are on the back page.

Details of the Lasting Power of Attorney (LPA)

Who is applying to register the LPA? ☐ the donor   ☐ the attorney(s)

Which type of LPA is being registered? ☐ Property and Affairs   ☐ Personal Welfare

(You must complete separate applications for each LPA you wish to register.)

On what date did the donor sign the LPA? D D M M Y Y Y Y

Details of the donor

Full name

Address

Telephone no.

Postcode

Details of the attorney(s)

Name of 1st attorney

Address

Telephone no.

Postcode

☐ solely   ☐ together and independently

☐ together   ☐ together in some matters and together and independently in others

Name of 2nd attorney

Address

Telephone no.

Postcode

☐ together   ☐ together and independently

☐ together in some matters and together and independently in others

Name of 3rd attorney

Address

Telephone no.

Postcode

☐ together   ☐ together and independently

☐ together in some matters and together and independently in others

Name of 4th attorney

Address

Telephone no.

Postcode

☐ together   ☐ together and independently

☐ together in some matters and together and independently in others

Signature and date ——————————————————————————————————————

This notice must be signed by all parties applying to register the lasting power of attorney.

Signed

Print name

Dated

D	D	M	M	Y	Y	Y	Y

How to object to the registering of a Lasting Power of Attorney (LPA)

You can ask the Office of the Public Guardian (OPG) to stop the LPA from being registered if one of the factual grounds at (A) below has occurred. You need to tell us by completing Form LPA7 which is available from the OPG and by providing evidence to accompany it. You must send us the completed LPA7 form **within five weeks** from the date this notice was given. Failure to tell us could result in the LPA being registered.

(A) Factual grounds – you can ask the Office of the Public Guardian to stop registration if:

- The Donor is bankrupt or interim bankrupt (for property and affairs LPAs only)
- The Attorney is bankrupt or interim bankrupt (for property and affairs LPAs only)
- The Attorney is a trust corporation and is wound up or dissolved (for property and affairs LPAs only)
- The Donor is dead
- The Attorney is dead
- That there has been dissolution or annulment of a marriage or civil partnership between the Donor and Attorney (except if the LPA provided that such an event should not affect the instrument)
- The Attorney(s) lack the capacity to be an attorney under the LPA
- The Attorney(s) have disclaimed their appointment

Form LPA7 is available from the OPG on 0845 330 2900 or www.publicguardian.gov.uk

You have the right to object to the Court of Protection about the registration of the LPA, but only on the grounds mentioned at (B) below. To do this you must contact the Court and complete the application to object form they will send you. Using that form, you must set out your reasons for objecting. They must receive the objection within five weeks from the date this notice was given. You must also notify the OPG when you object to the Court by using the separate form LPA8 that the Court will send you. Failure to notify the OPG of an objection may result in registration of the LPA.

Note: If you are objecting to the appointment of a specific attorney, it will not prevent registration if other attorneys or a substitute attorney have been appointed.

(B) Prescribed grounds – you can only object to the Court of Protection against registration of the LPA on the following grounds:

- That the power purported to be created by the instrument* is not valid as a LPA. e.g. the person objecting does not believe the donor had capacity to make an LPA.
- That the power created by the instrument no longer exists e.g. the donor revoked it at a time when he/she had capacity to do so.
- That fraud or undue pressure was used to induce the donor to make the power.
- The attorney proposes to behave in a way that would contravene his authority or would not be in the donor's best interests.

Note: * The instrument means the LPA made by the donor.

The Court will only consider objections made if they are made on the above grounds. To obtain a Court objection form please contact the Court of Protection at Archway Tower, 2 Junction Road, London N19 5SZ or Telephone 0845 330 2900.

┌─
LPA002 10.07 Office of the Public Guardian

Application to register a
Lasting Power of Attorney

Return your completed form to:
Office of the Public Guardian
Archway Tower
2 Junction Road
London N19 5SZ

Part 1 - The donor

Place a cross (x) against one option

Mr. ☐   Mrs. ☐   Ms. ☐   Miss ☐   Other ☐

If other, please specify ☐☐☐☐☐☐☐☐☐☐☐☐☐☐☐☐

Last name ☐☐☐☐☐☐☐☐☐☐☐☐☐☐☐☐☐☐☐☐☐☐☐☐☐☐

First name ☐☐☐☐☐☐☐☐☐☐☐☐☐☐☐☐☐☐☐☐☐☐☐☐☐☐

Middle name ☐☐☐☐☐☐☐☐☐☐☐☐☐☐☐☐☐☐☐☐☐☐☐☐☐☐

Address 1 ☐☐☐☐☐☐☐☐☐☐☐☐☐☐☐☐☐☐☐☐☐☐☐☐☐☐

Address 2 ☐☐☐☐☐☐☐☐☐☐☐☐☐☐☐☐☐☐☐☐☐☐☐☐☐☐

Address 3 ☐☐☐☐☐☐☐☐☐☐☐☐☐☐☐☐☐☐☐☐☐☐☐☐☐☐

Town/City ☐☐☐☐☐☐☐☐☐☐☐☐☐☐☐☐☐☐☐☐☐☐☐☐☐☐

County ☐☐☐☐☐☐☐☐☐☐☐☐☐☐☐☐☐☐☐☐☐☐☐☐☐☐

Postcode ☐☐☐☐☐☐☐   Daytime Tel. no. ☐☐☐☐☐☐☐☐☐☐☐☐☐

Date of birth ☐☐☐☐☐☐☐☐
D D M M Y Y Y Y

If the exact date is unknown please state the year of birth

e-mail address ☐☐☐☐☐☐☐☐☐☐☐☐☐☐☐☐☐☐☐☐☐☐☐☐☐☐

Please do not write below this line - For office use only

─┘

Part 2 - The persons making the application

Note: We need to know who is applying and how the attorney(s) have been appointed, please answer the questions in parts two and three carefully.

Place a cross (x) against one option

Is the donor applying to register the Lasting Power of Attorney? ☐ Yes

Is the attorney(s) applying to register the Lasting Power of Attorney? ☐ Yes

Part 3 - How have the attorney(s) been appointed?

The LPA states whether the attorney is to act soley, together or together and independently

Place a cross (x) against one option

There is only one attorney appointed ☐

There are attorneys appointed together and independently ☐

There are attorneys appointed together ☐

There are attorneys appointed together in some matters and together and independently in others ☐

Note: We need to know which, if any of the attorney(s) are making this application to register the LPA. You can tell us this by putting a cross in the box at the start of each attorney(s) details in section 4.

Part 4 - Attorney one

Place a cross (x) in this box if attorney one is applying to register ☐

Place a cross (x) against one option

Mr. ☐   Mrs. ☐   Ms. ☐   Miss ☐   Other ☐

If other, please specify

Last name

First name

Middle name

Company name *(if relevant)*

Address 1

Address 2

Address 3

Town/City

County

Postcode   DX number

Date of birth
D D M M Y Y Y Y   DX Exchange

Daytime Tel. no.

Occupation

e-mail address

Place a cross (x) against one option that best describes your relationship to the donor

Civil partner / Spouse ☐   Child ☐   Solicitor ☐   Other ☐   Other professional ☐

If 'Other' or 'Other professional', please specify

3

Part 4 - Attorney two

Place a cross (x) in this box if attorney two is applying to register ☐

Place a cross (x) against one option

Mr. ☐   Mrs. ☐   Ms. ☐   Miss ☐   Other ☐

If other, please specify ☐

Last name ☐

First name ☐

Middle name ☐

Company name *(if relevant)* ☐

Address 1 ☐

Address 2 ☐

Address 3 ☐

Town/City ☐

County ☐

Postcode ☐   DX number ☐

Date of birth ☐
D D M M Y Y Y Y   DX Exchange ☐

Daytime Tel. no. ☐

Occupation ☐

e-mail address ☐

Place a cross (x) against one option that best describes your relationship to the donor

Civil partner / Spouse ☐   Child ☐   Solicitor ☐   Other ☐   Other professional ☐

If 'Other' or 'Other professional', please specify ☐

4

Part 4 - Attorney three

Place a cross (x) in this box if attorney three is applying to register ☐

Place a cross (x) against one option

Mr. ☐   Mrs. ☐   Ms. ☐   Miss ☐   Other ☐

If other, please specify ☐☐☐☐☐☐☐☐☐☐☐☐☐☐☐☐☐☐

Last name ☐☐☐☐☐☐☐☐☐☐☐☐☐☐☐☐☐☐☐☐☐☐☐☐☐☐☐☐

First name ☐☐☐☐☐☐☐☐☐☐☐☐☐☐☐☐☐☐☐☐☐☐☐☐☐☐☐☐

Middle name ☐☐☐☐☐☐☐☐☐☐☐☐☐☐☐☐☐☐☐☐☐☐☐☐☐☐☐☐

Company name *(if relevant)* ☐☐☐☐☐☐☐☐☐☐☐☐☐☐☐☐☐☐☐☐☐☐☐☐☐☐☐☐

Address 1 ☐☐☐☐☐☐☐☐☐☐☐☐☐☐☐☐☐☐☐☐☐☐☐☐☐☐☐☐

Address 2 ☐☐☐☐☐☐☐☐☐☐☐☐☐☐☐☐☐☐☐☐☐☐☐☐☐☐☐☐

Address 3 ☐☐☐☐☐☐☐☐☐☐☐☐☐☐☐☐☐☐☐☐☐☐☐☐☐☐☐☐

Town/City ☐☐☐☐☐☐☐☐☐☐☐☐☐☐☐☐☐☐☐☐☐☐☐☐☐☐☐☐

County ☐☐☐☐☐☐☐☐☐☐☐☐☐☐☐☐☐☐☐☐☐☐☐☐☐☐☐☐

Postcode ☐☐☐☐☐☐☐   DX number ☐☐☐☐☐☐☐☐☐☐

Date of birth ☐☐☐☐☐☐☐☐   DX Exchange ☐☐☐☐☐☐☐☐☐☐☐☐☐☐
D D M M Y Y Y Y

Daytime Tel. no. ☐☐☐☐☐☐☐☐☐☐☐☐☐☐☐☐

Occupation ☐☐☐☐☐☐☐☐☐☐☐☐☐☐☐☐☐☐☐☐☐☐☐☐☐☐☐☐

e-mail address ☐☐☐☐☐☐☐☐☐☐☐☐☐☐☐☐☐☐☐☐☐☐☐☐☐☐☐☐

Place a cross (x) against one option that best describes your relationship to the donor

Civil partner / Spouse ☐   Child ☐   Solicitor ☐   Other ☐   Other professional ☐

If 'Other' or 'Other professional', please specify ☐☐☐☐☐☐☐☐☐☐☐☐☐☐

5

Part 4 - Attorney four

Place a cross (x) in this box if attorney four is applying to register ☐

> If there are additional attorneys, please provide the following details in the 'Additional information' section at the end of this form.

Place a cross (x) against one option

Mr. ☐   Mrs. ☐   Ms. ☐   Miss ☐   Other ☐

If other, please specify ☐☐☐☐☐☐☐☐☐☐☐☐☐☐☐☐

Last name ☐☐☐☐☐☐☐☐☐☐☐☐☐☐☐☐☐☐☐☐☐☐☐☐☐☐

First name ☐☐☐☐☐☐☐☐☐☐☐☐☐☐☐☐☐☐☐☐☐☐☐☐☐☐

Middle name ☐☐☐☐☐☐☐☐☐☐☐☐☐☐☐☐☐☐☐☐☐☐☐☐☐☐

Company name *(if relevant)* ☐☐☐☐☐☐☐☐☐☐☐☐☐☐☐☐☐☐☐☐☐☐☐☐☐☐

Address 1 ☐☐☐☐☐☐☐☐☐☐☐☐☐☐☐☐☐☐☐☐☐☐☐☐☐☐

Address 2 ☐☐☐☐☐☐☐☐☐☐☐☐☐☐☐☐☐☐☐☐☐☐☐☐☐☐

Address 3 ☐☐☐☐☐☐☐☐☐☐☐☐☐☐☐☐☐☐☐☐☐☐☐☐☐☐

Town/City ☐☐☐☐☐☐☐☐☐☐☐☐☐☐☐☐☐☐☐☐☐☐☐☐☐☐

County ☐☐☐☐☐☐☐☐☐☐☐☐☐☐☐☐☐☐☐☐☐☐☐☐☐☐

Postcode ☐☐☐☐☐☐☐   DX number ☐☐☐☐☐☐☐☐☐☐

Date of birth ☐☐☐☐☐☐☐☐   DX Exchange ☐☐☐☐☐☐☐☐☐☐☐☐☐☐
D D M M Y Y Y Y

Daytime Tel. no. ☐☐☐☐☐☐☐ ☐☐☐☐☐☐☐☐☐

Occupation ☐☐☐☐☐☐☐☐☐☐☐☐☐☐☐☐☐☐☐☐☐☐☐☐☐☐

e-mail address ☐☐☐☐☐☐☐☐☐☐☐☐☐☐☐☐☐☐☐☐☐☐☐☐☐☐

Place a cross (x) against one option that best describes your relationship to the donor

Civil partner / Spouse ☐   Child ☐   Solicitor ☐   Other ☐   Other professional ☐

If 'Other' or 'Other professional', please specify ☐☐☐☐☐☐☐☐☐☐☐☐☐☐

Part 5 - Notification of named persons

The donor or attorney(s) making the application must give notice to the named persons nominated by the donor in the section of the LPA marked 'Notifying others when an application to register your LPA is made'. The date on which the notice was given **must** be completed (which is the date it was posted or given to the named person). If the donor decided not to notify any named persons, please place a cross in the box provided.

The donor did not specify any named individuals in the LPA ☐

Place a cross (x) against one option

☐ I   ☐ We

have given notice to register in the prescribed form (LP1) to the following person(s):

Date notice given   ☐☐☐☐☐☐☐☐
D D M M Y Y Y Y

Last name

First name

Address 1

Address 2

Address 3

Town/City

County

Postcode

Part 5 - continued

Date notice given

D D M M Y Y Y Y

Last name

First name

Address 1

Address 2

Address 3

Town/City

County

Postcode

Date notice given

D D M M Y Y Y Y

Last name

First name

Address 1

Address 2

Address 3

Town/City

County

Postcode

Part 5 - continued

Date notice given

D D M M Y Y Y Y

Last name

First name

Address 1

Address 2

Address 3

Town/City

County

Postcode

Date notice given

D D M M Y Y Y Y

Last name

First name

Address 1

Address 2

Address 3

Town/City

County

Postcode

Part 6 - Fees

Guidelines on fee exemption and remission can be obtained from the Office of the Public Guardian.

Have you enclosed a cheque for the registration fee for this application?   ☐ Yes   ☐ No

Do you wish to apply for remission of the fee?   ☐ Yes   ☐ No

Do you wish to apply for exemption of the fee?   ☐ Yes   ☐ No

Do you wish to apply for postponement of the fee?   ☐ Yes   ☐ No

If you wish to apply for exemption, remission or postponement of all or part of the fee. You must complete the separate application form available from the Office of the Public Guardian.

Part 7 - Type of power

☐ I   ☐ We

apply to register the LPA (the original of which accompanies this application) made by the donor under the provisions of the Mental Capacity Act 2005.

What type of Lasting Power of Attorney are you applying to register?

☐ Property and affairs   **OR**   ☐ Personal welfare

Date that the **donor** signed the Lasting Power of Attorney   ☐☐☐☐☐☐☐☐
                                              D   D   M   M   Y   Y   Y   Y

To your knowledge, has the donor made any other Enduring Powers of Attorney or Lasting Power of Attorney?   ☐ Yes   ☐ No

If Yes, please give details below including registration date if applicable

Part 8 - Donor declaration

Note: This section should only be completed by the donor if they are applying for the registration of the Lasting Power of Attorney.

I apply to register the Lasting Power of Attorney (the original of which accompanies this application).

I certify that the above information is correct and that to the best of my knowledge and belief, I have completed the application in accordance with the provisions of the Mental Capacity Act 2005 and all statutory instruments made under it.

Signed

Date

D D M M Y Y Y Y

Last name

First name

Part 9 - Attorney(s) declaration

Note: This section should only be completed by the attorney(s) if they are applying for the registration of the Lasting Power of Attorney

☐ I ☐ We apply to register the Lasting Power of Attorney (the original of which accompanies this application).

☐ I ☐ We certify that the above information is correct to the best of my knowledge and belief.

☐ I ☐ We have completed the application within the provisions of the Mental Capacity Act 2005 and all statutory instruments made under it.

Signed

Date

D D M M Y Y Y Y

Last name

First name

Signed

Date

D D M M Y Y Y Y

Last name

First name

Part 9 - continued

Signed		Date								
			D	D	M	M	Y	Y	Y	Y

Last name

First name

Signed		Date								
			D	D	M	M	Y	Y	Y	Y

Last name

First name

Signed		Date								
			D	D	M	M	Y	Y	Y	Y

Last name

First name

Part 10 - Declaration by a trust corporation

If you are a trust corporation making this application please complete this declaration.

☐ I ☐ We

certify that the above information is correct and that to the best of my knowledge and belief, I have completed the application in accordance with the provisions of the Mental Capacity Act 2005 and all statutory instruments made under it.

Company name

Signature of authorised person(s)

Company seal (If applicable)

Last name

First name

12

Part 11 - Correspondence address

Place a cross (**x**) against one option

Mr. ☐   Mrs. ☐   Ms. ☐   Miss ☐   Other ☐

If other, please specify ☐☐☐☐☐☐☐☐☐☐☐☐☐☐☐

Last name ☐☐☐☐☐☐☐☐☐☐☐☐☐☐☐☐☐☐☐☐☐☐☐☐☐☐☐

First name ☐☐☐☐☐☐☐☐☐☐☐☐☐☐☐☐☐☐☐☐☐☐☐☐☐☐☐

Middle name ☐☐☐☐☐☐☐☐☐☐☐☐☐☐☐☐☐☐☐☐☐☐☐☐☐☐☐

Company name ☐☐☐☐☐☐☐☐☐☐☐☐☐☐☐☐☐☐☐☐☐☐☐☐☐☐☐

Company reference ☐☐☐☐☐☐☐☐☐☐☐☐☐☐☐☐☐☐☐☐☐☐☐☐☐☐☐

Address 1 ☐☐☐☐☐☐☐☐☐☐☐☐☐☐☐☐☐☐☐☐☐☐☐☐☐☐☐

Address 2 ☐☐☐☐☐☐☐☐☐☐☐☐☐☐☐☐☐☐☐☐☐☐☐☐☐☐☐

Address 3 ☐☐☐☐☐☐☐☐☐☐☐☐☐☐☐☐☐☐☐☐☐☐☐☐☐☐☐

Town/City ☐☐☐☐☐☐☐☐☐☐☐☐☐☐☐☐☐☐☐☐☐☐☐☐☐☐☐

County ☐☐☐☐☐☐☐☐☐☐☐☐☐☐☐☐☐☐☐☐☐☐☐☐☐☐☐

Postcode ☐☐☐☐☐☐☐   DX number ☐☐☐☐☐☐☐☐☐☐

DX Exchange ☐☐☐☐☐☐☐☐☐☐☐☐

Daytime Tel. no. ☐☐☐☐☐☐☐ ☐☐☐☐☐☐☐

e-mail address ☐☐☐☐☐☐☐☐☐☐☐☐☐☐☐☐☐☐☐☐☐☐☐☐☐☐☐

Part 12 - Additional information

Please write down any additional information to support this application in the space below. If necessary attach additional sheets.

LPA 003A **10.07**

Notice to an attorney of receipt of an application to register a Lasting Power of Attorney

Name of attorney

Take notice

An application to register a Lasting Power of Attorney (LPA) has been received by the Office of the Public Guardian.

We are sending you this notice because you are named as an attorney in the LPA and were not involved in the application to register.

You are hereby given notice of the proposed registration. **You have the right to object to the registration.** Details of how to do so are set out on page 2 of this notice. You have five weeks in which to object from the date this notice was given. (We will treat this notice as having been given two days after the date below.)

The names of the donor and the attorney(s) are set out below:

Donor's full name

The following attorney(s) have applied to register an LPA in the name of the above donor.

Attorney's full name

Attorney's full name

Attorney's full name

From

The Office of the Public Guardian
Archway Tower, 2 Junction Road
London N19 5SZ

Telephone 0845 330 2900

Dated

How to object to the registering of a Lasting Power of Attorney (LPA)

You can ask the Office of the Public Guardian (OPG) to stop the LPA from being registered if one of the factual grounds at (A) below has occurred. You need to tell us by completing Form LPA7 which is available from the OPG and by providing evidence to accompany it. You must send us the completed LPA7 form **within five weeks** from the date this notice was given. Failure to tell us could result in the LPA being registered.

(A) Factual grounds – you can ask the Office of the Public Guardian to stop registration if:

- The Donor is bankrupt or interim bankrupt (for property and affairs LPAs only)
- The Attorney is bankrupt or interim bankrupt (for property and affairs LPAs only)
- The Attorney is a trust corporation and is wound up or dissolved (for property and affairs LPAs only)
- The Donor is dead
- The Attorney is dead
- That there has been dissolution or annulment of a marriage or civil partnership between the Donor and Attorney (except if the LPA provided that such an event should not affect the instrument)
- The Attorney lacks the capacity to be an attorney under the LPA
- The Attorney disclaimed their appointment

Form LPA7 is available from the OPG on 0845 330 2900 or www.publicguardian.gov.uk

You have the right to object to the Court of Protection about the registration of the LPA, but only on the grounds mentioned at (B) below. To do this you must contact the Court and complete the application to object form they will send you. Using that form, you must set out your reasons for objecting. They must receive the objection within five weeks from the date this notice was given. You must also notify the OPG when you object to the Court by using the separate form LPA8 that the Court will send you. Failure to notify the OPG of an objection may result in registration of the LPA.

Note: If you are objecting to the appointment of a specific attorney, it will not prevent registration if other attorneys or substitute attorneys have been appointed.

(B) Prescribed grounds – you can only object to the Court of Protection against registration of the LPA on the following grounds:

- That the power purported to be created by the instrument* is not valid as a LPA. e.g. the person objecting does not believe the donor had capacity to make an LPA.
- That the power created by the instrument no longer exists e.g. the donor revoked it at a time when he/ she had capacity to do so.
- That fraud or undue pressure was used to induce the donor to make the power.
- The attorney proposes to behave in a way that would contravene his authority or would not be in the donor's best interests.

Note: * The instrument means the LPA made by the donor.

The Court will only consider objections made if they are made on the above grounds. To obtain a Court objection form please contact the Court of Protection at Archway Tower, 2 Junction Road, London N19 5SZ or telephone 0845 330 2900.

LPA 003B 10.07

Notice to donor of receipt of an application to register a Lasting Power of Attorney

Name of donor

Take notice

An application to register your Lasting Power of Attorney (LPA) has been received by the Office of the Public Guardian (OPG).

We are sending you this notice because your attorney(s) in the LPA has asked the OPG to register your LPA, so that it can be used.

You are hereby given notice of the proposed registration. **You have a right to object to the registration.** You have five weeks in which to object from the date this notice was given. (We will treat this notice as having been given two days after the date below). You can object by using form LPA6, which you can get from the OPG.

The names of your attorney(s) are set out below:

Attorney's full name

Attorney's full name

Attorney's full name

Attorney's full name

Dated

From
The Office of the Public Guardian
Archway Tower, 2 Junction Road
London N19 5SZ

Telephone 0845 330 2900

LPA 004 04 07

Notice of registration of a Lasting Power of Attorney

This notice is to confirm registration of a Lasting Power of Attorney.

Case no.

The donor

The attorney(s)

The Lasting Power of Attorney was entered into the register on

Notification of registration of the LPA is given as required in Schedule 1 Part 2 Paragraph 15 of the Mental Capacity Act 2005.

LPA 005 04.09

Disclaimer by a proposed or acting attorney under a Lasting Power of Attorney

Take notice that

☐ a proposed attorney

☐ an attorney acting under a Lasting Power of Attorney

has disclaimed appointment.

Details of attorney disclaiming appointment

Name

Address

Telephone no.

Postcode

Date of the Lasting Power of Attorney

On what date was the Lasting Power of Attorney made? D D M M Y Y Y Y

Signature and date

I disclaim my appointment as attorney under the Lasting Power of Attorney made by the donor.

Signed

Dated D D M M Y Y Y Y

Note: Where the LPA has been registered then a copy of this notice must be sent to the Office of the Public Guardian at: PO Box 15118, Birmingham, B16 6GX

Call OPG on 0845 330 2900 with any questions.

Details of the donor ————————————————————————————

Name

Address

Telephone no.

Postcode

Details of the other attorney(s) ————————————————————————

Name

Address

Telephone no.

Postcode

Name

Address

Telephone no.

Postcode

Name

Address

Telephone no.

Postcode

LPA 006 04:09

Objection by the donor to the registration of a lasting power of attorney

If you **do not want** your LPA to be registered then you need to complete and sign this form and return it to the Office of the Public Guardian. It would help if you tell us why you do not want your LPA registered by using the space below your signature but you do not have to give a reason.

Your full name

Date of birth

| D | D | M | M | Y | Y | Y | Y |

Case no. (if known)

Please sign to confirm your objection

Signed

Dated

| D | D | M | M | Y | Y | Y | Y |

Note: The registration of your LPA will be suspended by the Office of the Public Guardian upon receipt of this form. This means your attorney(s) will not be able to use the LPA, unless the attorney applies to the Court of Protection and the Court directs registration.

The reason(s) for your objection

Send your completed form to:
Office of the Public Guardian, PO Box 15118, Birmingham, B16 6GX

LPA 007 `04.09`

Objection to the Office of the Public Guardian of a proposed registration of a Lasting Power of Attorney on factual grounds

This form can only be used by the attorneys or named persons

Donors' full name

Date of birth (if known)   ☐ D ☐ D ☐ M ☐ M ☐ Y ☐ Y ☐ Y ☐ Y

Case no. (if known)

On what grounds are you objecting to the registration?

☐ The donor is bankrupt or interim bankrupt (Property and Affairs LPA only)

☐ The attorney is bankrupt or interim bankrupt

You must place an '**X**' in **at least one box** and provide evidence or proof of each ground to accompany this notice.

☐ The attorney is a trust corporation that has been wound up or dissolved

☐ The donor is dead

☐ The attorney is dead

☐ There has been dissolution or annulment of a marriage or civil partnership between the donor and attorney (and the LPA does not provide for this event)

☐ The attorney lacks capacity to act

☐ The attorney has disclaimed appointment

Please list opposite the evidence on which your objection is based and attach a copy to this form.

Signed   ☐ attorney

☐ named person

Full name

Dated   ☐ D ☐ D ☐ M ☐ M ☐ Y ☐ Y ☐ Y ☐ Y

Send your completed form and evidence to:
Office of the Public Guardian, PO Box 15118, Birmingham, B16 6GX

© Crown copyright 2009

LPA 008 04.09

Notice to the Office of the Public Guardian of an application to object to registration of a lasting power of attorney made to the Court of Protection

This notice is confirmation that I have applied to the Court of Protection to object to the registration of the lasting power of attorney, detailed below.

Note: You should notify the Office of the Public Guardian of an objection to the Court of Protection or the LPA may be registered.

Case no.
(if known)

Details of the donor

Your name

Address

Telephone no.

Postcode

Details of the person making the objection

Your name

Address

Telephone no.

Postcode

continued over

Reasons for making the objection ──────────────────────────────

Tell us here about the prescribed grounds on which you have objected to the Court of Protection about the registration of the LPA.

When did you send your objection to the Court of Protection? | D | D | M | M | Y | Y | Y | Y |

Signature and date ──────────────────────────────

Signed

Dated | D | D | M | M | Y | Y | Y | Y |

Send your completed form to:
Office of the Public Guardian, PO Box 15118, Birmingham, B16 6GX

ENDURING POWERS OF ATTORNEY FORMS

Form EP1PG

**Mental Capacity Act 2005
Enduring Power of Attorney**

> Notice of intention to apply for registration
> of an Enduring Power of Attorney

To..

Of..

This form may be adapted for use by three or more attorneys. Any attorney who is appointed to act jointly and severally, but who does not join in the application, must also be named.	**TAKE NOTICE THAT** I .... of .... and I .... of .... The attorney(s) of .... of .... intend to apply to the Public Guardian for registration of the enduring power of attorney appointing me (us) attorney(s) and made by the donor on the ....
Give the name and address of the donor	
The grounds upon which you can object are limited and are shown at 2 overleaf	1. You have the right to object to the proposed registration on one or more of the grounds set out below. If you object, you must notify the Office of the Public Guardian and state which of the grounds you are relying on within five weeks from the day this notice was given to you. You may make an application to the Court of Protection under rule [68] of the Court of Protection Rules 2007 for a decision on the matter. No fee is payable for such an application. If you do not make such an application, the Public Guardian may ask for the court's directions about registration.

Note: The instrument means the document used to make the enduring power of attorney made by the donor, which it is sought to register

The attorney(s) does not have to be a relative. Relatives are not entitled to know of the existence of the enduring power of attorney prior to being given this notice

Our staff will be able to assist with any questions you have regarding the objection (s). However, they cannot provide advice about your particular objection.

Note: Part 4 is addressed only to the donor

Note: This notice should be signed by every one of the attorneys who are applying to register the enduring power of attorney

Note:
The attorney(s) must keep a record of the date on which notice was given to the donor and to relatives. This information will be required from the attorney(s) when an application to register the EPA is made

2. The grounds on which you may object to the proposed registration are:

- That the power purported to be created by the instrument is not valid as an enduring power of attorney
- That the power created by the instrument no longer subsists
- That the application is premature because the donor is not yet becoming mentally incapable
- That fraud or undue pressure was used to induce the donor to make the power
- That the attorney is unsuitable to be the donor's attorney (having regard to all the circumstances and in particular the attorney's relationship to or connection with the donor).

3. You can obtain the necessary forms to object by.
- Writing to us at the address on the foot of this form
- Calling us on 0845 330 2900
- Downloading the forms from our website at www.publicguardian.gov.uk

4. You are informed that while the enduring power of attorney remains registered, you will not be able to revoke it until the Court of Protection confirms the revocation.

Signed: .... Dated: ....

Signed: .... Dated: ....

Please write to:
Office of the Public Guardian
PO Box 15118
Birmingham
B16 6GX

www.publicguardian.gov.uk

EP1PG – 02.10

Office of the Public Guardian
Mental Capacity Act 2005
Form EP2PG
Application for Registration of an Enduring
Power of Attorney

IMPORTANT: Please complete the form in <u>BLOCK CAPITALS</u> using a <u>black ball-point pen</u>. Place a clear cross 'X' mark inside square option boxes ⊠ - do not circle the option.

Part One - The Donor

Please state the full name and present address of the donor. State the donor's first name in 'Forename 1' and the donor's other forenames in full in 'Other Forenames'. Company Name should be completed with the name of the nursing/care home or hospital where applicable.

Mr   Mrs   Ms   Miss   Other
☐   ☐   ☐   ☐   ☐
Place a cross against one option ⊠   If Other, please specify here:

Last Name.

Forename 1.

Other Forenames:

Company Name:

Address 1:

Address 2:

Address 3:

Town/City:

County:

Postcode:

Donor Date of Birth: *If the exact date is unknown please state the year of birth*
D   D   M   M   Y   Y   Y   Y

Please do not write below this line - For Office Use Only

Produced in association with the
Office of the Public Guardian   © Crown Copyright 2007   Provider details

Page 1 of 7

Part Two - Attorney One

Please state the full name and present address of the attorney. Professionals e.g, Solicitors or Accountants, should complete the Company Name field.

Mr   Mrs   Ms   Miss   Other

☐   ☐   ☐   ☐   ☐   If Other, please

Place a cross against one option ☒   specify here:

Last Name:

Forename 1:

Other Forenames:

Company Name:

Address 1:

Address 2:

Address 3:

Town/City:

County:

Postcode: DX No.
(solicitors only):

DX Exchange
(solicitors only):

Attorney Date of Birth: Daytime Tel No.:

D   D   M   M   Y   Y   Y   Y   (STD Code):

Email Address:

Occupation:

Relationship to donor:

Civil Partner / Spouse   Child   Other Relation   No Relation   Solicitor   Other Professional   If 'Other Relation' or 'Other Professional', specify relationship:

☐   ☐   ☐   ☐   ☐   ☐

Place a cross against one option ☒

Part B of the Enduring Power of Attorney states whether the attorney is to act jointly, jointly and severally, or alone.

Appointment (*Place a cross against one option* ☒):   Jointly   ☐

                                                           Jointly and Severally   ☐

                                                           Alone   ☐

Part Three - Attorney Two

Please state the full name and present address of the attorney. Professionals e.g. Solicitors or Accountants, should complete the Company Name field.

Mr Mrs Ms Miss Other
☐   ☐   ☐   ☐   ☐
Place a cross against one option ☒

If Other, please specify here:

Last Name:

Forename 1:

Other Forenames:

Company Name:

Address 1:

Address 2:

Address 3:

Town/City:

County:

Postcode: DX No. (solicitors only):

DX Exchange (solicitors only):

Attorney Date of Birth: Daytime Tel No.:
D D M M Y Y Y Y   (STD Code):

Email Address:

Occupation:

Relationship to donor:

Civil Partner / Spouse | Child | Other Relation | No Relation | Solicitor | Other Professional
☐ | ☐ | ☐ | ☐ | ☐ | ☐
Place a cross against one option ☒

If 'Other Relation' or 'Other Professional', specify relationship:

Part Four - Attorney Three

Please state the full name and present address of the attorney. Professionals e.g. Solicitors or Accountants, should complete the Company Name field.

Mr Mrs Ms Miss Other
☐   ☐   ☐   ☐   ☐
Place a cross against one option ☒

If Other, please specify here:

Last Name:

Forename 1:

Part Four Continued Overleaf

Part Four - Attorney Three cont'd

Other Forenames:

Company Name:

Address 1:

Address 2:

Address 3:

Town/City:

County:

Postcode: DX No. (solicitors only):

DX Exchange (solicitors only):

Attorney Date of Birth: Daytime Tel No.:

D D M M Y Y Y Y   (STD Code):

Email Address:

Occupation:

Relationship to donor:

Civil Partner / Spouse	Child	Other Relation	No Relation	Solicitor	Other Professional	If 'Other Relation' or 'Other Professional', specify relationship:
☐	☐	☐	☐	☐	☐	

Place a cross against one option ☒

If there are additional attorneys, please complete the above details in the 'Additional Information' section (at the end of this form).

Part Five - The Enduring Power of Attorney

I (We) the attorney(s) apply to register the Enduring Power of Attorney made by the donor under the Enduring Powers of Attorney Act 1985, the original, or if the original is lost or destroyed, a certified copy of which accompanies this application.

I (We) have reason to believe that the donor is or is becoming mentally incapable.

Date that the **Donor** signed the Enduring Power of Attorney.
You can find this in Part B of the Enduring Power of Attorney.

D D M M Y Y Y Y

To your knowledge, has the Donor made any other Enduring Powers of Attorney?:

☐ ☐
Yes No
Place a cross against one option ☒

If 'Yes', please give details below including registration date if applicable:

Part Six - Notice of Application to Donor

Notice must be given personally to the donor. It should be made clear if someone other than the attorney(s) gives the notice. The date on which the notice was given MUST be completed.

I (We) have given notice of the application to register in the prescribed form (EP1PG) to the donor personally,

on this date: ☐☐☐☐☐☐☐☐

       D D M M Y Y Y Y

If someone other than the attorney gives notice to the donor please complete the name and address details below. Please also complete the date above:

Full Name: ....
Address 1: ....
Address 2: ....
Address 3: ....
Town/City: ....
County: .... Postcode: ....

Part Seven - Notice of Application to Relatives

Please complete details of all relatives entitled to notice.

Please place a cross in the box ☒ if no relatives are entitled to notice: ☐

I (We) have given notice to register in the prescribed form (EP1PG) to the following relatives of the donor:

Full Name: _____ Relationship to Donor: _____
Address: _____ Date notice given: ☐☐☐☐☐☐☐☐
    D D M M Y Y Y Y

Full Name: _____ Relationship to Donor: _____
Address: _____ Date notice given: ☐☐☐☐☐☐☐☐
    D D M M Y Y Y Y

Full Name: _____ Relationship to Donor: _____
Address: _____ Date notice given: ☐☐☐☐☐☐☐☐
    D D M M Y Y Y Y

Full Name: _____ Relationship to Donor: _____
Address: _____ Date notice given: ☐☐☐☐☐☐☐☐
    D D M M Y Y Y Y

Full Name: _____ Relationship to Donor: _____
Address: _____ Date notice given: ☐☐☐☐☐☐☐☐
    D D M M Y Y Y Y

If there are additional relatives please complete the Relative Name, Relationship, Address and Date details in the 'Additional Information' section (at the end of this form).

Part Eight - Notice of Application to Co-Attorney(s)

Do not complete this section if it does not apply. If there are additional co-attorneys please complete the Attorney Name, Relationship, Address and Date details in the 'Additional Information' section (at the end of this form).

Are all the attorneys applying to register?   Yes ☐   No ☐   *Place a cross against one option* ☒

If no, I (We) have given notice to my (our) co-attorney(s) as follows:

Full Name: _____   Relationship to Donor: _____

Address: _____   Date notice given:

D D M M Y Y Y Y

Full Name: _____   Relationship to Donor: _____

Address: _____   Date notice given:

D D M M Y Y Y Y

Part Nine - Fees

Guidelines on remission and postponement of fees can be obtained from the Office of the Public Guardian.

Have you enclosed a cheque for the registration fee for this application? Yes ☐ No ☐ *Place a cross against one option* ☒

Do you wish to apply for postponement, exemption or remission of the fee?   Yes ☐ No ☐ *Place a cross against one option* ☒

If yes, please complete the application for exemption or remission form.

Part Ten - Declaration

Note: The application should be signed by all attorneys who are making the application. This must not pre-date the date(s) when the notices were given.

I (We) certify that the above information is correct and that to the best of my (our) knowledge and belief I (We) have complied with the provisions of the Mental Capacity Act 2005.

Signed: _____   Dated:

D D M M Y Y Y Y

Signed: _____   Dated:

D D M M Y Y Y Y

Signed: _____   Dated:

D D M M Y Y Y Y

Part Eleven - Correspondence Address

Solicitors please note: The address to which the correspondence should be sent **MUST** be entered here if this is different to the address of Attorney One. State the full name and present address. Insert the name of the Solicitor's Firm in the Company Name field, if appropriate, and the correspondence reference in the Company Reference field.

Mr   Mrs   Ms   Miss   Other

☐   ☐   ☐   ☐   ☐

Place a cross against one option ☒

If Other, please specify here:

Last Name:

Forename 1:

Other Forenames:

Company Name:

Company Reference:

Address 1:

Address 2:

Address 3:

Town/City:

County:

Postcode:

DX No. (solicitors only):

DX Exchange (solicitors only):

Daytime Tel No..

(STD Code):

Email Address:

Part Twelve - Additional Information

Please write down any additional information to support this application in the space below. If necessary attach additional paper to the end of this form.

Guidance notes for completing form EP2PG: Application to register an Enduring Power of Attorney

Please complete every section of the form clearly in BLOCK CAPITALS using BLACK ink.

Part One – The Donor

- This section of the form covers the information we need to know about the Donor of the Enduring Power of Attorney (EPA). The Donor is the person who appointed the Attorney or Attorneys when the EPA was set up.

- Place a cross in the box that relates to the Donor's title or write it in the space provided.

- Last Name: The Donor's last name is their surname.

- Forename 1 and Other Forenames: Put the Donor's first name next to Forename 1, and put their second name and any other middle names next to Other Forenames.

- Company Name: If the Donor is living in, for example, a hospital or care home, write the name of that place in this section. If not, write 'not applicable'.

- Address 1- Address 3: When filling in the Donor's address, ensure that you don't write the town/city, county or postcode in this section.

- Town/City, County, Postcode: Ensure you only write the relevant information on each line.

- If the Donor's address on the EPA is different to the one you wrote on the EP2PG form, explain why this is the case under Part Twelve – Additional Information – the final section of the form.

- Donor Date of Birth: Complete the boxes requesting the Donor's date of birth, including the day, month and year. If you do not know this, you can find it in the EPA itself, under the Donor's name and address. If the date of birth you enter here is different from that on the EPA itself, explain the reason for the difference in Part Twelve – Additional Information and provide a copy of the birth certificate as evidence.

Part Five – The Enduring Power of Attorney

- Part Five is to record the date the Donor signed the original EPA. Please enter the day, month and year in the relevant boxes.

- If you know that the Donor has made other EPAs, put a cross in the relevant square.

Part Six – Notice of Application to Donor

- Part Six of the form covers the requirement to personally notify the Donor that you are registering the EPA. It asks you to record the details of when this happened, using the notice in form EP1PG.

- If someone other than the Attorney personally notifies the Donor, enter that person's full name and address. Input the actual date (using the day, month and year boxes) that the Donor was given the notice in person.

- Please note that in certain circumstances the Court of Protection (the 'Court') may consider dispensing with the requirement to notify the Donor. This will normally only happen if a doctor certifies that it will cause the Donor harm or distress. You would then need to contact the Court to make an application to dispense with notice and pay the Court application fee.

- Part Six of the form must be completed unless the Court has agreed that you are not required to notify the Donor. If this is the case you must explain this in Part 12 – Additional Information.

Part Seven – Notice of Application to Relatives

- Part Seven of the form covers the details of the relatives that you must notify that you intend to register the EPA.

- Input their Full Names, Relationship to Donor and their Addresses in the spaces provided.

- Next to each person's contact details, input the actual date that notice was given to that person, including the day, month and year.

- If more relatives need to be notified than you can fit in this section, attach additional sheets of papers to the form with their details.

- In certain circumstances the Court may consider dispensing with the requirement to notify relatives. You would need to contact the Court to make an application and pay the Court application fee.

IMPORTANT: You must send us the EP2PG application to register the EPA within 10 working days of serving the last notice on the Donor and relatives.

Part Five – The Enduring Power of Attorney

- Part Five is to record the date the Donor signed the original EPA. Please enter the day, month and year in the relevant boxes.

- If you know that the Donor has made other EPAs, put a cross in the relevant square.

Part Six – Notice of Application to Donor

- Part Six of the form covers the requirement to personally notify the Donor that you are registering the EPA. It asks you to record the details of when this happened, using the notice in form EP1PG.

- If someone other than the Attorney personally notifies the Donor, enter that person's full name and address. Input the actual date (using the day, month and year boxes) that the Donor was given the notice in person.

- Please note that in certain circumstances the Court of Protection (the 'Court') may consider dispensing with the requirement to notify the Donor. This will normally only happen if a doctor certifies that it will cause the Donor harm or distress. You would then need to contact the Court to make an application to dispense with notice and pay the Court application fee.

- Part Six of the form must be completed unless the Court has agreed that you are not required to notify the Donor. If this is the case you must explain this in Part 12 – Additional Information.

Part Seven – Notice of Application to Relatives

- Part Seven of the form covers the details of the relatives that you must notify that you intend to register the EPA.

- Input their Full Names, Relationship to Donor and their Addresses in the spaces provided.

- Next to each person's contact details, input the actual date that notice was given to that person, including the day, month and year.

- If more relatives need to be notified than you can fit in this section, attach additional sheets of papers to the form with their details.

- In certain circumstances the Court may consider dispensing with the requirement to notify relatives. You would need to contact the Court to make an application and pay the Court application fee.

IMPORTANT: You must send us the EP2PG application to register the EPA within 10 working days of serving the last notice on the Donor and relatives.

Part Eight – Notice of Application to Co-Attorney(s)

- Part Eight of the form is to be used only if there is more than one Attorney and the other Attorney(s) are not making this application with you. The details of those Attorney(s) are to be entered in this section.

- This section does not apply if the Attorneys are appointed jointly – as this would mean that they would both (or all) have had to make the application with you because the Donor appointed you to act together.

Part Nine – Fees

- This section of the form covers fee information. There is separate guidance available from the Office of the Public Guardian (OPG) on fees, exemptions and remissions. If you wish to apply for a postponement, exemption or remission of the fee, you should fill in the appropriate box. You will also need to complete the relevant application form.

- If the OPG provided you with the EP2PG registration application form, you should have received our fees guidance at the same time. You can also download it from our website.

Part Ten – Declaration

- Part Ten is the Attorney(s) declaration. This is where you or the Attorney(s) certify that you have complied with the provisions of the Mental Capacity Act 2005 and all the relevant statutory instruments made under it. Please note that false declarations may make the signatory liable to criminal prosecution.

- Input the date that you signed the application, including day, month and year.

Part Eleven – Correspondence Address

- Part Eleven of the form requests the address for all correspondence. This information is vital to your application and care should be taken to ensure accuracy.

- The registered EPA will be returned to this address. If this section is left blank, all correspondence will be sent to Attorney One.

- The boxes entitled DX Exchange are for those wishing to use Document Exchange as an alternative to the postal service.

- The telephone number and email address should be completed if applicable.

Part Twelve – Additional Information

- Part Twelve is for any additional information. For instance if there are more than three Attorneys, the details of the additional Attorney(s) should be entered here.

Further Assistance

- The OPG publishes guidance about EPAs, Lasting Powers of Attorney (LPA) and the role of the Attorney. These are available to download from our website or you can call us for a hard copy.

- If you need further help in completing the EP2PG form please contact us.

Contact Us

Office of the Public Guardian
PO Box 15118
Birmingham B16 6GX

Phone Number: 0300 456 0300

Fax Number: 020 7664 7705

Email: customerservices@publicguardian.gsi.gov.uk

Website: www.publicguardian.gov.uk

DX: 744240 Birmingham 79

Textphone: 020 7664 7755 (If you have speech or hearing difficulties and have access to a textphone, you can call the OPG textphone for assistance.)

International Calls: +44 20 7664 7000

International Faxes: +44 20 7664 7705

Disclaimer

OPG and Court staff can provide advice about OPG and Court processes only and cannot provide legal advice or services. We recommend that you seek independent legal advice where appropriate. Information in this publication is believed to be correct at the time of printing, however we do not accept liability for any error it may contain.

DEPRIVATION OF LIBERTY FORMS

COP DLA 04.09 Court of Protection	Case no.
Deprivation of liberty	Date of application
Application form	Date of issue

For urgent consideration

To the applicant(s) and interested party(ies). Representations as to the urgency of the claim may be made by applicant or interested parties to the Deprivation of Liberty Officer by fax: 020 7664 7712

SEAL

If a standard/urgent authorisation has been given please fill in this two boxes.

Date of urgent/ standard authorisation   ☐☐/☐☐/☐☐☐☐   Date of effective detention ☐☐/☐☐/☐☐☐☐

Section 1 – Contact details

Applicant

Name

Address   Telephone no.

Mobile no.

Postcode ☐☐☐☐ ☐☐☐☐

Email

What is the appliant's relationship to the relevant person? (This is the person that the application is about)

Applicant's solicitor or representatives

Name

Address   Telephone no.

Mobile no.

Fax no.

Postcode ☐☐☐☐ ☐☐☐☐

Email

1

Counsel *(if known)*

Name

Address　　　　　　　　　　　　　　　　　Telephone no.

　　　　　　　　　　　　　　　　　　　　　Mobile no.

　　　　　　　　　　　　　　　　　　　　　Fax no.

Postcode

Email

Relevant person's details if not applicant

Name

Address　　　　　　　　　　　　　　　　　Telephone no.

　　　　　　　　　　　　　　　　　　　　　Mobile no.

　　　　　　　　　　　　　　　　　　　　　Fax no.

Postcode

Email

Supervisory body PCT/LA

Name

Address　　　　　　　　　　　　　　　　　Telephone no.

　　　　　　　　　　　　　　　　　　　　　Mobile no.

　　　　　　　　　　　　　　　　　　　　　Fax no.

Postcode

Email

Managing Authority/Hospital/Care Home

Name

Address

Telephone no.

Mobile no.

Fax no.

Postcode

Email

IMCA

Name

Address

Telephone no.

Mobile no.

Fax no.

Postcode

Email

Relevant person's representative

Name

Address

Telephone no.

Mobile no.

Fax no.

Postcode

Email

Section 2 – Details of other interested parties

Name	

Address		Telephone no.
		Fax no.
		DX no.

Postcode [ ][ ][ ][ ] [ ][ ][ ][ ]

Email

Name	

Address		Telephone no.
		Fax no.
		DX no.

Postcode [ ][ ][ ][ ] [ ][ ][ ][ ]

Email

Section 3 – Details of issue to be challenged

3.1   Date of decision [ ][ ] / [ ][ ] / [ ][ ][ ][ ]

3.2   Where an **urgent** authorisation has been given, the court may determine any question relating to any of the following matters:

☐ whether the urgent authorisation should have been given

☐ the period during which the urgent authorisation is to be in force

☐ the purpose for which the urgent authorisation is given

☐ other

3.3   Where a **standard** authorisation has been given, the court may determine any question relating to any of the following matters:

       ☐ whether the relevant person meets one or more of the qualifying requirements

       ☐ the period during which the standard authorisation is to be in force

       ☐ the purpose for which the standard authorisation is given

       ☐ the conditions subject to which the standard authorisation is given

       ☐ other

3.4   Do you require permission?   ☐ Yes   ☐ No

       If Yes, complete form **COP DLC Permission Form**

3.5   Other issues that may arise

       Are you making an interim application?   ☐ Yes   ☐ No

       Do you intend to bring other applications if this application succeeds in whole or in part?   ☐ Yes   ☐ No

       Do you intend to bring other applications if this application fails?   ☐ Yes   ☐ No

Section 4 – Detailed statement of grounds

       ☐ Set out below   ☐ Attached

Section 5 – Other issues of the case

5.1   Are there other issues that will arise for determination in respect of the relevant
      person and any applications that you have made or intend to make in respect of   ☐ Yes   ☐ No
      them?

      If Yes, please give details below

Section 6 – Other applications

6.1 Are you aware of any previous application(s) to the Court of Protection regarding ☐ Yes ☐ No
the person to whom this application relates?

If Yes, please give as much of the following information as you can. If there has
been more than one previous application please attach the information about
other previous applications on a separate sheet of paper.

The name of the applicant

[   ]

The date of the order

[ ] [ ] / [ ] [ ] / [ ] [ ] [ ] [ ]

Case number

[   ]

Please attach a copy of the order(s), if available.

☐ Copy attached   ☐ Not available

Section 7 - Attending court hearings

7.1 If the court requires you to attend a hearing do you need any special ☐ Yes ☐ No
assistance or facilities?

If Yes, please say what your requirements are. If necessary,
court staff may contact you about your requirements.

[   ]

7

Section 8 – Statement of facts relied on

Section 9 - Statement of truth

The statement of truth is to be signed by you, your solicitor or your litigation friend.

*(I believe) (The applicant believes) that the facts stated in this application form and its annex(es) are true.

Signed | | Date | ☐☐ / ☐☐ / ☐☐☐☐ |

Name | |

Name of firm | | Position or office held | |

Section 10 - Supporting documents

10.1   Which of the following documents are you filing with this application and any you will be filing later?

☐ Standard authorisation

☐ Urgent authorisation

☐ Age assessment

☐ No refusals assessment

☐ Mental capacity assessment

☐ Mental health assessment

☐ Eligibility assessment

☐ Best interests assessment

☐ Form COP DLB Declaration of exceptional urgency

☐ Form COP DLC Permission Form (if applicable)

☐ Form COP 24 Witness Statement

☐ A copy of the Legal Aid or CSLF certificate (if legally represented)

☐ Copies of any relevant statutory material

☐ Draft Order or Directions

10.2   The following documents not being in my possession. I request   the Supervisory Body/ Managing Authority, to file copies of the following documents with their acknowledgment of service

☐ Standard authorisation

☐ Urgent authorisation

☐ Age assessment

☐ No refusals assessment

☐ Mental capacity assessment

☐ Mental health assessment

☐ Eligibility assessment

☐ Best interests assessment

☐ Care plan

10.3   Please explain why you have not supplied a document and a date when you expect it to be available:

Signed .... Applicant's Solicitor ....

9

COP
DLB
04.09 Court of Protection
Deprivation of liberty

Declaration of
exceptional urgency

Case no.	
Date of application	
Date of issue	

To the applicant(s) and interested party(ies). Representations as to the urgency of the claim may be made by applicant or interested parties to the Deprivation of Liberty Officer by fax: 020 7664 7712

Full name of person to whom the application relates
(this is the name of the person who is deprived/will be deprived of their liberty)

Date of urgent/
standard authorisation ☐☐/☐☐/☐☐☐☐   Date of effective detention ☐☐/☐☐/☐☐☐☐

Section 1 - Reasons for urgency

1.1   Please give reasons for the urgency

1.2   Please state what interim relief is sought and why?

Signed   Dated ☐☐/☐☐/☐☐☐☐

Section 2 - Proposed timetable

2.1   Please tick the boxes that apply

☐ The application for interim relief should be
  considered within   ☐ hours
                                                             ☐ days

☐ The form DLC Application for permission should be
  considered within   ☐ hours
                                                             ☐ days

☐ Abridgement of time is sought for the lodging of
  acknowledgments of service

☐ If permission granted, a substantive hearing is sought by ☐☐/☐☐/☐☐☐☐

1   © Crown Copyright 2009

Section 3 – Service

3.1   On whom have you served a copy of this form?

☐ **Relevant person**

Date served

☐☐/☐☐/☐☐☐☐

☐ by fax machine

Fax no.

Time sent

☐ by e-mail (please give address below)

☐ by handing it to or leaving it with

Name

☐ **Managing Authority**

Date served

☐☐/☐☐/☐☐☐☐

☐ by fax machine

Fax no.

Time sent

☐ by e-mail (please give address below)

☐ by handing it to or leaving it with

Name

☐ **Supervisory Body**

Date served

☐☐/☐☐/☐☐☐☐

☐ by fax machine

Fax no.

Time sent

☐ by e-mail (please give address below)

☐ by handing it to or leaving it with

Name

☐ **IMCA**

Date served

☐☐/☐☐/☐☐☐☐

☐ by fax machine

Fax no.

Time sent

☐ by e-mail (please give address below)

☐ by handing it to or leaving it with

Name

☐ **Relevant persons representative**

Date served

☐☐/☐☐/☐☐☐☐

☐ by fax machine

Fax no.

Time sent

☐ by e-mail (please give address below)

☐ by handing it to or leaving it with

Name

☐ **Interested parties**

Date served

☐☐/☐☐/☐☐☐☐

☐ by fax machine

Fax no.

Time sent

☐ by e-mail (please give address below)

☐ by handing it to or leaving it with

Name

CCP DLC 04.09 Court of Protection	For office use only	
Deprivation of liberty	Date received	
Permission form	Case no.	
	Date issued	

Full name of person to whom the application relates
(this is the name of the person who is deprived/will be deprived of their liberty)

SEAL

Section 1 - Your details (the applicant)

Applicant's full name

Address   Telephone no.

Postcode

Email

1.1   I seek permission for the following reason(s)

continued over the page ➡

1

1.1 continued

Statement of truth

The statement of truth is to be signed by you, your solicitor or your litigation friend.

(I believe) (The applicant believes) that the facts stated in this permission form are true.

Signed		Date	
	Applicant('s litigation friend)('s solicitor)		

Name	

Name of firm		Position or office held	

COP DLD 04.09 Court of Protection **Deprivation of liberty** **Certificate of service/ non-service** **Certificate of notification/ non-notification**	Case no. Name of applicant Name of respondent Filed by Date

Full name of person to whom the application relates
(this is the person who is deprived/will be deprived of their liberty)

Section 1 – Details of the person served/notified

1.1   Name of the person(s) served/notified:

Name   Date served/notified

Name   Date served/notified

Name   Date served/notified

Name   Date served/notified

Section 2 – Document served

2.1   Title or description of the document (tick only **one** box)

☐ application form

☐ other (please give details)

© Crown Copyright 2009

Section 3 – Person(s) not served or notified

3.1 Name of the person(s) who have not been served/notified:

Name

Reason

Name

Reason

Name

Reason

Name

Reason

Section 4 – Statement of truth

The statement of truth must be signed by the person who served/provided notification.

I believe that the facts stated in this certificate are true.

Signed   Date ☐☐/☐☐/☐☐☐☐

Name

Name of firm   Position or office held

2

COP DLE 04.09   Court of Protection

Deprivation of liberty
Acknowledgment of service/notification

Case no.	
Name of applicant	
Name of respondent	
Name of party acknowledging	
Date	

Full name of person to whom the application relates
(this is the name of the person who is deprived/will be deprived of their liberty)

Section 1 - The person served/notified

1.1   Your details   ☐ Mr.   ☐ Mrs.   ☐ Miss   ☐ Ms.   ☐ Other _____

     First name

     Last name

1.2   Address (including postcode)   Telephone no.

     E-mail address

1.3   Is a solicitor representing you?   ☐ Yes   ☐ No

     If Yes, please give the solicitor's details.

     Name

     Address (including postcode)   Telephone no.

     Fax no.

     DX no.

     E-mail address

1.4   Which address should official documentation be sent to?

☐ Your address

☐ Solicitor's address

☐ Other address (please provide details)

Section 2 – Attending court hearings

2.1   If the court requires you to attend a hearing do you need any special
       assistance or facilities?   ☐ Yes   ☐ No

       If Yes, please say what your requirements are. If necessary, court staff may
       contact you about your requirements.

Section 3 – Signature

Signed   Date served/ ☐☐/☐☐/☐☐☐☐
                                                    notified

Person served/notified ('s solicitor) ('s litigation friend)

Name

Name   Position or
of firm   office held

Section 4 – Supervisory Body or Managing Authority only

4.1   I am serving and filing the following documents:

1.

2.

3.

4.

Signed   **Date** ☐☐/☐☐/☐☐☐☐

2

INDEX

References are to paragraph numbers.